DARE TO BIRD

DARE TO

Photos and Text by Melissa Hafting

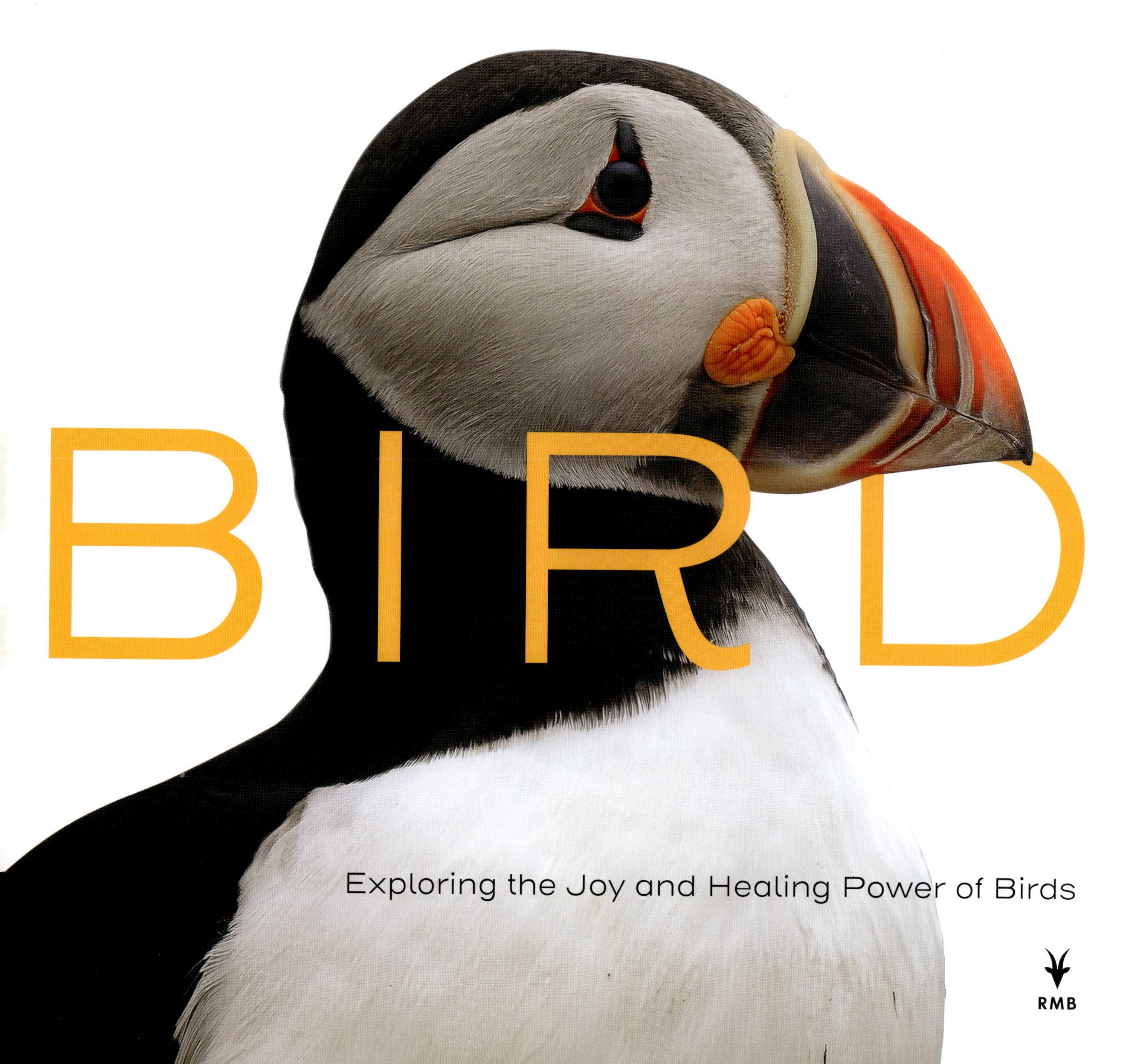
BIRD
Exploring the Joy and Healing Power of Birds
RMB

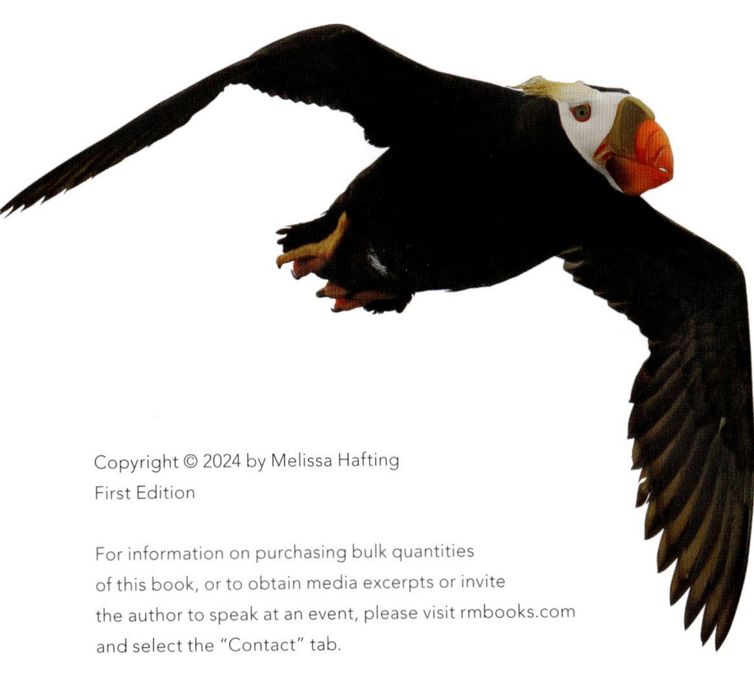

First Edition

For information on purchasing bulk quantities of this book, or to obtain media excerpts or invite the author to speak at an event, please visit rmbooks.com and select the "Contact" tab.

RMB | Rocky Mountain Books Ltd.
rmbooks.com
@rmbooks
facebook.com/rmbooks

Cataloguing data available from Library and Archives Canada
ISBN 9781771606547 (hardcover)
ISBN 9781771606554 (electronic)

All photographs are by Melissa Hafting unless otherwise noted.

Design: Lara Minja

Printed and bound in China

We would like to take this opportunity to acknowledge the Traditional Territories upon which we live and work. In Calgary, Alberta, we acknowledge the Niitsítapi (Blackfoot) and the people of the Treaty 7 region in Southern Alberta, which includes the Siksika, the Piikuni, the Kainai, the Tsuut'ina, and the Stoney Nakoda First Nations, including Chiniki, Bearpaw, and Wesley First Nations. The City of Calgary is also home to Métis Nation of Alberta, Region III. In Victoria, British Columbia, we acknowledge the Traditional Territories of the Lkwungen (Esquimalt and Songhees), Malahat, Pacheedaht, Scia'new, T'Sou-ke, and W̱SÁNEĆ (Pauquachin, Tsartlip, Tsawout, Tseycum) Peoples.

We acknowledge the financial support of the Government of Canada through the Canada Book Fund and the Canada Council for the Arts, and of the province of British Columbia through the British Columbia Arts Council and the Book Publishing Tax Credit.

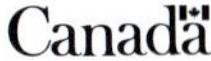

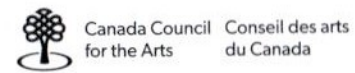

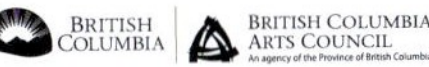

Above:

AN ADULT TUFTED PUFFIN TAKES FLIGHT IN TOFINO, BC.

I dedicate this book to my mother, Valerie, who passed on Christmas Eve, 2021. She always believed in me and taught me how to love and how to be a strong Black woman. I also dedicate this book to my father, Arne, who passed away on my mother's birthday in 2023. He sparked my love and interest in birds by showing me my first Black-capped Chickadee and fostered my love of the outdoors and respect for nature. I was blessed to have their unwavering support and unconditional love.

— MELISSA HAFTING

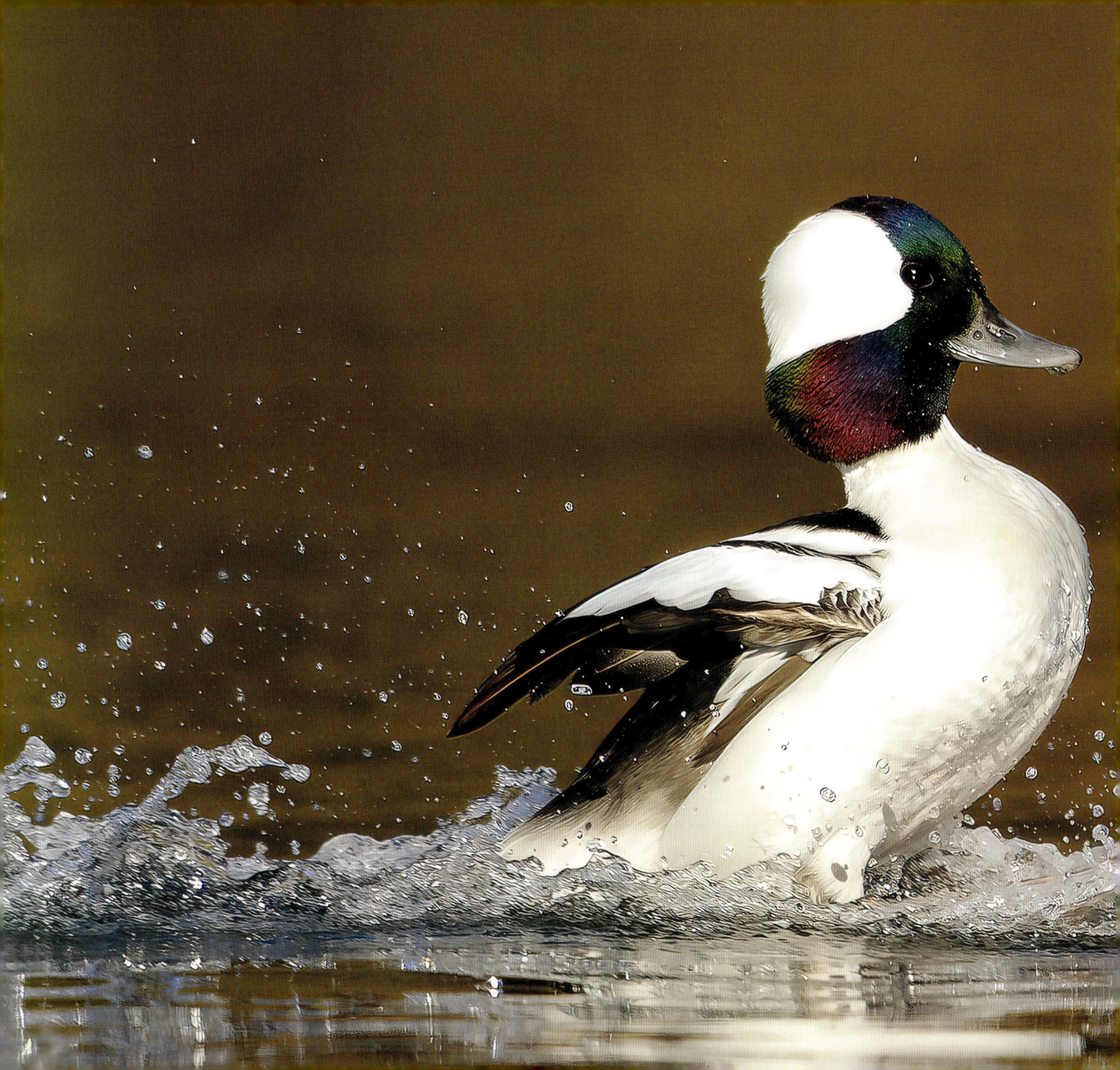

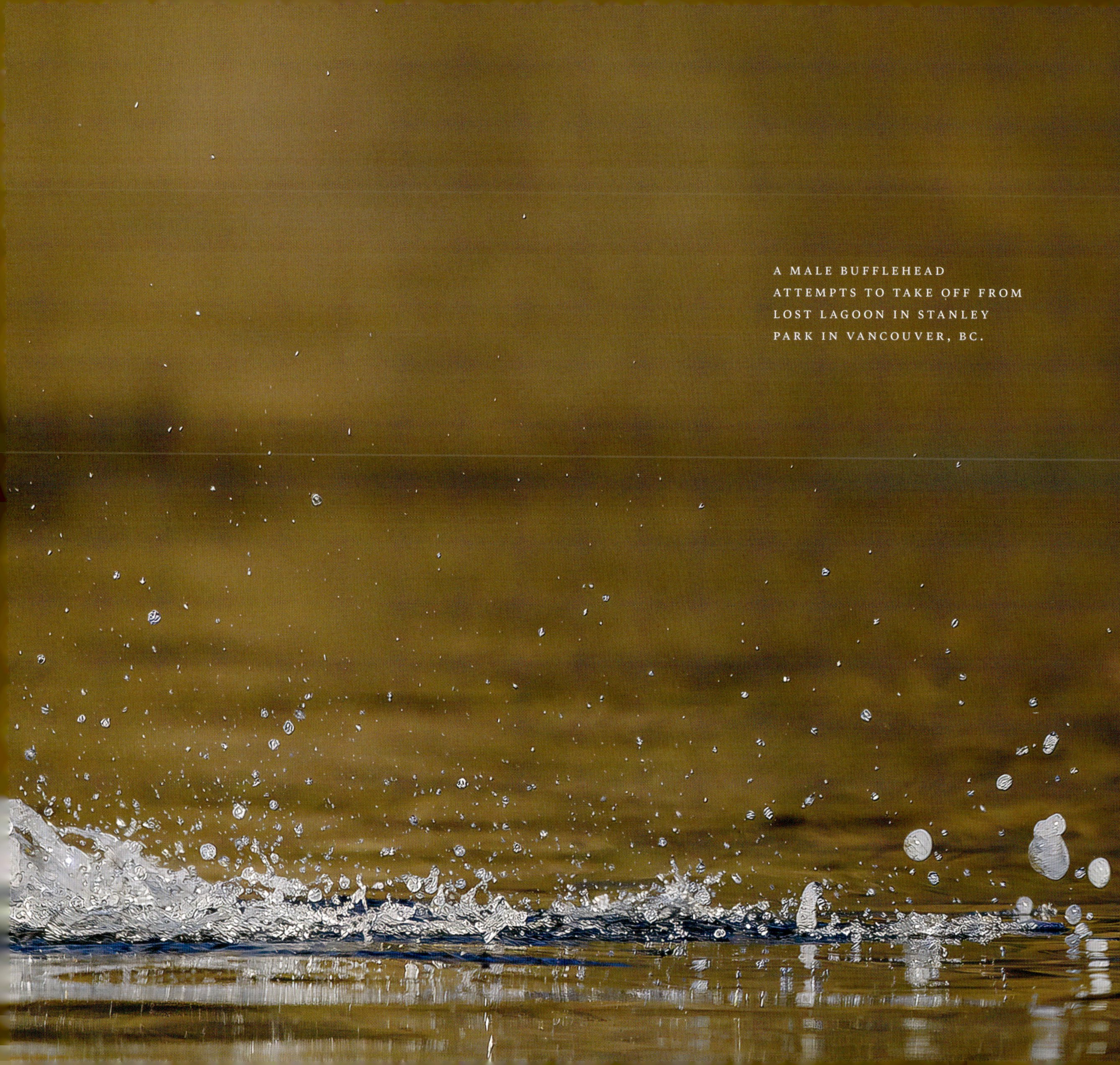

A MALE BUFFLEHEAD ATTEMPTS TO TAKE OFF FROM LOST LAGOON IN STANLEY PARK IN VANCOUVER, BC.

I want people to look at birds and admire them, adore them. But then I want them to take their binoculars down and look around and understand why things are as they are. And then ask what they've done to either make things better or make them worse.

—J. DREW LANHAM

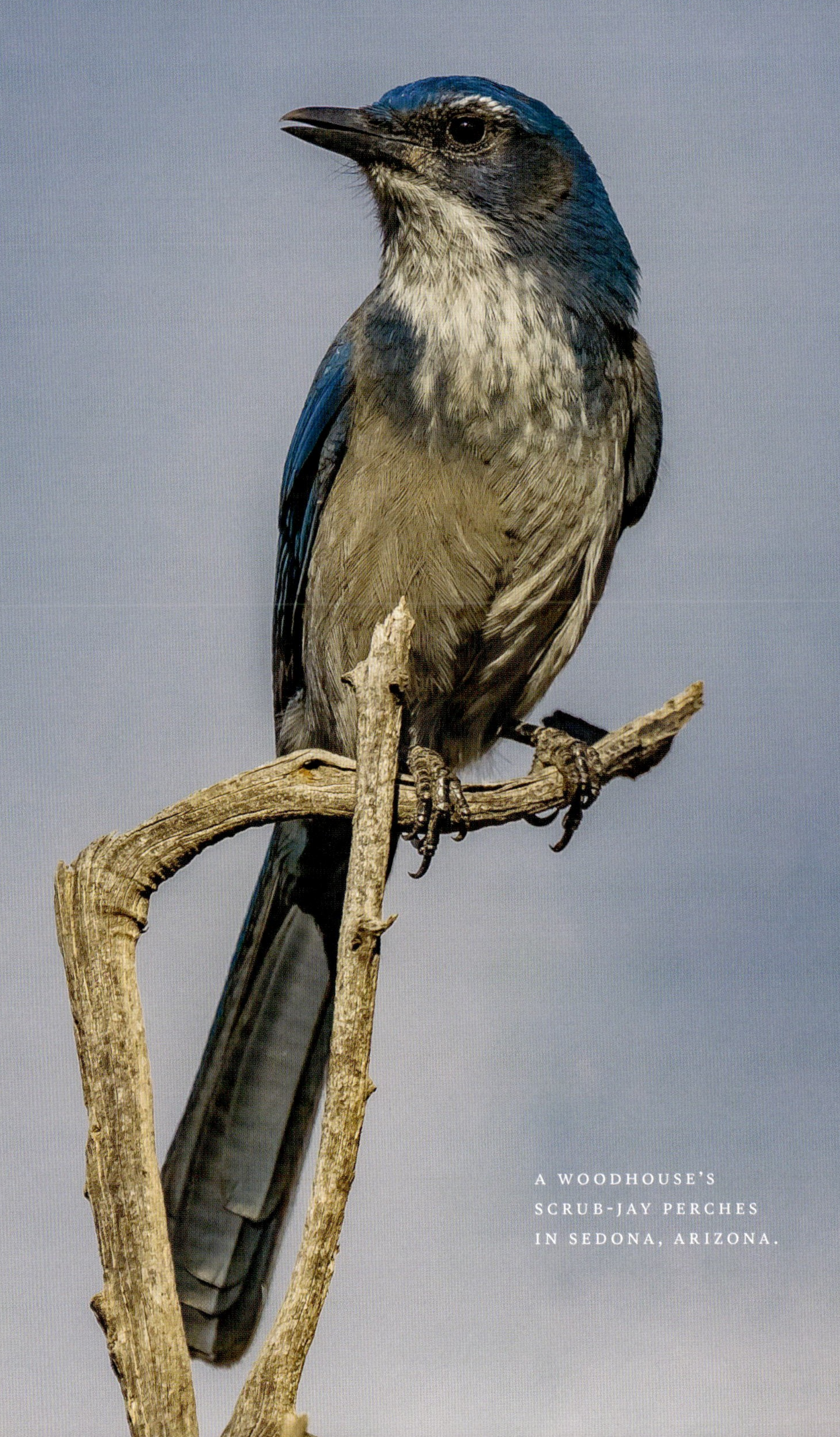

A WOODHOUSE'S SCRUB-JAY PERCHES IN SEDONA, ARIZONA.

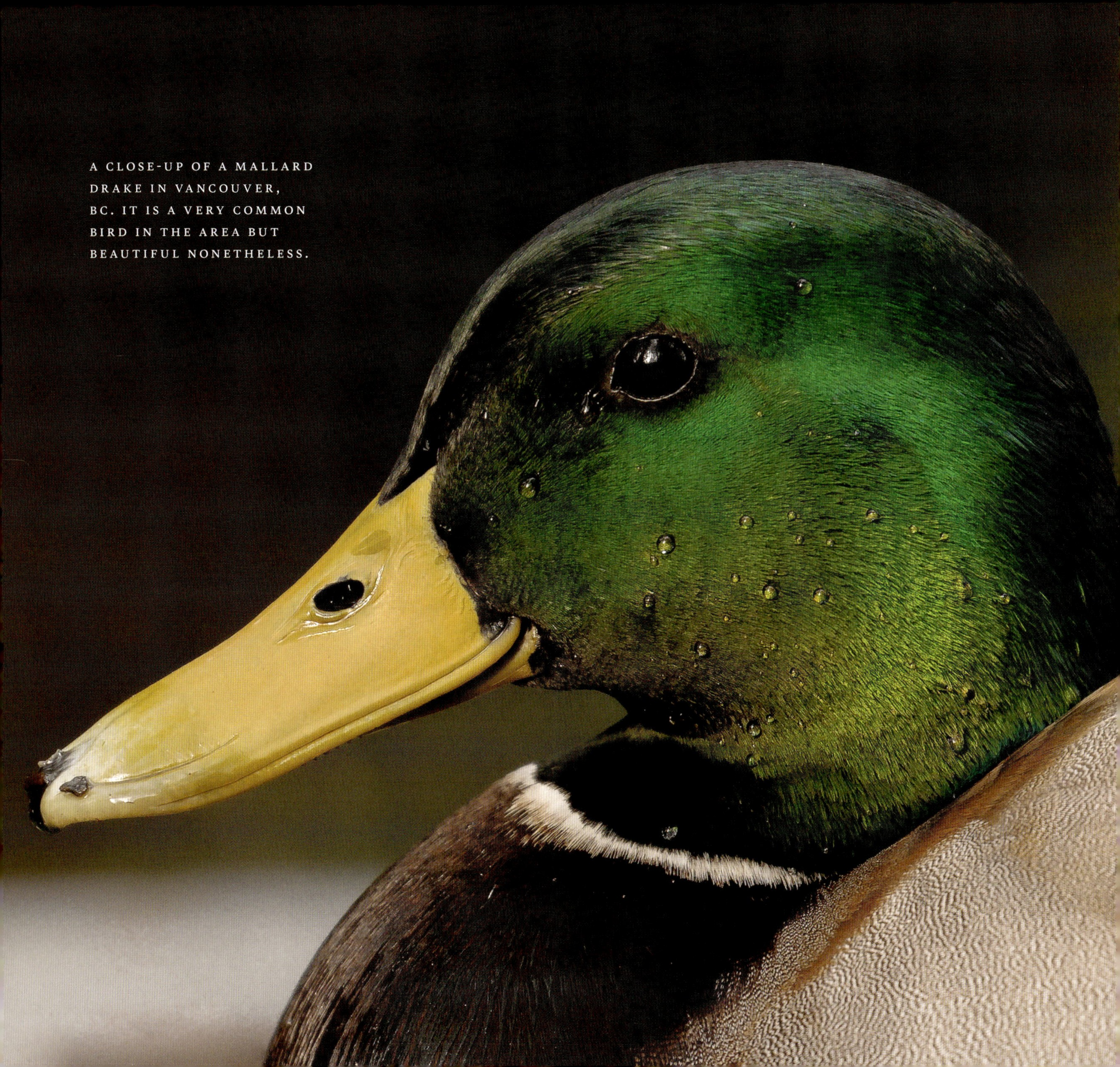

A CLOSE-UP OF A MALLARD DRAKE IN VANCOUVER, BC. IT IS A VERY COMMON BIRD IN THE AREA BUT BEAUTIFUL NONETHELESS.

CONTENTS

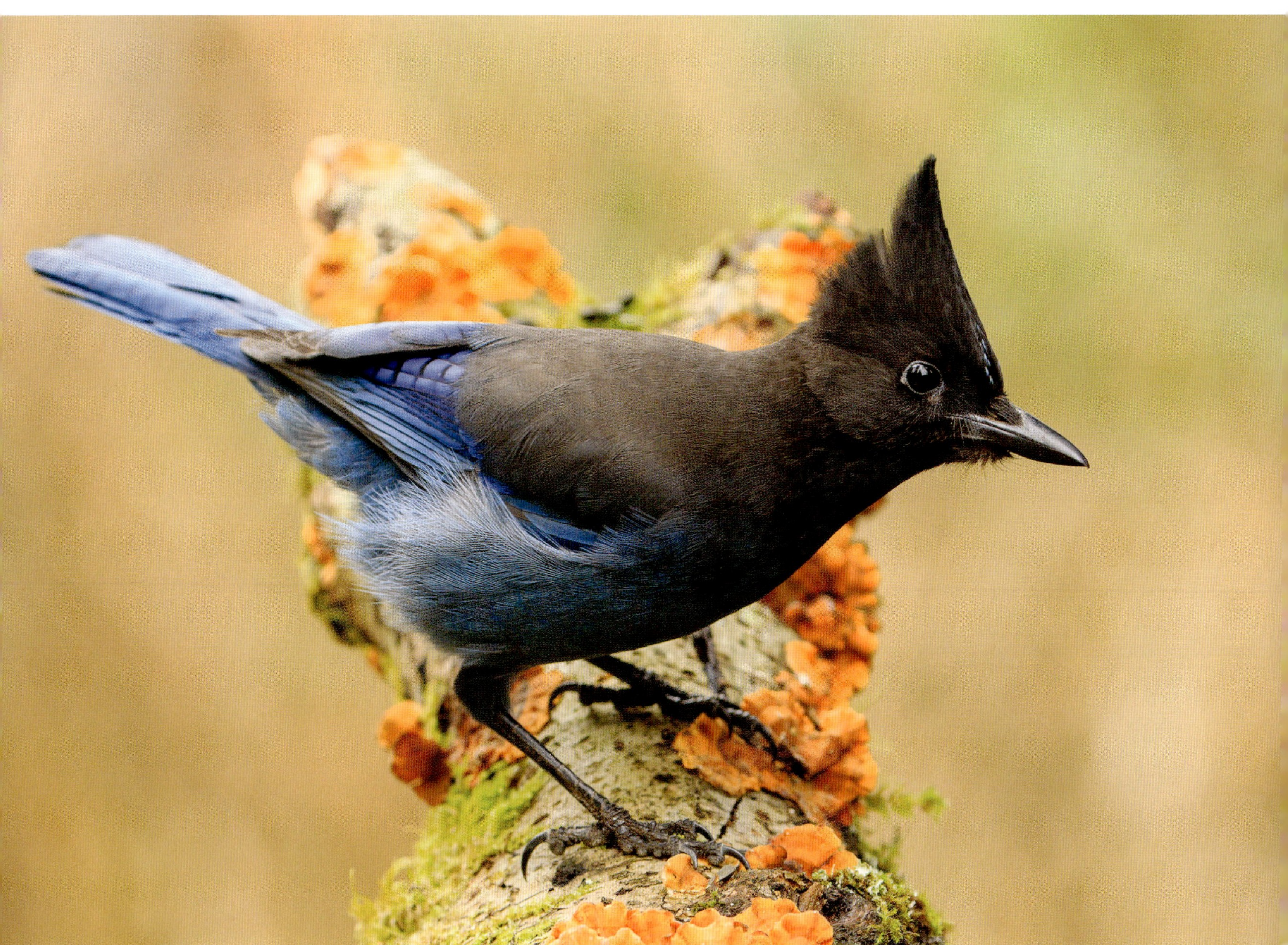

ACKNOWLEDGEMENTS

Opposite:

A STELLER'S JAY POSES ATOP A FUNGI-COVERED LOG AT STANLEY PARK IN VANCOUVER, BC.

I would like to thank publisher Don Gorman and the rest of the Rocky Mountain Books team (specifically social media manager Grace Gorman, publicist James Faccinto, editor Kirsten Craven, and graphic designer Lara Minja) for asking me to write this book, for publishing it, and for being gracious in giving me extra time to complete it after my father died. I also want to thank Ian Harland for taking my author photo for the book.

I would like to thank my sister, Meghan Grove, for her unwavering support and love always through anything and for her valuable input. I want to thank her for believing in me and pushing me to achieve my goals. I would also like to thank Ilya Povalyaev for supporting me as I finished the book and for reading my second and third drafts.

I want to thank all the young birders I have worked with over the years for inspiring me every day and bringing me so much joy and purpose. I would also like to thank all the birders in British Columbia and elsewhere who have supported me and to thank them for the lasting friendships we have made. I want to thank all my birding friends who held me up when I felt I would break after first my mother and then my father died, 14 months apart. I will never forget your support and you know who you are. I would like to personally thank, in no particular order, Kevin Louth, Melissa Groo, Nate Swift, Drew Lanham, Yousif Attia, Colleen Gara, Russell Cannings, Liron Gertsman, Bridget Spencer, Joshua Brown, Alice Sun, Maxime Vezina-Legare, Steve Hampton, Molly Adams, Paul Riss, Krista DeGroot, Danielle Belleny, Kelly-Sue O'Connor, Brian Stech, Alecia Smith, Jeremy Gatten, Quentin Brown, Rob Lyske, John Reynolds, Barry Price, Sabine Decamp, Monica Nugent, Sheryl Spencer, Rob Butler, Chris Charlesworth,

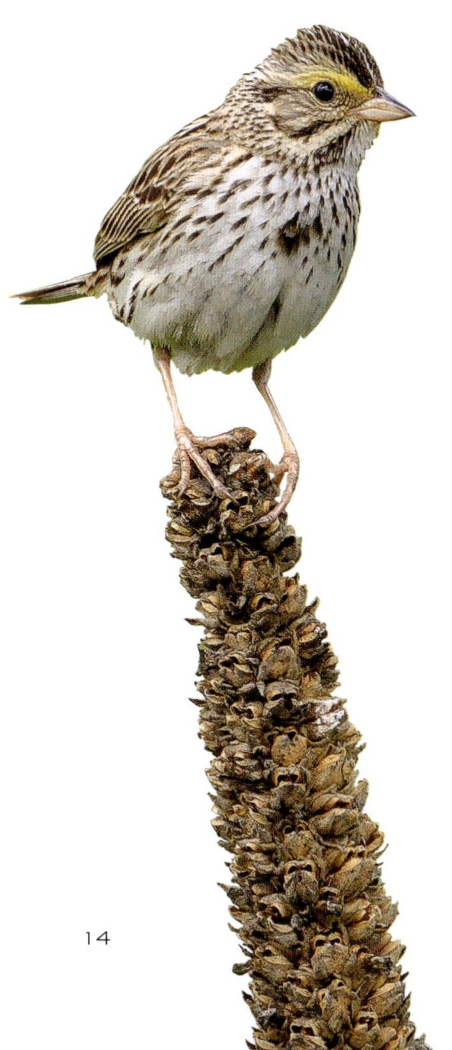

Cameron Eckert, George Clulow, and all my friends (too many to list here) for being so supportive of this book project.

I want to thank Rich Kenny and the City of Richmond for their support of my Tree Swallow and Purple Martin projects. I want to thank the Canadian Museum of Nature and BC Nature for their support of my work with youth. I want to thank the Stanley Park Ecology Society for its inclusive BIPOC (Black, Indigenous, and people of colour) and LGBTQ2SIA+ (lesbian, gay, bisexual, transgender, queer, Two-Spirit, intersex, asexual, plus) bird walks, which I have led over the years as part of its Birding with Me series. I want to thank the CBC for amplifying my work on radio and TV and publishing my essays on how birding can help with mental health and my swallow project. I want to thank the American Birding Association and editor Ted Floyd for publishing my essays in their *Birding* magazine and for featuring a photo I took on the cover, and to Noah Strycker for interviewing me for the magazine. I also want to thank Nate Swick for having me as a guest on the *American Birding Podcast*, and to Birds Canada for having me as a guest on *The Warblers* podcast to discuss how birds can help with grief and mental health.

I want to thank everyone who reads this book and finds some peace, joy, and inspiration in these pages. For anyone who is grieving, like me, please know you are not alone, and when you feel alone, just get outside and listen to those birds who are telling you, "We got you."

I want to thank everyone fighting to make the world and this hobby a more inclusive, safe, accessible, and friendly space. I must also thank all those who are fighting to protect birds, animals, and their habitats. I thank the birds for all the beauty they have brought into my life. Most of all, I would like to thank my beloved parents who instilled in me the value of respect and love for nature and who loved me unconditionally and supported me through absolutely everything. I truly hope I have made them proud.

INTRODUCTION

Opposite:

A SAVANNAH SPARROW SITS ATOP ITS PERCH IN THE GRASSLANDS OF QUILCHENA, BC.

Birds are so unique that, if you look at them for too long, they can draw you in, and once you are hooked under their spell, there really is no way to get out from their grasp. Who could have guessed a White-throated Sparrow held so much power? When it opens its beak and begins to sing, you quickly understand. They come in drab colours, from a brown Song Sparrow to the bright red of a Vermilion Flycatcher. They live in all habitats on Earth, from hot deserts to cold Antarctica.

Birds are resilient beings, and I think that is why I find such a kinship with them. I have been through some difficult struggles in my life (as I'm sure many of you reading this book have), and the birds help and inspire me to keep going. They help me to dust myself off and start all over again.

When I lost my mother to breast cancer on Christmas Eve, 2021, I wondered how I would ever be able to go on. Then when I lost my dad just over a year later, when he died on her birthday in 2023, I thought for sure I would not survive it. But I did and I'm here to tell my story.

My story begins as a little girl of 5 who got introduced to birds by her father and fell in love with them even more than he did. My friends started to call me "Birdergirl," and that name has stuck into adulthood. As I grew up, I got my bachelor of science in university and my love for birds didn't wane. I continued to love birds even more each day. I became more and more passionate about environmental issues that affected them and began spreading awareness to help their plight.

I have a passion for working with youth and sharing the joys of the natural world with them. They have enriched my life with their love of birds and passion for conservation. I feel it is essential to mentor young people. I never had a mentor in the birding community and wanted to

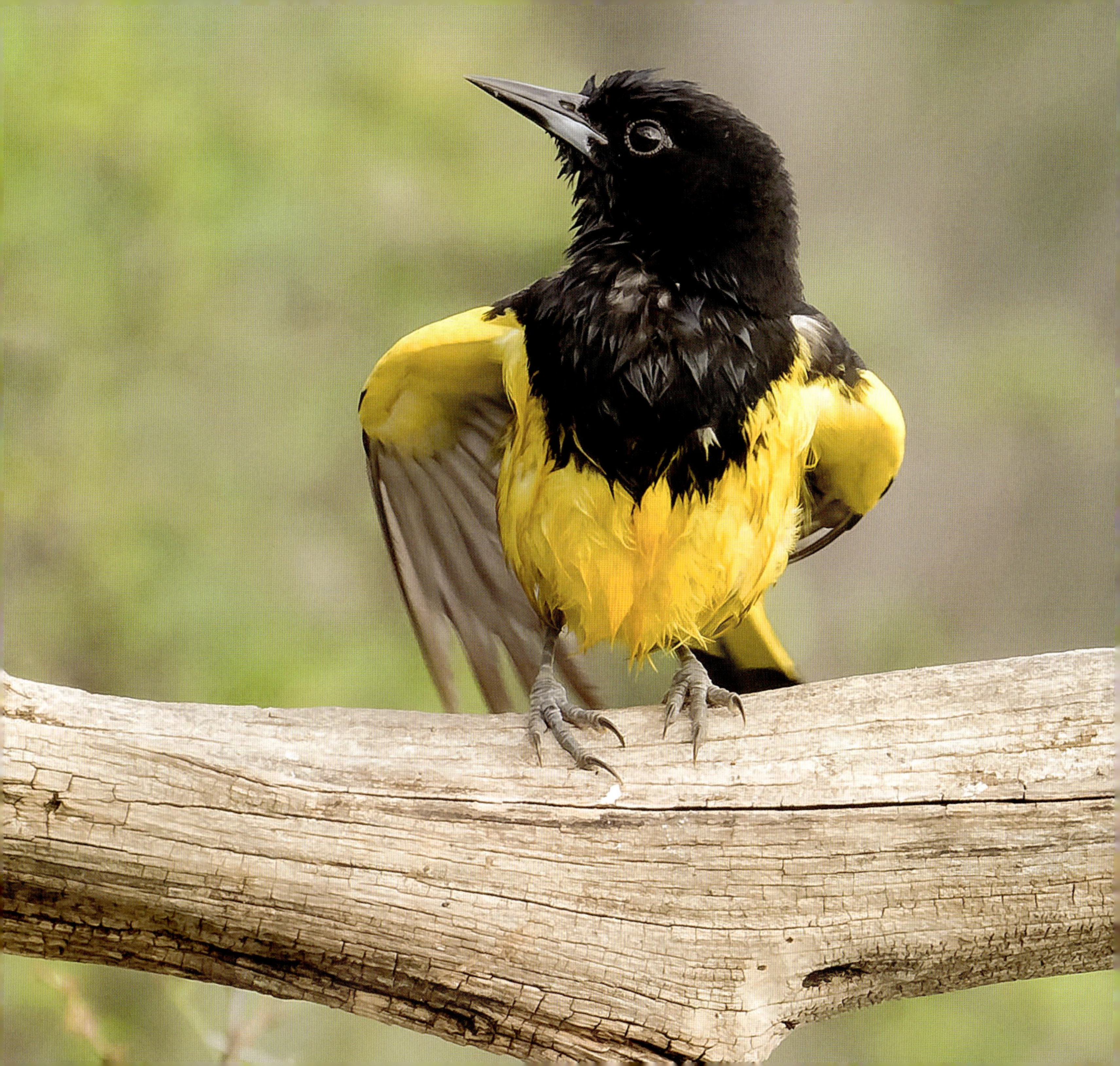

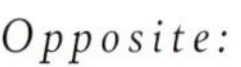

Opposite:

A MALE SCOTT'S ORIOLE DRIES OFF ON A PERCH AFTER A BATHING SESSION IN UVALDE, TEXAS.

ensure every kid felt welcome and wanted. I wanted to share my knowledge of birds with them and show them birds they didn't see in their everyday neighbourhoods, while also making them aware how special the birds in their own backyards were. I formed the BC Young Birders Program in 2014 and got the youth out into nature on field trips close and afar. At the same time, the youth brought such joy and purpose to my life, and I too have learned so much from them.

I took over running the BC Rare Bird Alert (RBA) website from my friend Russell Cannings because of my passion for rare birds and identification. My role as a provincial eBird reviewer has helped me to keep my skills sharp as I review photos daily. I enjoy helping other birders with their identification questions and encourage them to email me. I also have written a few identification tutorials for birders. I believe in bringing the community together through the sharing of sightings on the RBA website. I help others as much as I can to see as many birds as possible. I truly believe it is important to share as much knowledge as you can and to pay it forward. The universe will reward you tenfold in return.

I believe in the power of kindness. I also believe in birds and why it is so important to protect them. Birds do show us that, if we listen to them and protect them and their habitats, they can survive and even thrive and bounce back. The Short-tailed Albatross that was almost hunted to extinction for its feathers is just one example of this, or Bald Eagles and Peregrines who almost went extinct because of DDT and who have now rebounded to record numbers. Whooping Cranes were also hunted to near extinction, but thanks to changes we humans have made, after advocating on their behalf, they too have rebounded.

Birds are truly indicator species that tell us we must reflect and change what we are doing now if we want them to continue to live with us on this planet tomorrow. They also warn us that, if we don't make changes, especially as the climate continues to warm, we won't be lasting here on this planet much longer either. Our impacts on the environment and birds matter. We really need to listen to them before it is too late. It is our responsibility to ensure that each of us leaves a positive, lasting impact on the birds that we so love to look at. We need to realize that, by protecting birds and their habitats, we are also protecting ourselves.

After losing my mother and father, whom I loved so incredibly much, I know how important it is to not sit by and idle our time away but to try and make the planet better for birds and animals while we still can. Who knows how many tomorrows I have left in my life, but all my tomorrows will be for the birds.

Birds have literally saved me after my parents' deaths. They have kept me going and have brought incredible people into my life, from the young birders to friends and opportunities all over the world. I will never stop paying forward what I can. I have started a Tree Swallow and Purple Martin conservation project in Richmond, BC, and petitioned my hometown to ban rodenticides. I was successful in this and did the same in several other municipalities and was part of a group of people who successfully fought hard to get a provincial ban on rodenticides. This ban came into effect in BC for second-generation rodenticides in 2023. I have also donated much of my time to bring education and awareness to the public and to fight for conservation issues that affect birds across the province.

There really is so much to love about birds; they awaken in us all five senses. There is no right or wrong way to bird, from mindful, casual birding to fast-paced, hard-core birding to listing. That is what is so great about this hobby! There is truly something for everyone. There is a place for all of us and we are all welcome. I truly believe in making everyone feel welcome in the birding community, no matter what age, class, race, sexual identity, or gender expression. I want to bring awareness to the barriers faced by Black, Indigenous, and people of colour in this hobby as well and continue to promote diversity and inclusion.

Birding is a hobby that is not ageist and helps connect birders from every age group, ethnicity, and gender. Birding has brought so much joy into my life and so many great friends and experiences I will always treasure. From memorable rare bird chases with friends across the province I won't ever forget, to casual shorebirding moments with a group of friends at the local BC shorebird spot called Boundary Bay. I am blessed by how many friends birding has brought me, but I also love birding solo and the tranquility it brings me.

I am also a photographer who loves to photograph birds. I know the power of a photograph. Photos can make people feel empowered to save birds and to conserve their habitats. I find it also allows me to relive the moment with the bird or birds repeatedly. Photos flood my brain with wondrous, moving, and magical moments in nature. I am truly passionate about educating the public about ethical photography practices.

I wrote this book in the hope it will help all birders deepen their connection to nature. I wrote this book for those who suffer from grief and loss or mental illness, or who feel alone. I want you to know you are never alone when you are with birds. I also wrote this book for anyone who has experienced racism while birding and for those who just love birds and can see through my experiences just how much joy is possible through this hobby.

Birding is truly my way of life and I'm so grateful I can share my passion with you all. Thank you for taking the time to buy and read this book, it means the world to me.

I hope you enjoy this book about the healing power of birds. Hopefully, it showcases how birds can enhance and bring joy to our lives.

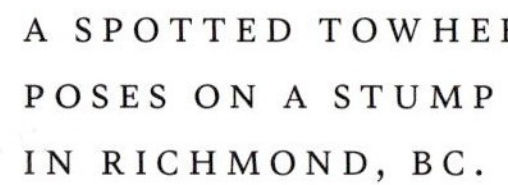

A SPOTTED TOWHEE POSES ON A STUMP IN RICHMOND, BC.

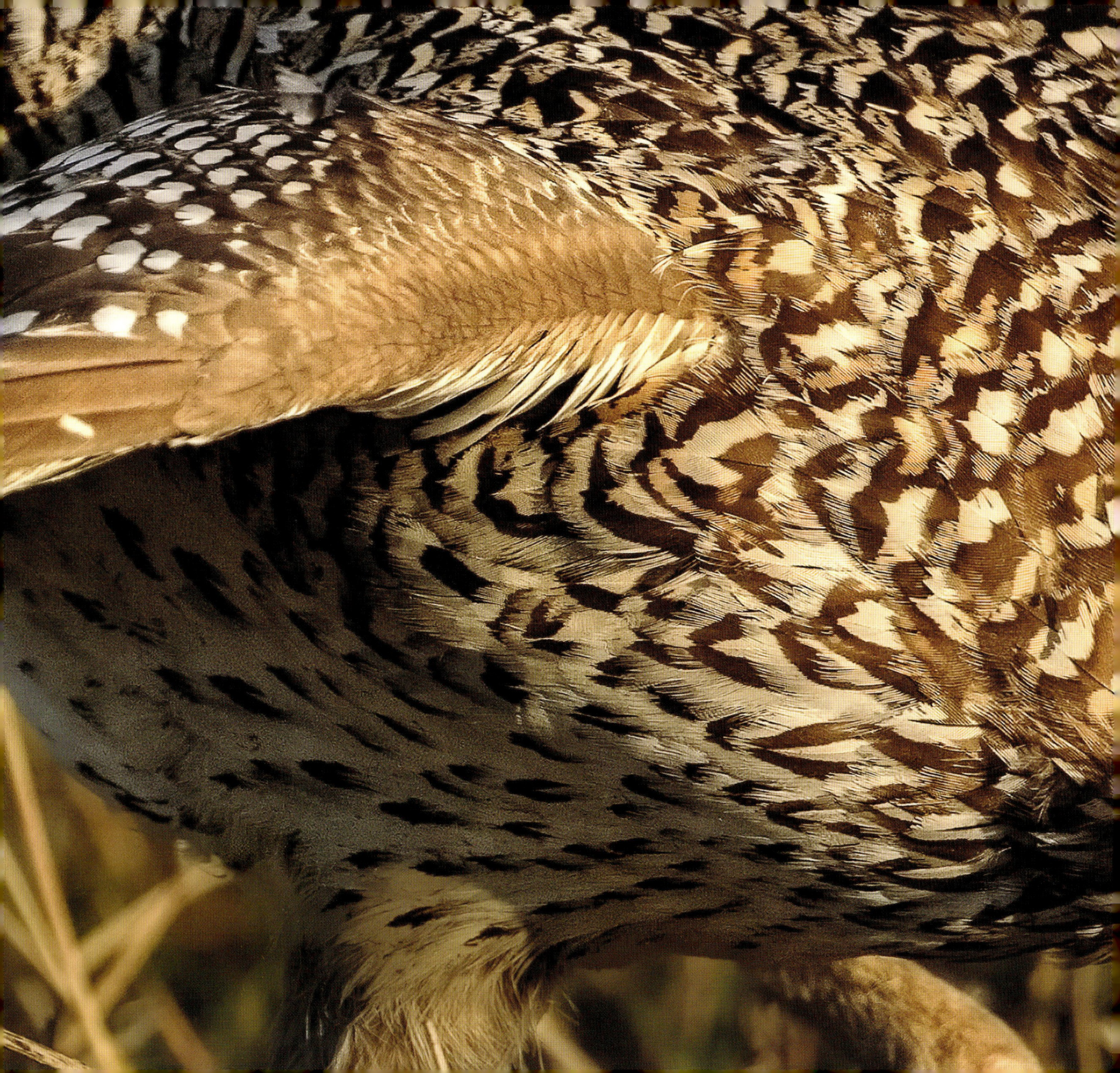

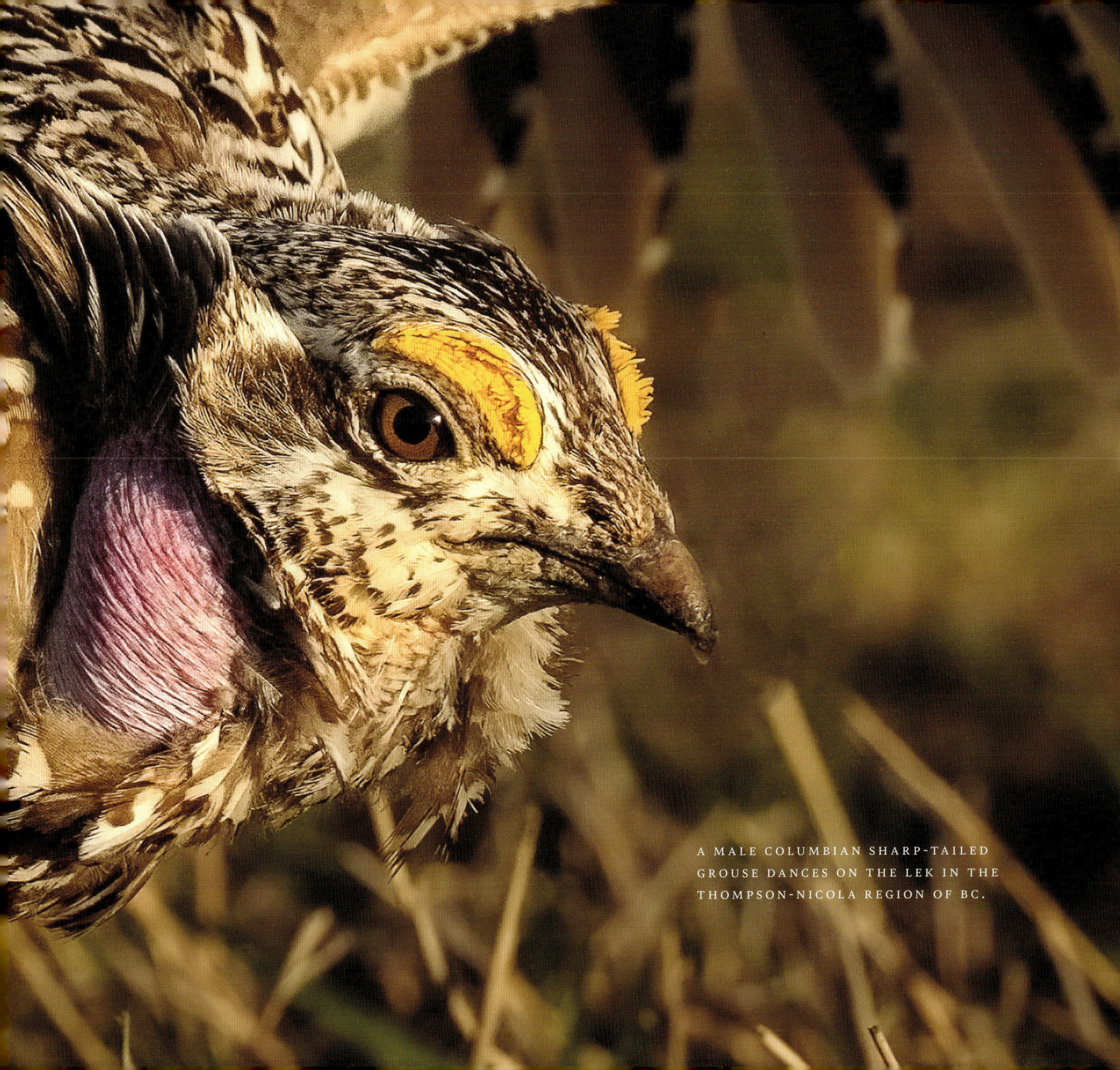

A MALE COLUMBIAN SHARP-TAILED GROUSE DANCES ON THE LEK IN THE THOMPSON-NICOLA REGION OF BC.

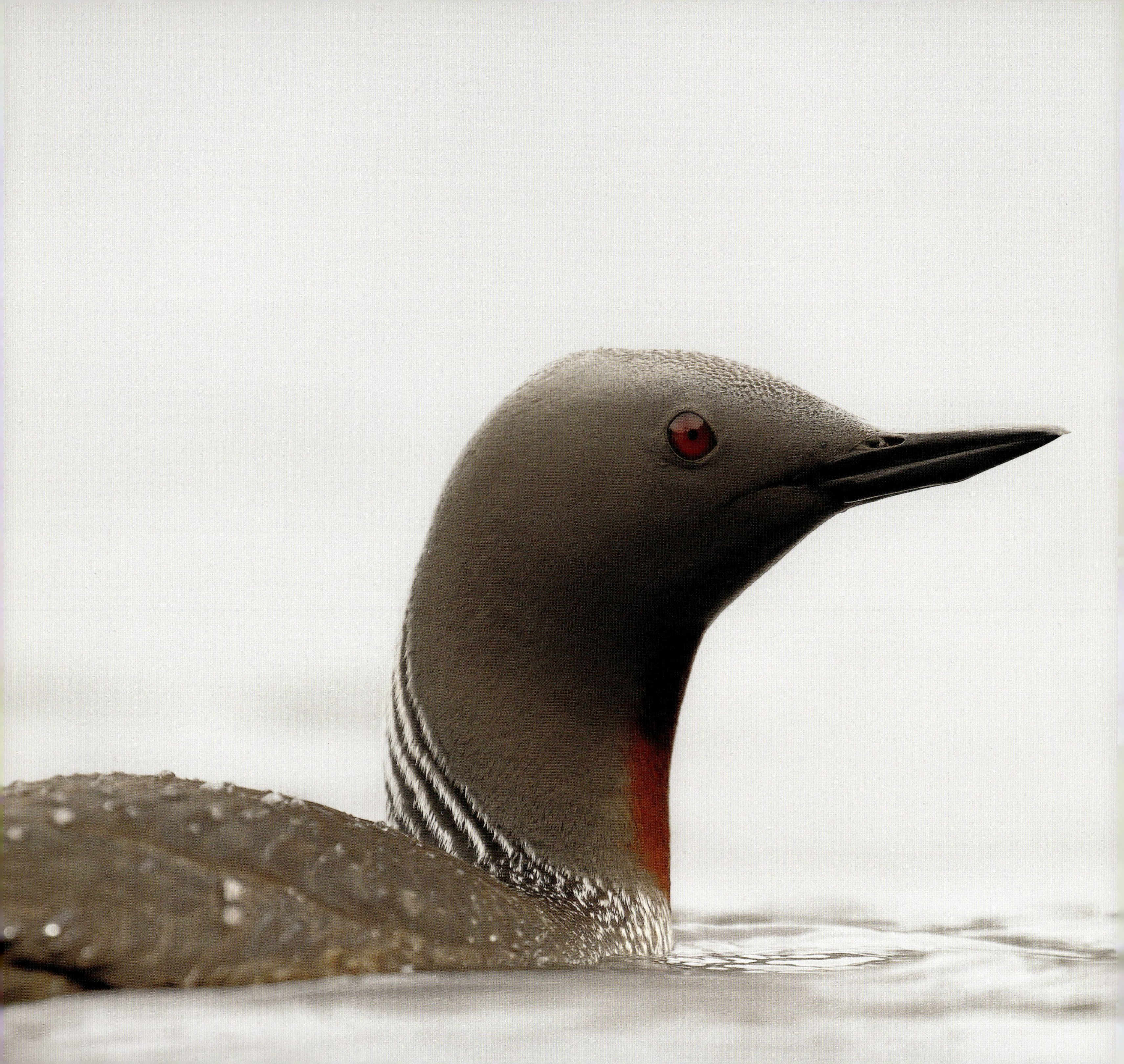

1

The Importance of Diversity and Inclusion

I formed the BC Young Birders Program to take young people out into nature and teach them the importance of birds and their habitats and to give them a safe space where they can interact with other young birders. I especially encourage and am inclusive of BIPOC and LGBTQ2SIA+ birders who are traditionally under-represented in birding.

Opposite:

A RED-THROATED LOON IN BREEDING PLUMAGE SWIMS CLOSE TO ME IN WHISTLER, BC.

Birding is unfortunately not as safe and as welcoming a space as it could be, and I hope one day it will change to be more inclusive for all people. However, positive strides have certainly been made due to education, awareness, and acknowledgement on the issue. There is still a lot left to do through concrete action and not just empty words to make people of colour feel safe, welcome, and included in this space.

When I started birding, I didn't see anyone who looked like me. I am half Black and half white. Birding was mostly a white, male-dominated hobby when I began. I still don't see enough people that look like me but have started to see more women and more younger women of colour getting involved. Since it is a traditionally male-dominated hobby, it is harder for females to be taken as seriously as their male counterparts. I've definitely experienced racism while birding, and I am actively working to make sure young birders coming up don't go through the same racism and sexism I did.

One male Black birder in my young birder program was birding alone in Richmond one day, when a white woman called the RCMP on him because he appeared suspicious to her. At the time he was birding inside a fenced-off sewage lagoon. Little did she know that Metro Vancouver Regional Parks had an agreement with birders to bird inside the area. She clearly only assumed the young man was suspicious because of his skin colour. The police came out and spoke to him and were polite and let him go once they understood the situation, as he was

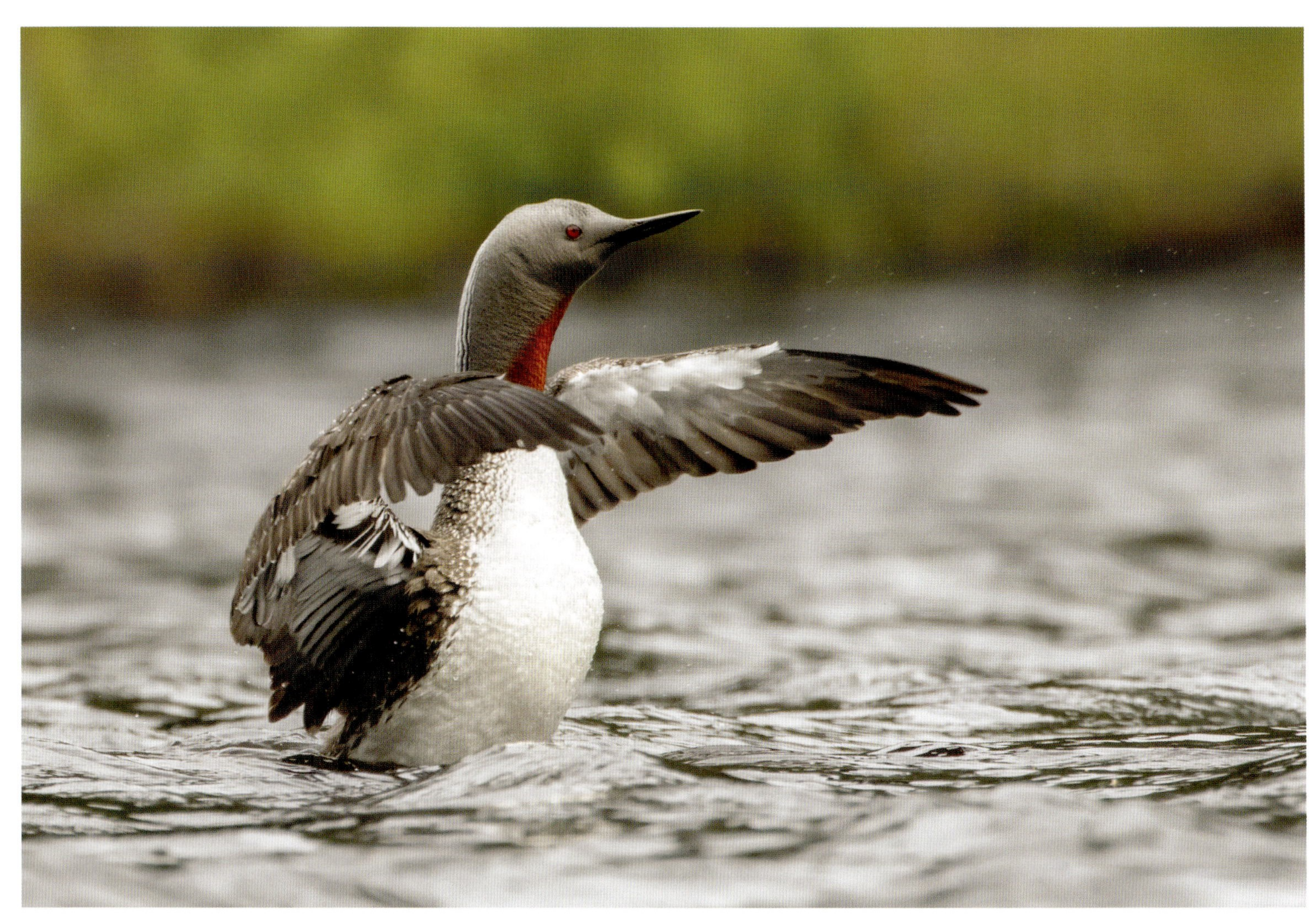

AN ELEGANT RED-THROATED LOON FLAPS ITS WINGS IN WHISTLER, BC.

doing nothing illegal. Unfortunately, this happens to Black birders too much in North America. Another South Asian young birder in my program was publicly called a racial slur on a local birding website by a white man who was quickly condemned by several birders. It is important we always stand up to racism when we see it and especially protect children affected by it.

Since the COVID pandemic there has been an increase in Anti-Asian racism. During the pandemic, a white woman threw a cup of coffee at two birders and called them a racist slur at a Richmond park. Also, I have personally heard other birders say racist things, while I was present, about certain ethnic groups, and I have been subjected to racist hate speech to my face while birding and via emails. I have struggled to get some birding organizations to use the term BIPOC and to capitalize the words "Black" and "Indigenous" and have asked them to include LGBTQ2SIA+ inclusive language. There is still resistance in modern times to inclusive language. You quickly get accused of being political, despite this being a civil rights issue. While birding on public land, I have been followed by white people in vehicles wondering what I was doing and why I was there. During one of these instances, they tried to intimidate me by asking me if they could help me in a very unfriendly tone while I had full legal right to be there birding and looking at an American Kestrel. They continued to follow me, but I stood my ground and eventually they gave up their intimidation tactics and left. All of these things could turn off a BIPOC person from wanting to bird. This is why I truly believe we must do better in making everyone feel included.

BIPOC and other marginalized people have historically been denied entry into birding and conservation, even though they tend to be the first people to be disproportionately affected by environmental disasters and impacts from climate change. I believe it is imperative to fight both systemic and environmental racism, which are very much still present in Canada and the United States.

Christian Cooper is a Black birder who made headlines in 2020 for birding in New York City's Central Park. He was verbally attacked and threatened, then the police were called on him after a white woman provided a false story, lying that he had attacked her. Cooper's experience helped to bring awareness to the plight of BIPOC birders. Events like Black Birders Week, where Black birders share their experiences being outdoors, show how unsafe and unwelcoming it can be out there when we simply want to go out and look at birds and nature.

I have led several BIPOC birding walks for the Stanley Park Ecology Society, the Canadian Wildlife Service, and Birds Canada and found that every year we get more participants and a wider representation of ages and ethnicities. Black people and Indigenous Peoples are still the most under-represented in our hobby. It is hard to feel welcome when there are no overt welcoming signs on websites (which is a simple and easy thing to do) or walks for people that look like you. Organizations must no longer assume everyone feels welcome but do active work to make them feel welcome and encourage BIPOC participation. Some

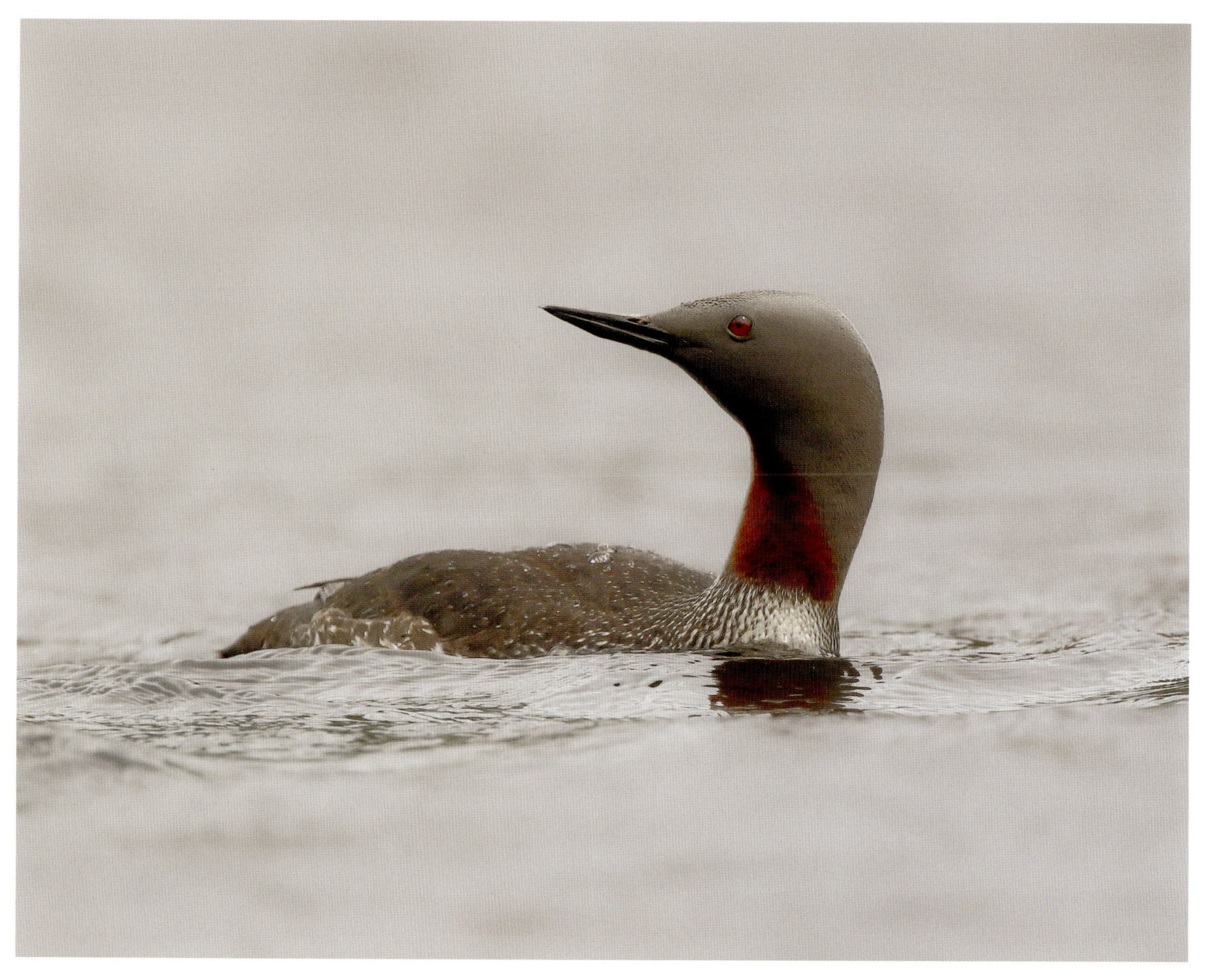

A RED-THROATED LOON ON THE WATER IN WHISTLER, BC.

birding organizations have recognized this and are striving to achieve balance in representation, working to be more welcoming to BIPOC and LGBTQ2SIA+ birders. Having BIPOC birders lead walks, getting paid for their time, energy, and work, and having them sit on boards and committees in leadership positions are what is needed. Having BIPOC and LGBTQ2SIA+ inclusive activities and walks are also key to making them feel safe and welcome.

To the best of my ability, I have tried to make BIPOC birders feel welcome and encourage BIPOC participation and will continue to do so in the BC birding community. I will NEVER GIVE UP on this or the youth I work with, and I certainly will NEVER give up on birds. It is up to us to ensure the future of birds is a bright one. All of us hold the power within us to make the planet a more beautiful place.

With all the injustices and atrocities and losses in the world today, it is vital we have the birds to help heal the world of its anger and negative energy. When the world wants to pull us down and we feel like drowning, the birds are there to lift us up. They watch over us and guide us and help to connect us to one another. No one owns the birds – they are here for all of us.

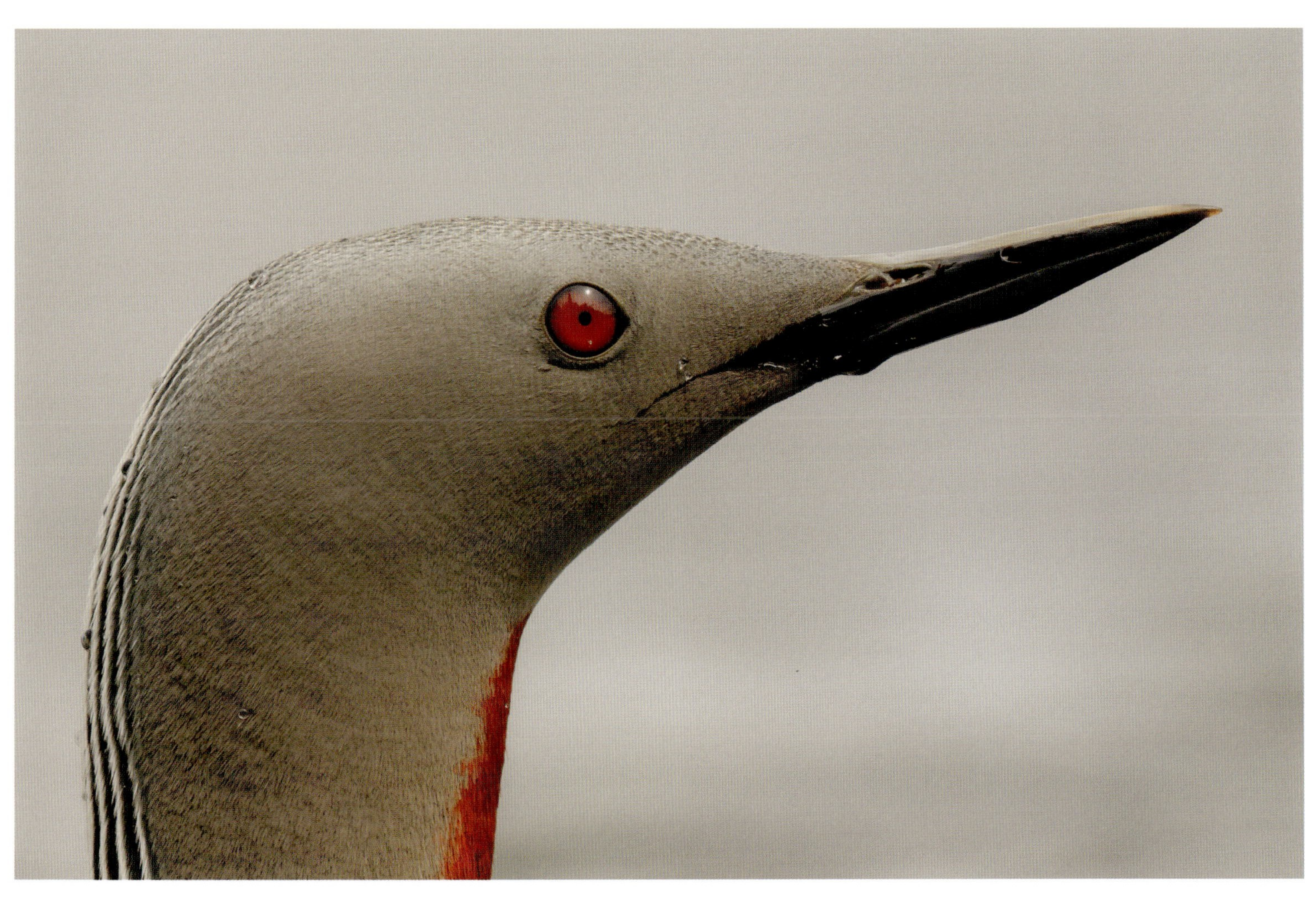

A CLOSE-UP PORTRAIT OF THE FACIAL DETAILS OF A RED-THROATED LOON IN WHISTLER, BC.

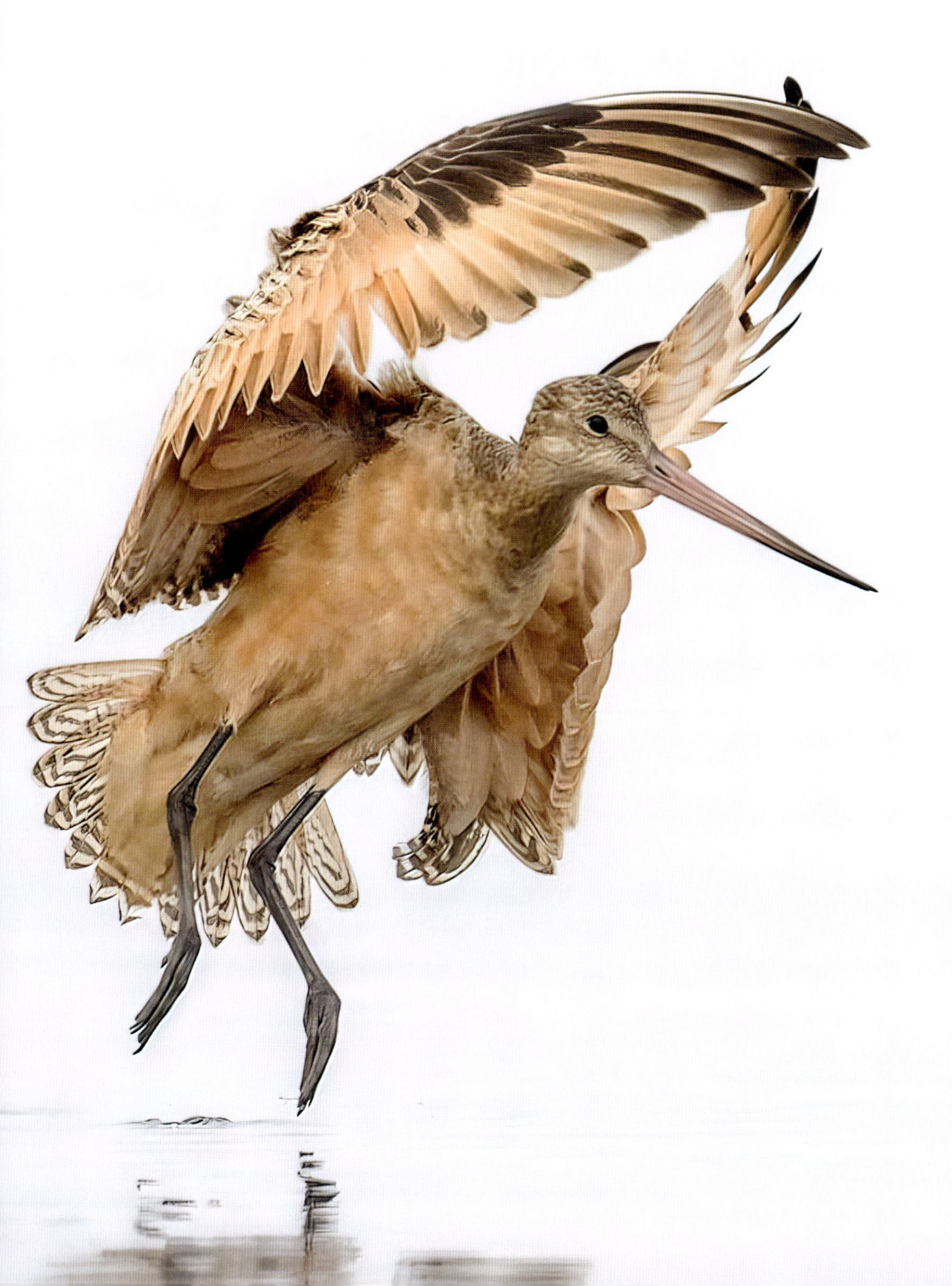

2

Flight

Whenever I look at birds in flight, I am instantly overcome with a sense of peace and fascination. Who doesn't want to fly? Since before airplanes were invented, humans wanted to figure out how we could soar above the oceans and plains. We wanted to feel free. We don't want to feel chained down, we want to open our wings and fly. That is why Maya Angelou said she wanted to know why the caged bird sings.

Opposite:

A MARBLED GODWIT (A LARGE SHOREBIRD) ELEGANTLY PICKS UP ITS WINGS IN FLIGHT IN SURREY, BC.

I can stare at a flock of birds twirling and swirling around for hours, especially at a flock of Snow Geese or shorebirds in murmuration. Birds are so graceful and elegant when they fly. I will often go to the beach and sit on a log or rock and just take it all in. I remember one cold winter day watching them. These white geese with black wing tips always stop me in my tracks because they are stunning to look at. I was watching them at the time with some of the most important people in my life, making it that more special. The sound of them calling with their honking cries, at sunset with the Salish Sea in the background, and watching them take up in flight all together and land in front of you is something you don't ever forget. When you are grieving, it is hard to focus on anything, but birds help centre me and bring me back to a sense of feeling grounded, despite the pain in my heart.

Some birds are normally solitary or hang out in pairs but form large flocks in the winter, like Steller's Jays or Bushtits. Watching a bird in flight – like the fastest bird in the world, a Peregrine Falcon, diving in a flock of shorebirds – although the bane of shorebirders, is a spectacular sight, especially when its aerial acrobatics pay off and it gets its hard-earned meal. From seeing a Bald Eagle in flight as it narrows in on its salmon meal in BC's Fraser Valley, to a gorgeous Red-tailed Tropicbird, with its long trailing red tail flying over the ocean in Oahu while I sat on a rocky bluff watching, are memories to treasure forever.

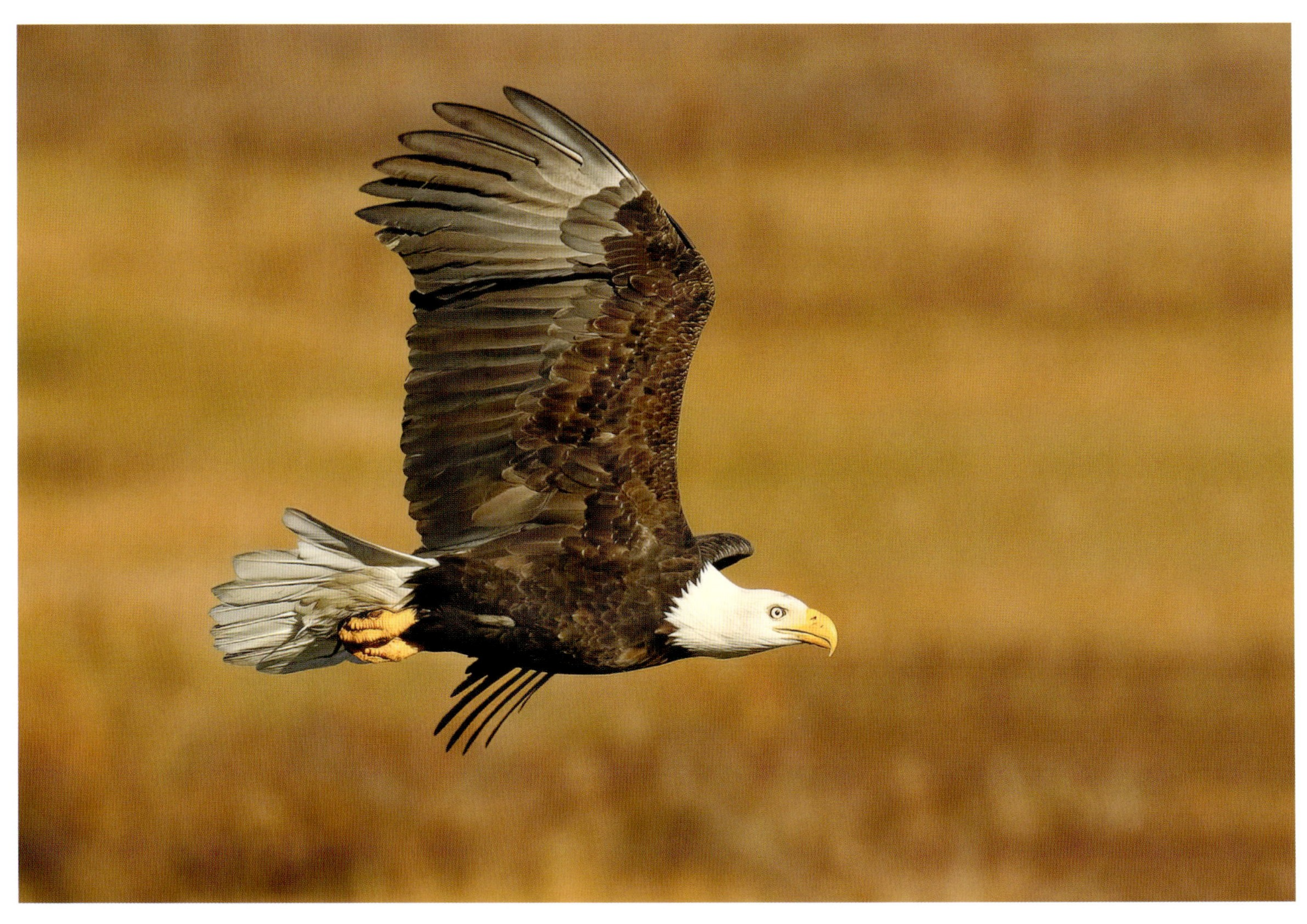

ADULT BALD EAGLES ARE POWERFUL BIRDS THAT ARE AWE-INSPIRING. HERE ONE IS FLYING OVER HARRISON MILLS, BC.

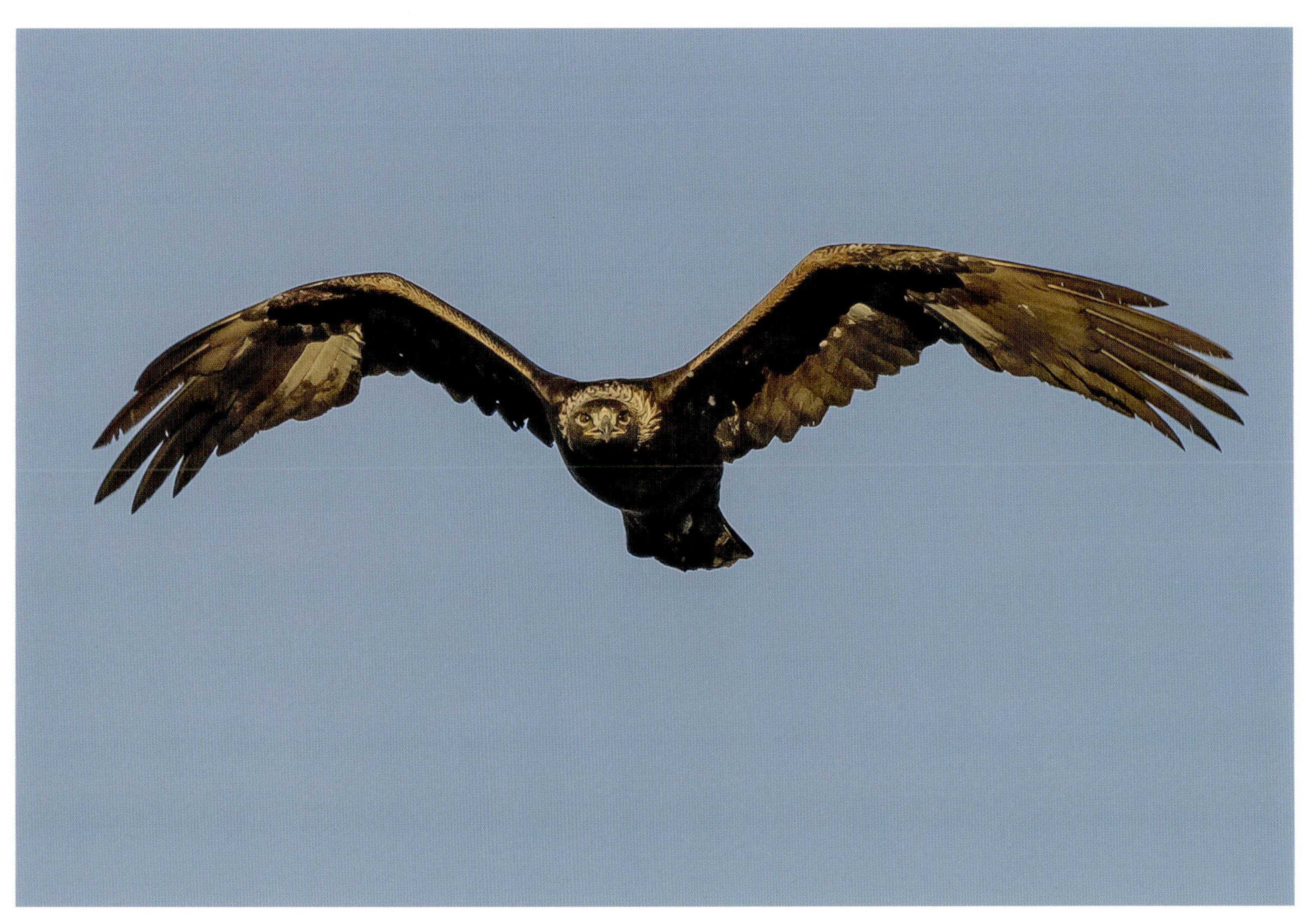

A GOLDEN EAGLE FLIES OVERHEAD IN DELTA, BC.

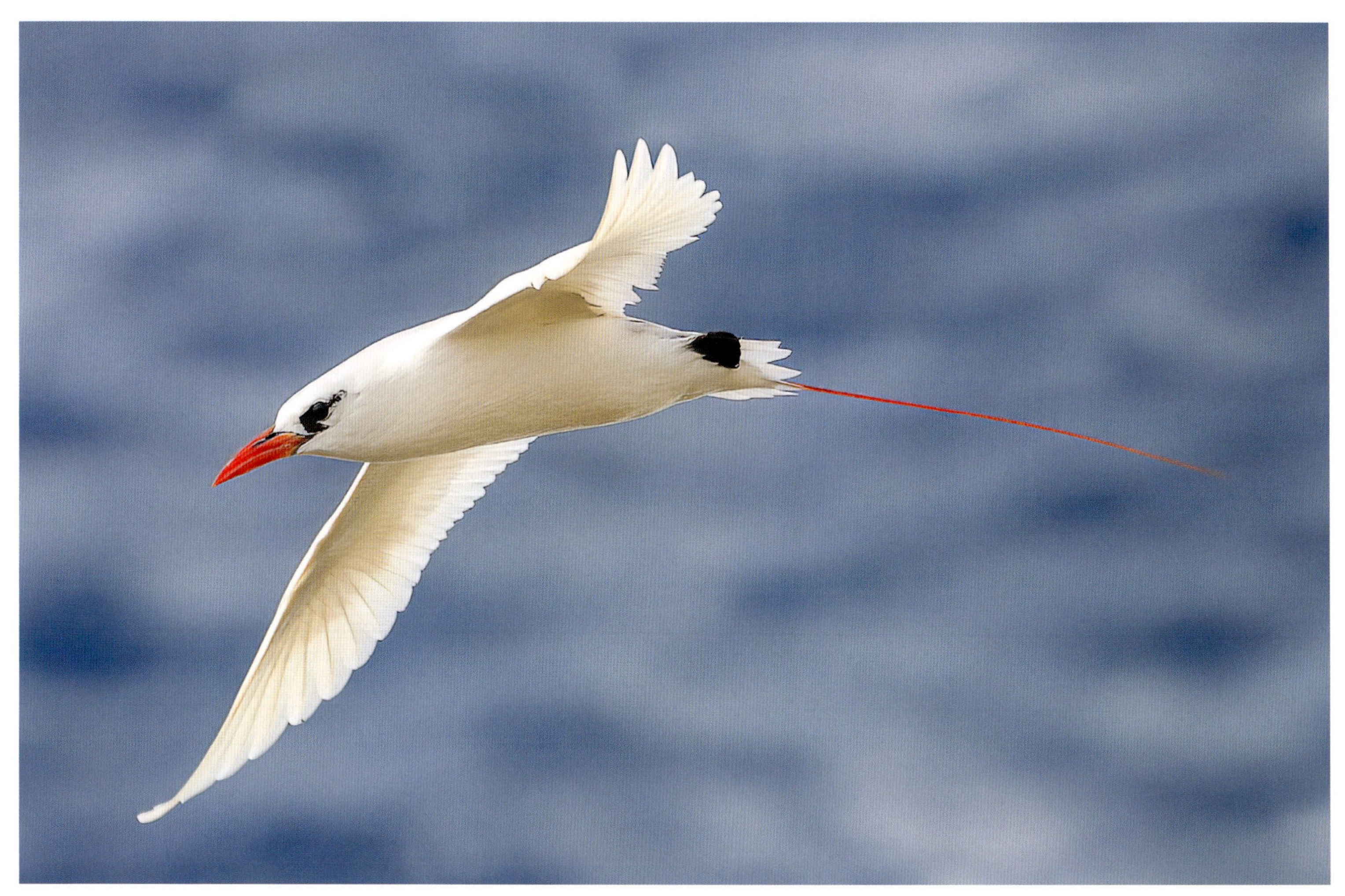

A STUNNING RED-TAILED TROPICBIRD, OR KOA'E'ULA, FLIES OVER HONOLULU ON OAHU, HAWAII.

A JUVENILE SNOW GOOSE FLIES OVER TERRA NOVA PARK IN RICHMOND, BC.

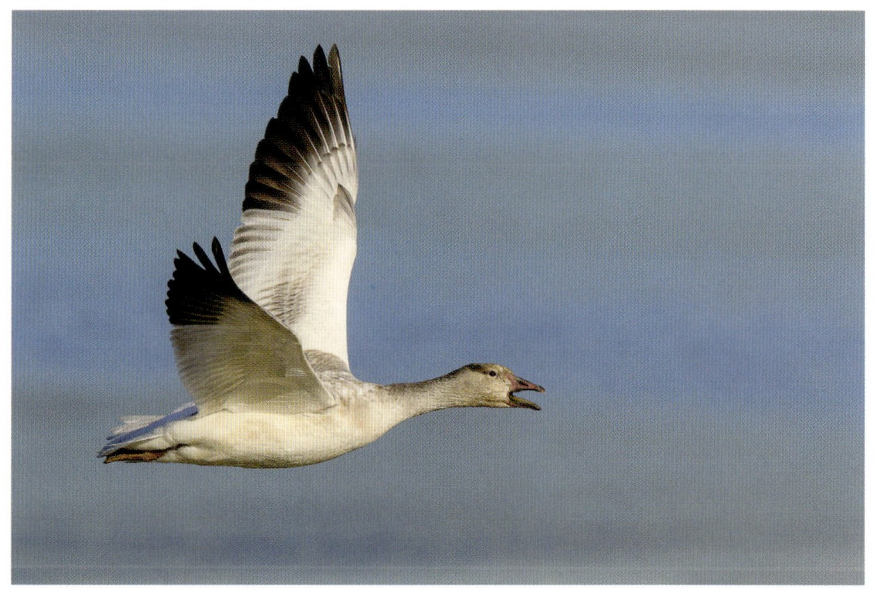

AN ADULT SNOW GOOSE FLIES OVER A FIELD IN DELTA, BC, WITH BEAUTIFUL FALL COLOURS IN THE BACKGROUND. SNOW GEESE WINTER IN MASSIVE NUMBERS IN SOUTHERN BC AND WASHINGTON STATE AFTER MIGRATING FROM RUSSIA AND ALASKA.

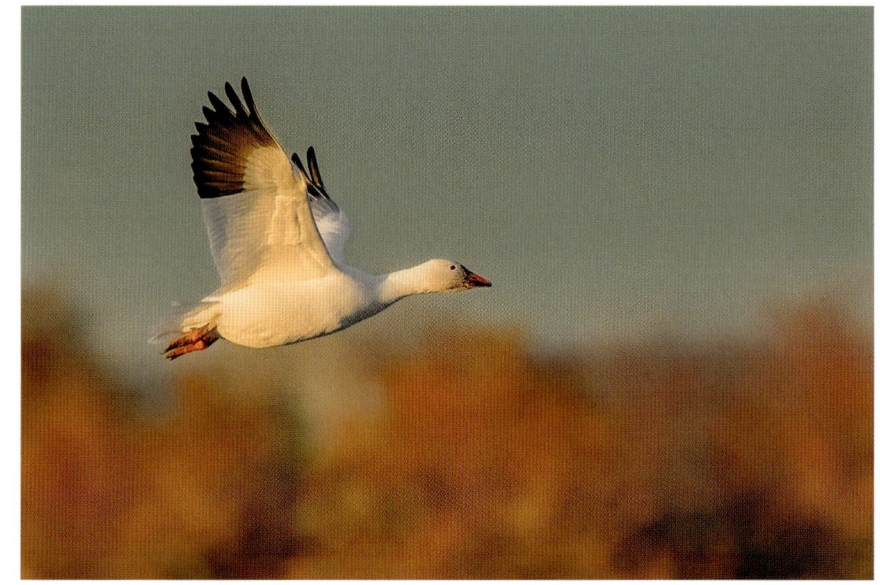

I WATCH IN AWE WITH OTHERS AS THIS SUB-ADULT NORTHERN GANNET FLEW BY US AT CAPE ST. MARY'S COLONY IN ST. BRIDE'S, NEWFOUNDLAND.

When I led a seven-day bird tour for Avocet Tours in Newfoundland, we visited Cape St. Mary's Ecological Reserve and saw one of the largest Northern Gannet colonies in Canada. Our collective jaws dropped as these beautiful birds flew right in front, above, and around us on the impressive cliffs where they nest. When I say the cliffs were impressive, I mean it. The cliffs at this location are sheer vertical and towering. If you have vertigo, this is not the place to visit! The sound of the crashing waves way down beneath you and listening to the cries of the braying Gannets and other seabirds is impressive. The cries of the Murres, Razorbills, Kittiwakes, Guillemots, and Gannets carry through the thick fog that often surrounds this mystical place.

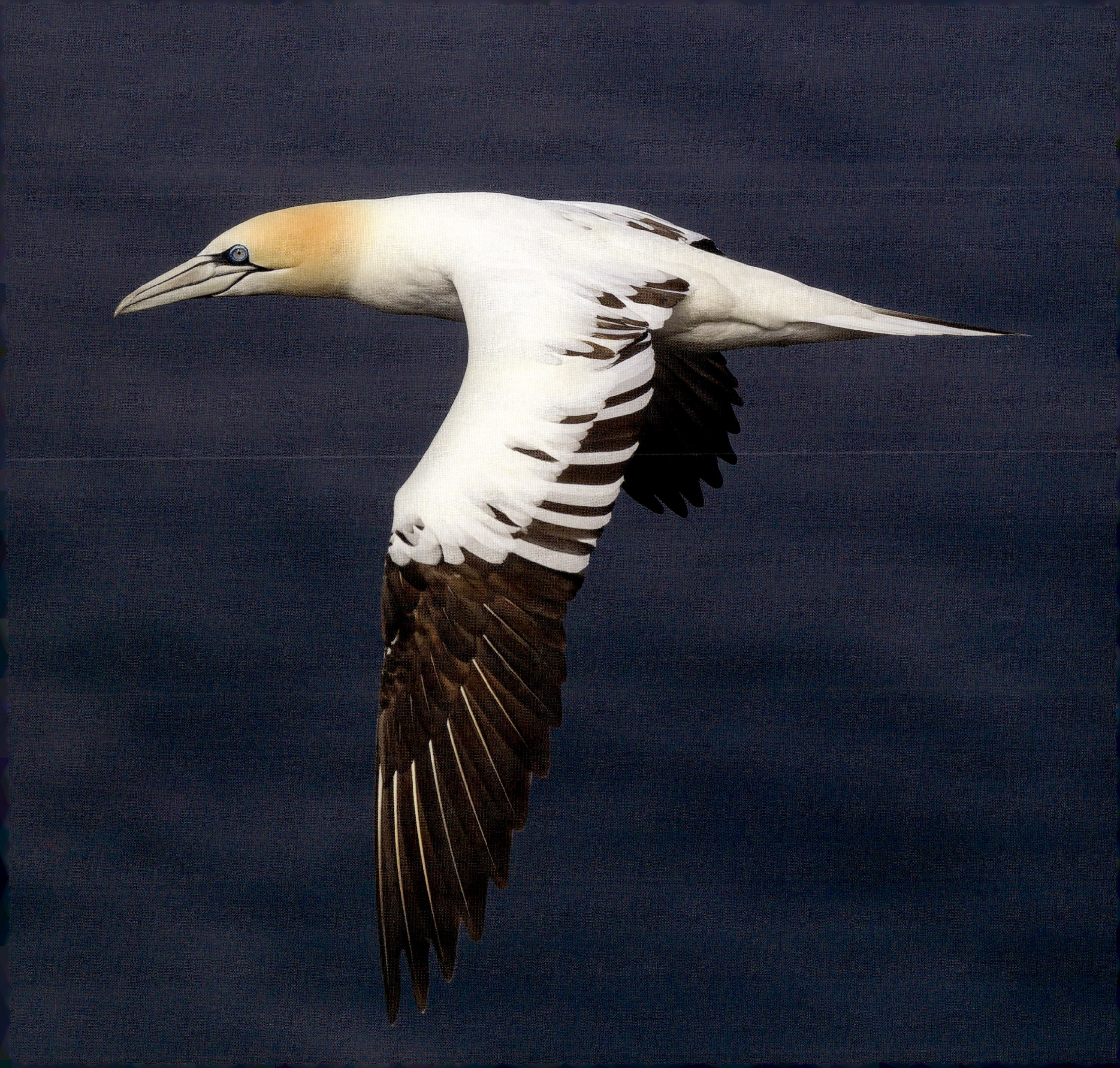

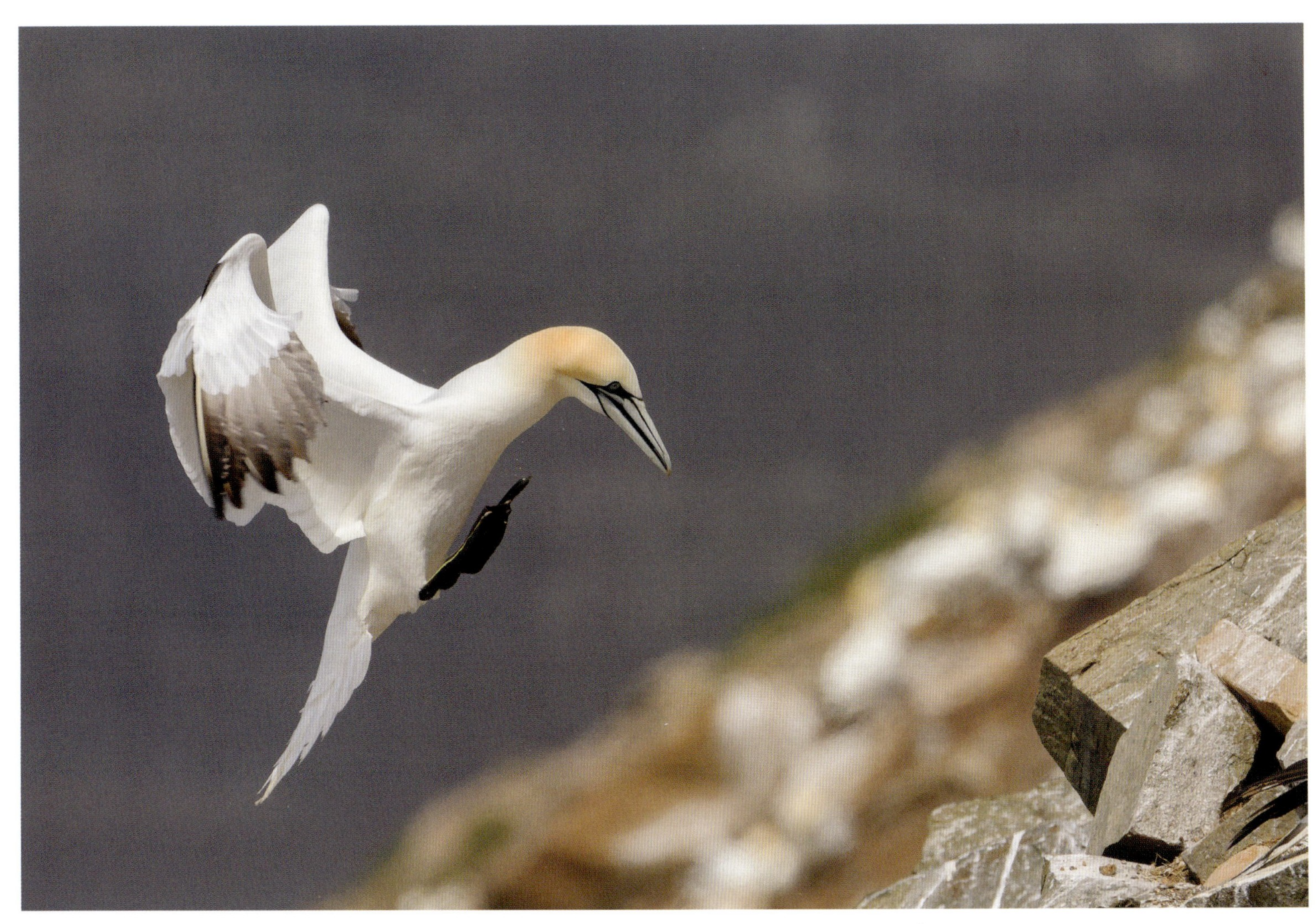

A NORTHERN GANNET VISITING ITS NEST AT THE CAPE ST. MARY'S COLONY IN NEWFOUNDLAND.

Blackpoll Warblers fly an average of 2540 km nonstop over an average of 62 hours, up to 3 days straight. Scientists have proven this by putting tiny geolocators on the birds' backs. They fly at a rate of 41 km per hour! They fly from their breeding grounds, which stretch from Alaska down through Canada to the northeastern United States, to their wintering grounds in the Caribbean and South America. What is even more fascinating about Blackpoll Warblers is that the birds that breed in Alaska fly the farthest of any Blackpoll Warbler and actually have developed longer wings to help them get to their wintering grounds faster. Leach's Storm-Petrels fly over 32,000 km every year as well. Pacific Golden-Plovers fly from Alaska all the way to Hawaii. Bar-tailed Godwits are the world record holders for the longest nonstop flight from Alaska to Tasmania. The bird can fly up to 11 days straight at a distance of 13,560 km! Most Bar-tailed Godwits migrate from Alaska to New Zealand and lose half of their body weight during their flights. Their internal organs also alter during their flights to make the long journey. It is imperative to protect migratory stopover points for shorebirds that use these critical grounds to rest and feed during long migrations. In Delta, BC, birds like Western Sandpipers use the critical stopover points in the Fraser River Estuary during their migration.

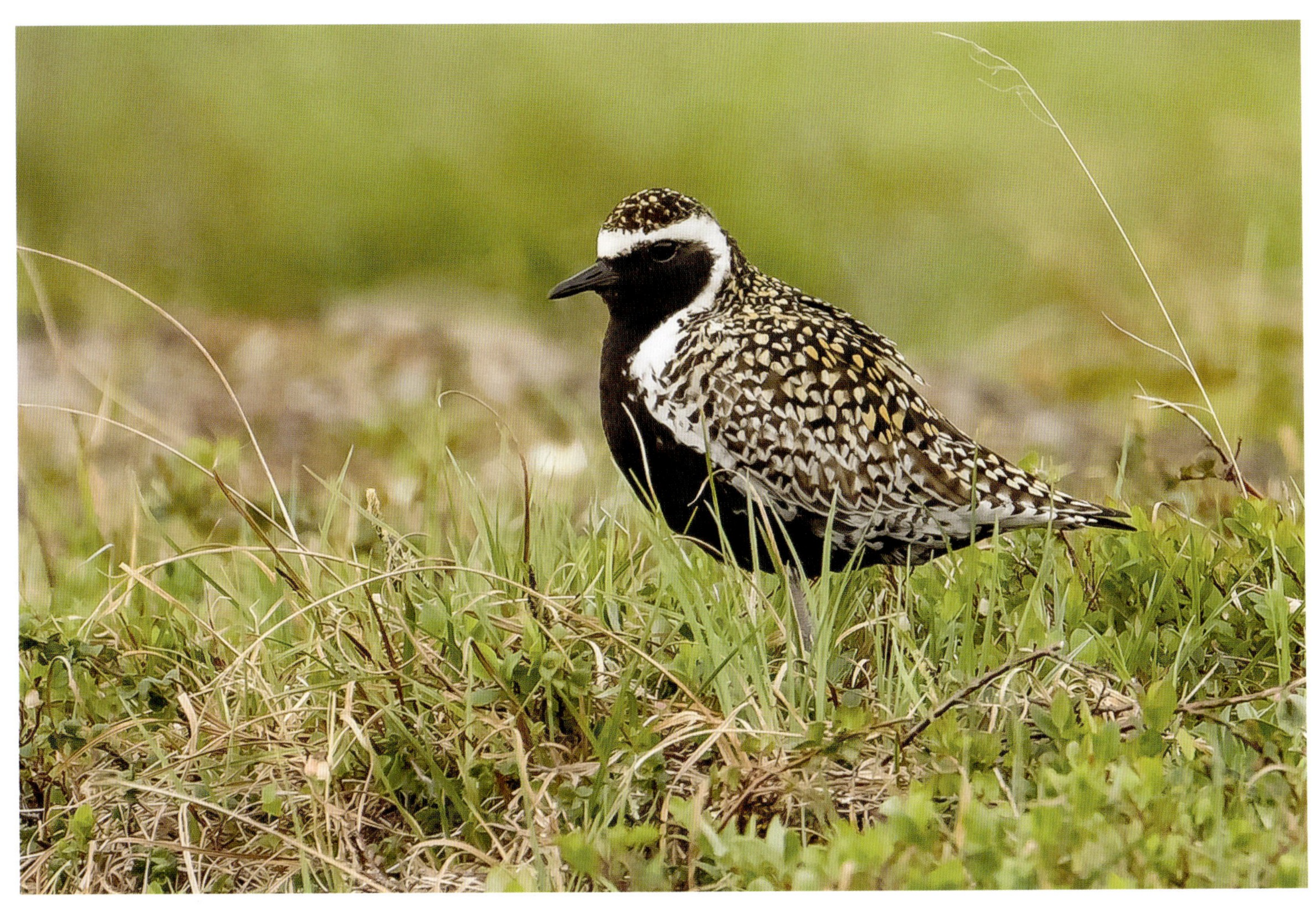

A PACIFIC GOLDEN-PLOVER IN BREEDING PLUMAGE AT ITS NESTING GROUNDS IN NOME, ALASKA.

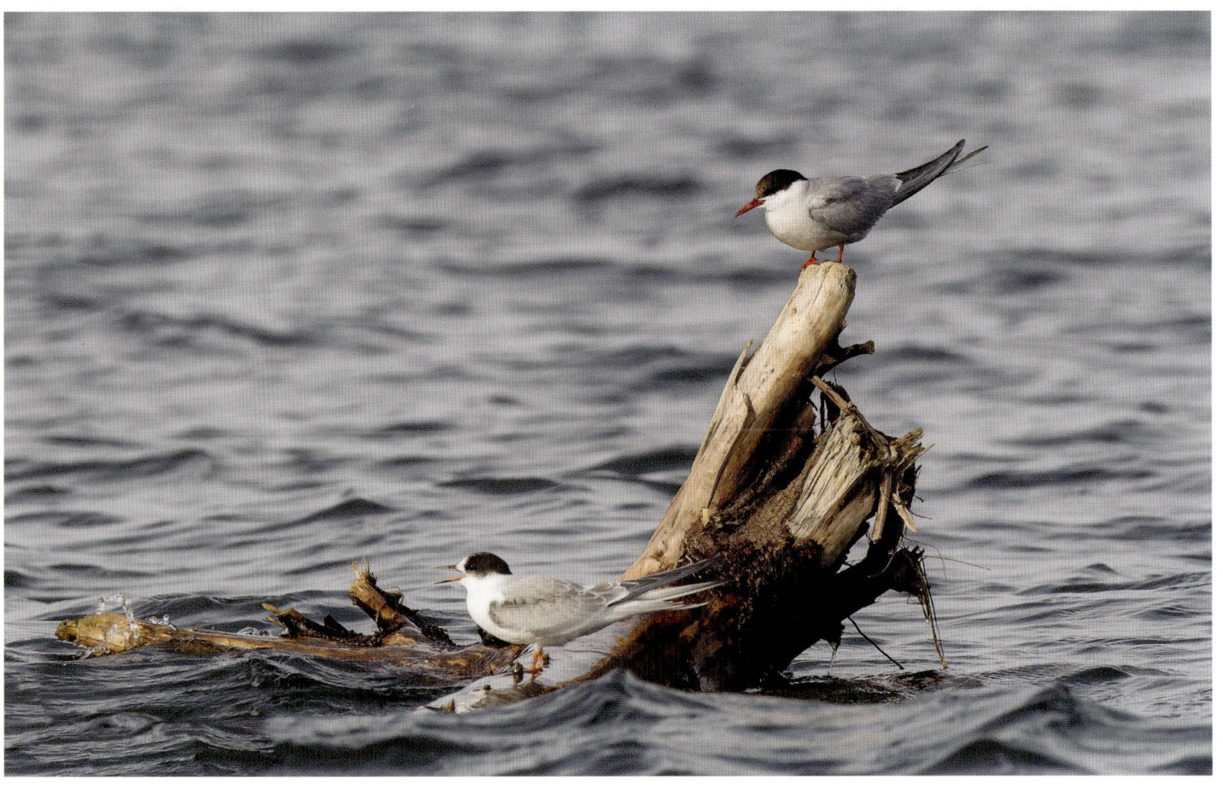

ARCTIC TERNS ARE RARELY SEEN OFFSHORE FROM VANCOUVER, BC.

Another fascinating flier is the Arctic Tern. Arctic Terns migrate from the Arctic where they breed to spend the winter in Antarctica and fly about 40,000 km! It is the farthest yearly journey of any bird. One day, I was out with my friends on a boat off Richmond, BC, and was lucky enough to see a rare and special treat – a juvenile Arctic Tern who was begging the adult to feed it. The offspring must have travelled with its parent, which is the first record of one doing so in the Metro Vancouver area.

AN ADULT ARCTIC TERN IS A RARE OCCURRENCE IN GREATER VANCOUVER WATERS. THIS ONE PERCHED IN FRONT OF THE BOAT I WAS IN OFF RICHMOND, BC.

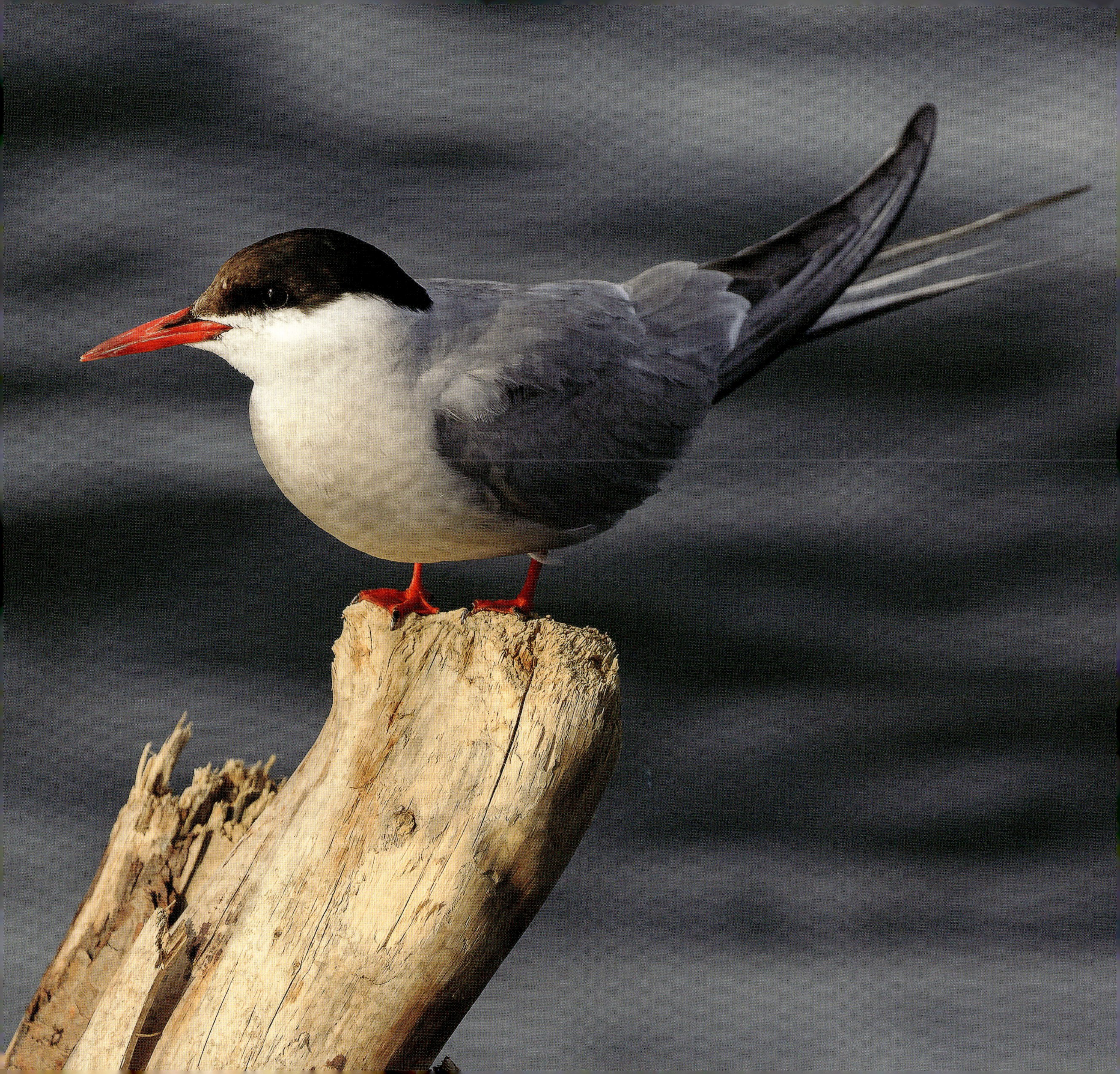

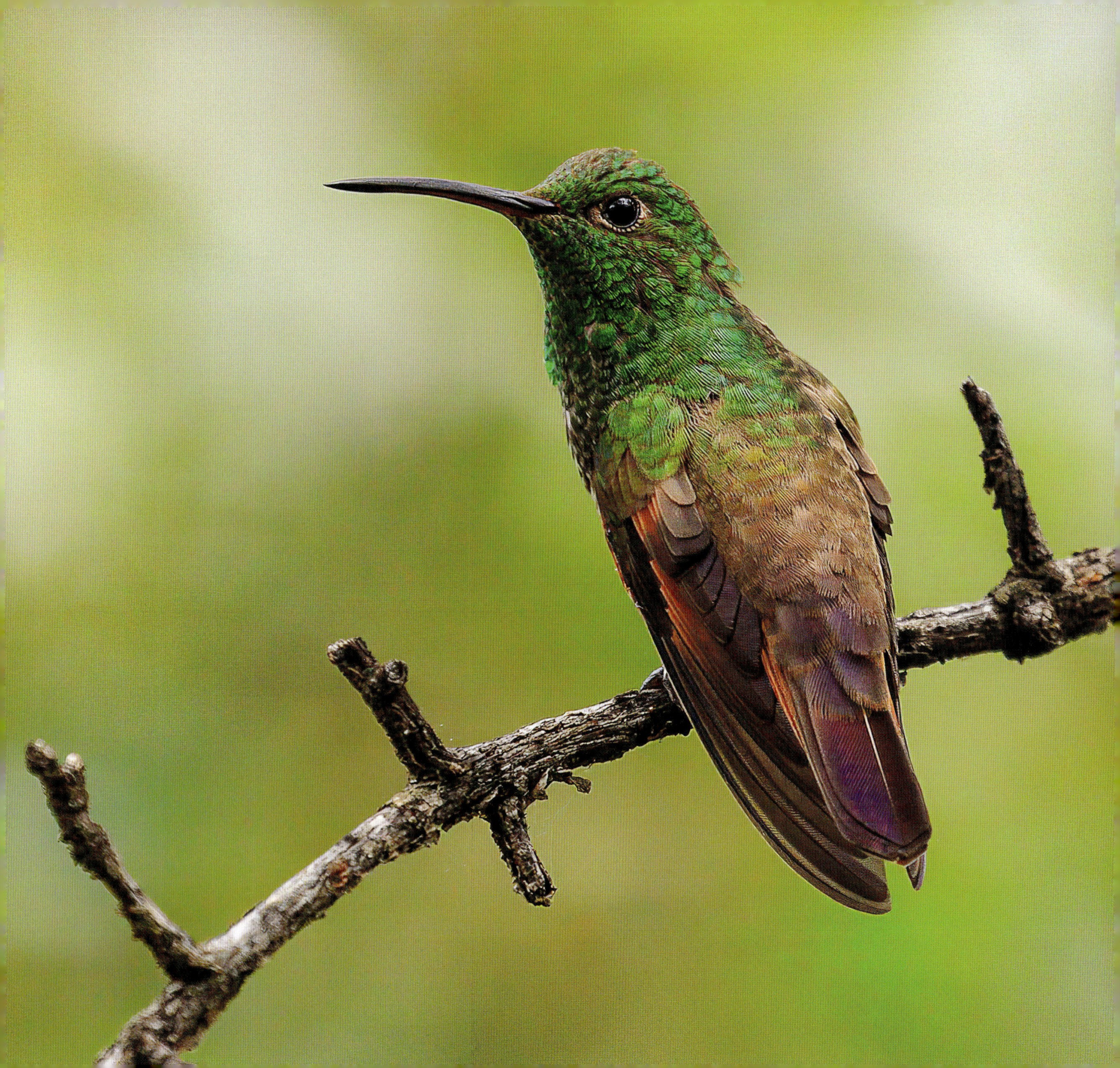

3

Hummingbirds – the Prismatic Gems

I like to call hummingbirds "prismatic gems." They are tiny jewels that shine so brightly in the right light when the sun hits their gorget. My mother loved hummingbirds and so do I. They are inspiring. Such tiny birds, yet they are fast and fierce. They will defend their territory and food source to the death if they have to. They migrate long distances. Take the Rufous Hummingbird, for instance, that winters in Mexico and summers as far north as Alaska! The heart of an Anna's Hummingbird can beat up to 1,200 times per minute when it is flying. When they go into torpor, their heart rate plummets to 50 times per minute. Anna's Hummingbirds now stay all year in south coastal BC. Some hummingbirds that migrate fly over 960 km of open bodies of water to get to and from their breeding grounds each year during migration.

Opposite:

A BERYLLINE HUMMINGBIRD IN PORTAL, ARIZONA. SEEING THIS HUMMINGBIRD WAS ONE OF THE MOST MAGICAL MOMENTS I'VE HAD WHILE BIRDING.

As I said before, birds are fascinating. Although hummingbirds are tiny, they leave you in complete wonder at their fierce and incredible personalities, not to mention their stunning iridescent gorget colours. In BC, we are spoiled with several species of hummingbirds: Black-chinned, Anna's, Rufous, and Calliope.

Arizona is one of my favourite places to bird in North America, not only because it has so many diverse species and rarities but also because I LOVE HUMMERS! There are so many more brilliant hummingbird species in Arizona than in BC because it is further south and closer to Mexico. When I went to Ecuador and saw all the hummers, my jaw dropped. I saw almost 50 species of hummers, and one even tapped my red nail polish on my hands, trying to feed from my fingers (but that's another story for another book). I will never tire of looking at hummingbirds. After my mom died, a female Rufous Hummingbird visited my yard frequently in the summer. Even though I live in Vancouver, where there are many Rufous Hummingbirds, they seldom visit my yard, so this was unusual. It would fly up and pause in front of my face and follow me around the yard, and as it did so a feeling of warmth would

Opposite:

A BLUE-THROATED MOUNTAIN-GEM IN PORTAL, ARIZONA.

come over me. I believe it was a sign from my mother, but of course I can't prove it. Even for those who have never lost anyone, seeing a hummingbird will bring a type of joy into your life that you have never known.

One of the best moments I have had while birding was on a fall trip to Arizona. I went to Portal to see a Berylline Hummingbird. I was told to dress in red to attract the bird, so I wore a red shirt. Birding really does take you to some beautiful and unique places. The trail I walked to find the Berylline was small and narrow and led me through a pine-clad canyon high in the Chiricahua Mountains. Surprisingly, I was all alone. Almost immediately, a beautiful Berylline Hummingbird zipped to me. I could hear it buzzing as it looked at my shirt, trying to figure out how it could feed from it. It perched and posed for me, then, just like that, it was gone. A magical moment shared with one of the tiniest birds on the planet.

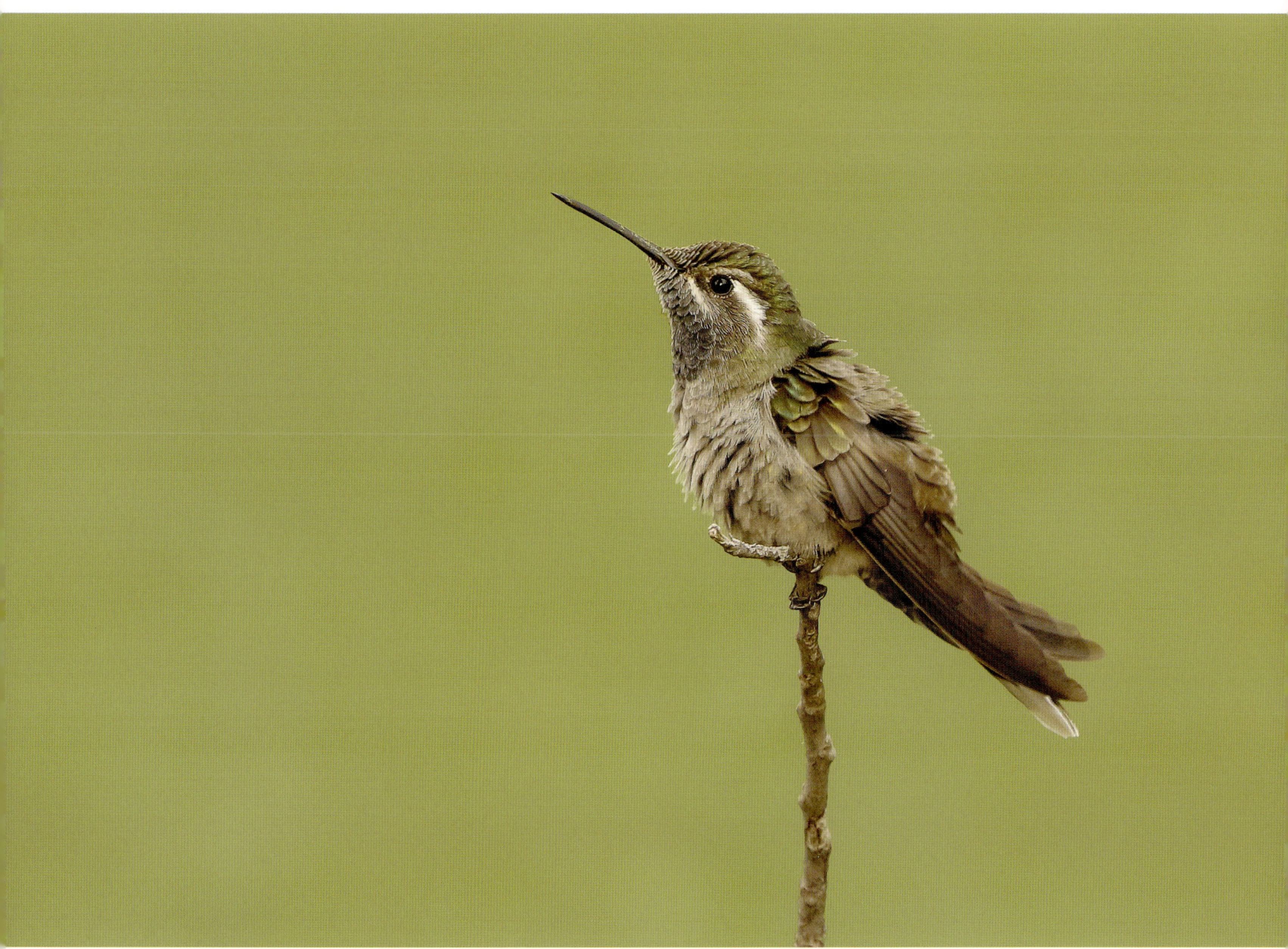

A FEMALE ANNA'S HUMMINGBIRD TAKING NATURAL NECTAR FROM FLOWERS IN RICHMOND, BC.

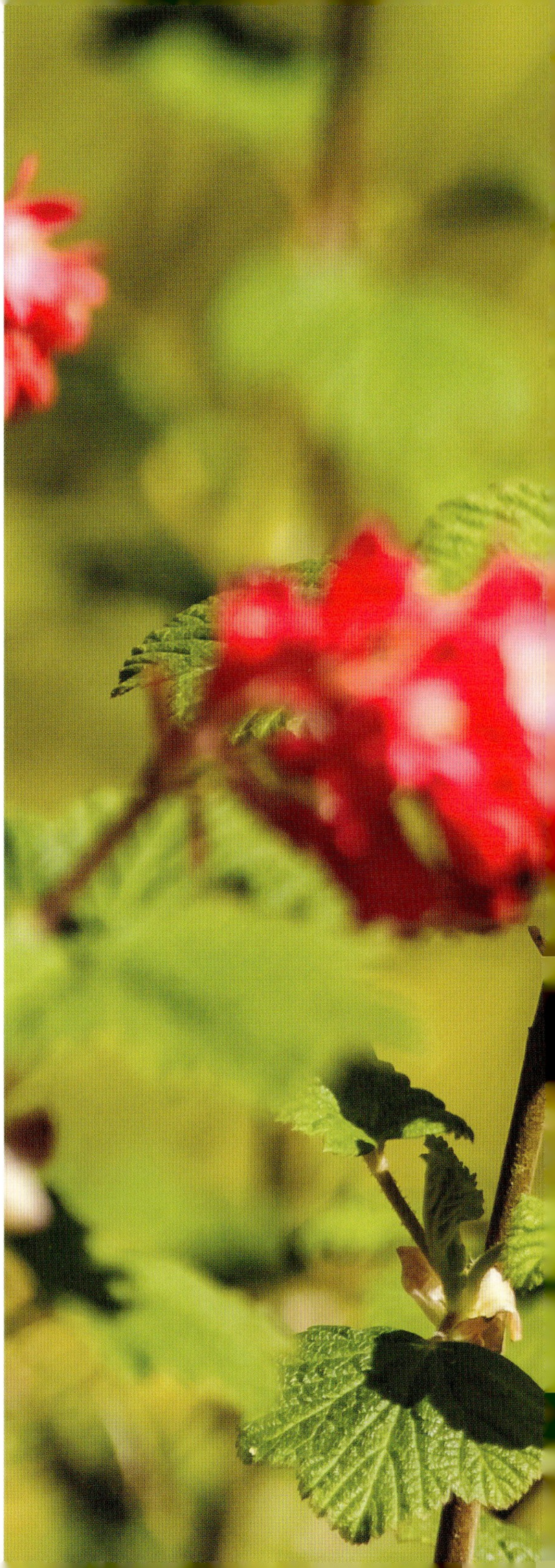

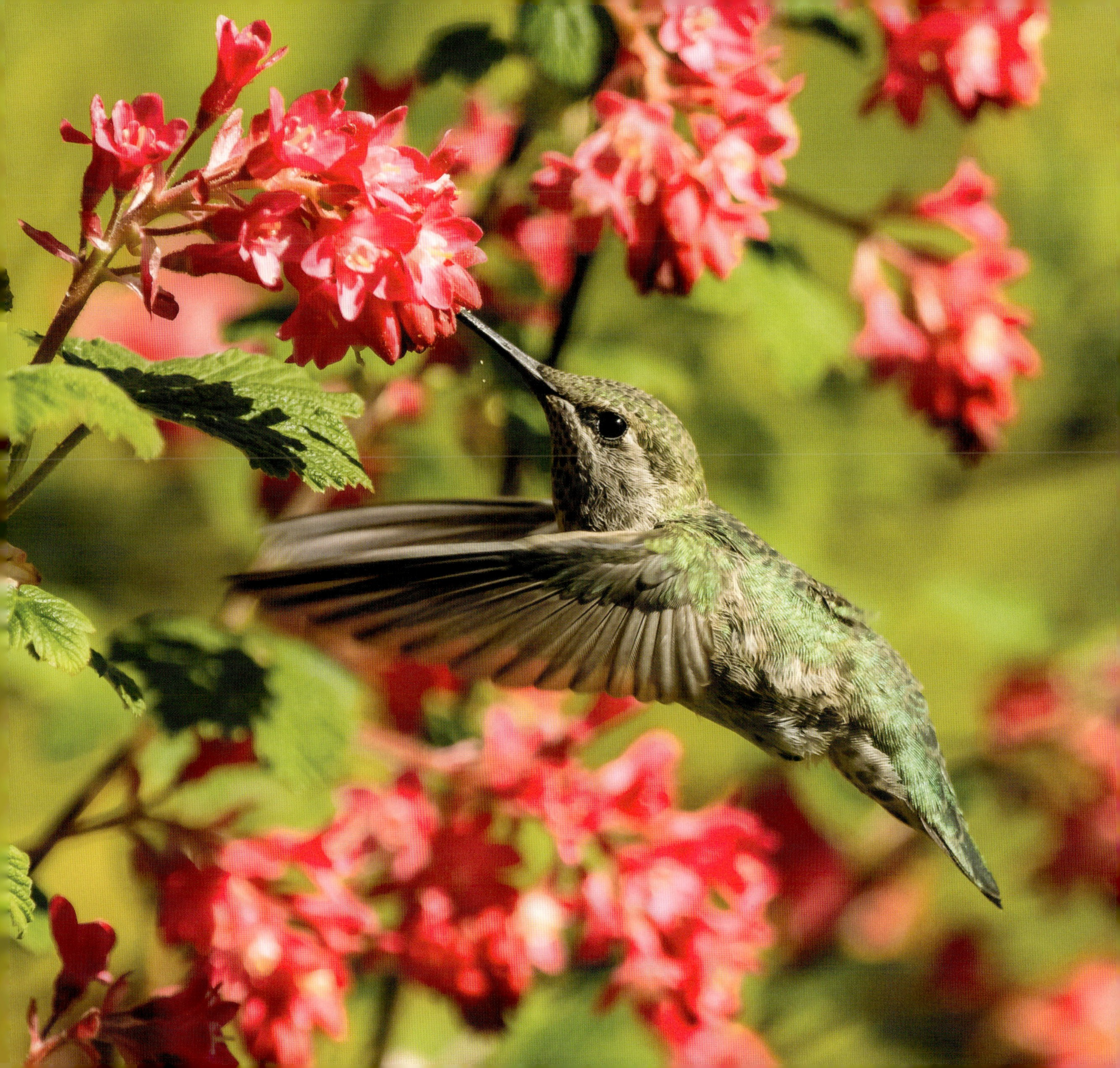

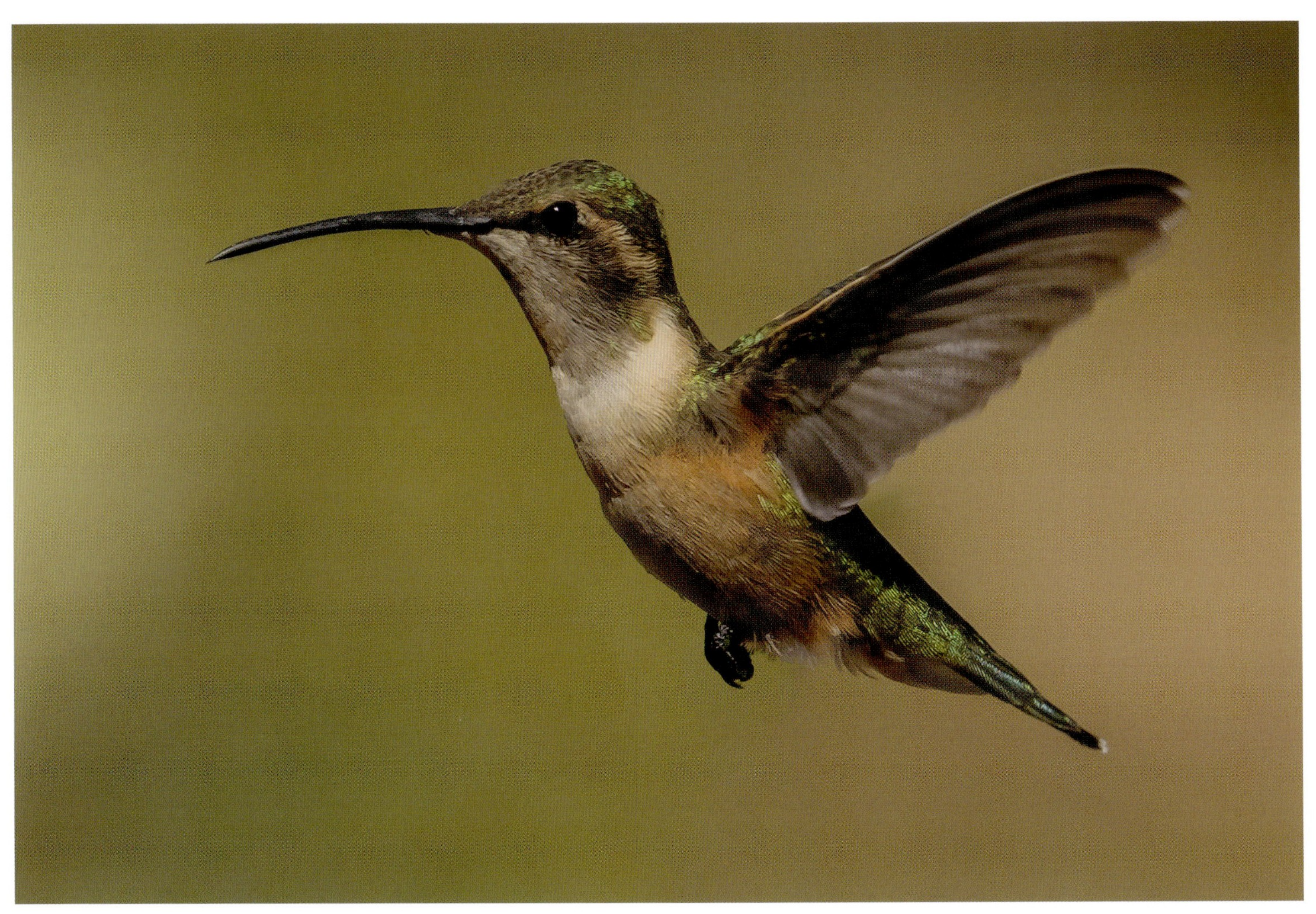

A FEMALE LUCIFER HUMMINGBIRD FLIES IN FRONT OF MY FOLKS AND ME IN HEREFORD, ARIZONA.

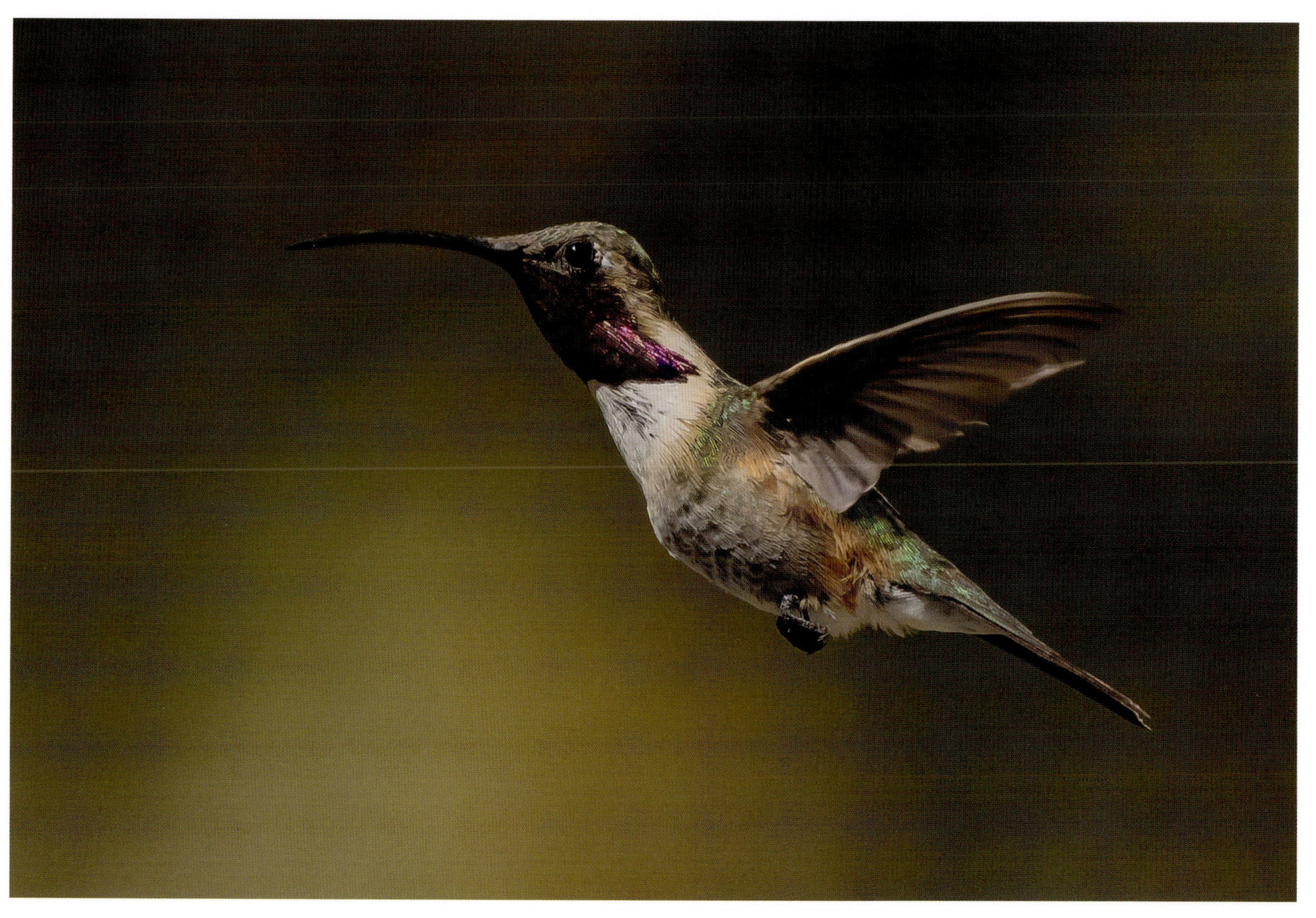

A MALE LUCIFER HUMMINGBIRD HOVERS IN FRONT OF MY PARENTS AND ME IN HEREFORD, ARIZONA.

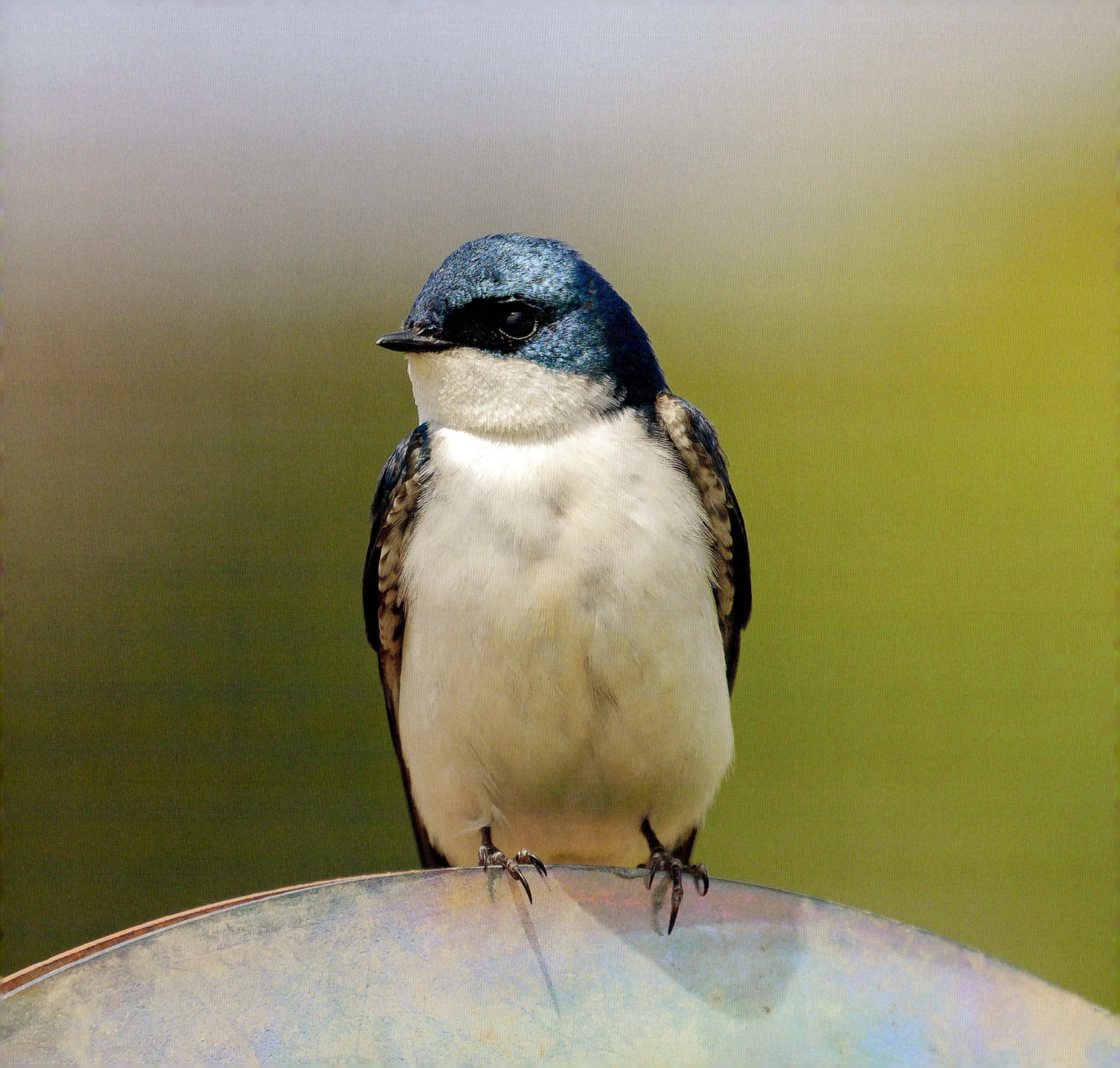

4

Connection

As humans, we all strive for connection. Do you ever sit and ponder just how we are all connected? Birds connect us and reflect how we are connected to those we love. The Tree Swallows and Purple Martins I work with show us just how intertwined that connection is. I started a project by petitioning the City of Richmond to put Tree Swallow nest boxes up in local parks and said I would monitor and maintain them. The city agreed, and we now have over 60 boxes in four parks and are in our third year. The project has been very successful and has fledged hundreds of young. However, until we retrofitted our nest boxes, we were losing too many young to the effects of human-induced climate change. During two consecutive years, we went through heat waves in the Metro Vancouver area, and we lost young due to temperatures that were over 40 degrees Celsius. We have painted the boxes white and added heat shields and more ventilation holes this year, in order to help cool the boxes to prevent further losses of chicks to the heat.

Opposite:

A MALE TREE SWALLOW IN RICHMOND, BC, PERCHES NEAR ITS NEST, WHICH IT IS GUARDING AGAINST PREDATORS.

I have also added 20 Purple Martin nest boxes with the help of the City of Richmond in the Steveston area. My friend Rob Lyske helped build the boxes, and my friend John Reynolds helped me to get the boxes up with Rob by using his boat. The federal government also granted permission for us to place the boxes on their lands. It was a great collaboration effort and an important issue, since this species is blue-listed in BC and in such decline.

My mom loved to go for evening walks with me to watch hundreds of swallows fly and feed over water. She was mesmerized by the sight of the Tree Swallows, especially as these blue and white elegant dazzling creatures flew over us in their acrobatic flight style, twisting and turning low over the water. This helped to forge our connection even deeper over our mutual love of these incredible creatures. Now that she is gone, they carry my heart on their wings every time I see them.

Swallows are an indicator species. We have noticed that, with a warming planet, some birds are coming back to their breeding grounds too early and not finding enough food, and, in turn, some of their

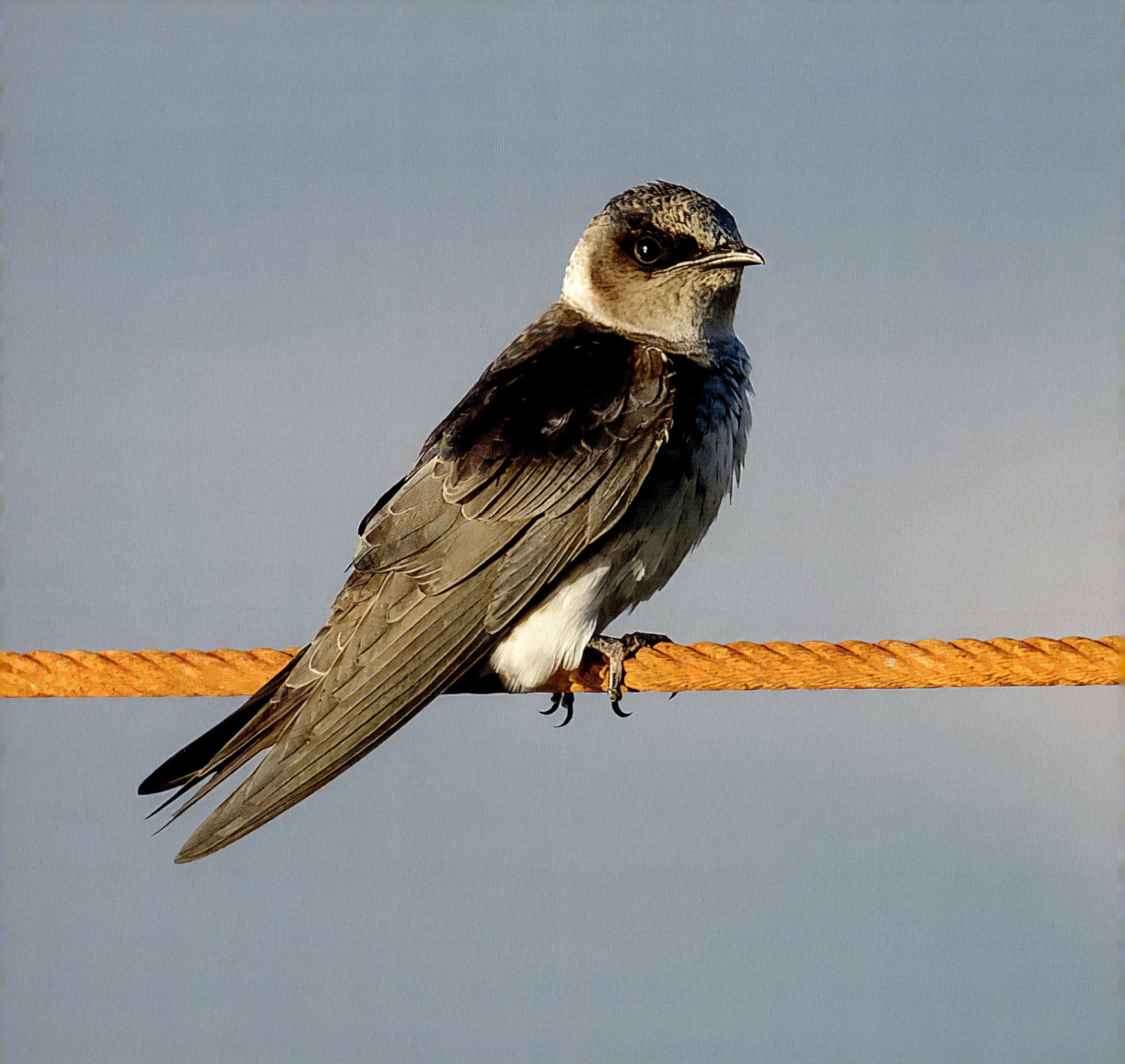

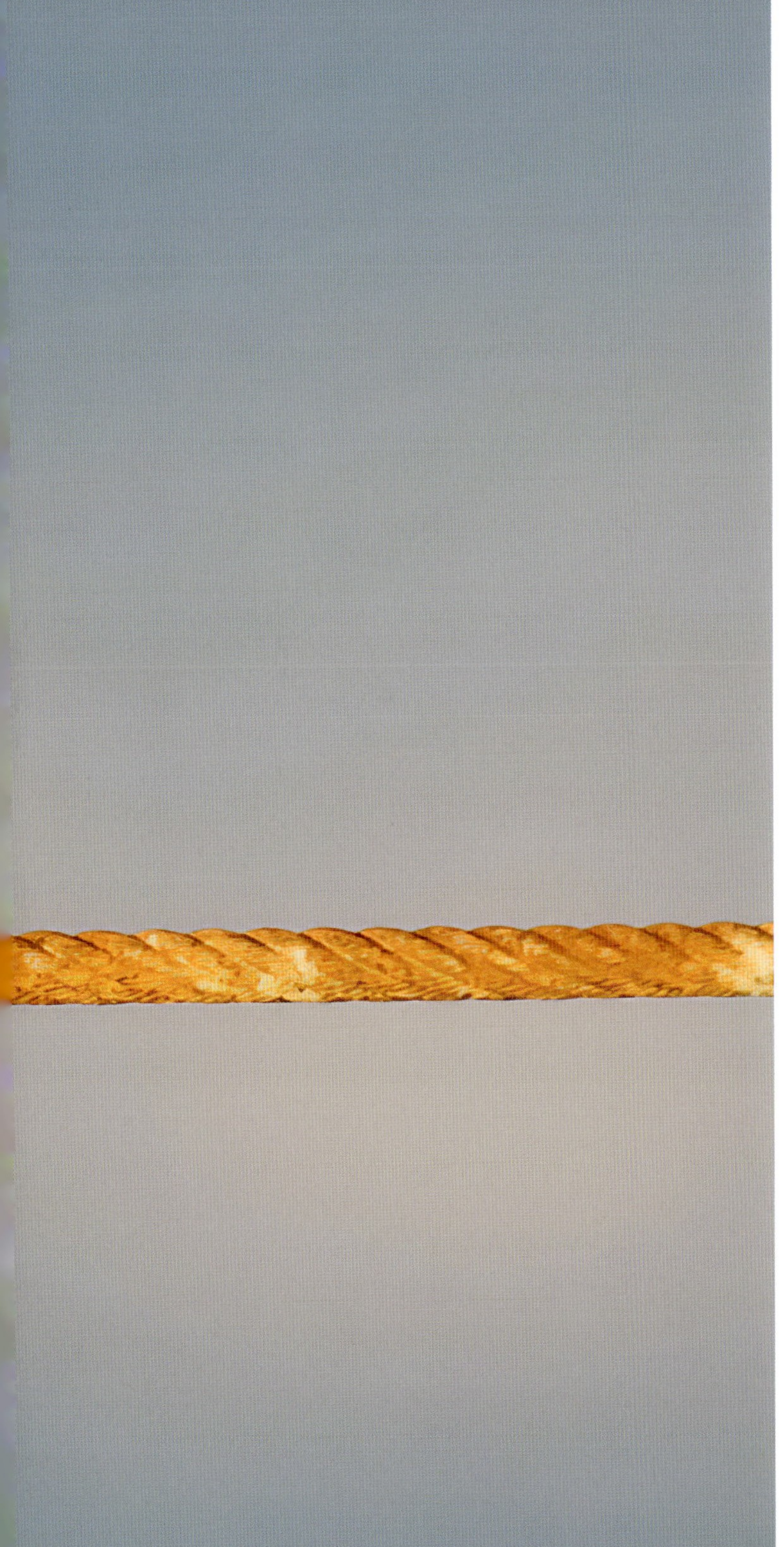

A FEMALE PURPLE MARTIN PERCHES ON A WIRE AT IONA BEACH REGIONAL PARK IN RICHMOND, BC. I HAVE STARTED A NEST BOX PROJECT IN COLLABORATION WITH THE CITY OF RICHMOND TO HELP PROTECT THESE BIRDS FROM FURTHER DECLINE.

young don't make it either. We are seeing a shift on new eBird trend maps, which are showing that many species are moving north as the climate warms. This should be alerting us that our behaviours are impacting these birds in a negative light. Tree Swallows and Purple Martins used to nest in natural tree cavities, but due to logging and urban development, they have lost many of their natural nesting sites. Humans have helped them by installing nest boxes. Purple Martins were almost extirpated from BC, but because of human intervention they have made a dramatic comeback. Humans have the power to do

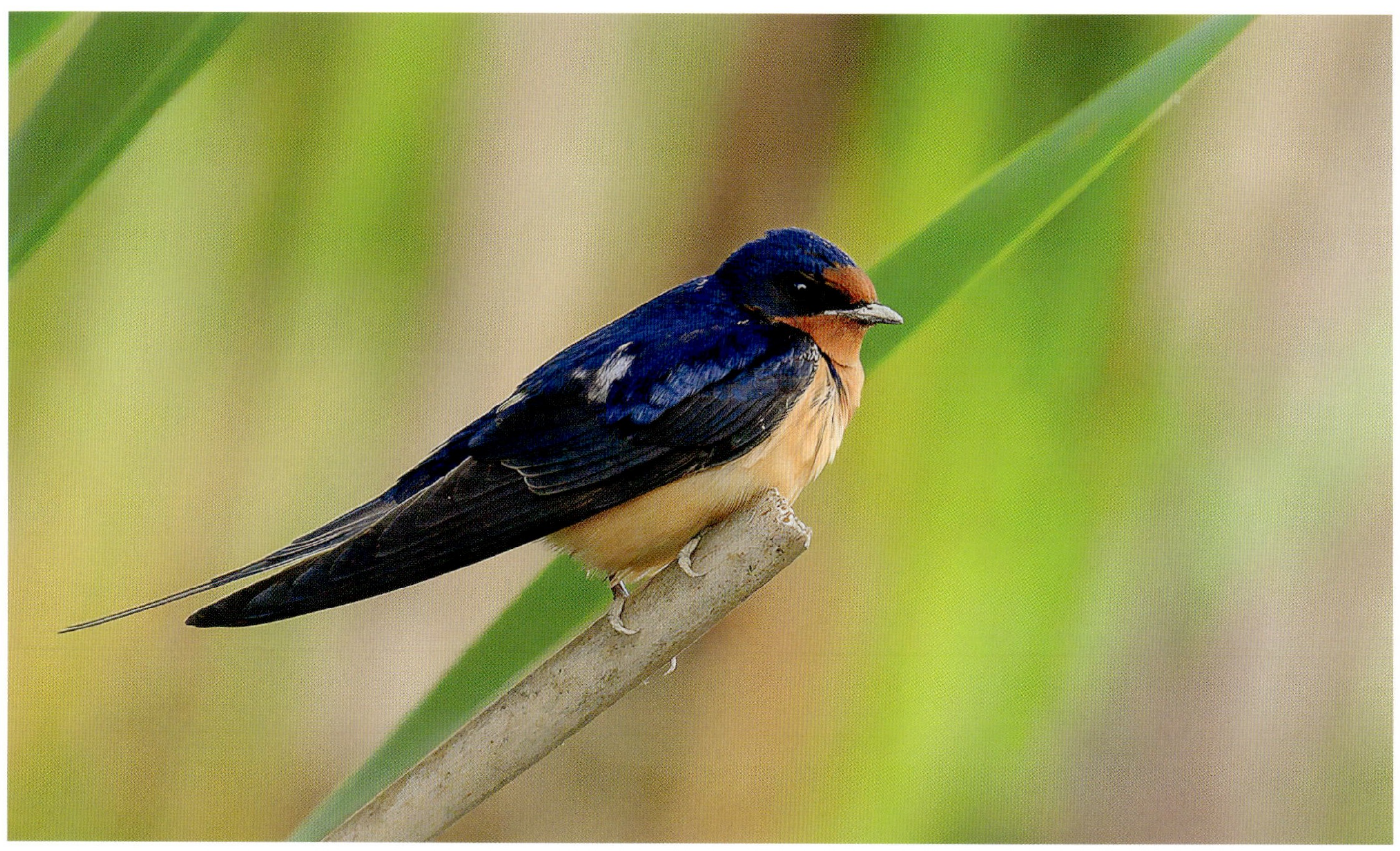

AN ADULT BARN SWALLOW PERCHES ON REEDS IN A POND IN RICHMOND, BC.

so much good for birds, but also in the same hands we hold the power to hurt them. Both humans and birds use the same keys for survival – air, water, and shelter – to thrive and survive. Like I said, we are so connected. It is up to us to decide how to positively nurture that connection. We definitely must do better for the birds that bring us so much joy.

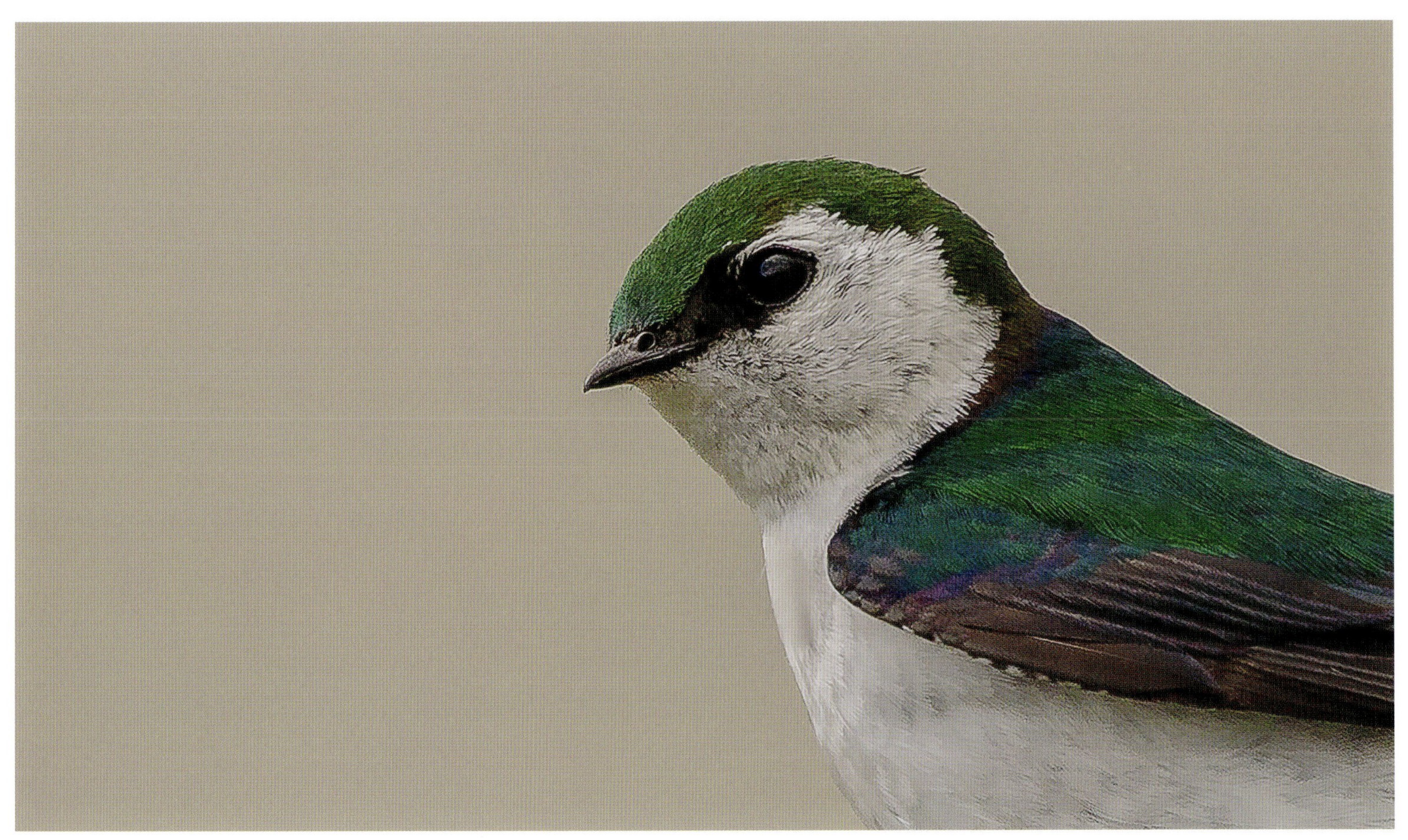

A MALE VIOLET-GREEN SWALLOW LOOKS AT ME IN DELTA, BC. THESE SWALLOWS HAVE HUES OF STUNNING GREEN AND BRONZE ON THEIR WINGS AND BACK AND BRIGHT PURPLE ON THEIR TAILS BELOW THEIR DISTINCTIVE WHITE RUMP PATCHES KNOWN AS "SADDLEBAGS."

A MALE TREE SWALLOW SITS ON AN UNUSUAL PERCH, A CONIFER IN RICHMOND, BC.

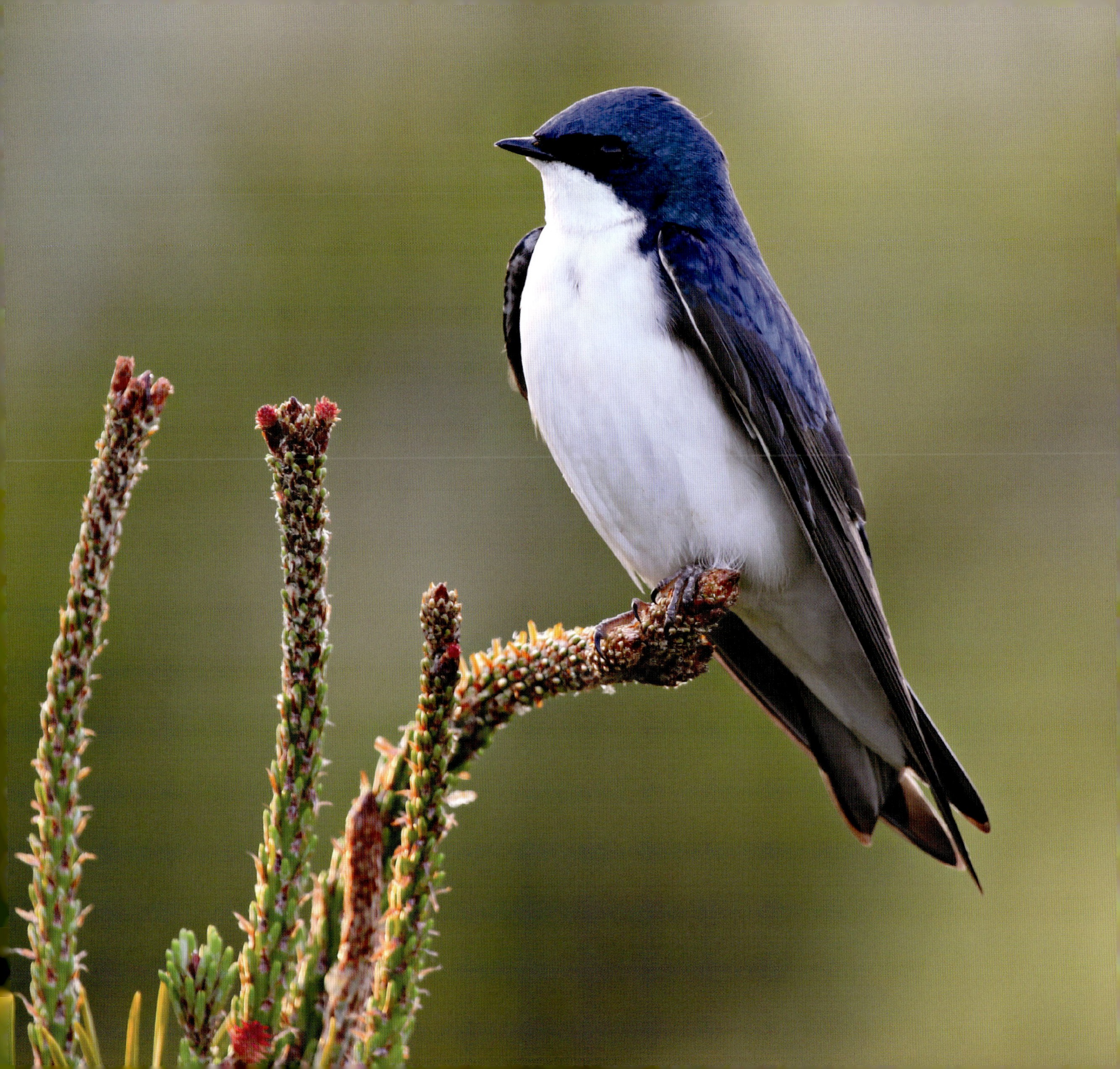

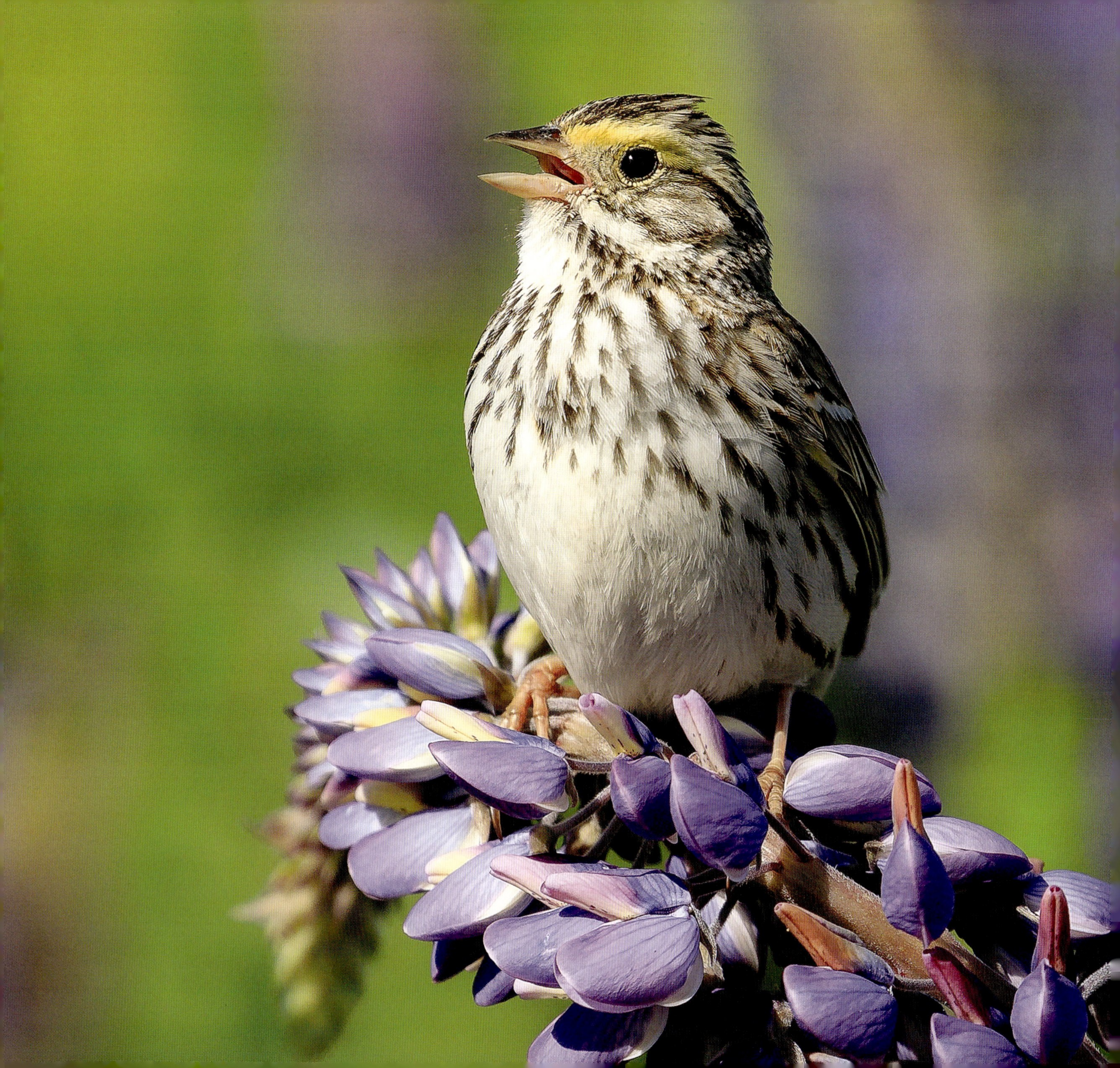

5

The Healing Power of Bird Sounds and Song

Birdsong is pure joy; when I hear it, the heavy burden of life and grief lightens just a little. When I am feeling very sad, my best remedy is to get out in nature and look at birds.

Opposite:

A SAVANNAH SPARROW SINGS FROM A PURPLE LUPINE FLOWER AT GARRY POINT PARK IN RICHMOND, BC.

The sweet song of warblers in the spring is what I yearn for all winter. You may be surprised to learn how much we move through the world using our sense of hearing over sight. I truly could not imagine a world devoid of birdsong, could you? Imagine seeing a Ruffed Grouse display but not hearing the drumming sounds of its wings. Ruffed Grouse will flap their wings vigorously forward and backward against the air, creating a low-pitched, intensifyingly rapid thumping sound. Or seeing a declining Western Meadowlark perched on sagebrush but not hearing its gorgeous song. All grassland songbirds are in dramatic decline and habitat loss is one of the biggest reasons why. I would hate to walk through a Hawaiian forest and not hear the lovely song of the endemic Hawaiian honeycreepers. There are many people and organizations working hard day in and day out to prevent that from happening. Could you imagine watching a flight of Snow Geese flying in without hearing their honking cries? No, neither could I. To not hear the bugling call of a Sandhill Crane would break my heart. It is a true gift to hear the sounds of birds. Sometimes it is just nice to go out in the forest and bird by ear and identify all the sounds around you, even if you can't see all the birds.

Did you know that many birds mimic other birds' sounds, like the Northern Mockingbird or the European Starling? Some birds have distinctive regional dialects as well. Many songs are extremely complex and others are not. Some sing staying hidden deep in forest brush,

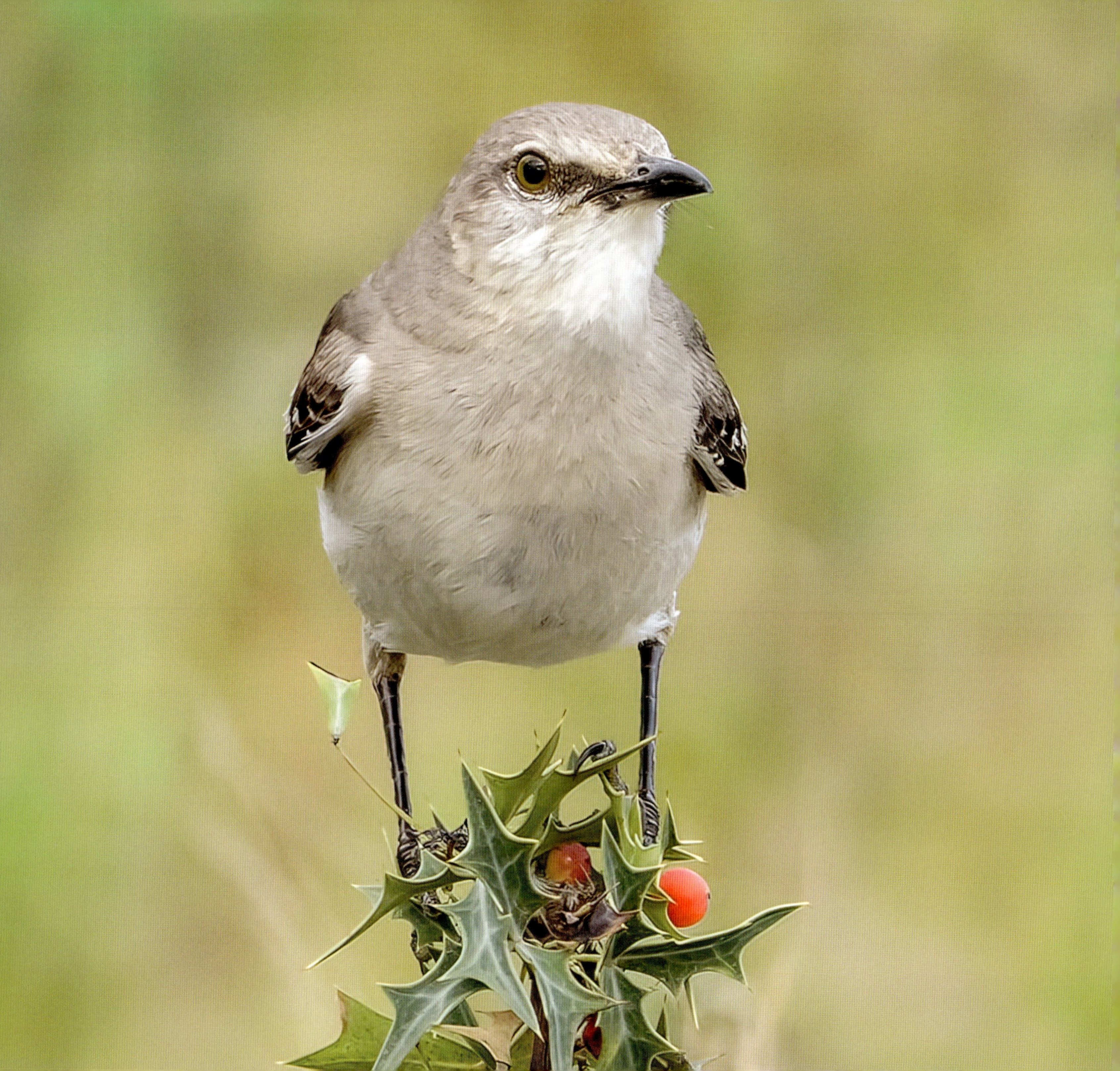

A NORTHERN MOCKINGBIRD IN BRACKETTVILLE, TEXAS.

like Pacific Wrens, and others sing from exposed perches, like a Meadowlark or Song Sparrow. Some birds do displays while they sing, like Lapland Longspurs on their arctic breeding grounds. It is a misnomer that birdsong is only attributed to male birds. Some female birds sing just as loud as the males. The world of birdsong is a fascinating one.

We have a small breeding population of Yellow-headed Blackbirds at Iona Beach Regional Park near my house in Richmond. Every spring I love to go see the returning males. Each year we are getting less and less of these breeding birds, and I am afraid one day they will not return, but for now I will keep listening to their songs. This species has a very unique song and call. They do a harsh, buzzy, screeching song. These vocalizations may not be melodious to most, but to me it is a song I wait for every spring.

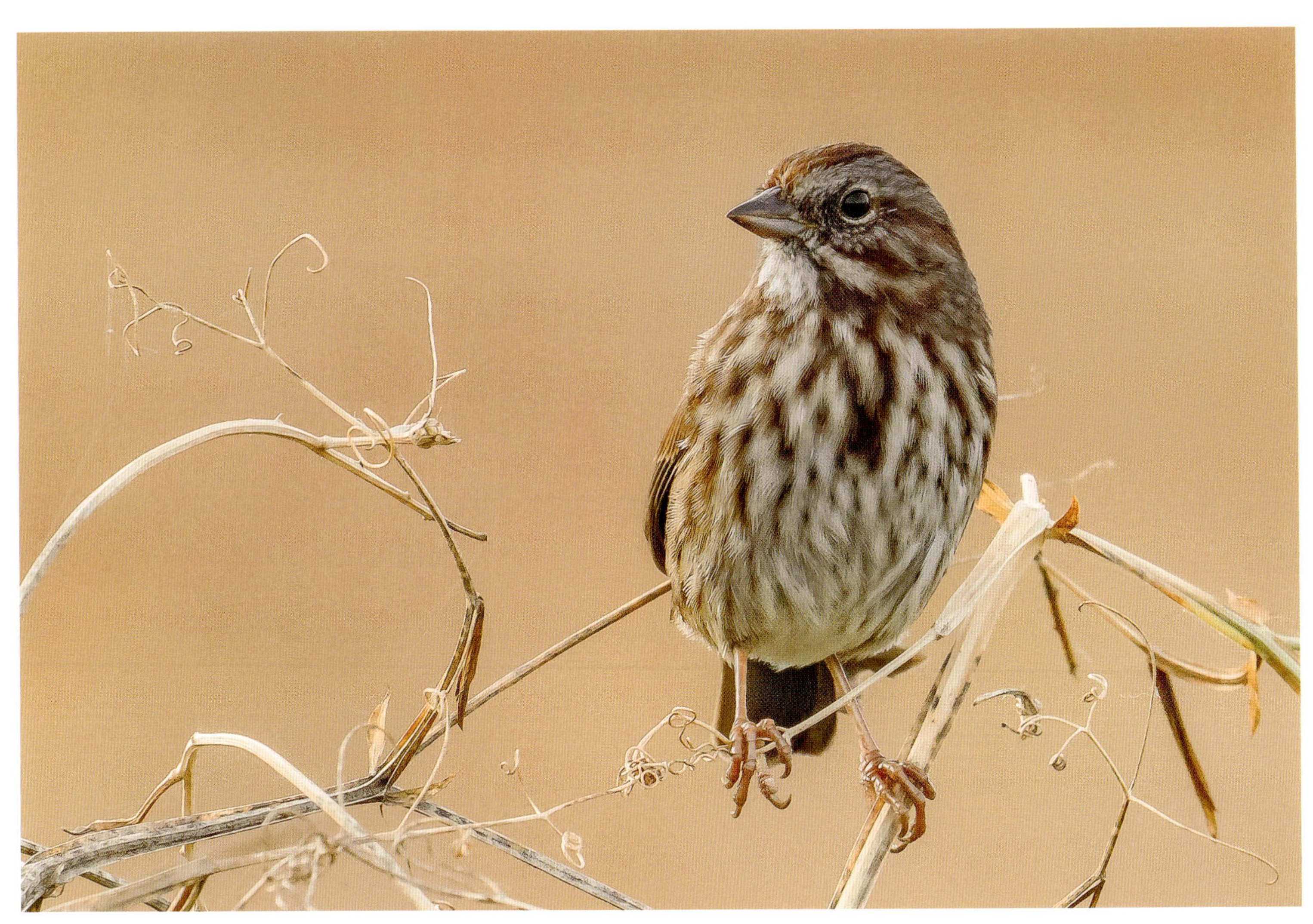

A SONG SPARROW IN DELTA, BC.

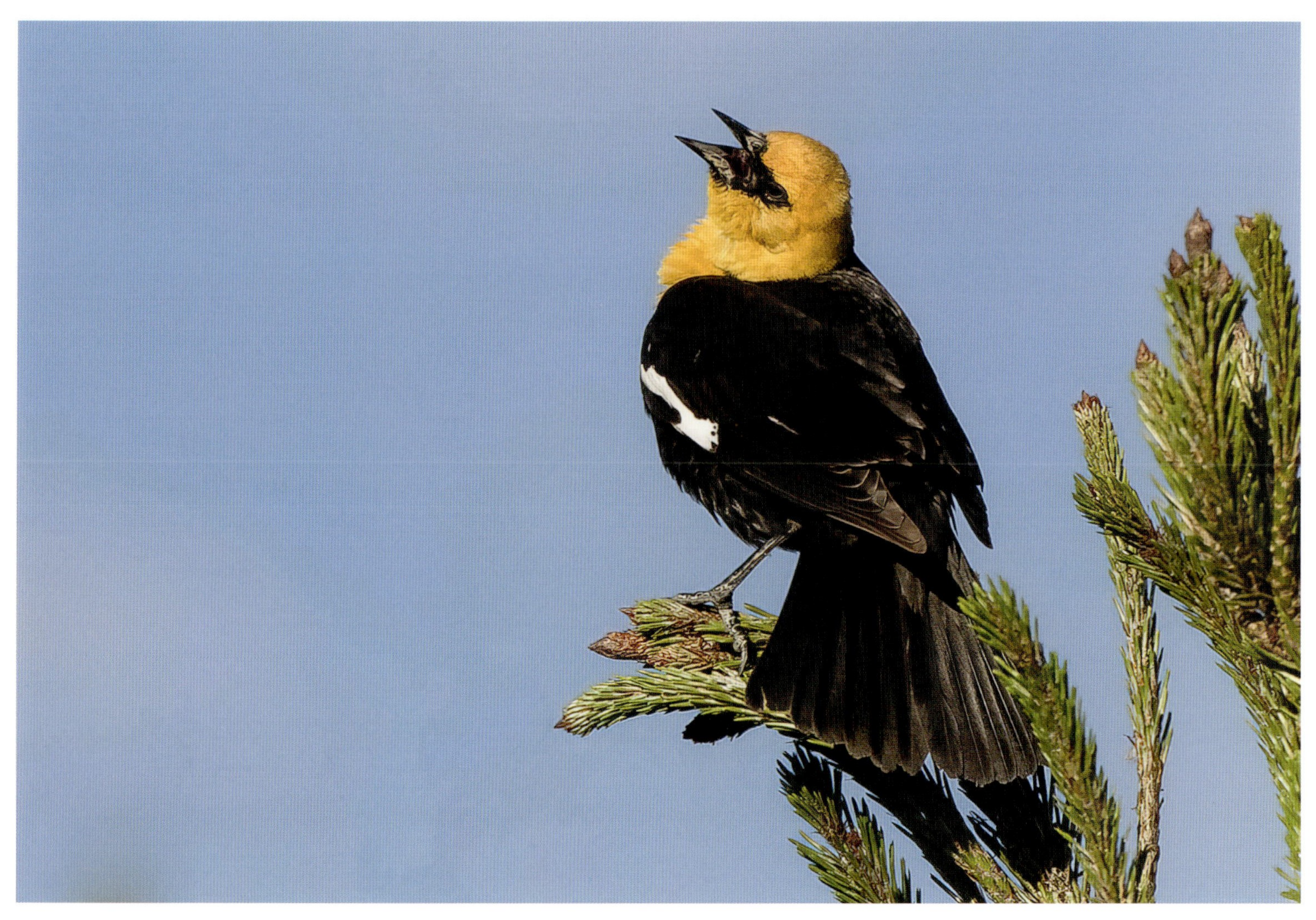

A MALE YELLOW-HEADED BLACKBIRD SINGS FROM ITS BREEDING GROUNDS AT IONA BEACH REGIONAL PARK IN RICHMOND, BC.

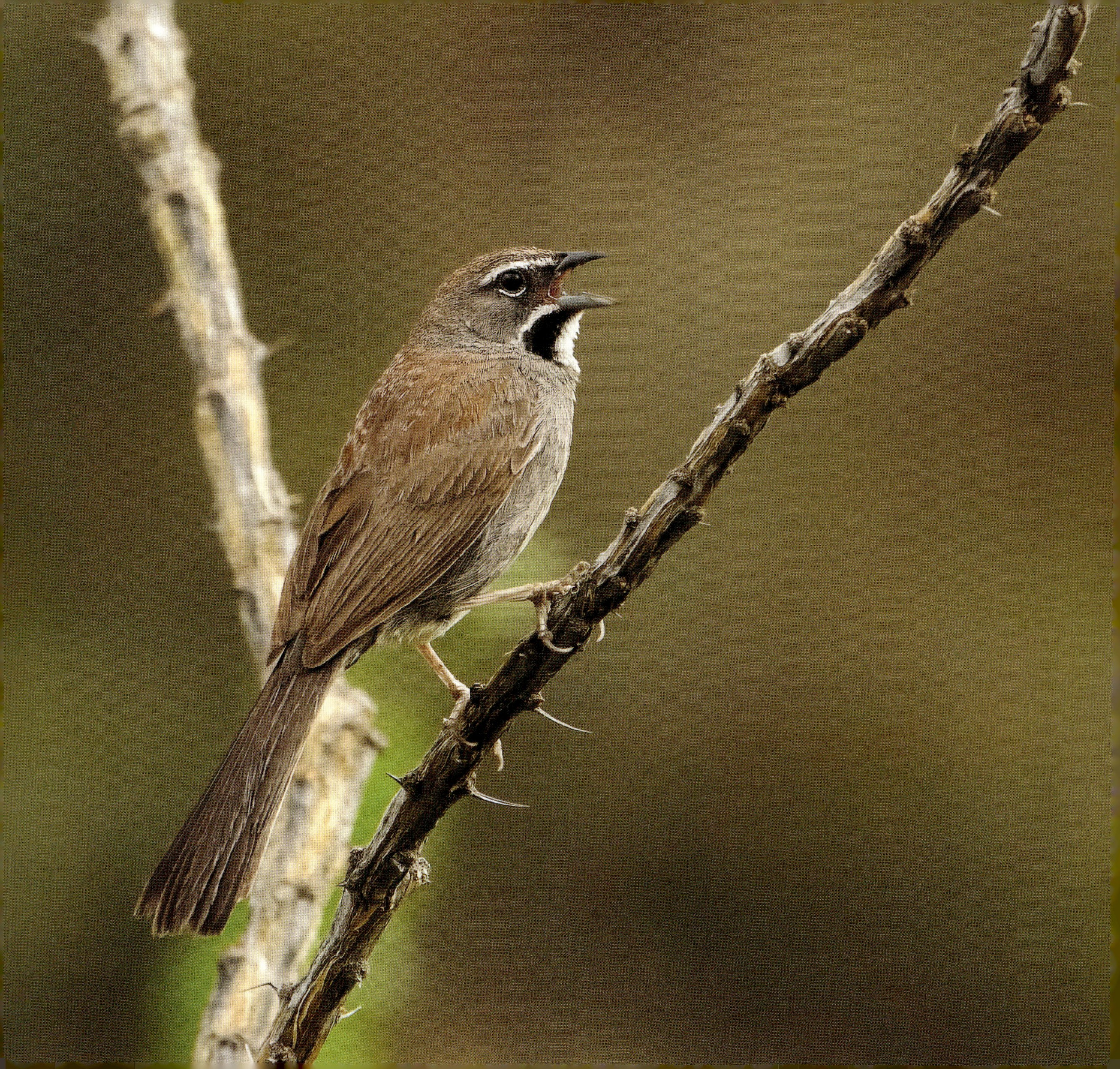

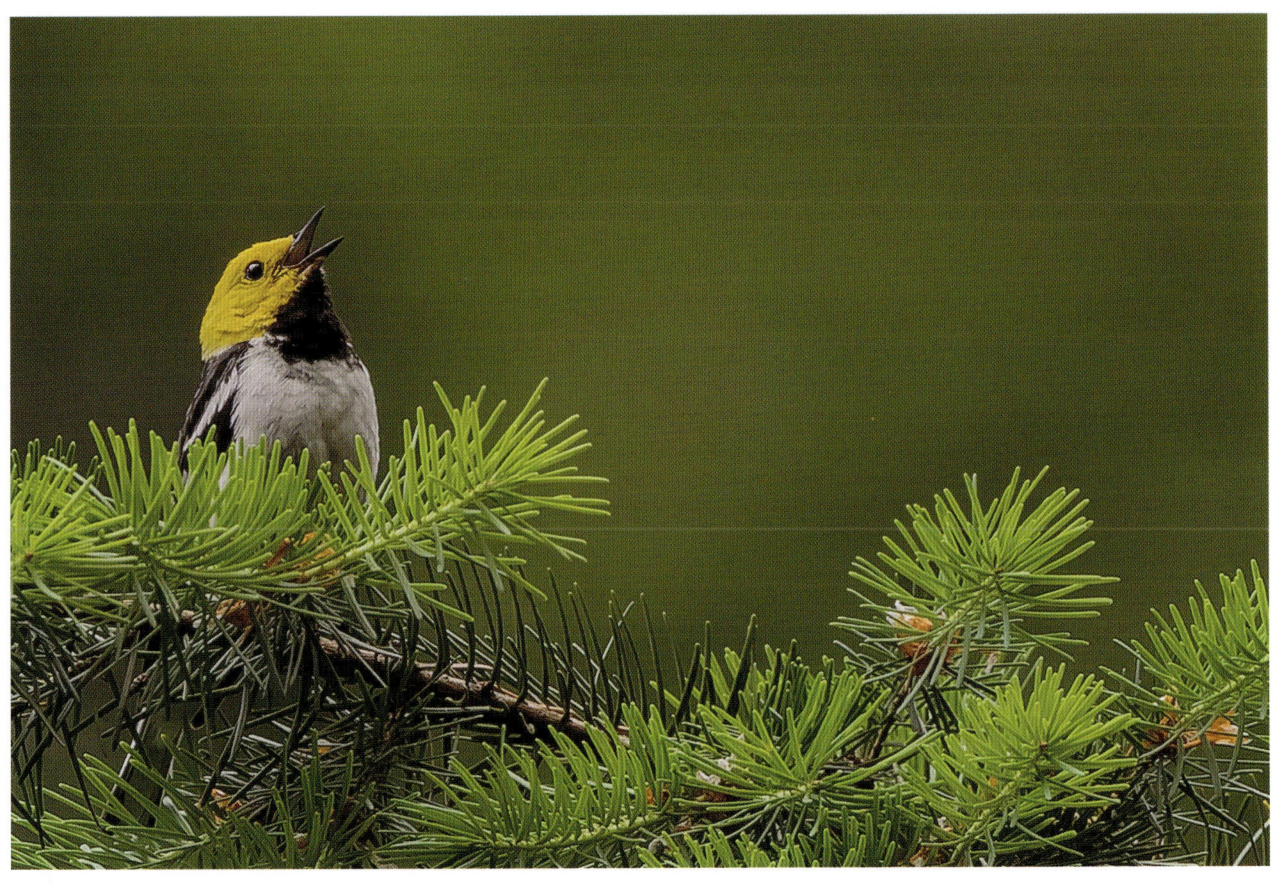

Opposite:

A SINGING FIVE-STRIPED SPARROW IN FLORIDA CANYON, ARIZONA. IT IS A BIRD MUCH SOUGHT AFTER BY BIRDERS, SINCE IT IS ONLY FOUND IN SOUTHEASTERN ARIZONA, IN AREAS SOUTH OF TUCSON ALONG THE MEXICAN BORDER.

Above:

I FIRST DETECTED THIS MALE HERMIT WARBLER BY ITS DISTINCTIVE SONG. TAKEN IN CHEHALIS, WASHINGTON.

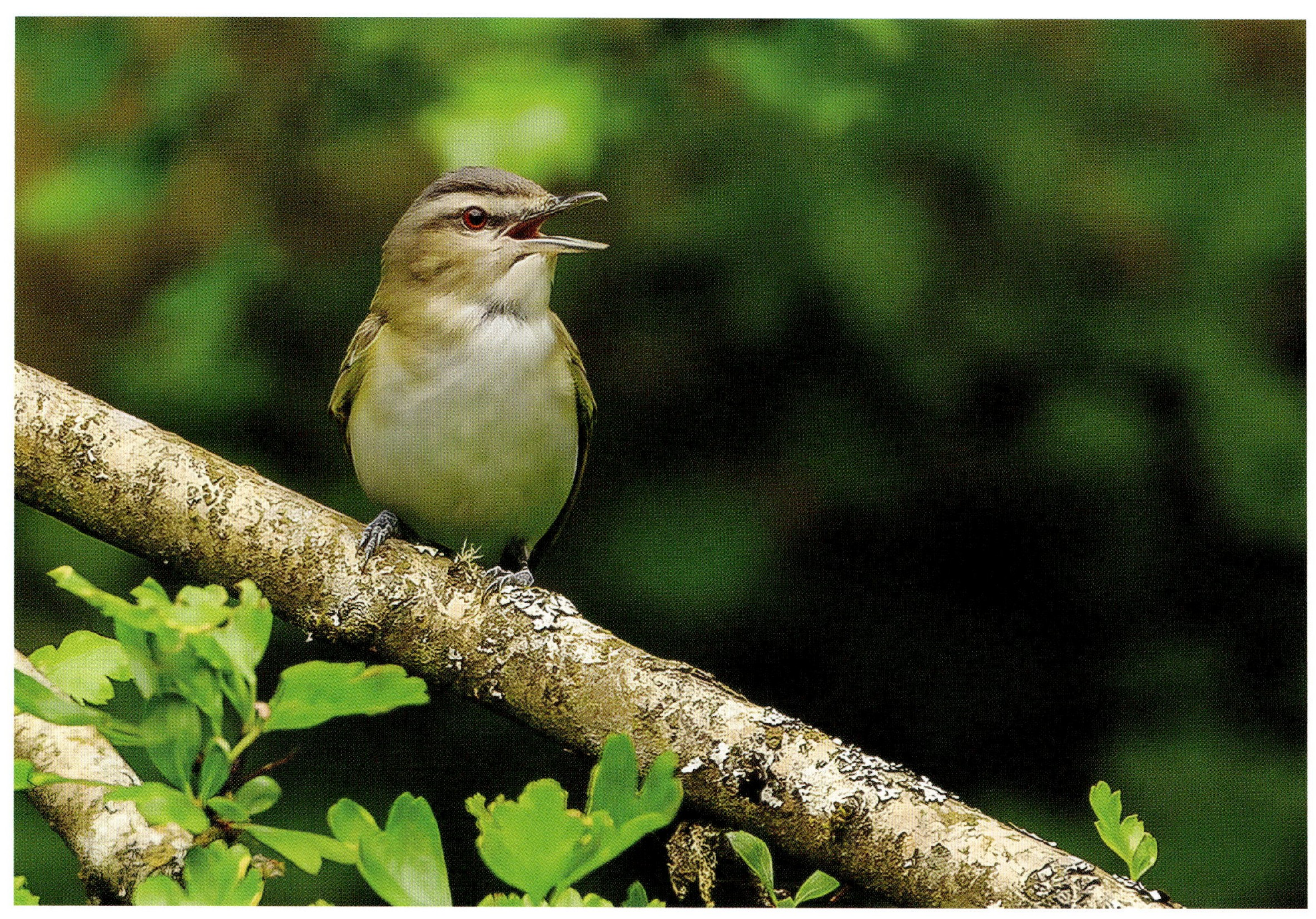

SINGING RED-EYED VIREOS ARE ONE OF THE LATEST BREEDING MIGRANTS TO RETURN TO THE VANCOUVER AREA EACH SPRING. THEY ARE USUALLY FIRST FOUND BY BIRDERS THROUGH THEIR TIRELESS, LOVELY SONG, WHICH GIVES AWAY THEIR PRESENCE HIGH IN THE CANOPY.

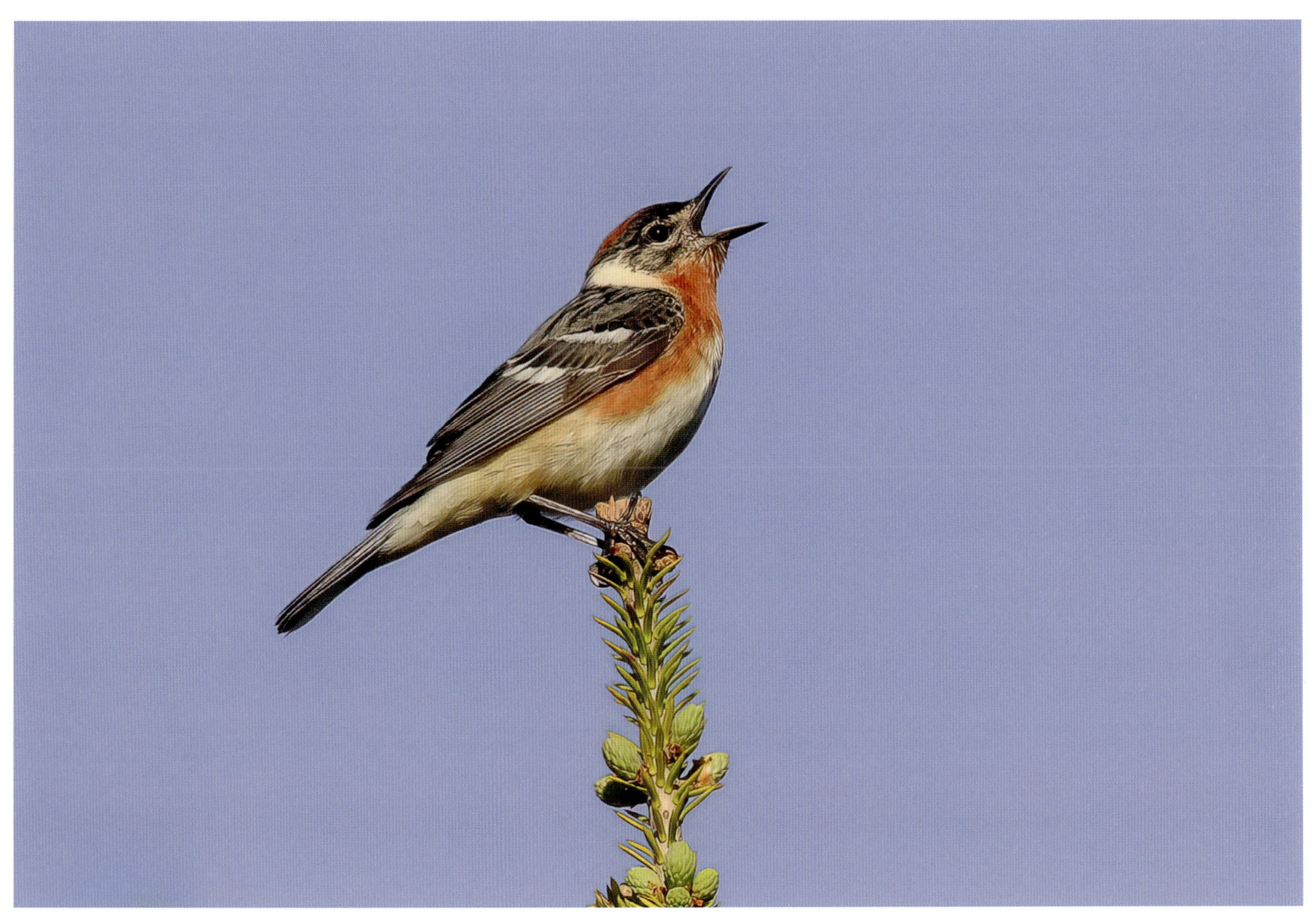

AN EYE-CATCHING MALE BAY-BREASTED WARBLER IS ONE OF THE WARBLERS THAT BIRDERS SEEK ALL OVER NORTH AMERICA DUE TO ITS BEAUTIFUL SONG AND PLUMAGE. TAKEN IN CAPE BRETON, NOVA SCOTIA.

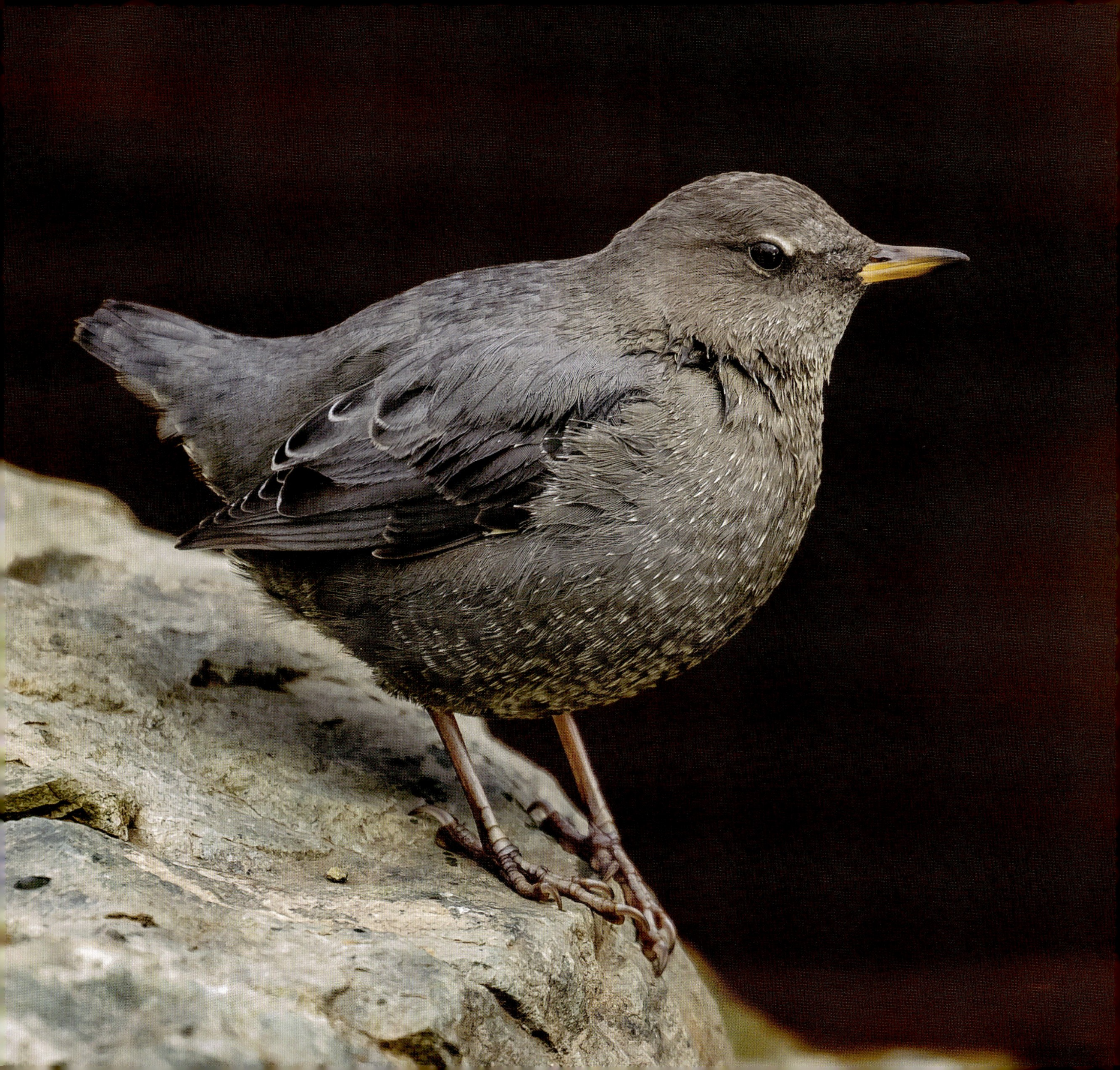

6

Birding with Mom

My mom was not a hard-core birder, but she liked to go see birds with me anytime. One of my fondest memories was going up Mount Seymour with my mom to photograph a couple of American Dippers. We sat by a small lake and watched them feed, sing, and swim. American Dippers are the only aquatic songbird in North America. We also loved watching Common Loons together as they swam on a lake with their young riding on their backs on their nesting grounds in Kamloops, BC.

Opposite:

A JUVENILE AMERICAN DIPPER POSES IN FRONT OF MY MOM AND ME ON MOUNT SEYMOUR IN NORTH VANCOUVER, BC.

I hated watching how my mom suffered during her battle with breast cancer. She had fought so hard to beat it, enduring surgery, radiation, and difficult chemotherapy. When it spread to her liver, she bled out a lot and that was hard to see. She died at home with me giving her hospice care with a palliative care team overseeing it. I gave her all her medications and all of her needed care and was constantly by her side. It took all my strength, but I am so glad I was able to fulfill her last wishes and be with her at the moment she died, so close to Christmas. When she passed away in my arms, I lay with her, unable to move, and wept profoundly as my heart was wrenching from complete and utter pain like I had never experienced before. I thought I would be prepared for her death, since she was deemed terminal, but it hit me like a ton of bricks. The reality that she was *really gone* had sunk in.

What I would give to bird one more day with her. To talk to her, touch her, and see her beautiful smiling face and hear that incredible laugh. Her death has made me appreciate the power of birds even more.

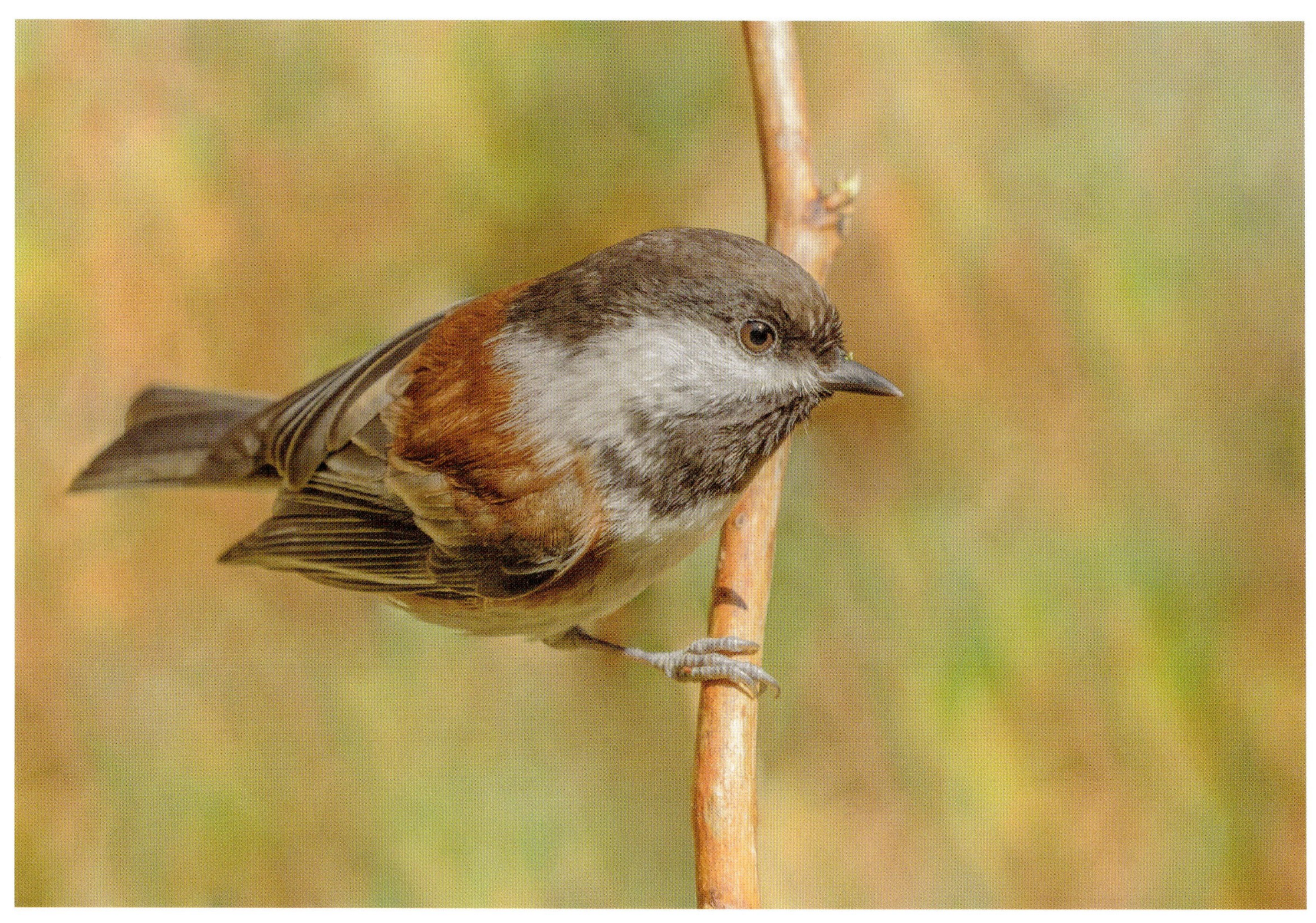

A CHESTNUT-BACKED CHICKADEE PERCHES IN FRONT OF MY MOM AND ME AT BEAVER LAKE IN VANCOUVER, BC.

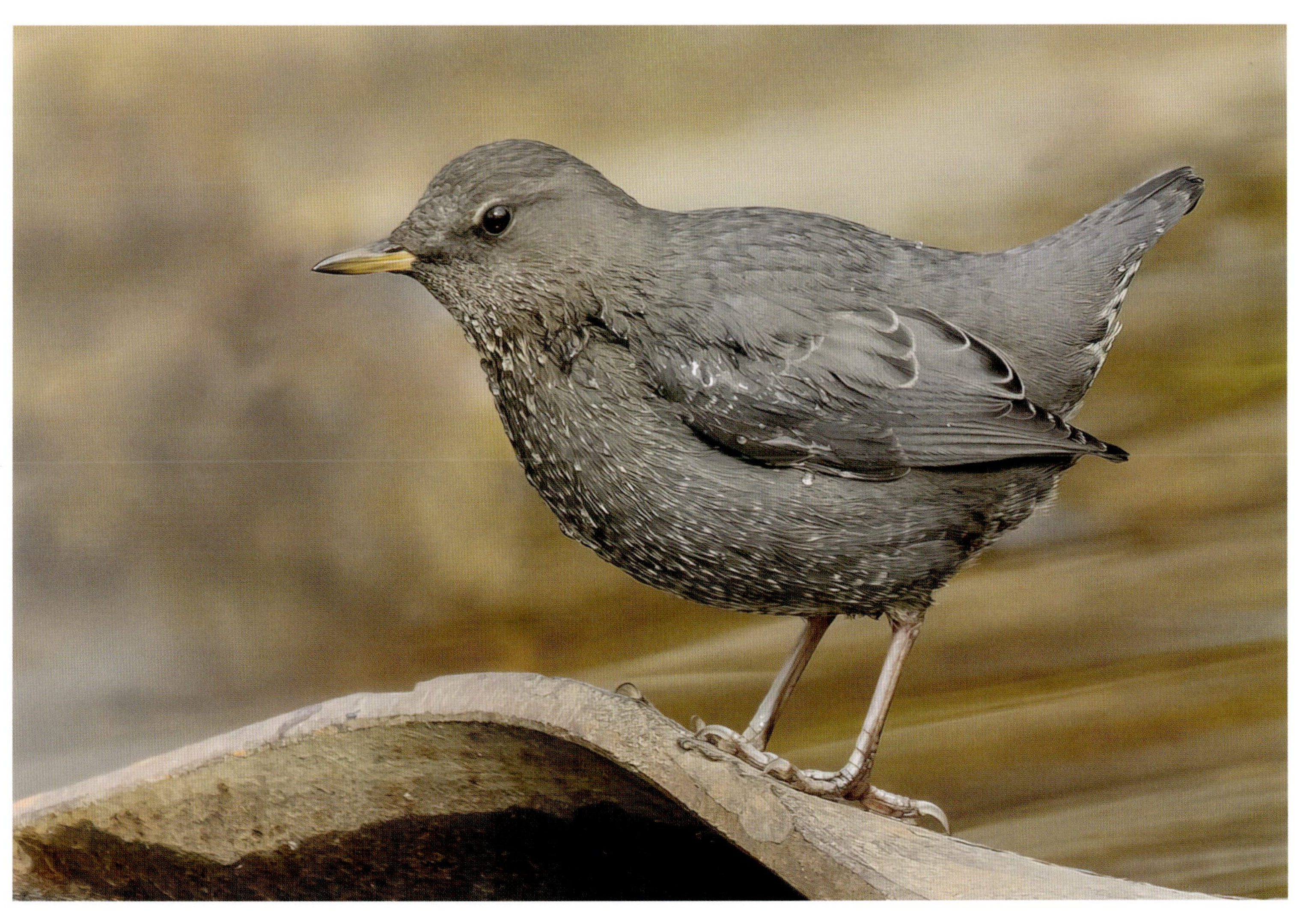

AS HE HUNTED FOR ROE IN NORTH VANCOUVER, BC, A MALE AMERICAN DIPPER GREW VERY CURIOUS ABOUT MY MOM AND ME AND CAME CLOSE TO CHECK US OUT.

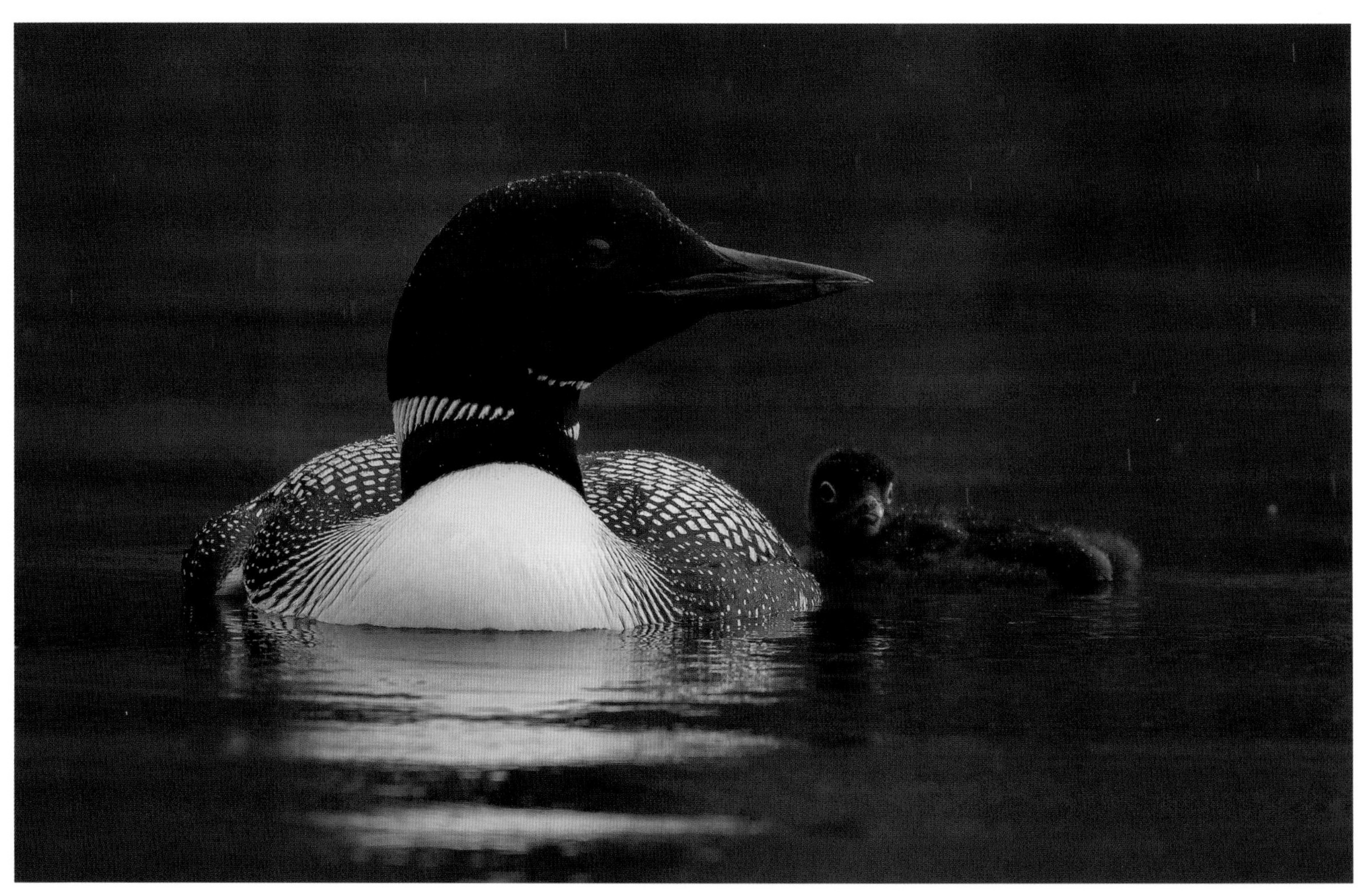

A COMMON LOON WITH HER YOUNG CLOSE BY IN KAMLOOPS, BC. COMMON LOONS ARE EXTREMELY DEVOTED PARENTS TO THEIR CHICKS, WHO RIDE ON THEIR BACKS WHEN THEY ARE SMALL. COMMON LOONS ARE SADLY SUSCEPTIBLE TO ENTANGLEMENT FROM FISHING LINE AND POISONING FROM LEAD WEIGHTS.

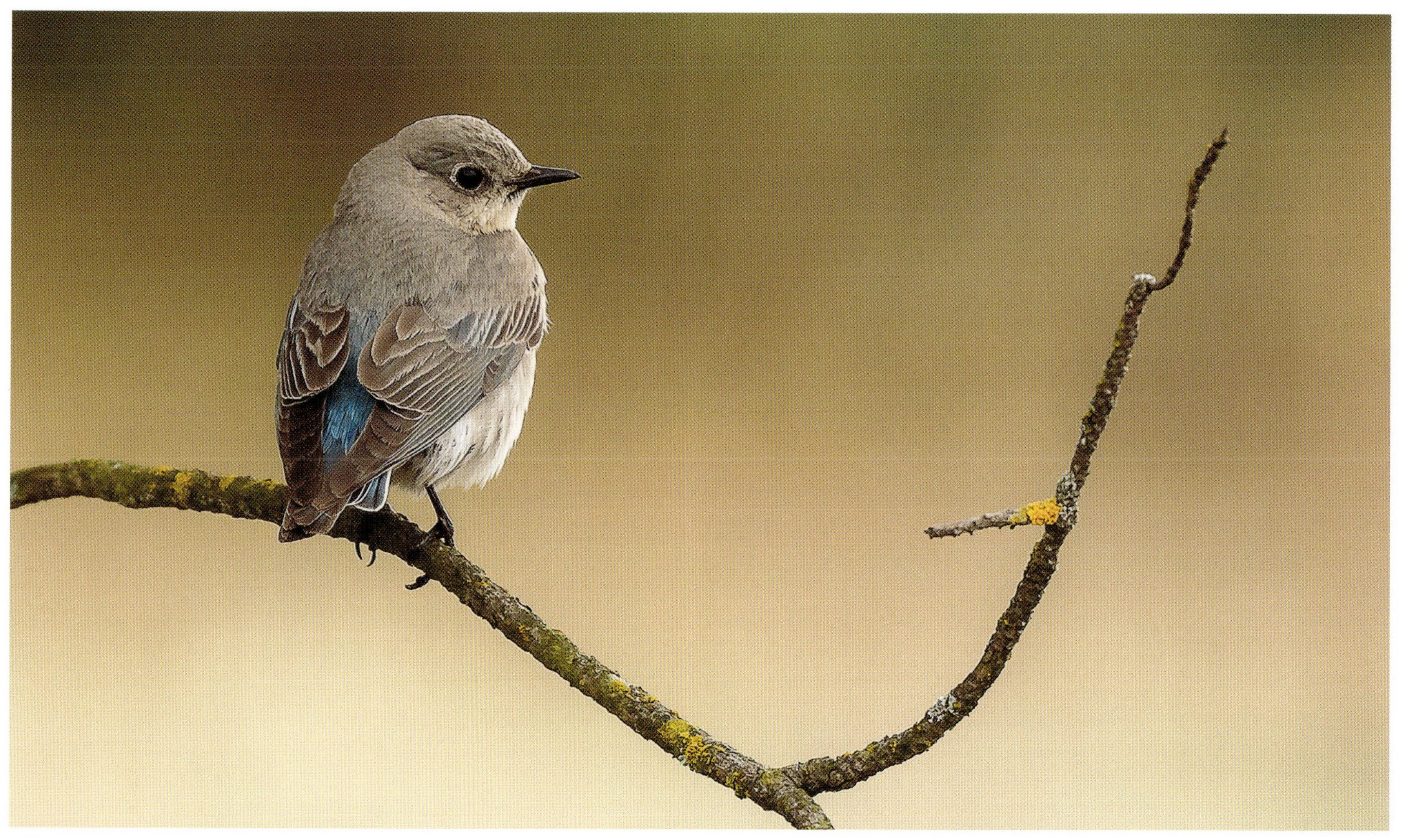

A BLUEBIRD REALLY CARRIES THE SKY ON ITS BACK. A FEMALE MOUNTAIN BLUEBIRD PERCHES ON A SNAG AT IONA BEACH REGIONAL PARK IN RICHMOND, BC. MY MOM AND I WERE WATCHING THE BIRD TOGETHER WHEN THE PHOTO WAS TAKEN.

One thing my mom loved to see was Mountain Bluebirds. Whenever one was reported, we would go out together to look at them. In coastal BC each spring we have a brief passage of them. The closest breeding population to Vancouver is in Merritt, BC, and every year we would travel there to see them. Whenever I see a bluebird, I think of her and all the wonderful trips we had together looking at these beautiful blue thrushes.

Opposite:

A WOODHOUSE'S SCRUB-JAY POSES AGAINST THE RED-ROCK EARTH OF SEDONA, ARIZONA.

We also travelled together looking at birds, including to places like Arizona. We saw so many incredible birds there together, from dazzling hummingbirds to Varied Buntings. On one trip, I took her to Sedona and we got to see Woodhouse's Scrub-Jays. We even saw one fight with a Crissal Thrasher. First off, I had never seen a Crissal Thrasher outside of strictly desert habitat, so seeing one at this high elevation in a treed setting was odd for me, but it is not rare for the area. Secondly, the thing that was really strange was to see it going at it with a territorial Woodhouse's Scrub-Jay. Both were calling and then started fighting – I've never seen anything like it and probably never will again. The jay appeared to be the victor.

The last birding trip I took with my mom was to the Cariboo region in BC. We watched American White Pelicans together and saw many Yellow-headed Blackbirds that she loved, as well as bluebirds, Bobolinks, Black Terns, warblers, and many ducks with their young, from Blue-winged Teals to Canvasbacks. I am so glad I got to experience that last trip with her. Even though she was so sick that she could barely leave the car, she was delighted to see these beautiful creatures, and it made her heart lift and her face smile.

I will always treasure the wonderful memories I shared with my mother while birding. They will stay with me forever, and I am lucky to have so many.

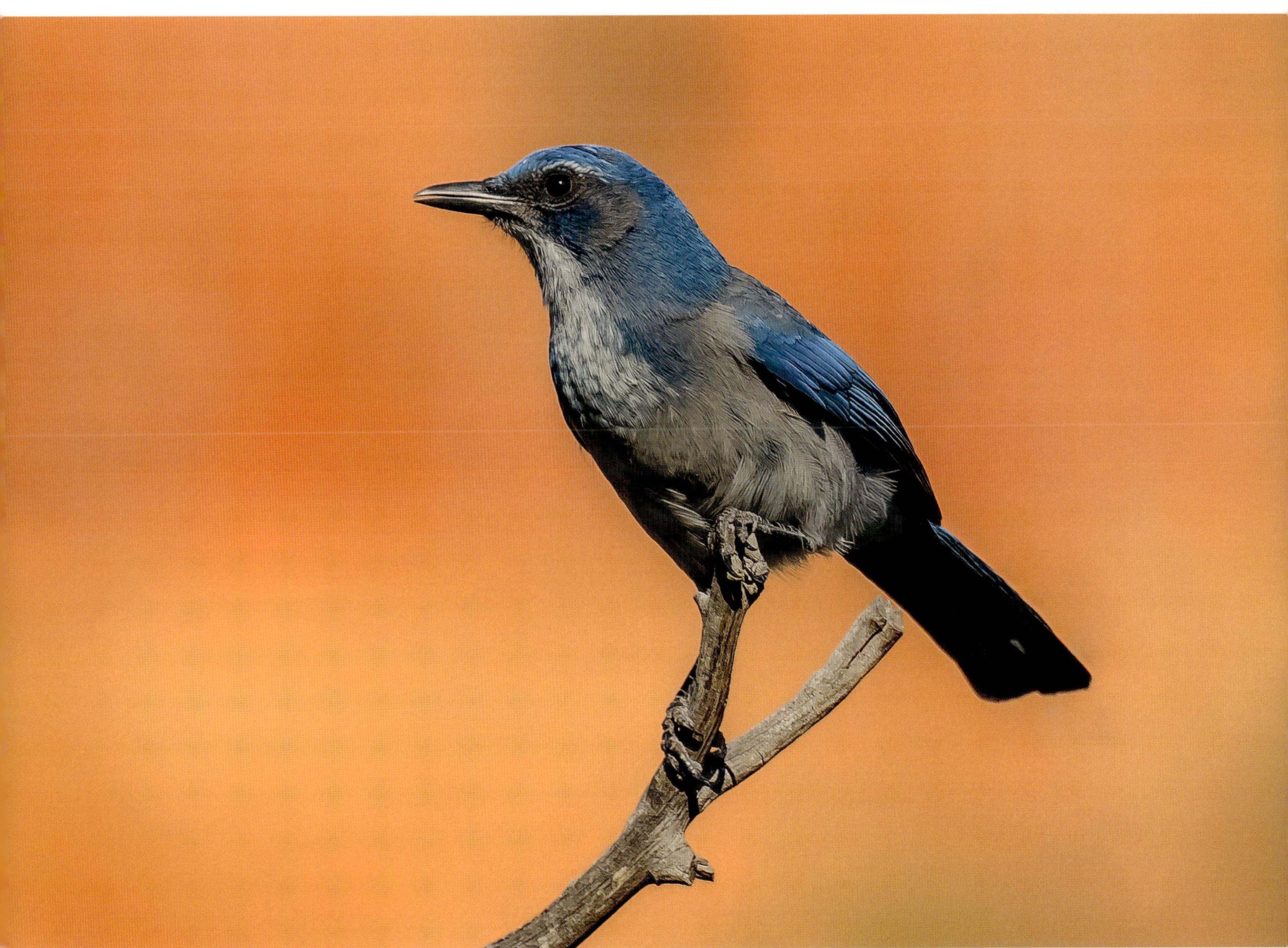

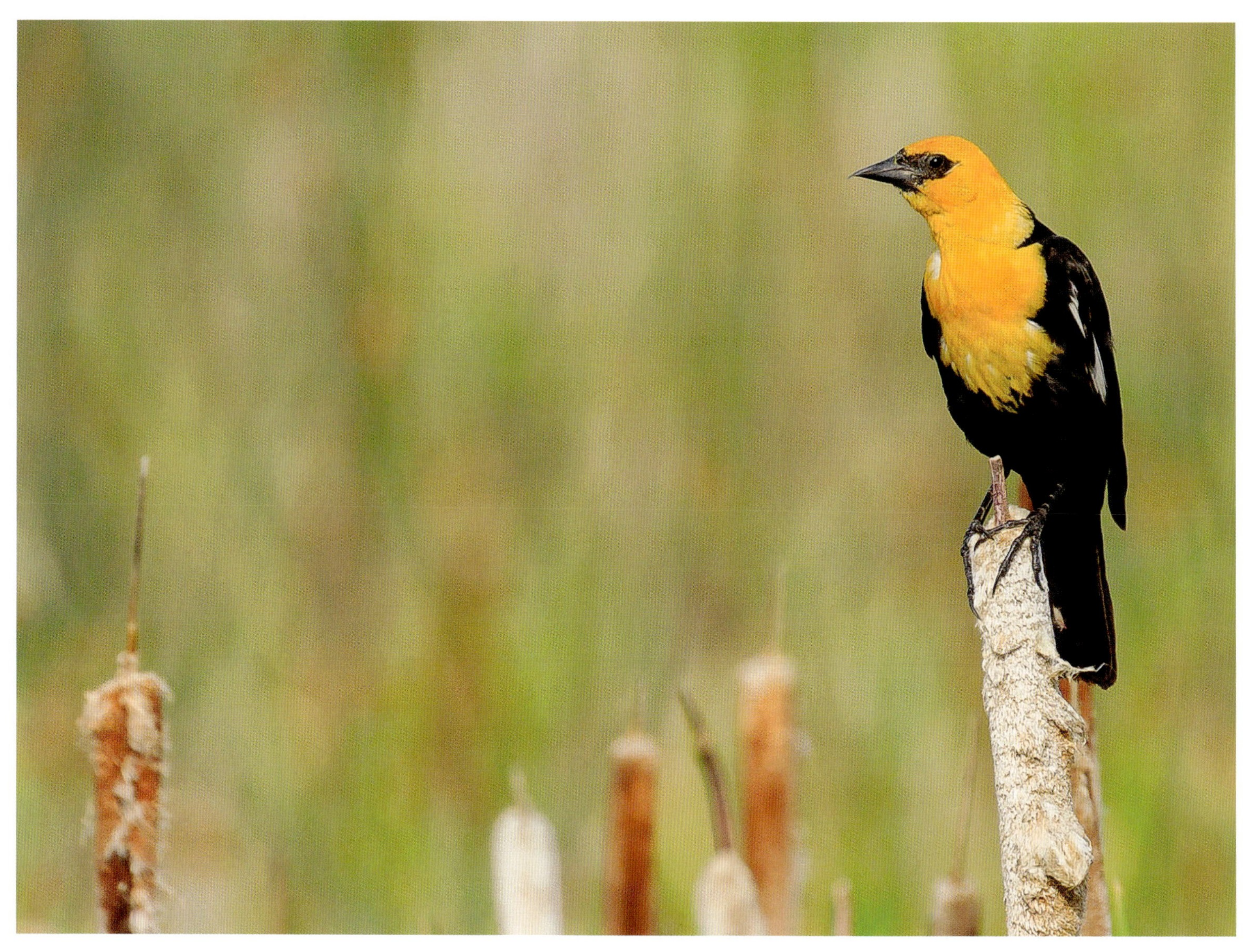

A MALE YELLOW-HEADED BLACKBIRD POSES FOR MY MOM AND ME NEAR 100 MILE HOUSE IN THE CARIBOO REGION OF BC.

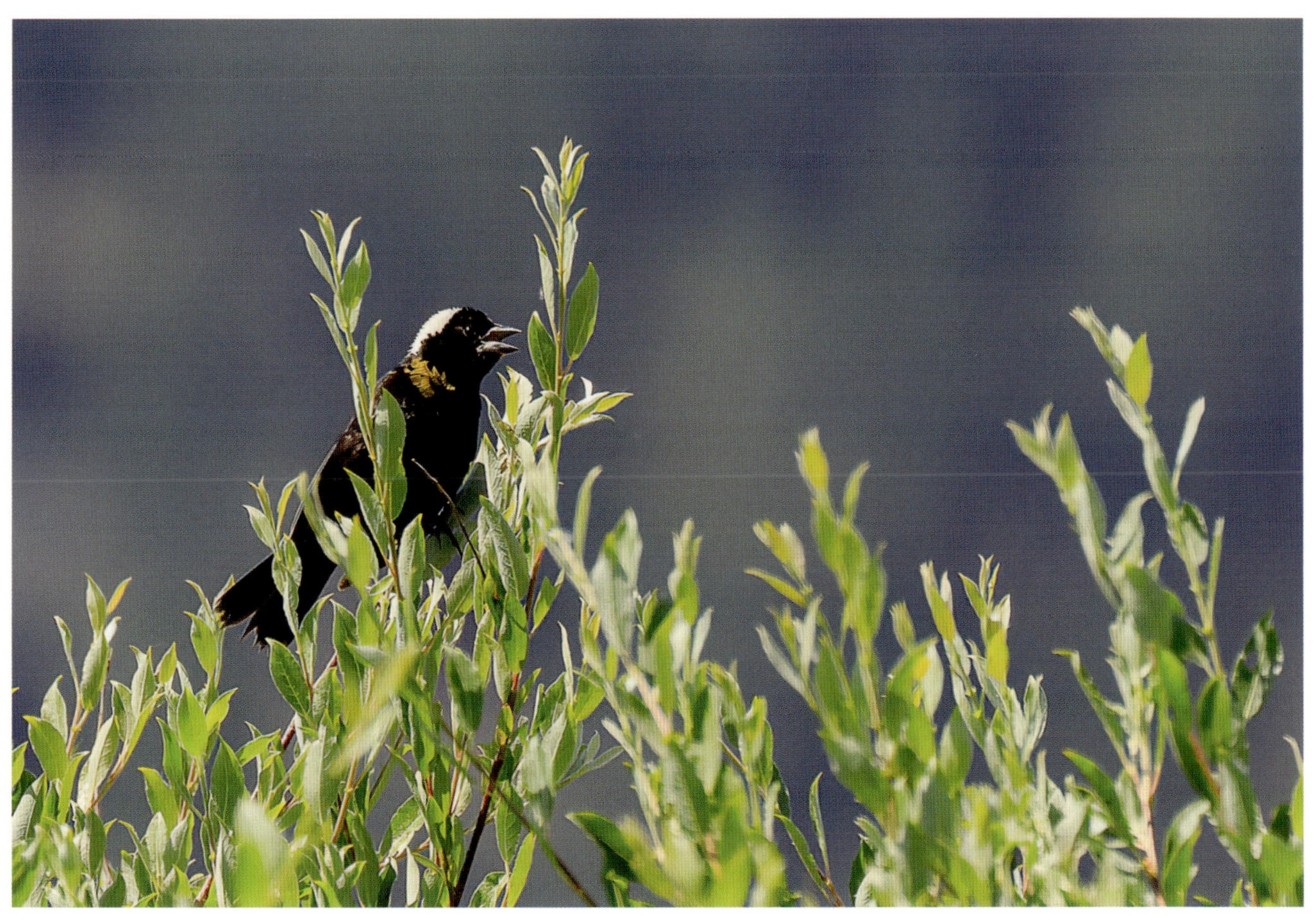

THIS MALE BOBOLINK FASCINATED MY MOM AND ME. THREATENED GRASSLAND SONGBIRDS, BOBOLINKS ARE FREQUENTLY KILLED WHEN FARMERS CUT GRASS WHERE THEY NEST DURING AGRICULTURAL OPERATIONS. THEY ALSO SUFFER FROM HABITAT LOSS, PESTICIDES, AND BIRD CONTROL WHERE THEY WINTER.

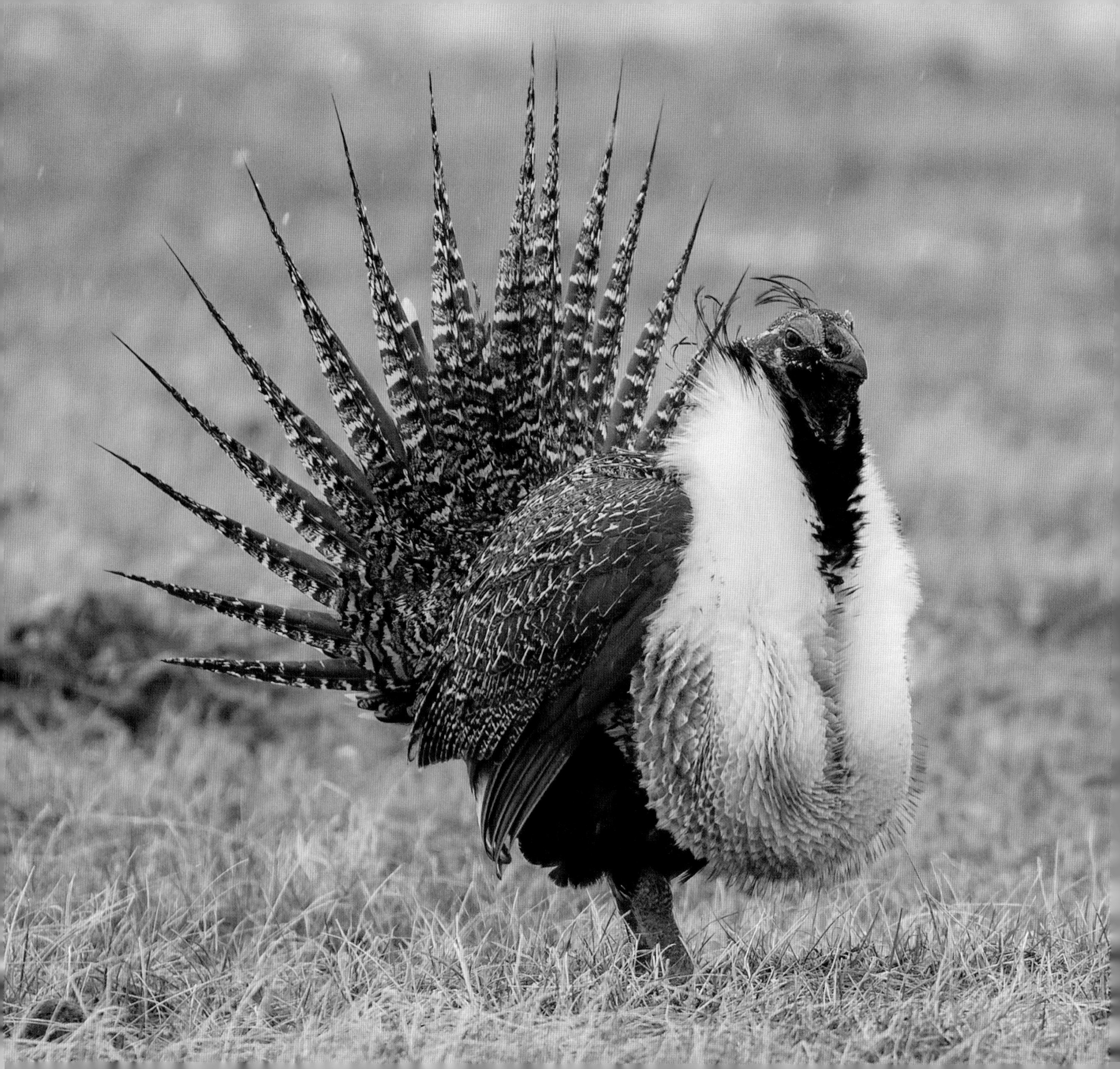

7

The Dance

One of the best trips I ever took was to travel alone to Colorado and Kansas one April for the so-called Chicken Run. The Chicken Run takes you all through Colorado looking at Gunnison Sage-Grouse, Greater Sage-Grouse, Sharp-tailed Grouse, White-tailed Ptarmigan, Dusky Grouse, Scaled Quail, and Greater and Lesser Prairie-Chickens.

Opposite:

A MALE GREATER SAGE-GROUSE PREPARES TO DANCE ON A LEK IN WALDEN, COLORADO.

I just love grouse and game birds; they are one of my favourite bird families. Watching the males dance on the lek for the females was truly life-changing. A lek is a collection of male birds that gather in an area to do elaborate courtship displays or dances to impress and entice a female to mate with them. The comparatively drab females are in control of the mating decision and select the fittest and most virile male in their eyes. The males expend tremendous amounts of energy displaying for females twice a day for months on end during the breeding season (between March and May).

The dance starts early, and any hopeful observer must be in position before dawn. I used my car as a blind to avoid disturbing the grouse. To watch these Greater Sage-Grouse, I left the hotel just after 4 a.m. and was on site by 5 a.m., just as the sun was about to cast its first rays of light over the grouses' stage.

Greater Sage-Grouse are the largest grouse in North America and are truly imposing birds as they strut around on the lek. They are declining due to habitat loss of vital grasslands. They completely depend on sagebrush for food and their nesting habitat.

I watched the females bunched up in the middle of all the males on the lek. The hens were as dazzled as I was by the show. The males with their long head plumes; yellow eyebrows; tail feathers pointing straight out like stars; and yellow, eye-popping, expanding breast sacs are fascinating to see. The males would inflate and bounce their

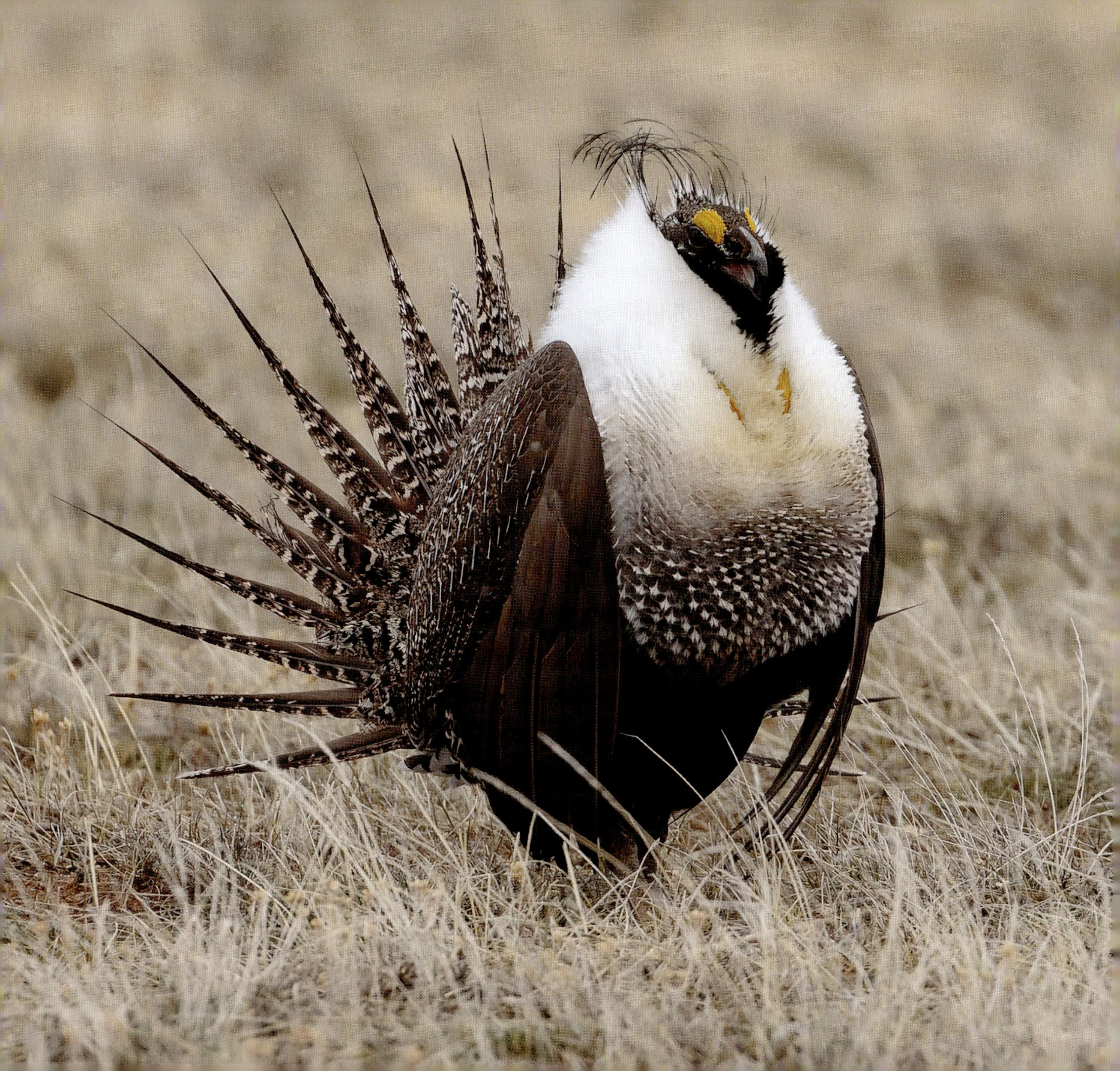

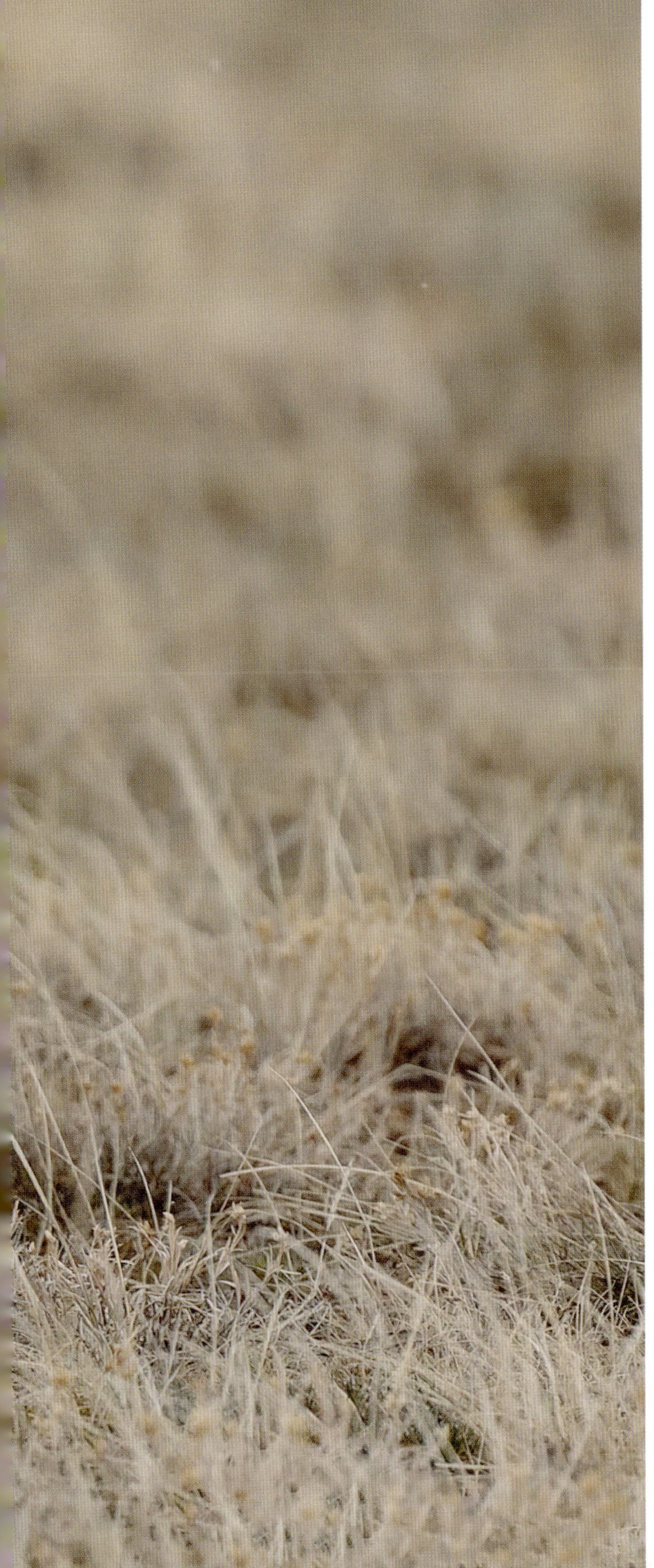

A MALE GREATER SAGE-GROUSE CALLS OUT WITH COOS AS HE STRUTS ON THE LEK HOPING TO ATTRACT A FEMALE IN WALDEN, COLORADO.

air sacs with a swoosh and popping sound as they attempted to impress the females. Very few of the females actually mate with the males, but I did see some successfully copulate. Some of the males would fight viciously at times too.

The last bird left the lek at 8:15 a.m., then I left. You must never leave a lek before the last bird leaves, in order to ensure the lek doesn't get disturbed, causing the birds to flush and possibly never return *again*. Seeing these birds during my first Colorado snow was a dream for me. It was cold sitting in the car, but watching these threatened grouse dance in the falling snow in the sagebrush just made my whole trip right there. I was moved to happy tears watching them.

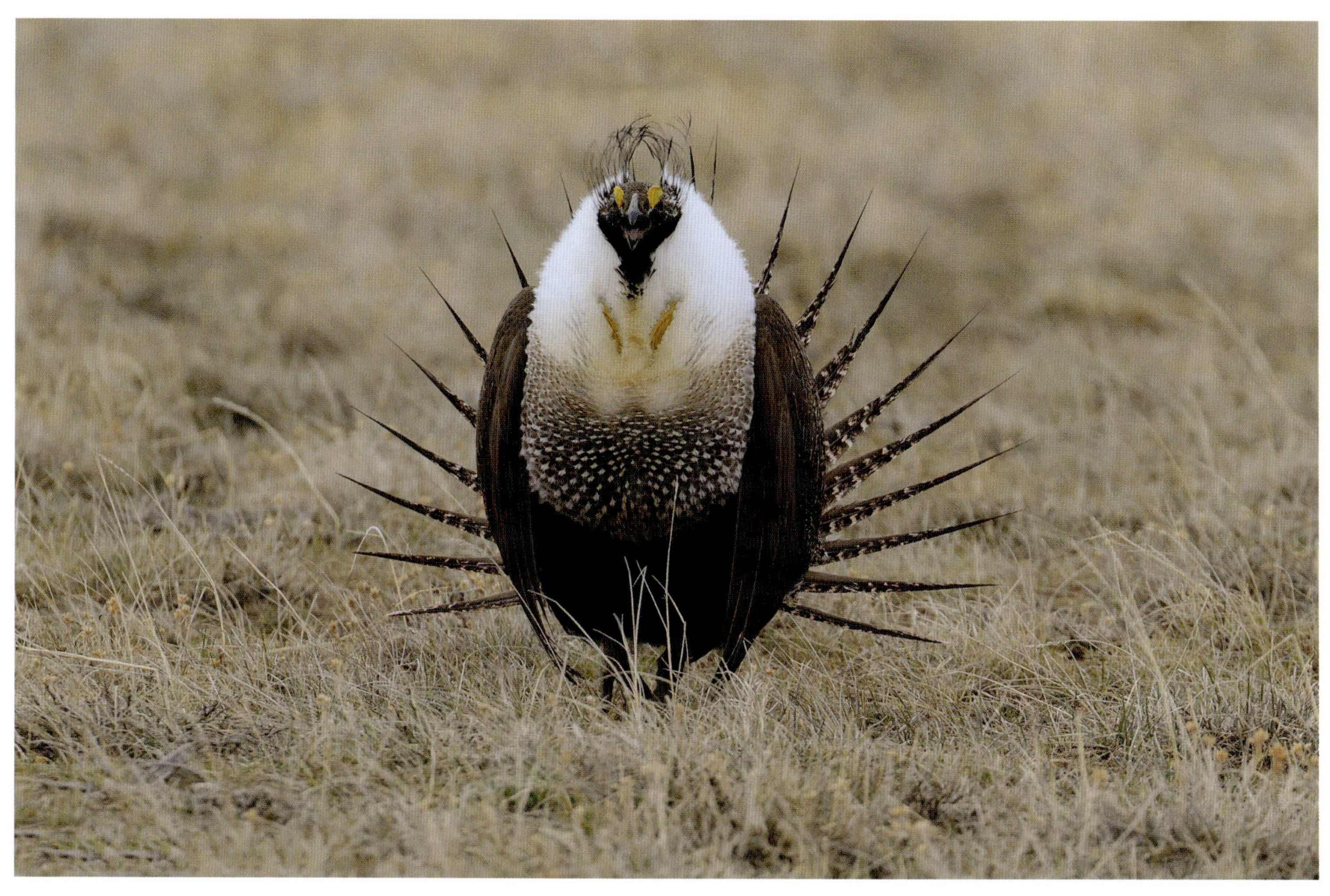

A MALE GREATER SAGE-GROUSE DISPLAYS FOR A FEMALE BY SPREADING OUT HIS BEAUTIFUL POINTED TAIL FEATHERS ON THE LEK IN WALDEN, COLORADO.

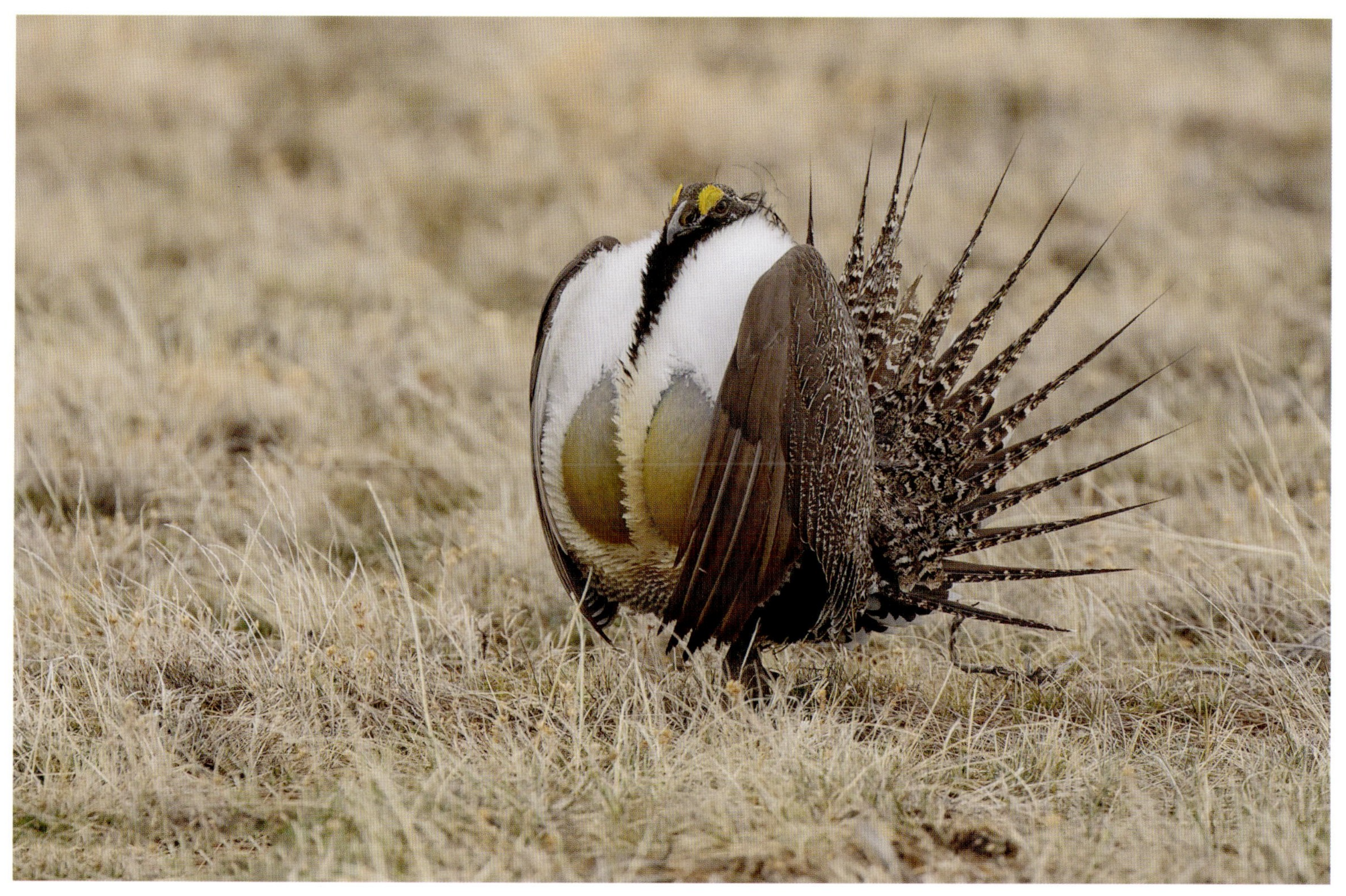

A MALE GREATER SAGE-GROUSE PUFFS OUT THE YELLOW AIR SACS ON HIS BREAST IN ORDER TO ATTRACT A FEMALE TO MATE WITH HIM ON THE LEK IN WALDEN, COLORADO. THE AIR SACS MAKE STRANGE POPPING AND WHISTLING SOUNDS WHEN HE DOES THIS.

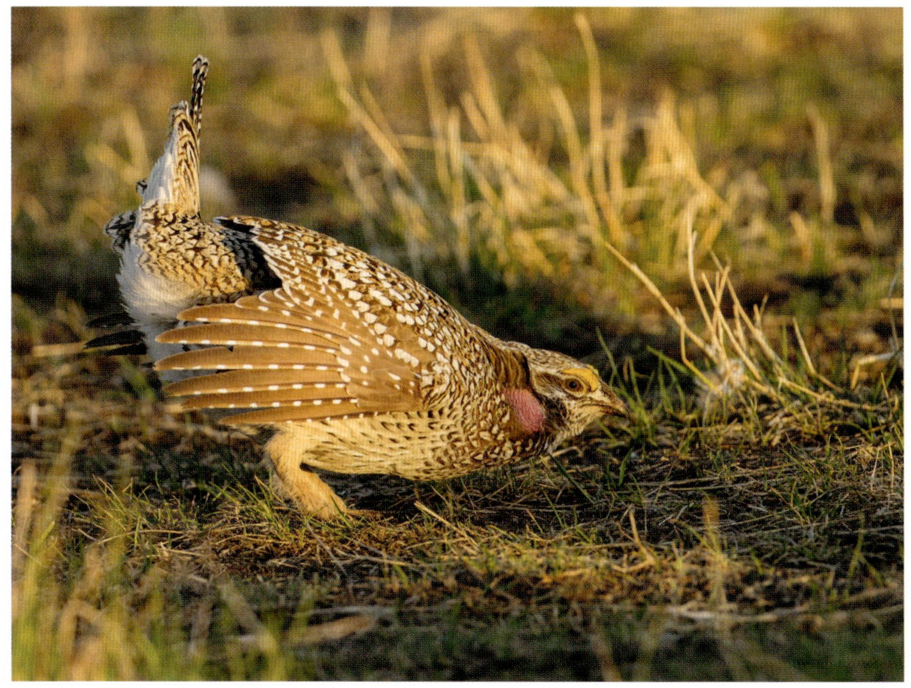

A MALE COLUMBIAN SHARP-TAILED GROUSE GETS READY TO DANCE ON THE LEK IN THE THOMPSON-NICOLA REGION OF BC.

Since Lesser Prairie-Chickens are virtually extirpated in Colorado, I had to drive to Oakley, Kansas, to see this threatened species on the lek on Nature Conservancy land. I photographed these not from my car, as I did with the Greater Sage-Grouse, but from a physical blind. The blind I used in this case was a trailer with window holes cut out to view the birds without causing any disturbance. At the lek there were 20 birds (18 males and 2 hens), including one Greater Prairie-Chicken. Greaters and Lessers often interbreed. They were making popping and clicking sounds and doing these little flight hops like the Greater Prairie-Chickens do. However, the Greater Prairie-Chickens sound more like doves to me. The Lessers could easily be told apart when the males were displaying, as they showed off their red air sacs on the sides of their necks. This contrasts with the yellow air sacs on the necks of Greater Prairie-Chickens. The Lessers would go frantic when one of the two hens passed by and some of the males would begin fighting.

Since so many grouse species are declining, threatened, or endangered, it is imperative we preserve critical grassland habitat in order to ensure the dance goes on for many generations to come.

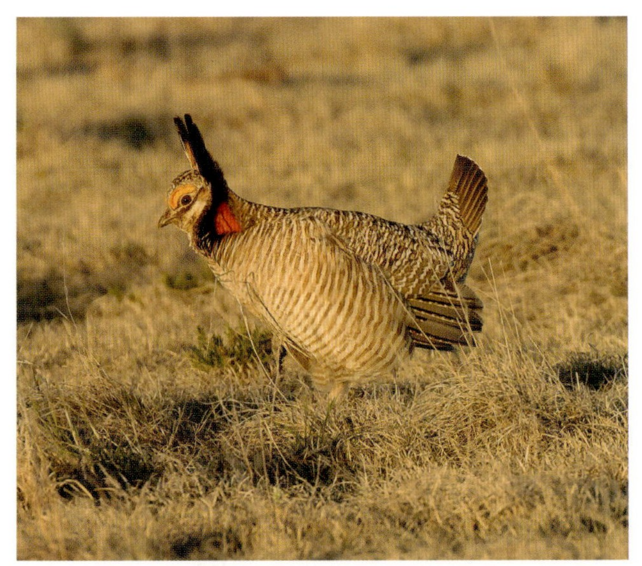

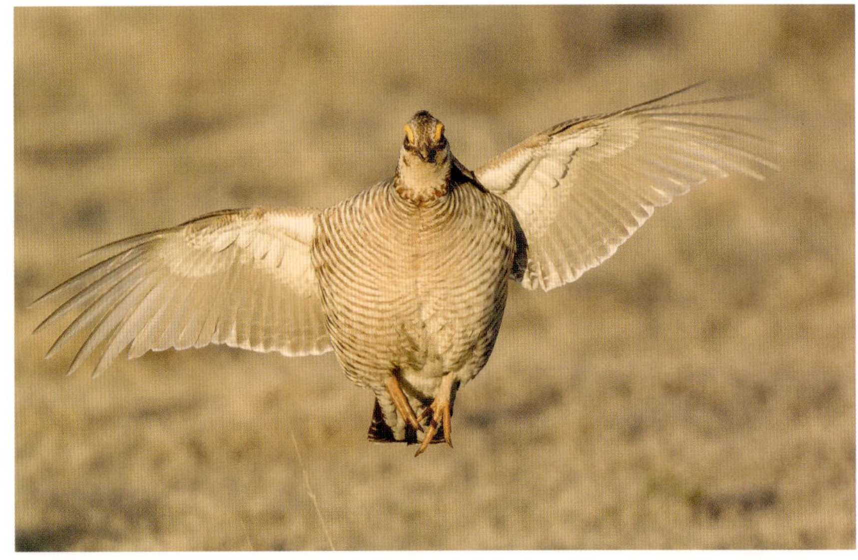

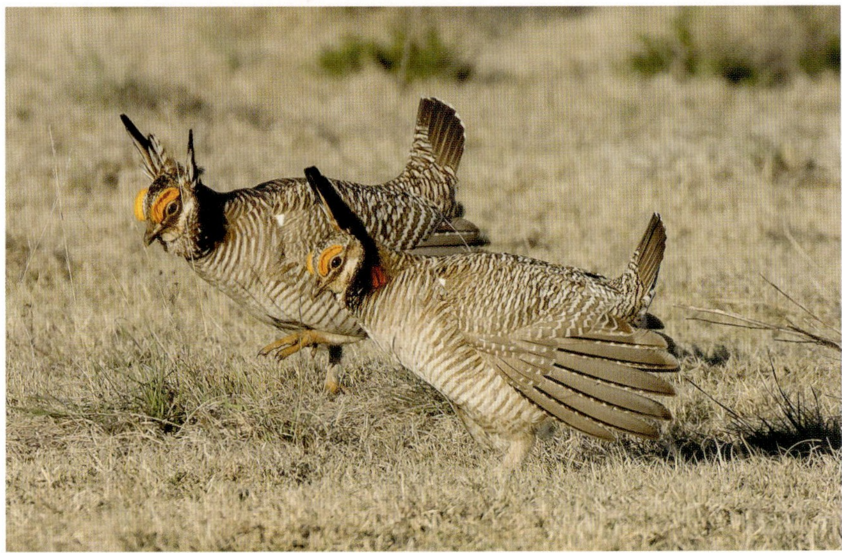

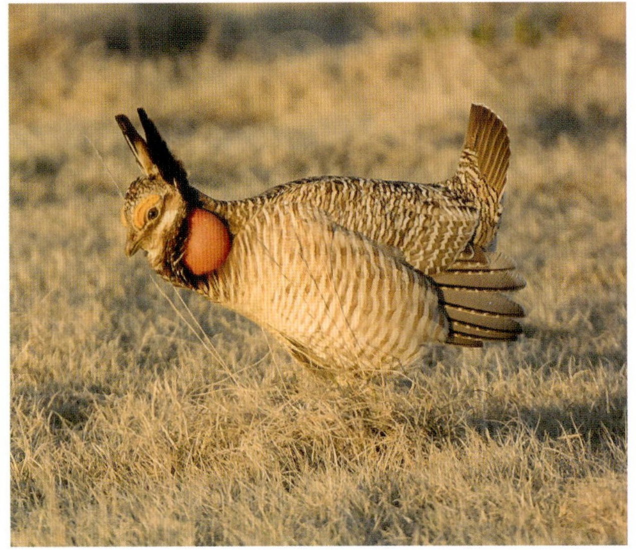

AN ENDANGERED LESSER PRAIRIE-CHICKEN DANCES ON A LEK IN OAKLEY, KANSAS.

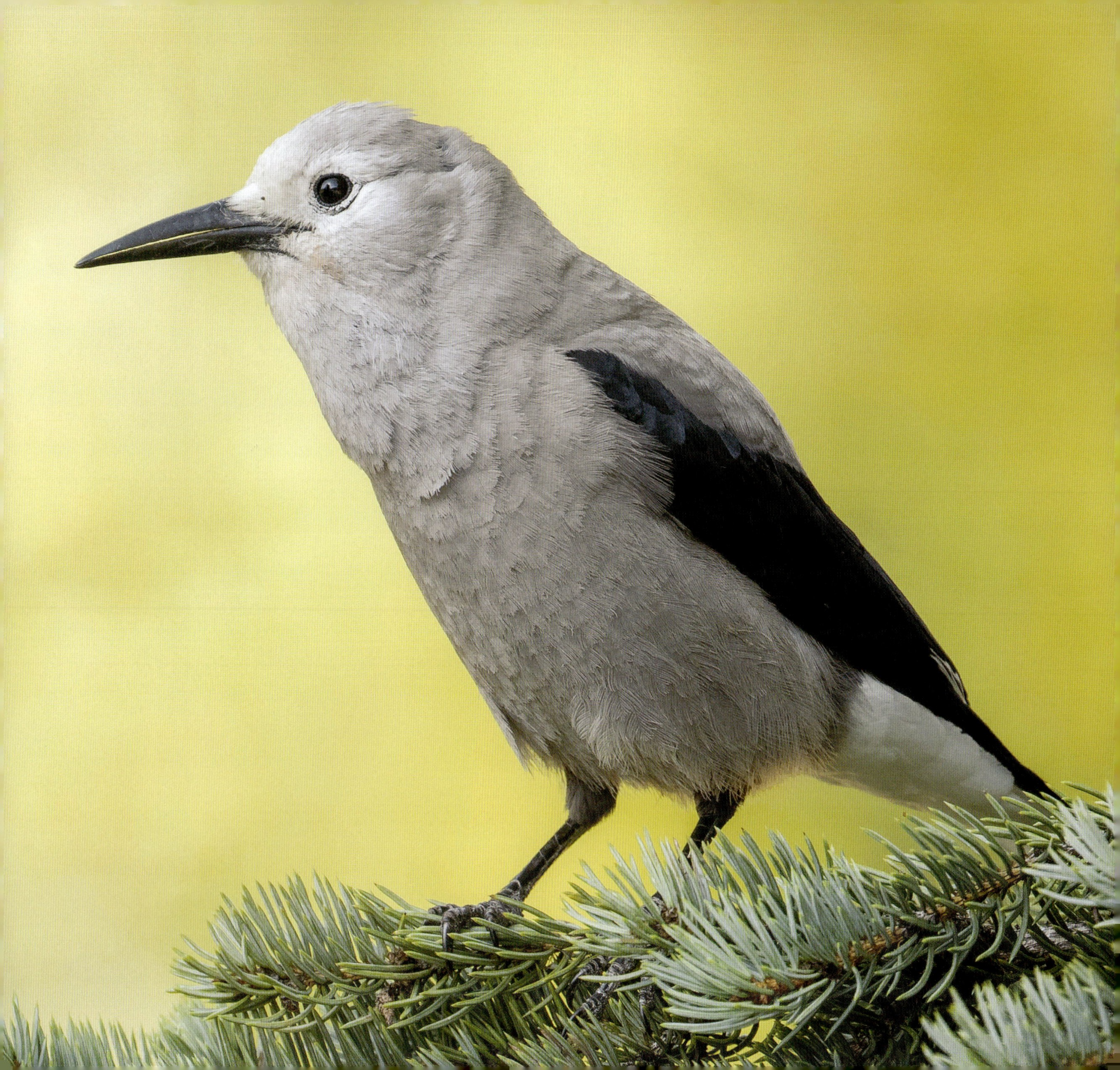

The Secrets of Birds

8

I believe birds are the holders of secrets. They sing of things we will never know or quite understand. As they flit along, going about their business, it lifts my spirit that these creatures holding secrets can delight so many. There is so much yet to discover about birds. One of the greatest things about birding is that you are continuously learning.

Opposite:

A CLARK'S NUTCRACKER AT E.C. MANNING PARK, NORTH OF HOPE, BC.

Sometimes I look at birds and hear music, a symphony of sweet jazz music (my favourite genre) when the birds aren't even singing. For me, it truly is a spiritual experience. I am so grateful the birds have been so generous with me. I feel blessed that they share little glimpses and allow me into their secretive and amazing lives.

Birds come in so many diverse colours, shapes, and sizes and live in such drastically different landscapes, just like us humans. They have the power to truly connect us to their world. Once they draw you in, you want to protect and save them and their habitats in order that future generations will be able to see these incredible creatures too. Even birds far away from our immediate home that are in peril we want to fight for, or at least learn more about. Scientists are still learning about and discovering new species and migration routes.

The 'Akiapōlā'au is an example of the wondrous and mysterious lives of birds. It is sometimes called the Hawaiian Woodpecker. It is an endangered, endemic Hawaiian honeycreeper that has evolved to fill the niche of woodpeckers. They use their short, thick lower mandible to bore into the bark of trees and use their long, thin, down-curved upper mandible to pull out the grubs to eat. They can also drink sap from the holes they drill in the wood with their beaks.

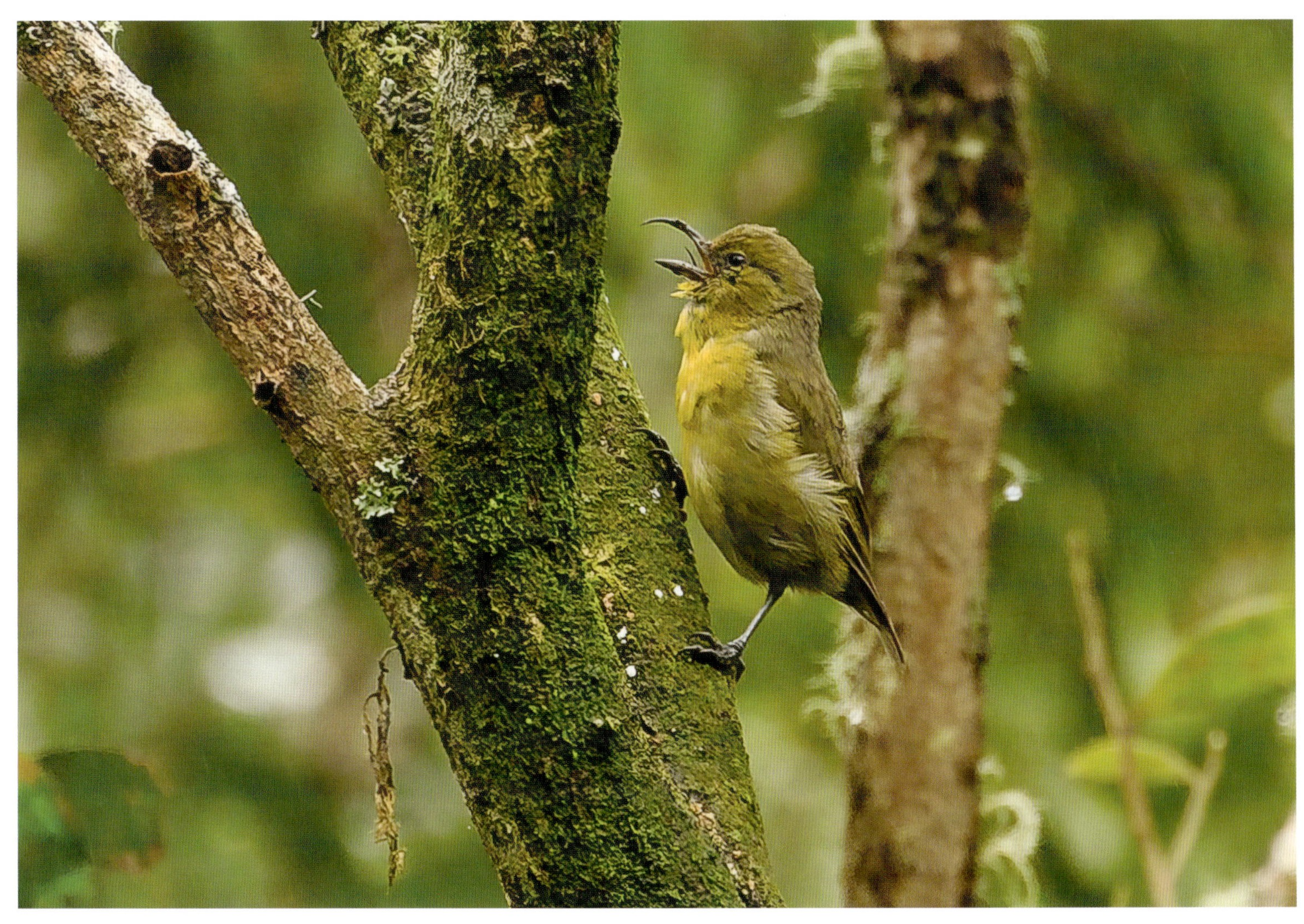

AN ENDANGERED FEMALE ʻAKIAPŌLĀʻAU SINGS FROM ITS PERCH ON THE BIG ISLAND OF HAWAII.

As well as the little-known species, there are the species birders don't get to see very often in the day, such as nightjars. Nightjars are nocturnal and blend into their backgrounds because of their camouflage. We also have birds like the incredible Buff-breasted Sandpiper, which is one of only a few shorebirds like the Ruff to dance in a congregation of males for the females on a lek. Much like the Greater Sage-Grouse I spoke about in the previous chapter. There is also the intriguing Harris's Hawk that literally hunts its prey in packs like a wolf, but unlike wolves it allows the weakest and youngest to feed first. Common Ravens and parrots have learned to imitate human language, speaking words just like us. And, like humans, Ravens can perform complex tasks. Ravens are one of the birds that like to fly and play with each other, making sounds, twirling, and having fun. They are so amazing to watch! There are so many secrets these incredible birds hold. They keep us constantly intrigued as we try to discover more about them.

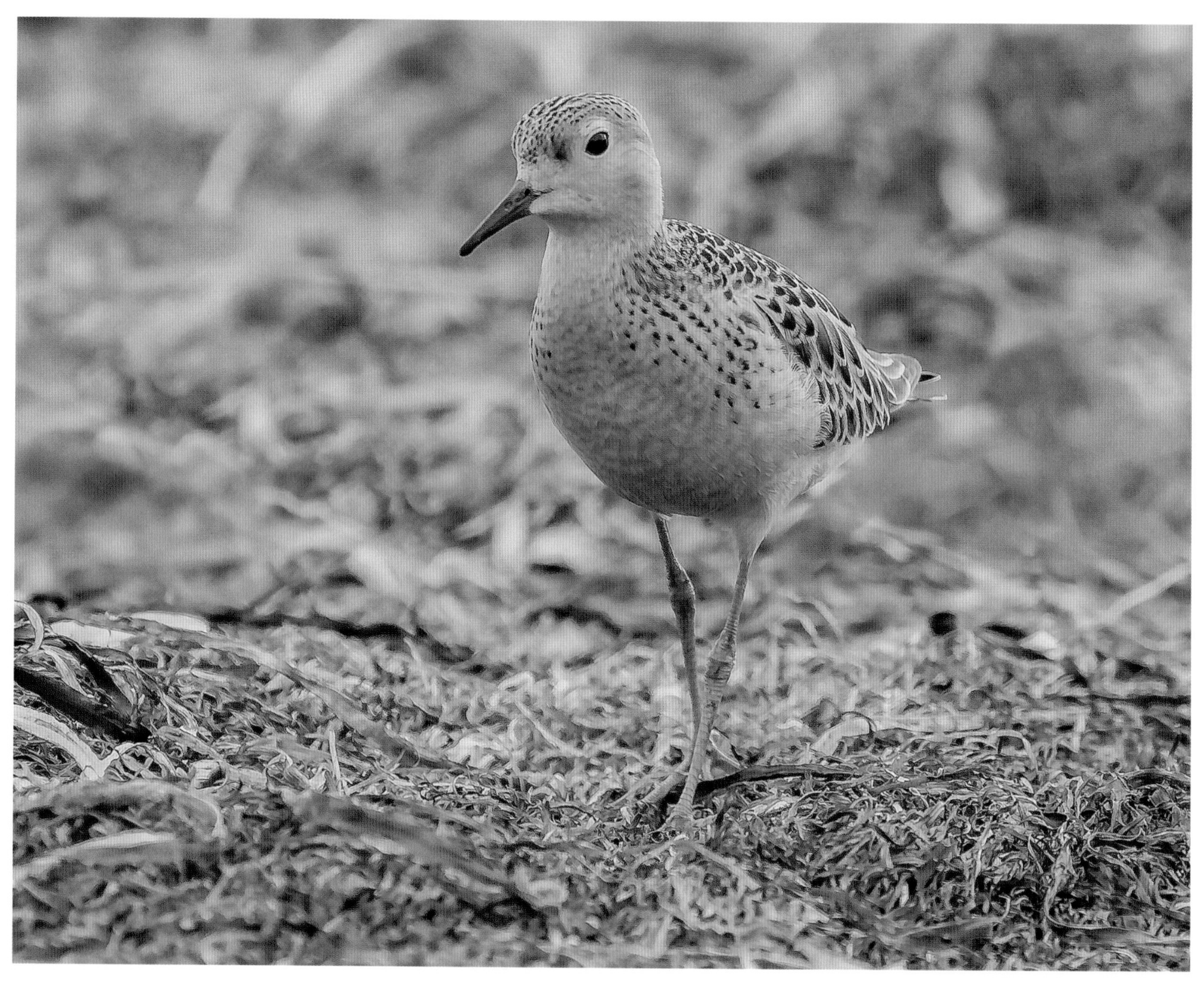

AN ELEGANT, DOVE-LIKE BUFF-BREASTED SANDPIPER IN DELTA, BC.

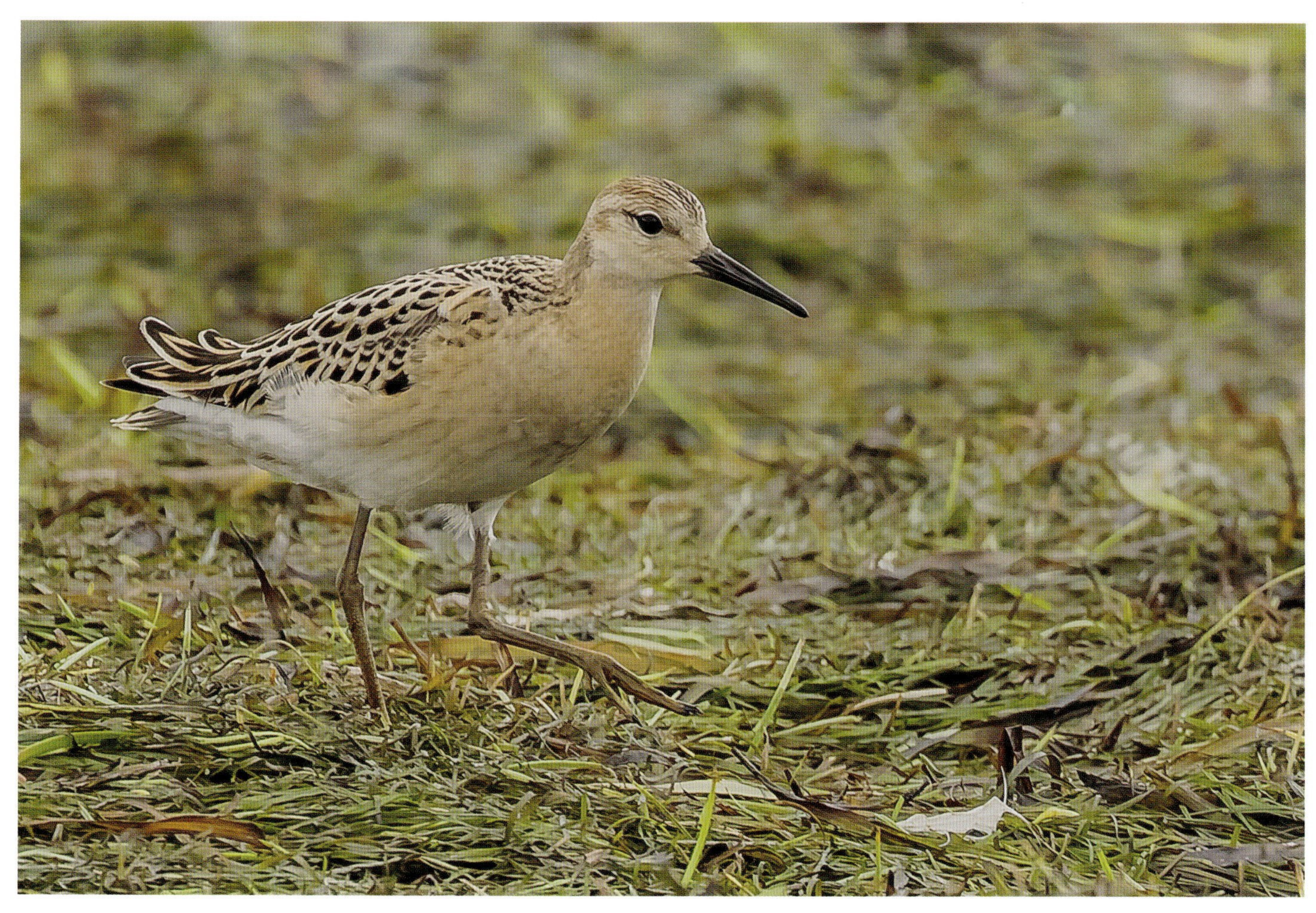

A JUVENILE RUFF AT BOUNDARY BAY IN DELTA, BC. IN THE BREEDING SEASON, THESE BIRDS DEVELOP EXTRAVAGANT FEATHERS AND BOLD COLOURS TO ATTRACT FEMALES TO MATE.

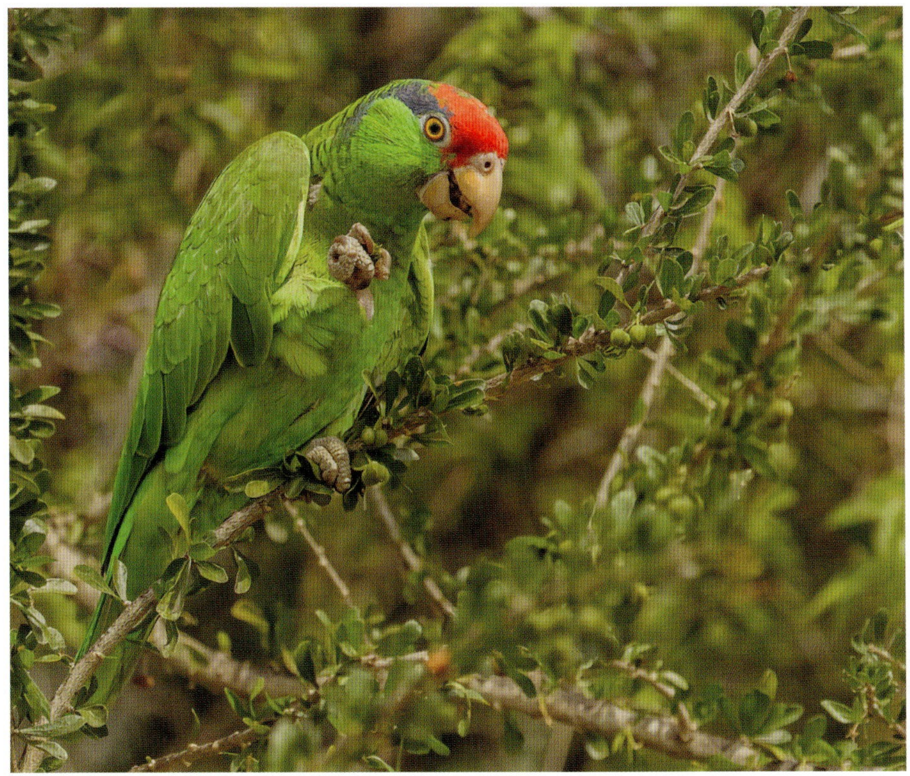

A RED-CROWNED PARROT IN WESLACO, TEXAS.

Clark's Nutcrackers are one of very few members of the corvid family where the males incubate the eggs during nesting. With corvids, egg rearing is usually only done by the female. The male Clark's Nutcracker develops a brood patch like the female and keeps the eggs warm while the female finds food. Clark's Nutcrackers also have a pouch under their tongue that they use to transport seeds. In this pouch, they can store up to 150 pine seeds! They cache thousands of seeds in the ground every year. They and all corvids have excellent memories and can remember where they have cached most of the pine seeds even nine months later. They can even retrieve seeds in the ground that are buried under a metre of snow. Clark's Nutcrackers only select the best seeds by colour and test them out in their bill for quality. They have developed a codependent relationship with Whitebark Pines because the birds help disperse their seeds. The shape of the pine seeds and the shape of the trees and their cones have changed due to their relationship with this bird species, in comparison to other pine trees whose seeds rely on wind dispersal.

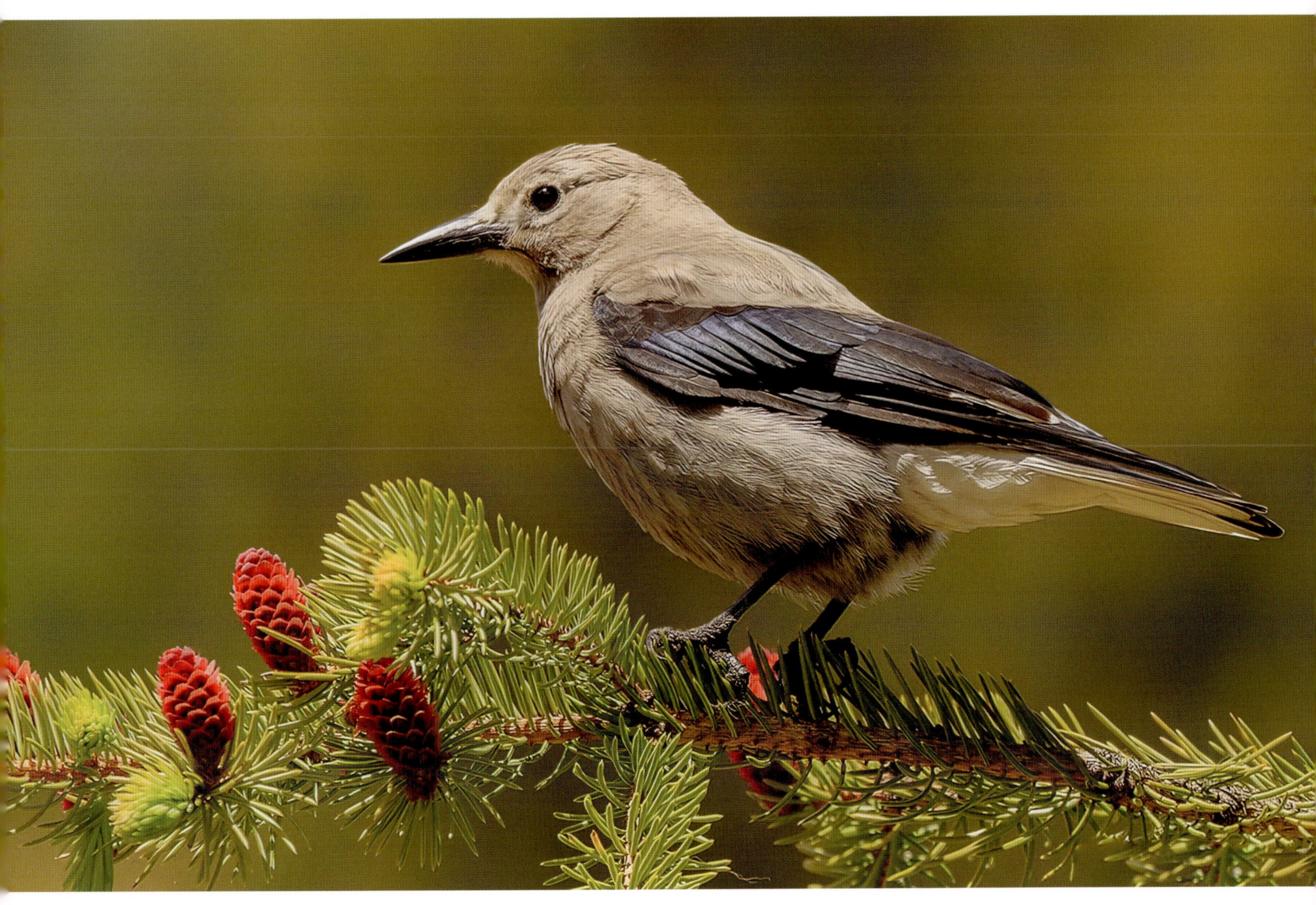

I LOVE TO HAND-FEED CLARK'S NUTCRACKERS AT E.C. MANNING PARK, BC.

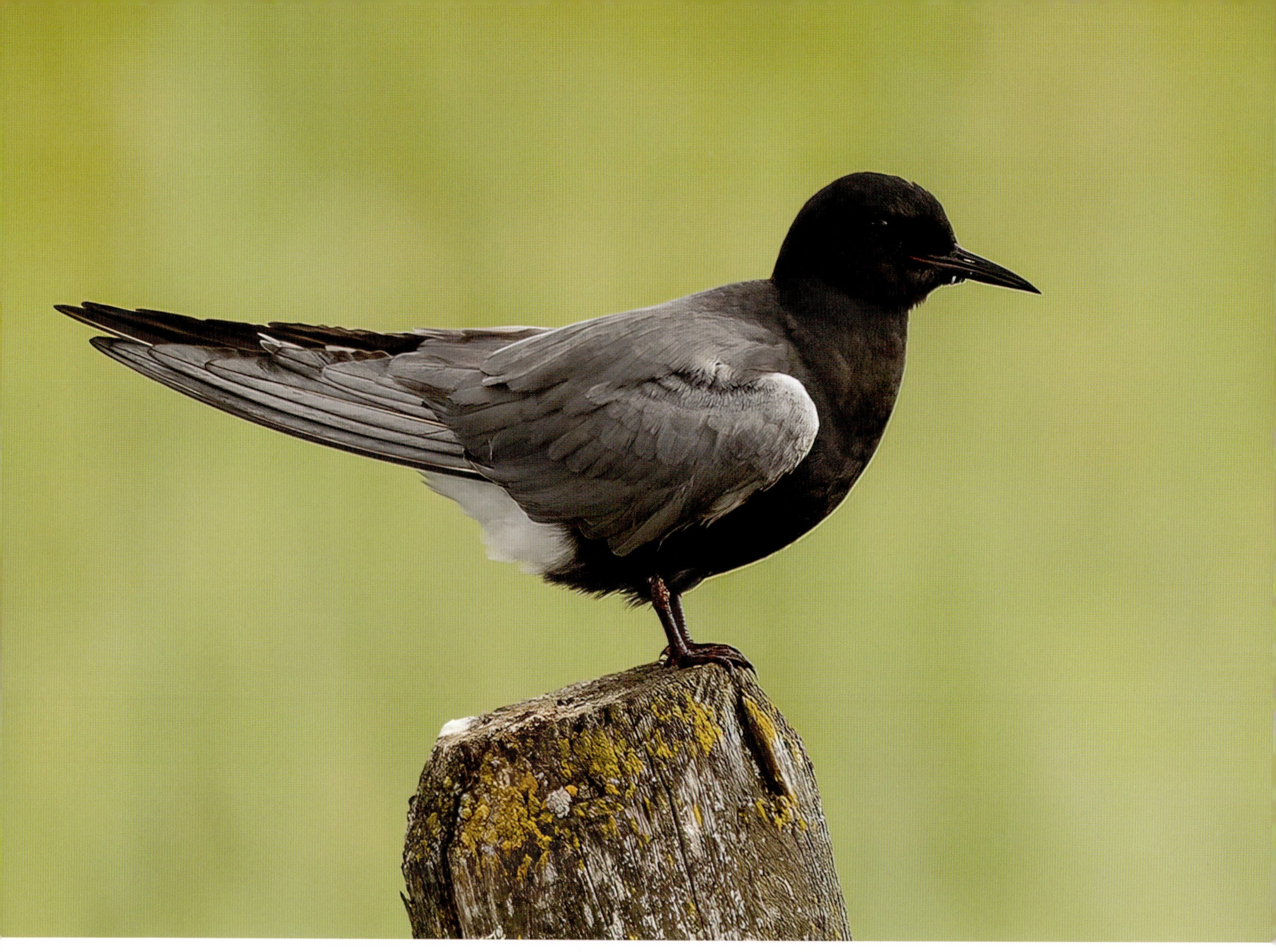

A BLACK TERN APPEARS TO SMILE IN COLD LAKE, ALBERTA.

When I was birding in Cold Lake, Alberta, I watched a Black Tern on a post above its nest. It almost seemed as if it were smiling, and I wondered what secret it knew but wasn't telling. Black Terns nest deep in reeds and tall grasses on floating vegetation on freshwater wetlands. Black Terns are affected by climate change by way of changes in precipitation. Periods of drought can strand nests or make them accessible to predators, and periods of heavy rain can flood them, killing nestlings.

I couldn't see the cute nestlings but watched the adults bring food over and over. The adults would swoop down, gracefully skimming the water, catching fish and insects they brought back to their begging young. It is nice to get a little glimpse into the life of birds, even though we will never truly know all their secrets.

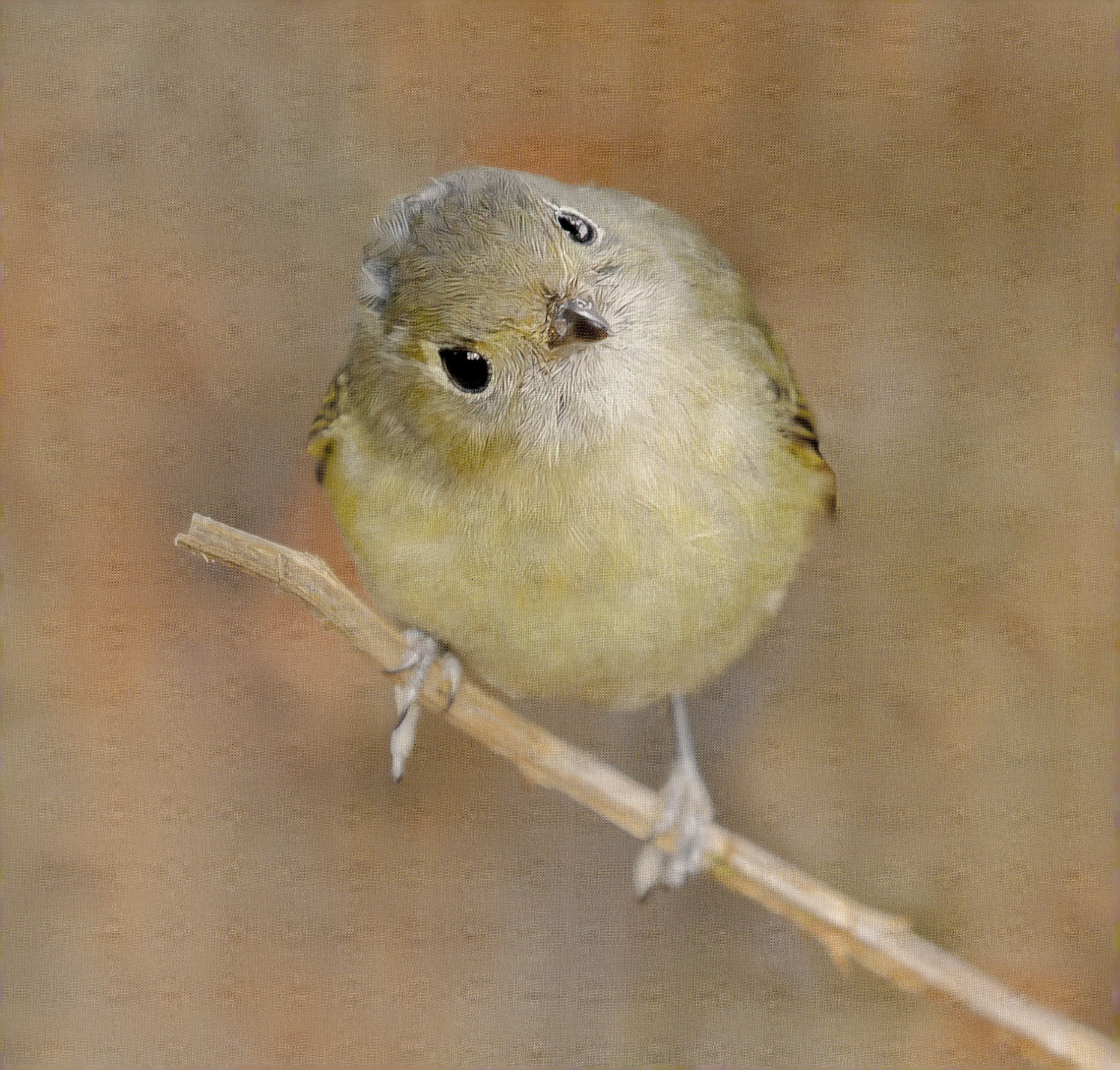

A HUTTON'S VIREO CHEEKILY STARES AT THE CAMERA IN DELTA, BC.

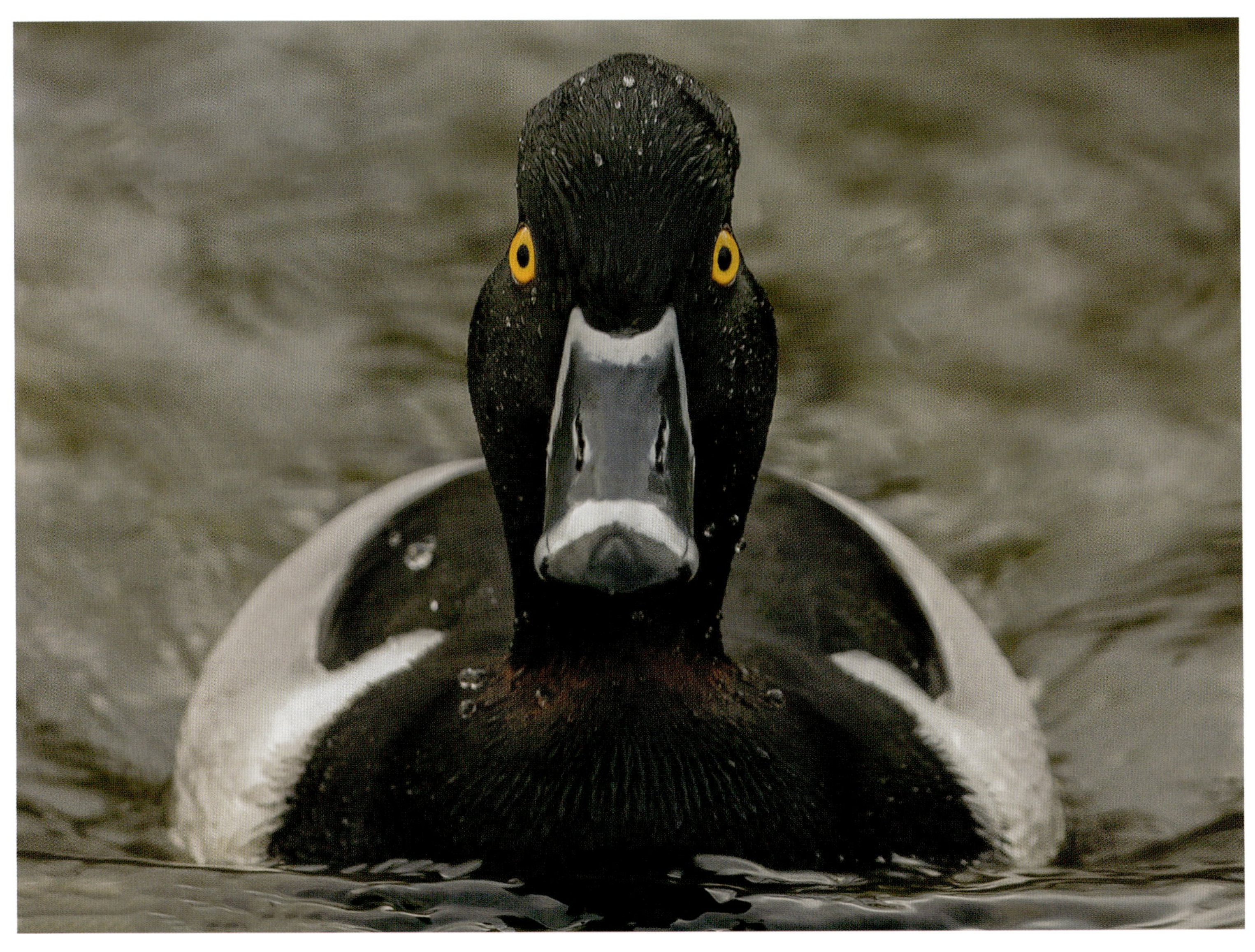

A RING-NECKED DUCK DRAKE SWIMS TOWARD ME AS I COME EYE TO EYE WITH IT AT THE GEORGE C. REIFEL MIGRATORY BIRD SANCTUARY IN DELTA, BC.

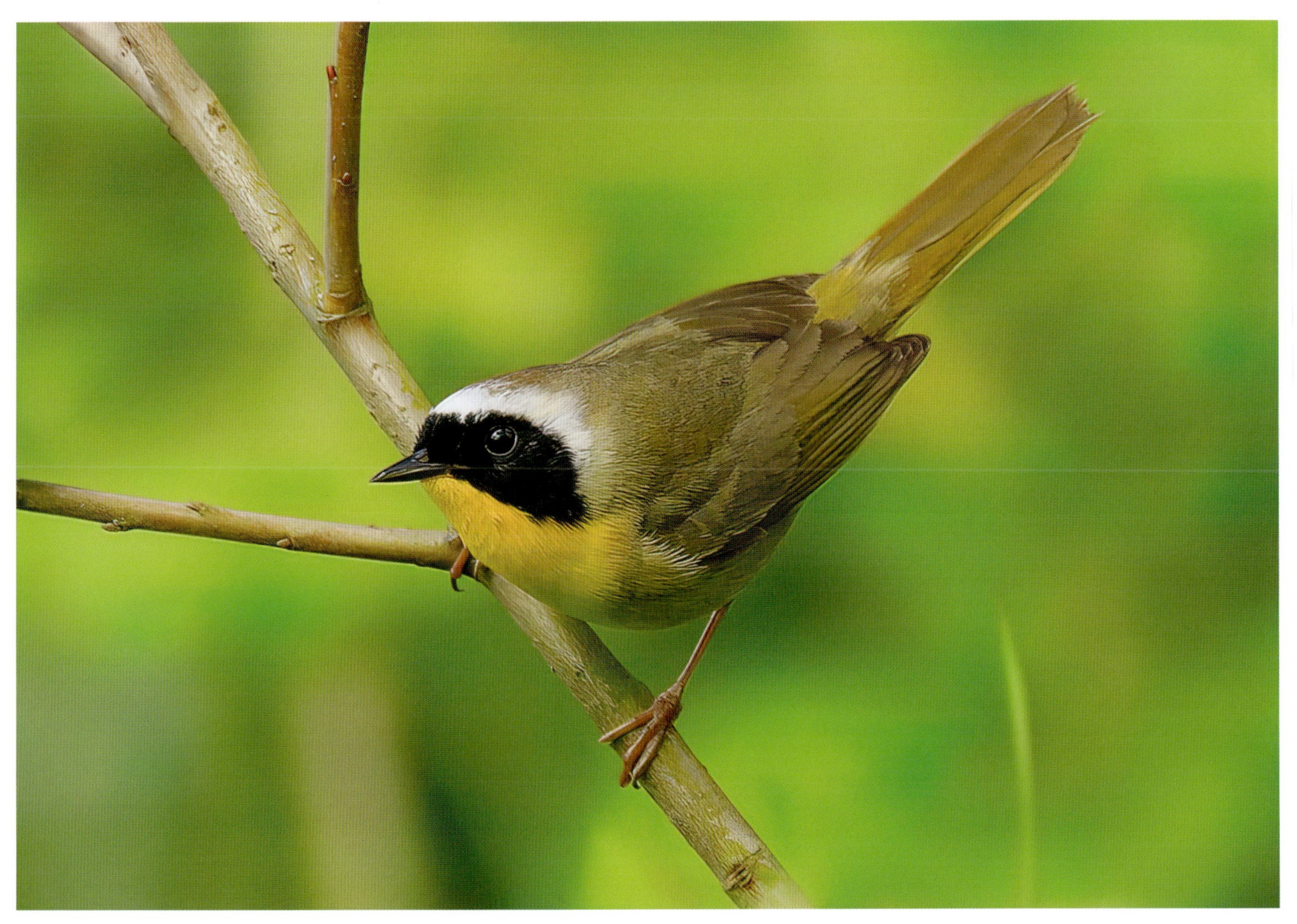

A COMMON YELLOWTHROAT PAUSES TO LOOK AT ME THROUGH THE REEDS IN RICHMOND, BC.

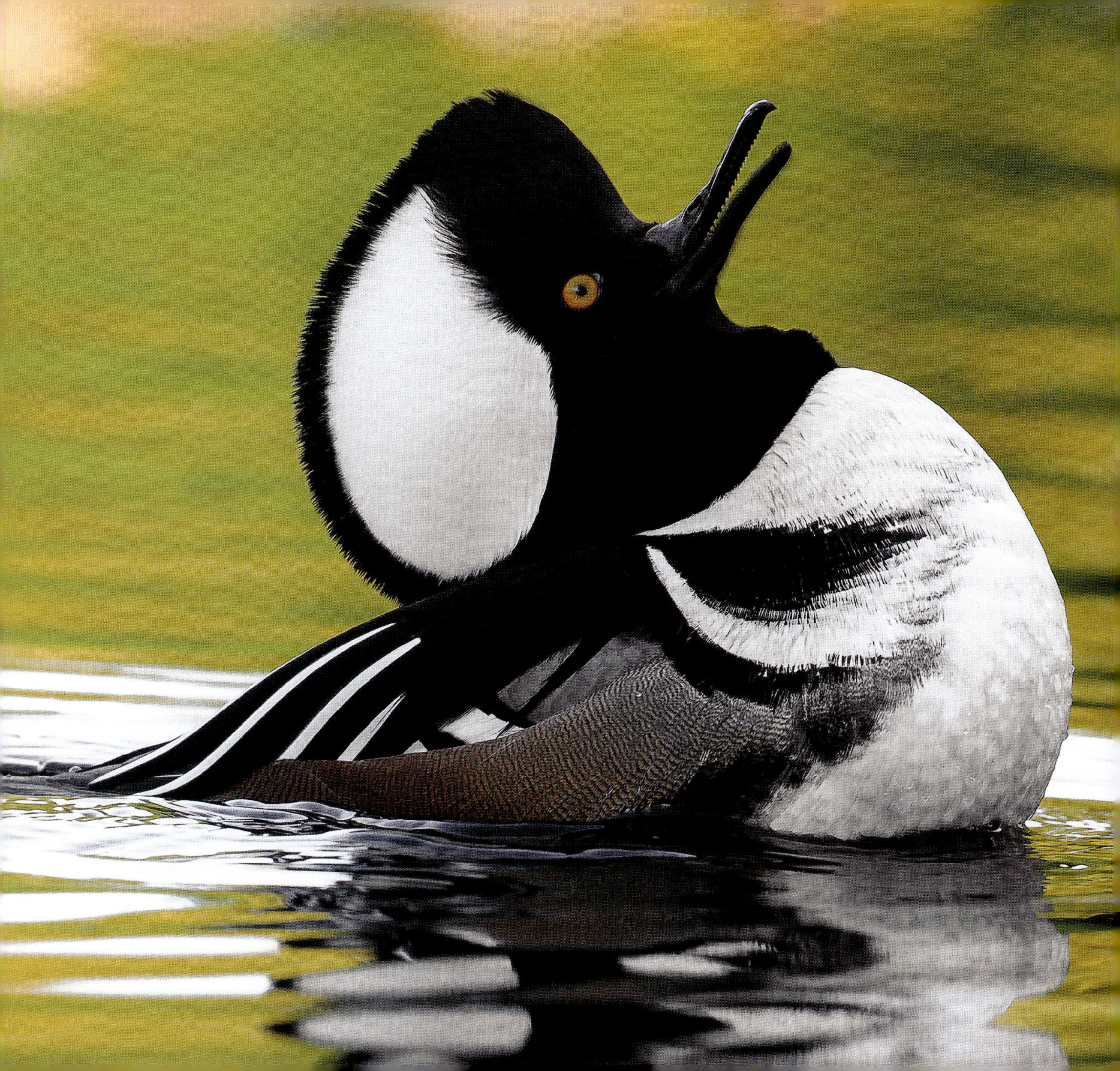

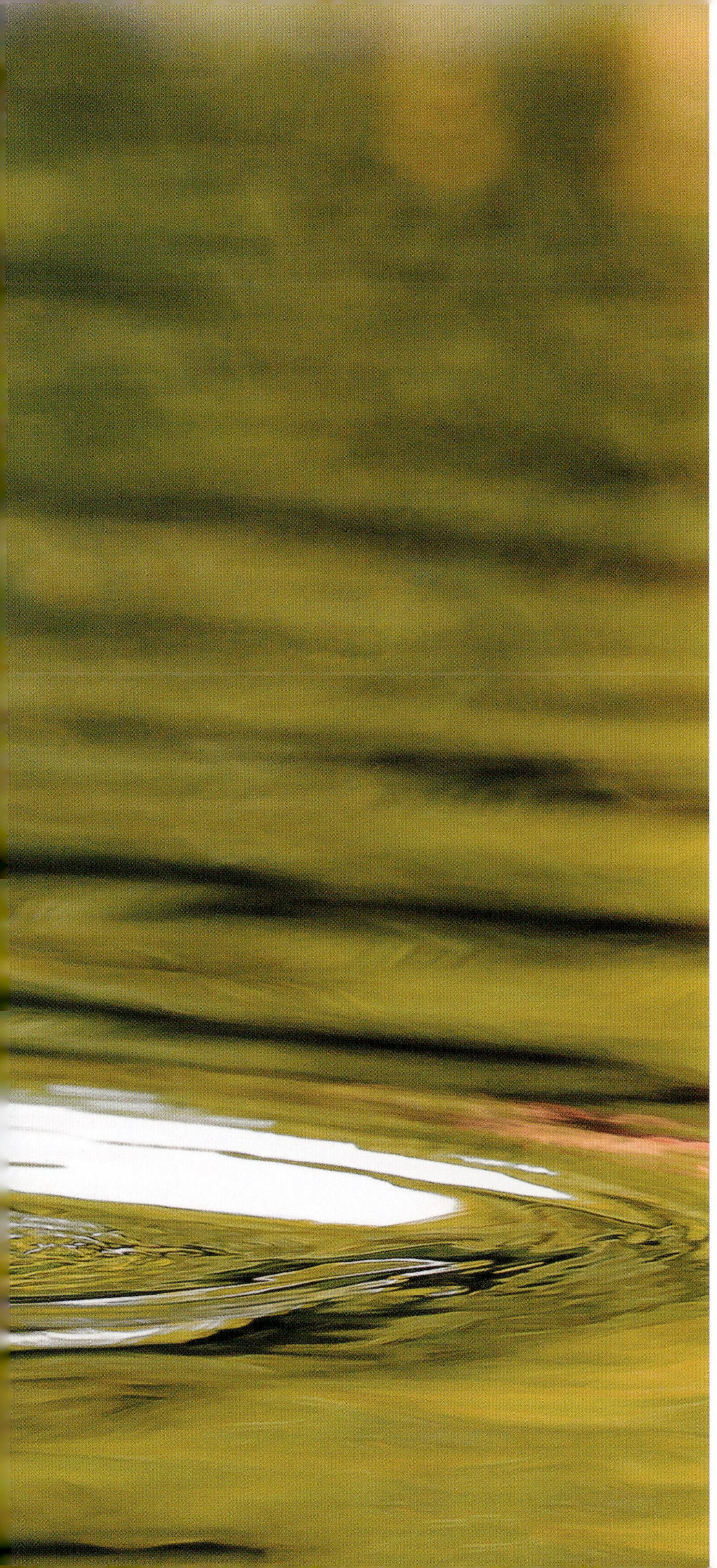

A HOODED MERGANSER DRAKE DOES A COURTSHIP DISPLAY FOR FEMALES IN VANCOUVER, BC. MALE HOODED MERGANSERS MAKE LOUD GRUNTING SOUNDS AND POP THEIR CRESTS ON THEIR HEADS BACK AND FORTH DURING THE DISPLAY.

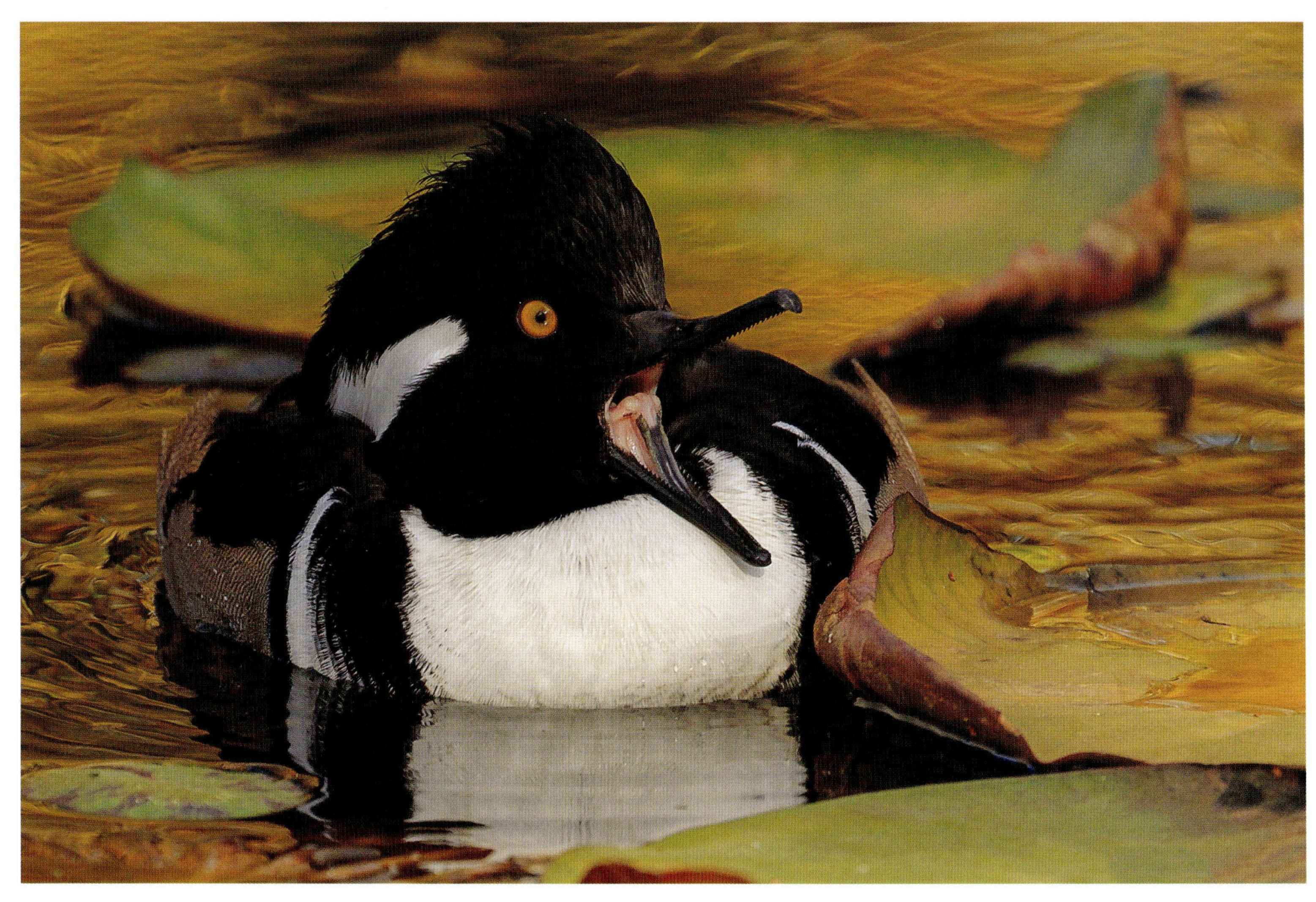

A HOODED MERGANSER YAWNS FOR THE CAMERA IN VANCOUVER, BC.

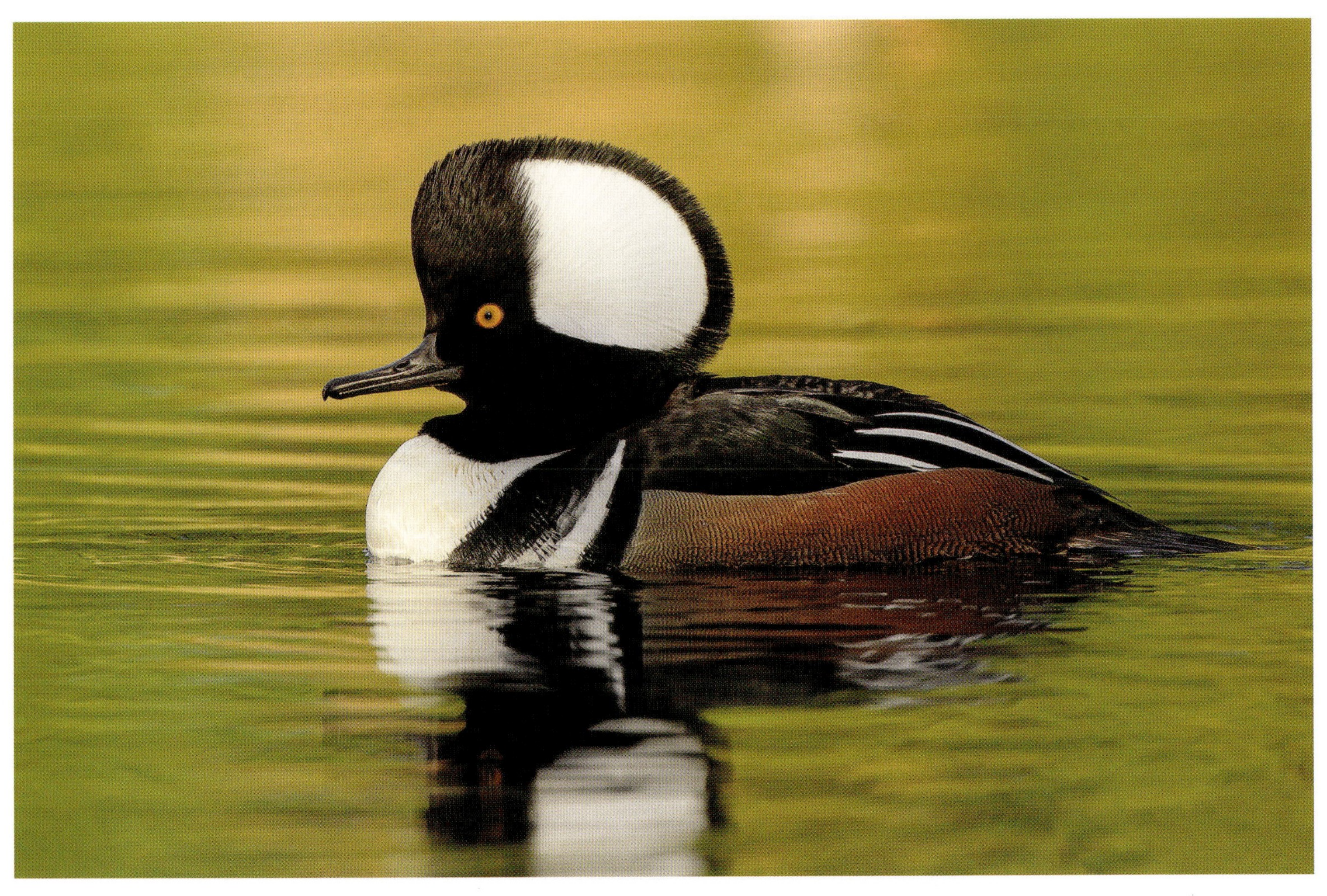

A MALE HOODED MERGANSER SWIMS ON A GOLDEN-COLOURED POND IN BETWEEN ITS ELABORATE COURTSHIP DISPLAY FOR A FEMALE IN VANCOUVER, BC.

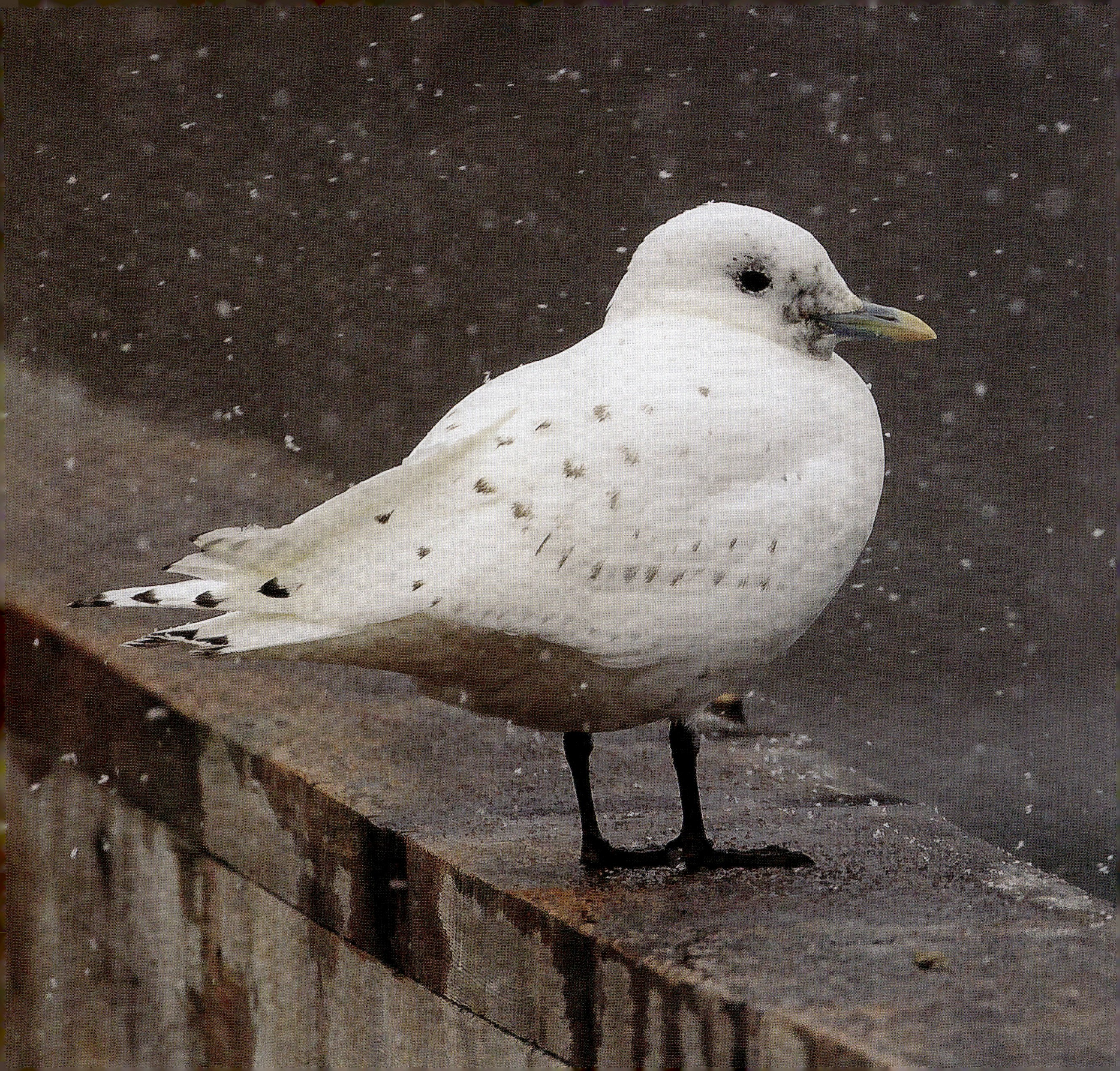

9

Rare Bird Alert

I run the BC Rare Bird Alert website, and I love to "twitch" or chase rare birds. It is exciting to see what cool vagrants turn up from Asia, Europe, or another part of North America or elsewhere in the world.

Opposite:

I DROVE TEN HOURS TO POLSON, MONTANA, TO SEE THIS RARE IVORY GULL.

Birds undertake tremendous migrations and at times get blown off course. Others may be born with faulty navigation systems and undertake migration in the opposite direction from the rest of their conspecifics. The possibility of finding or seeing these vagrants is one facet of birding that many people find appealing. For example, there was the Ivory Gull I saw that turned up in a small lake in Polson, Montana, when it should have been in the High Arctic in Alaska or in extreme northern Canada. This bird even spends its winters there, surviving off carrion from the remains of Polar Bear kills.

Both Polar Bears and Ivory Gulls are connected in another way: climate change. Ivory Gulls are dramatically affected by climate change. Their populations have dropped more than 80 per cent. They make nests on High Arctic ice mountains that are melting, therefore making them more susceptible to Arctic Fox predation. These endangered gulls breed the farthest north of any other bird in the world. They are also affected by pollution in the ocean and air. They have been shown to have high levels of DDT, mercury, and other pollutants in their bodies. I drove ten hours to Montana to see this amazing and stunning snow white-coloured gull with a yellow and blue bill. It was one of the best twitches I ever went on. Seeing this bird with the snow falling all around it left me speechless.

I've driven 14 hours to see a Crested Caracara eating flies in Bella Coola that should have been in places like Arizona and Texas. I have also had a lot of fun seeing vagrants near my hometown, such as a Tufted Duck that showed up at Burnaby Lake. I have so many amazing memories

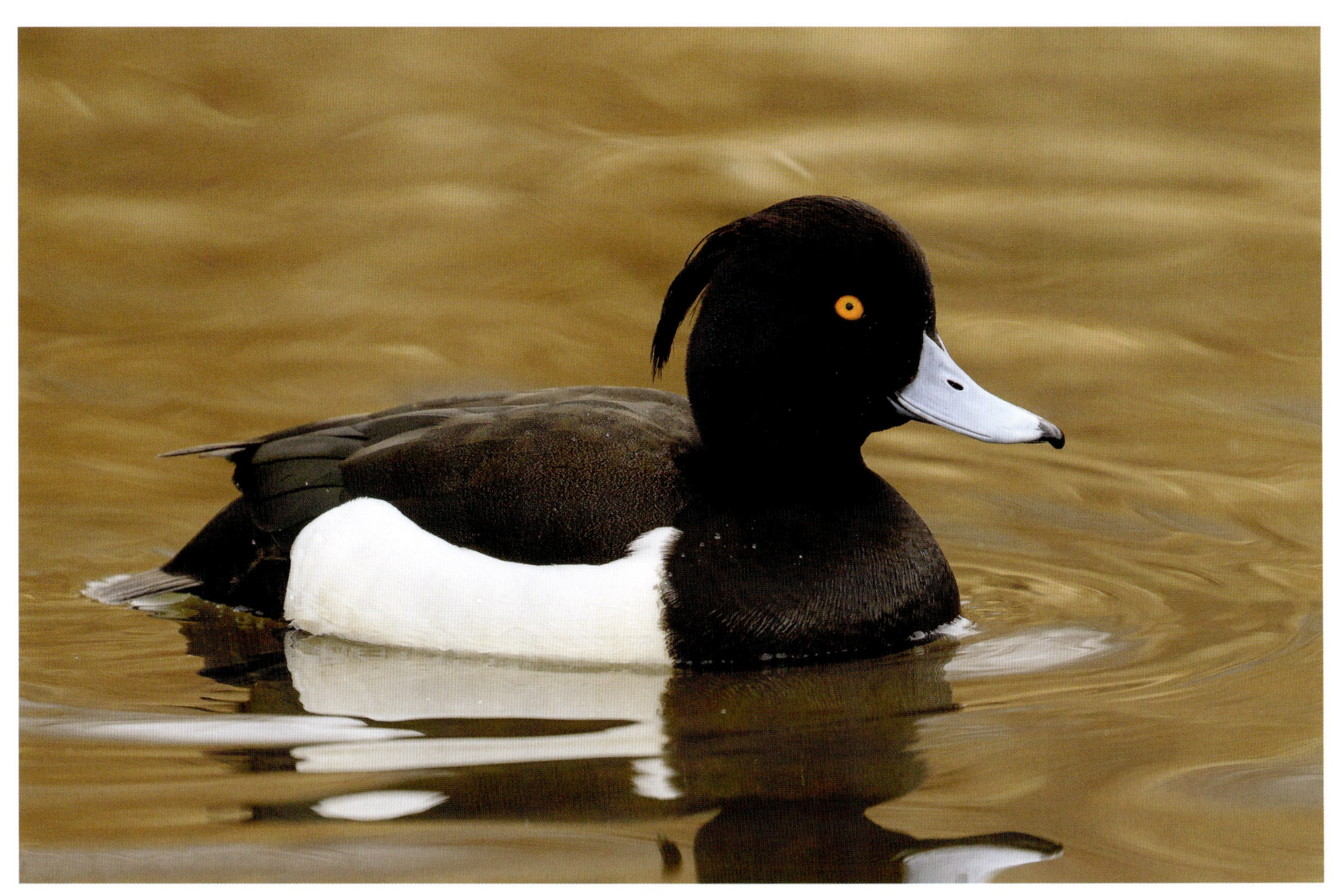

A RARE TUFTED DUCK THAT SHOWED UP IN BURNABY, BC.

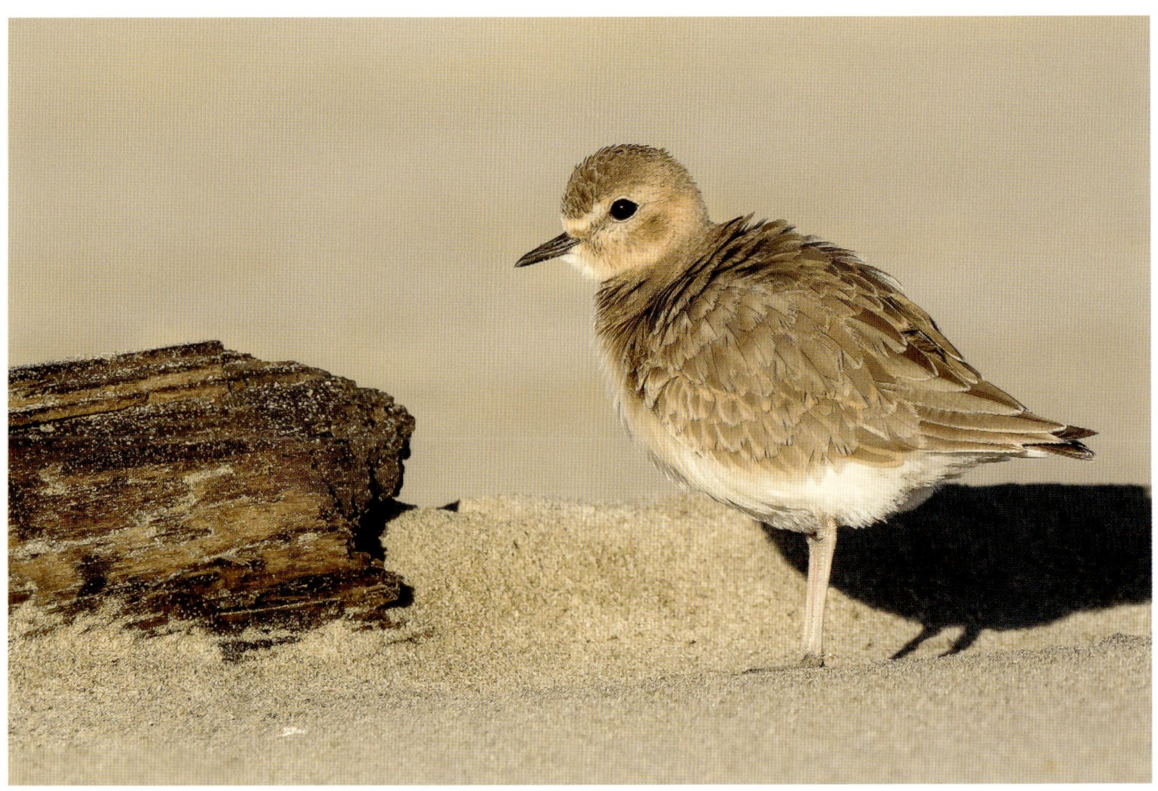

A JUVENILE MOUNTAIN PLOVER ON A BEACH IN NEWPORT, OREGON.

of twitching rare birds. So many fun road trips with friends, as well as the cool people I meet when I see the bird. Of course, sometimes you don't see the bird, like with a recent Pallas's Bunting I chased, which is called "dipping," but that's all part of the fun. If you got the bird every time, it would be too easy! Birding is a cool hobby because it's for people who like to drive near and far to see a rare bird, but it is equally for those who like to watch the birds right in their own backyard. I like to do both, but my passion is certainly for seeing rare birds.

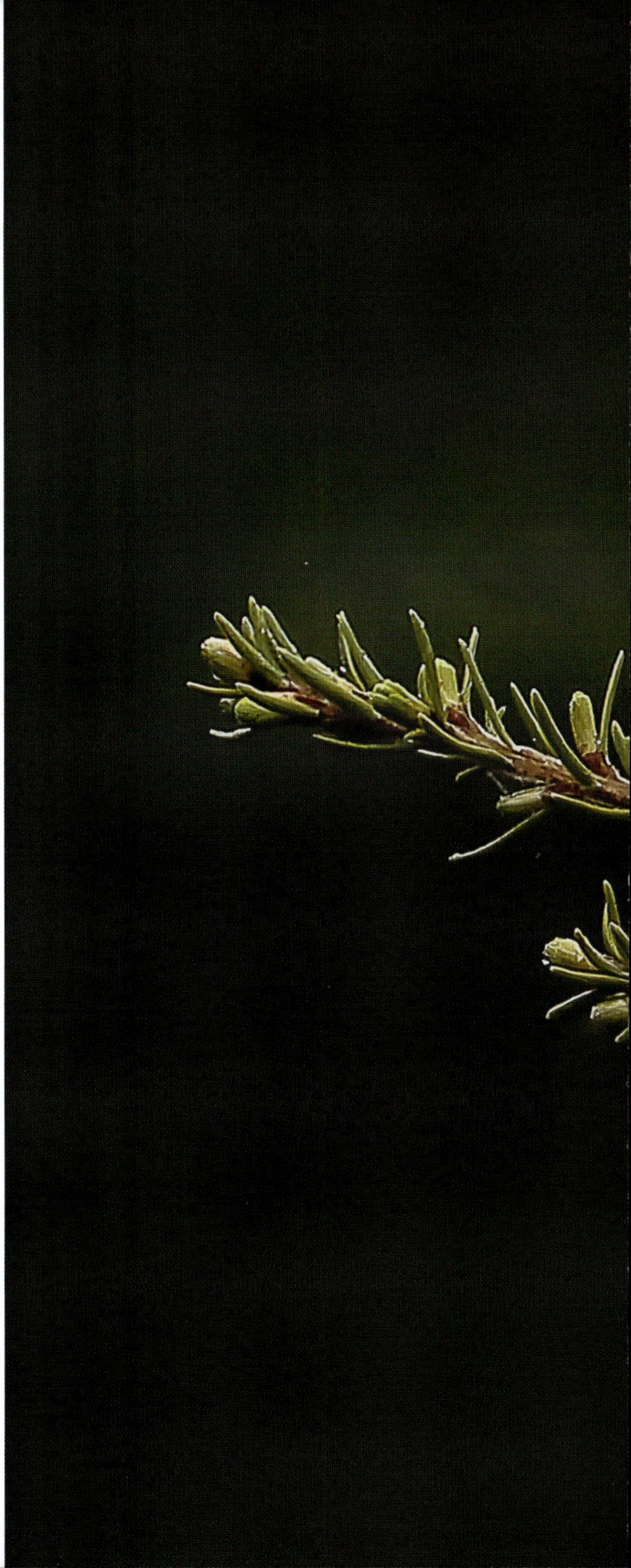

A MALE HERMIT WARBLER
IN COURTENAY ON
VANCOUVER ISLAND, BC.

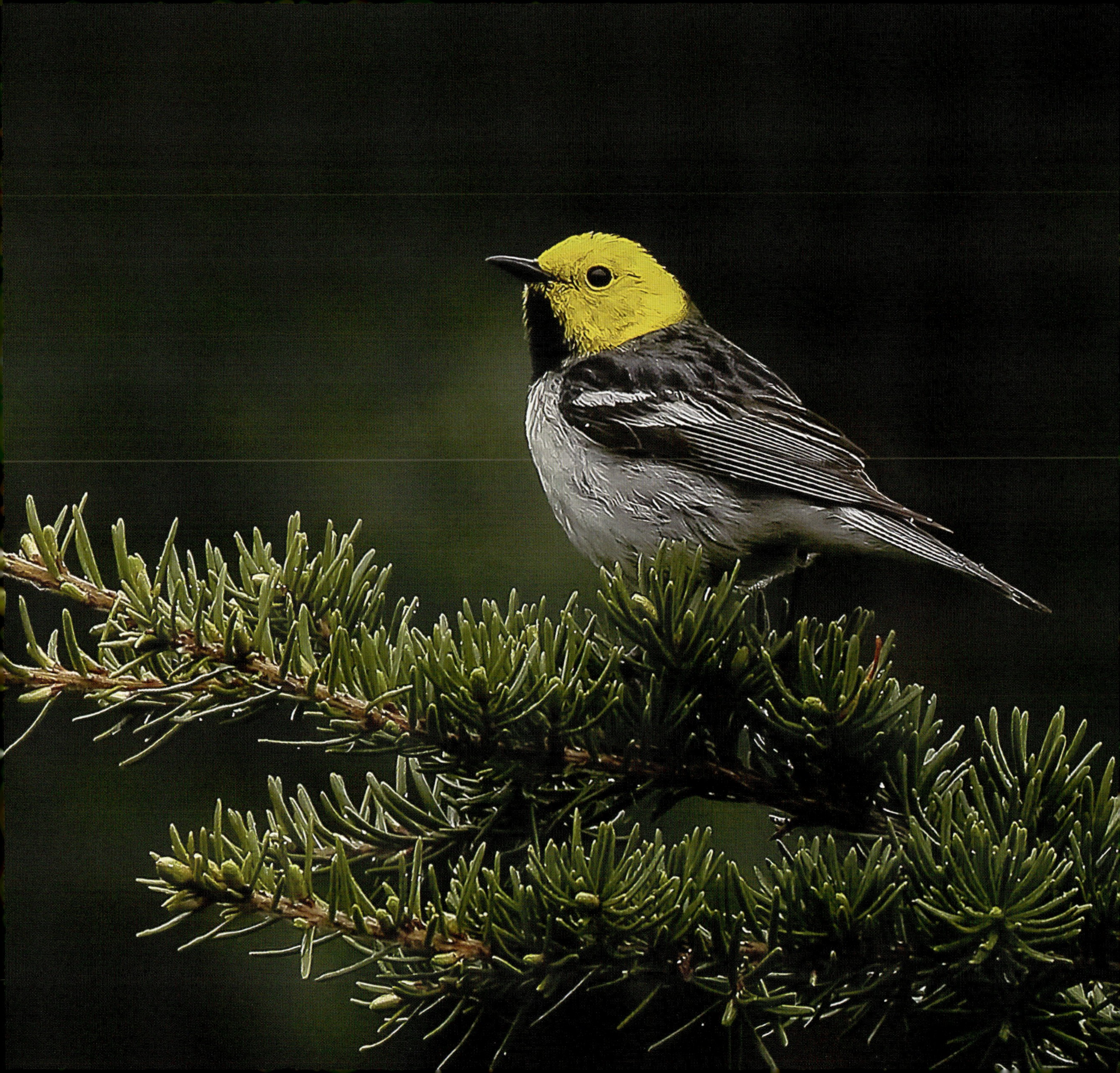

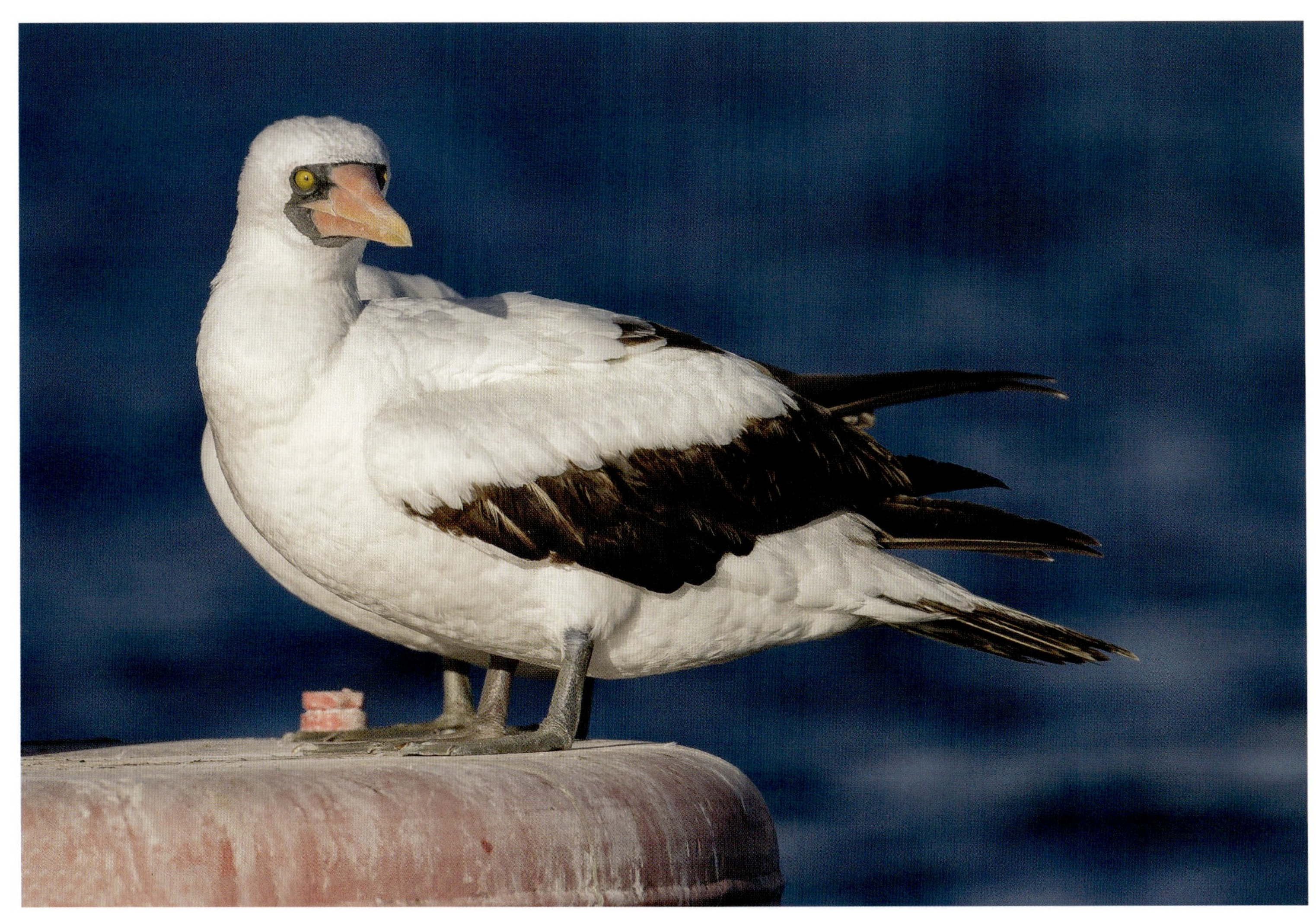

I RENTED A BOAT AND DROVE IT OUT IN CORONADO BAY TO SEE TWO RARE NAZCA BOOBIES IN SAN DIEGO, CALIFORNIA.

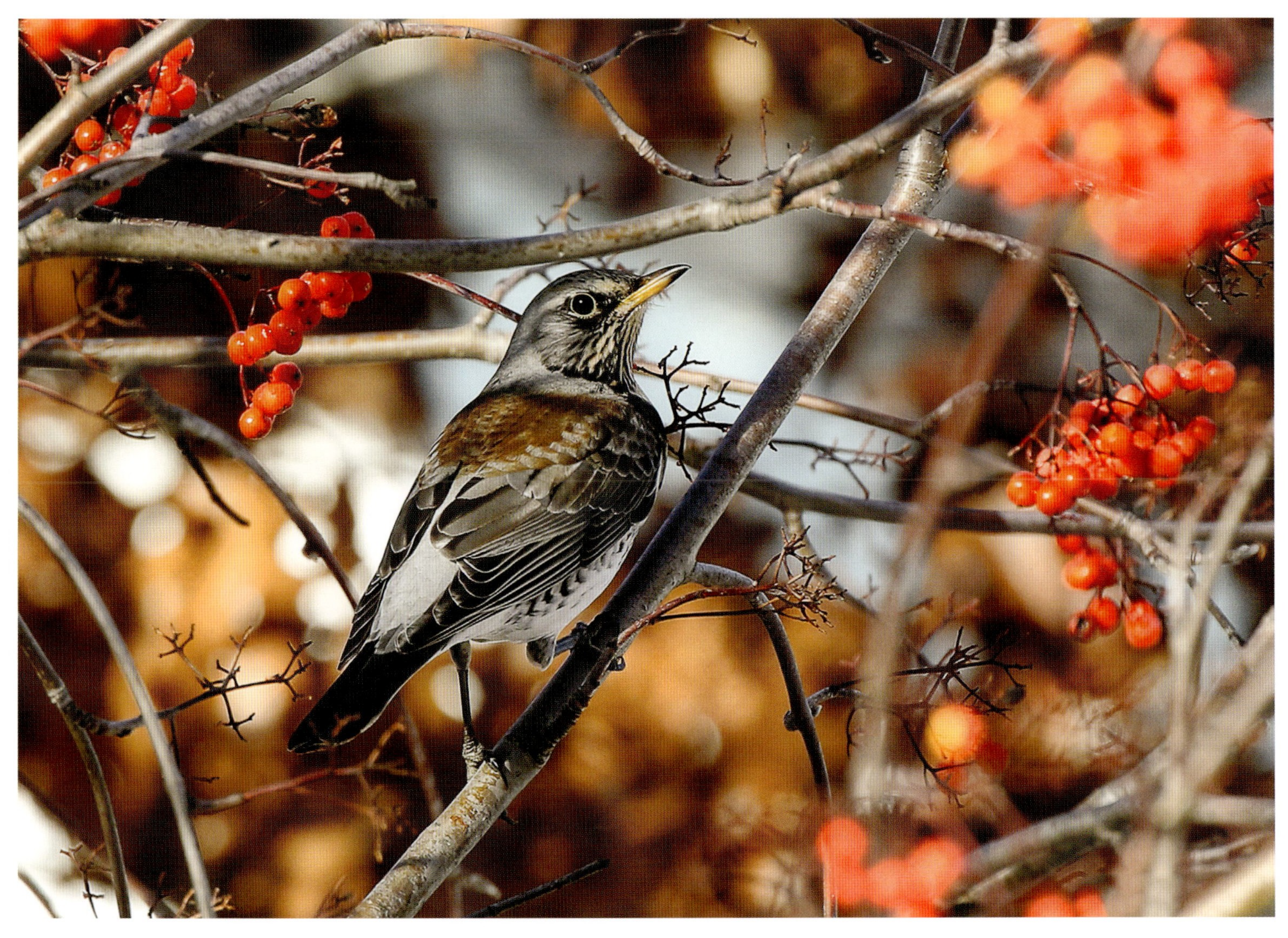

A VERY RARE EUROPEAN THRUSH CALLED A FIELDFARE VISITED SALMON ARM, BC, AND DELIGHTED HOARDS OF BIRDERS.

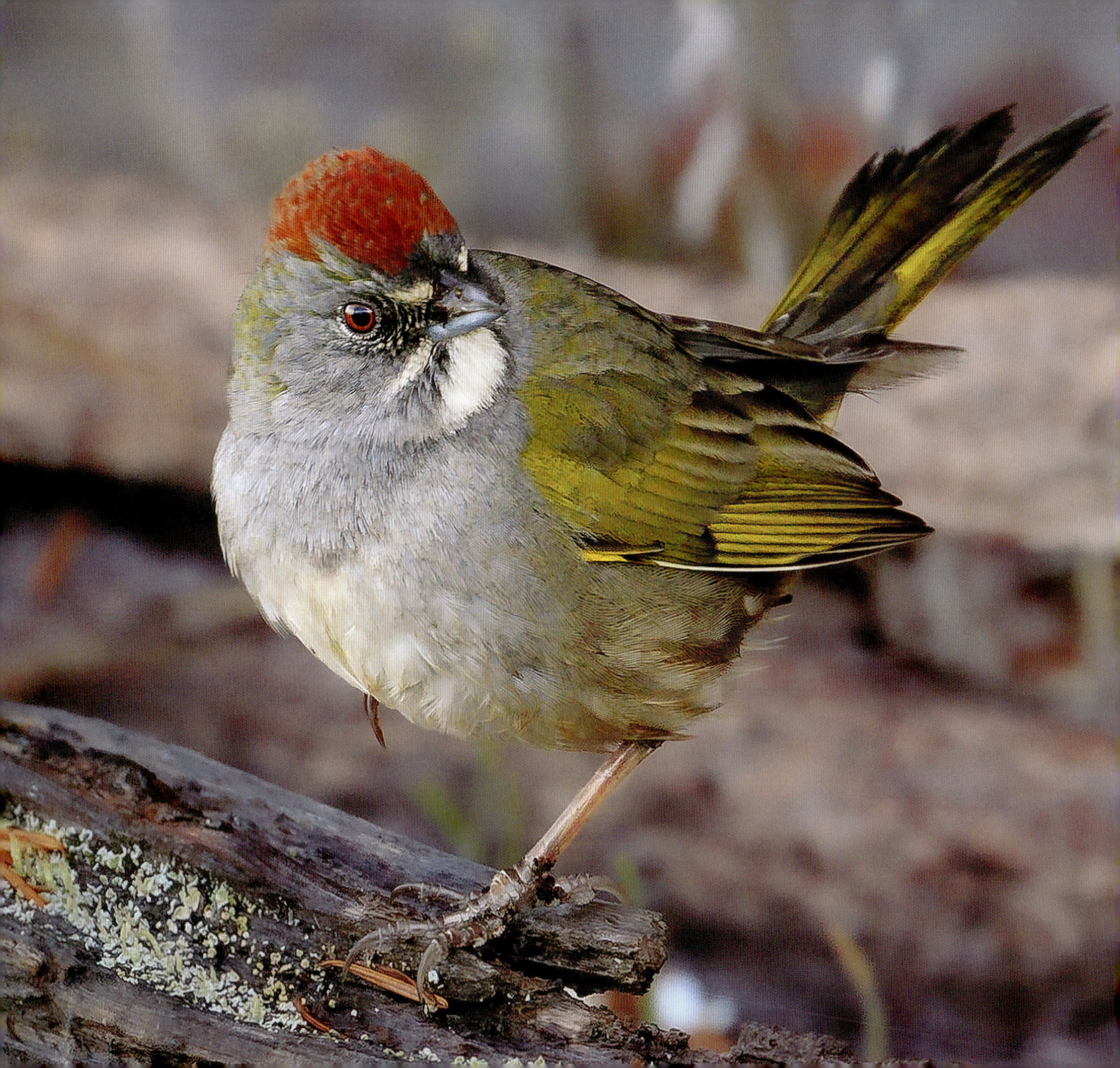

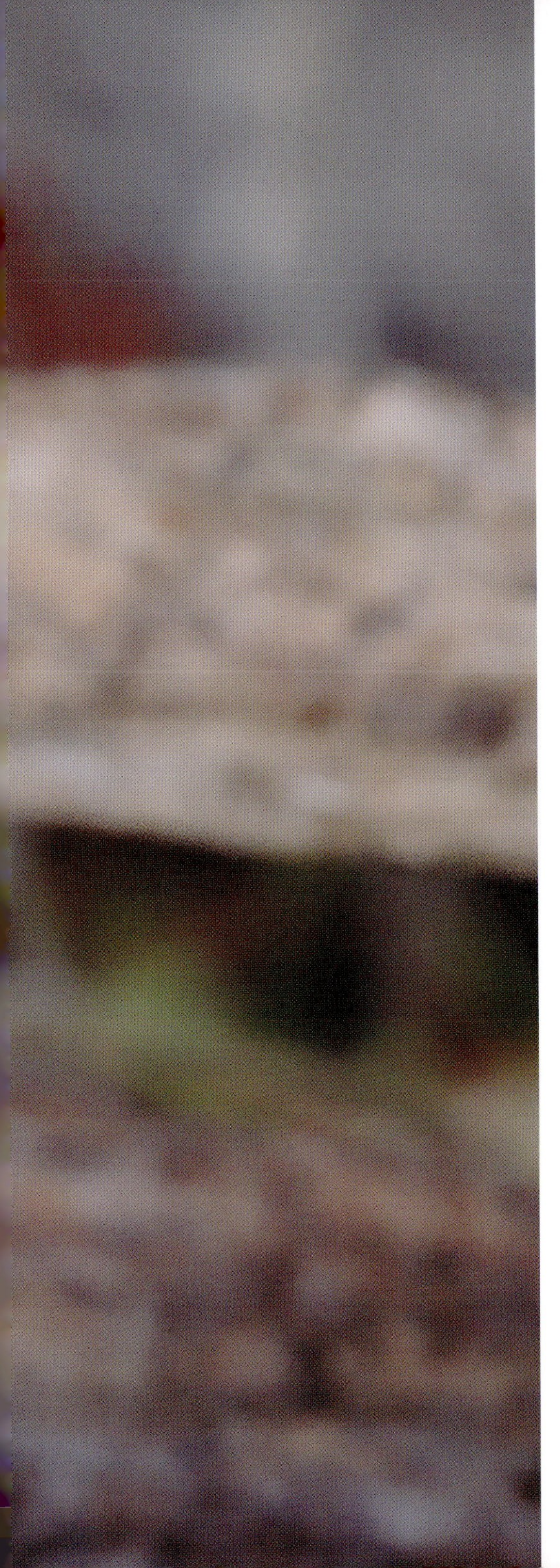

A RARE GREEN-TAILED TOWHEE DELIGHTED MANY BIRDERS ON DENMAN ISLAND, BC. IT WAS THE FIRST TIME I SAW THE BIRD IN THE PROVINCE.

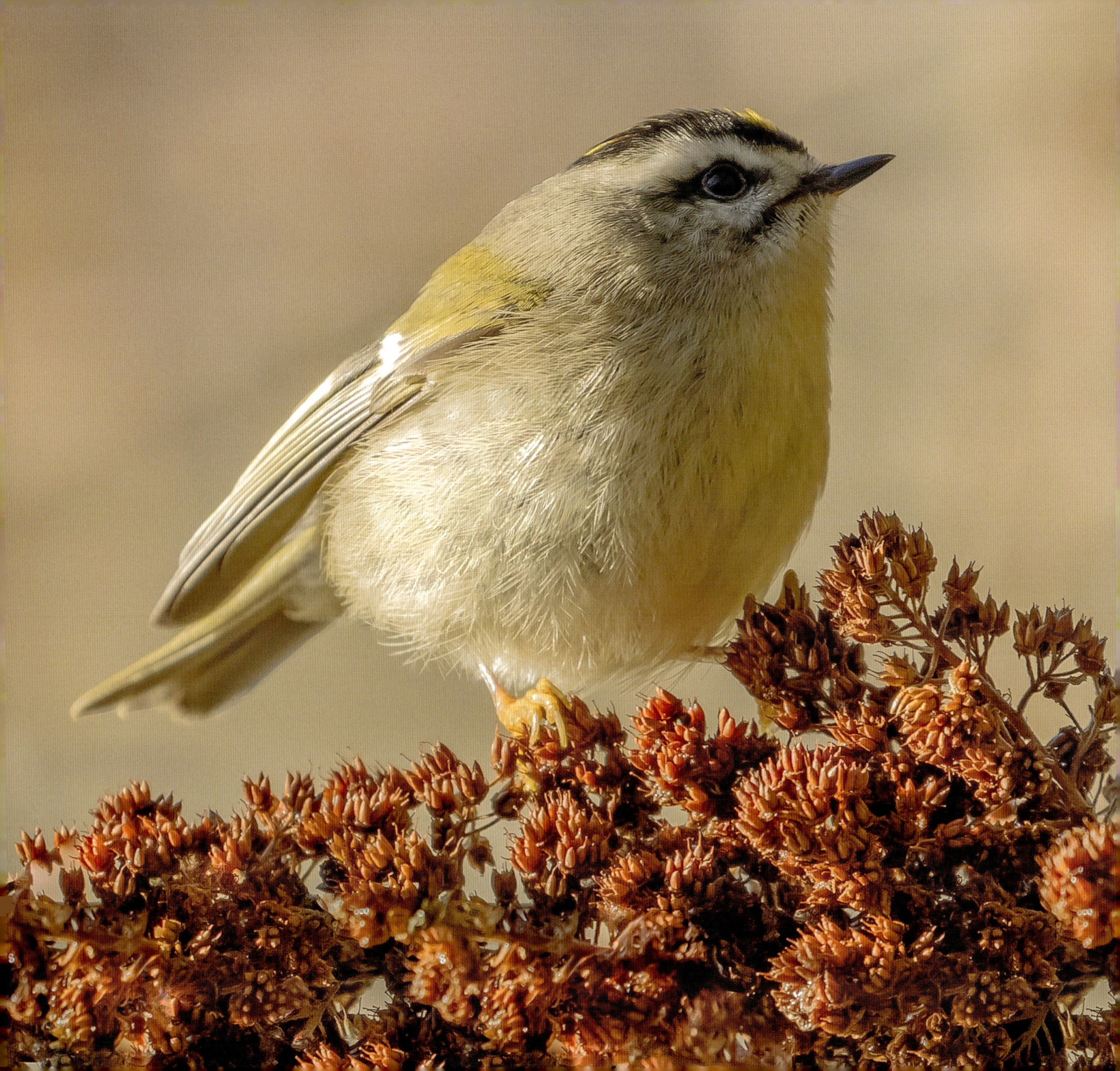

10

In My Solitude

Birding is a hobby that one can do alone or in a group. I very much enjoy birding alone because it gives me time to reflect and think and get away from stress. It is also a good way to distract the mind from distressing or painful things. When you are focusing on birds, especially when you are grieving, it helps you think of something more peaceful and less heavy. Don't be afraid to do a solo birding trip either! I love travelling solo. It opens your life up to nature in a way you never knew possible.

Opposite:

A GOLDEN-CROWNED KINGLET IN VANCOUVER, BC.

One of my favourite places to go solo is in the forested coastal mountains of BC. Don't ever let the rain stop you from getting out there either. There is beauty in the rain and the sound it makes as it hits the leaves. Being alone isn't lonely. I enjoy long walks in the forest, and it is nice to see no other human out there. I am just enveloped by the trees and the birds as they sing and there is comfort in that. So even though there are no other people there, I am never alone. I feel the warm embrace of the woods and all the creatures therein. The trees laden with birds can hold a person in a way no human can. You can disappear and get away from all the noise and only be seen by the birds. It is a grounding feeling like no other. You often don't see many birds in the forest, but even if you don't see them, there is magic in simply hearing them.

Birding solo can also surprisingly help with loneliness as well. When you are alone or feeling lonely and see a beautiful bird, you feel connected and you don't feel alone. I never feel lonely while birding solo and that's a wonderful thing. I can distract myself for a few hours and focus on the beauty in front of me. Mindful birding like this is a part of my daily life. Often, I will go down to the ocean and just sit there alone, watching the ducks and shorebirds. It makes me feel safe and at peace as I take in all the wonderful bird glory.

A STELLER'S JAY POSES FOR A PHOTO ATOP CYPRESS MOUNTAIN IN WEST VANCOUVER, BC.

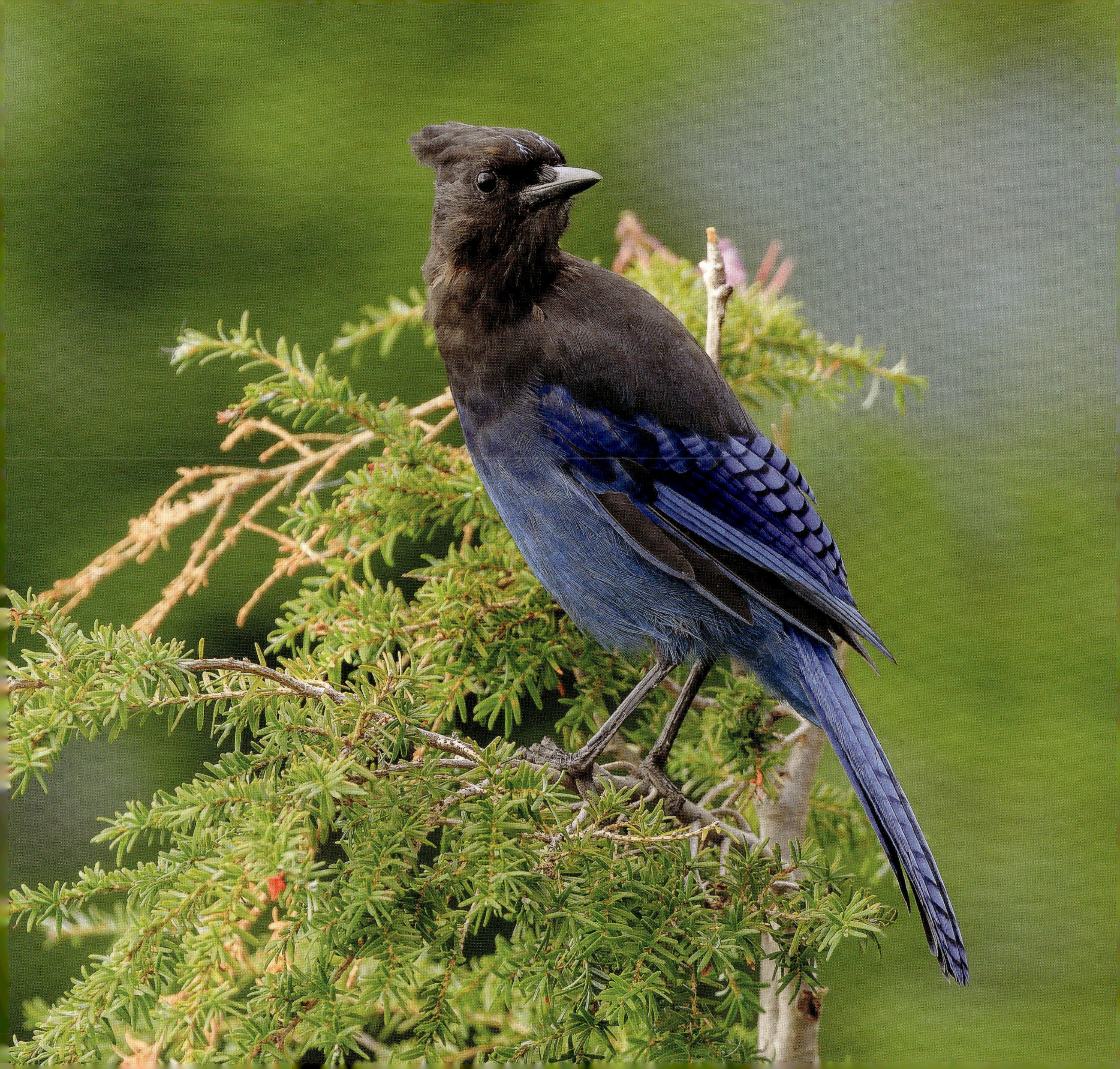

A SEMIPALMATED PLOVER ON ITS BREEDING GROUNDS IN NOME, ALASKA, SITS IN FRONT OF ME ON THE ARCTIC TUNDRA.

Overleaf:

A LONG-BILLED CURLEW, LISTED AS VULNERABLE IN BC DUE IN PART TO GRASSLAND HABITAT LOSS, STANDS IN THE PACIFIC OCEAN AT BLACKIE SPIT PARK IN SURREY, BC.

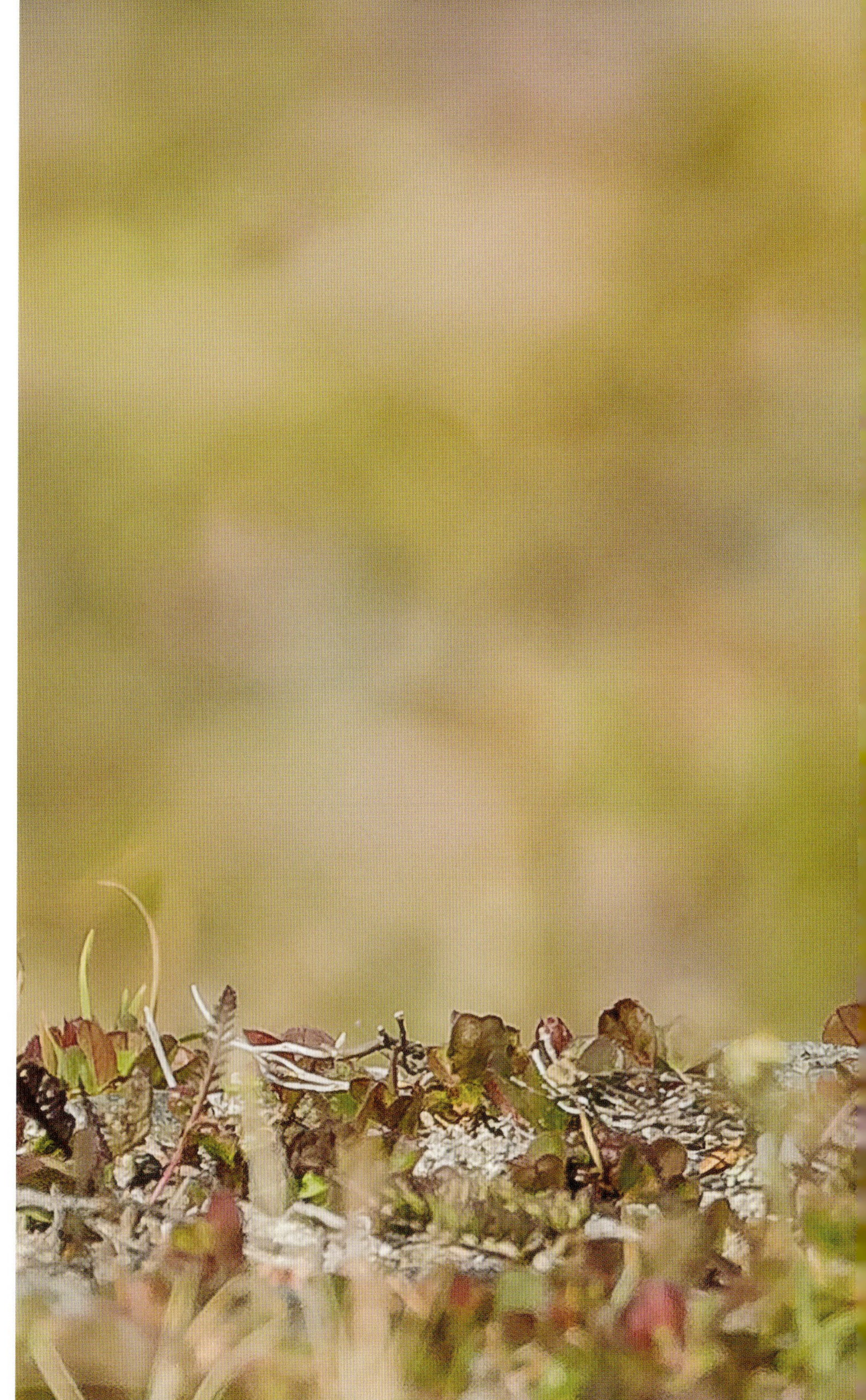

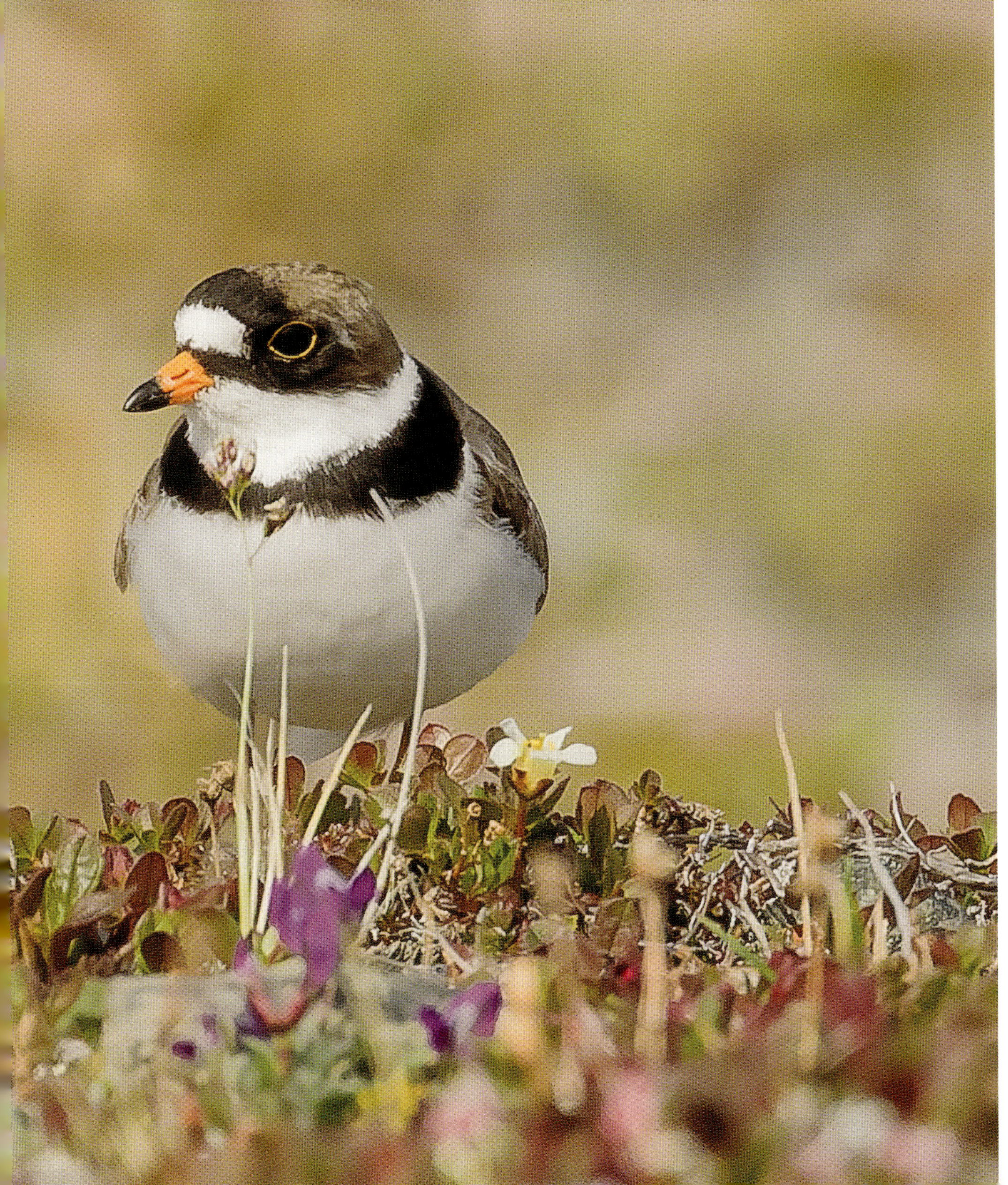

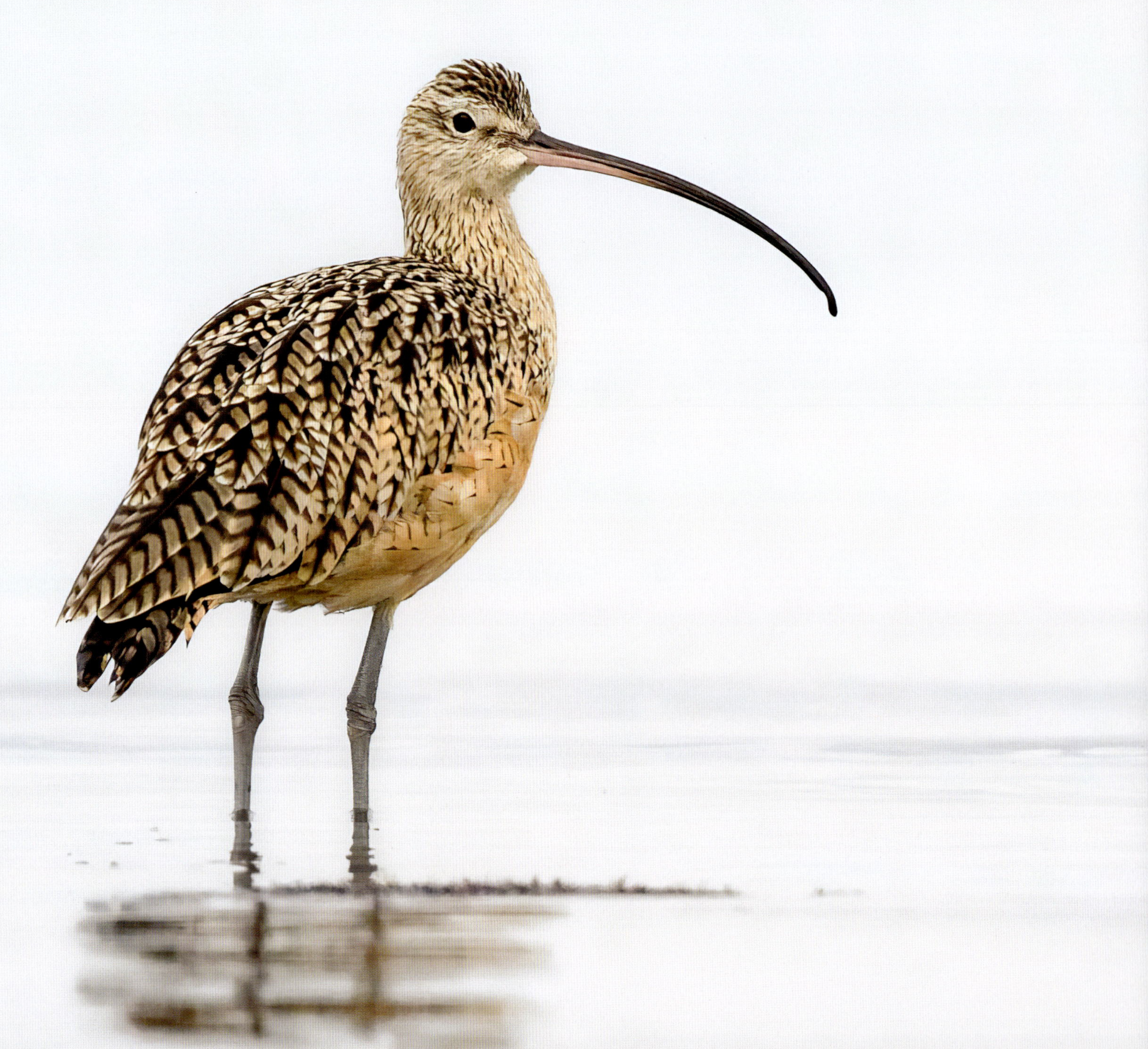

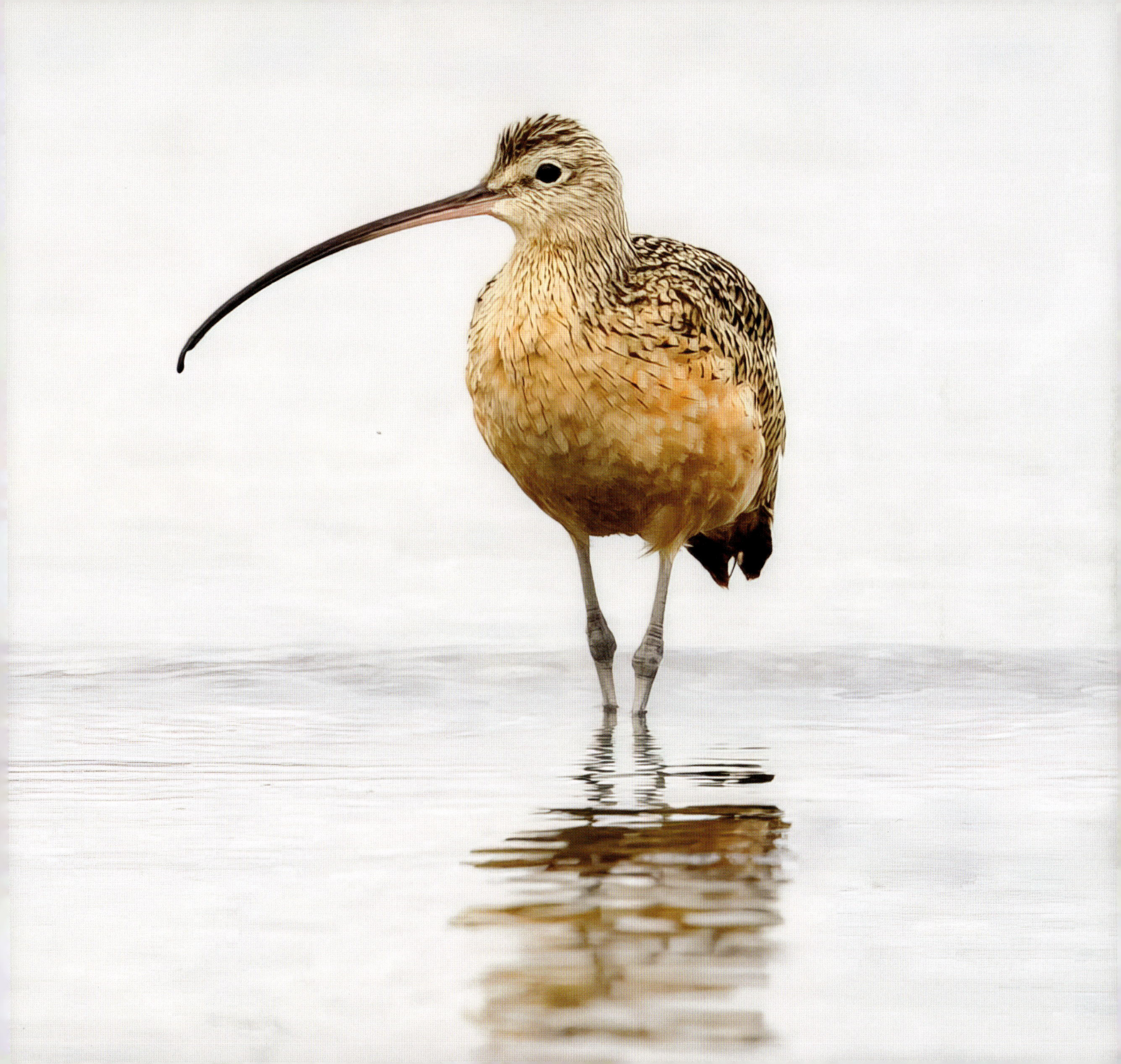

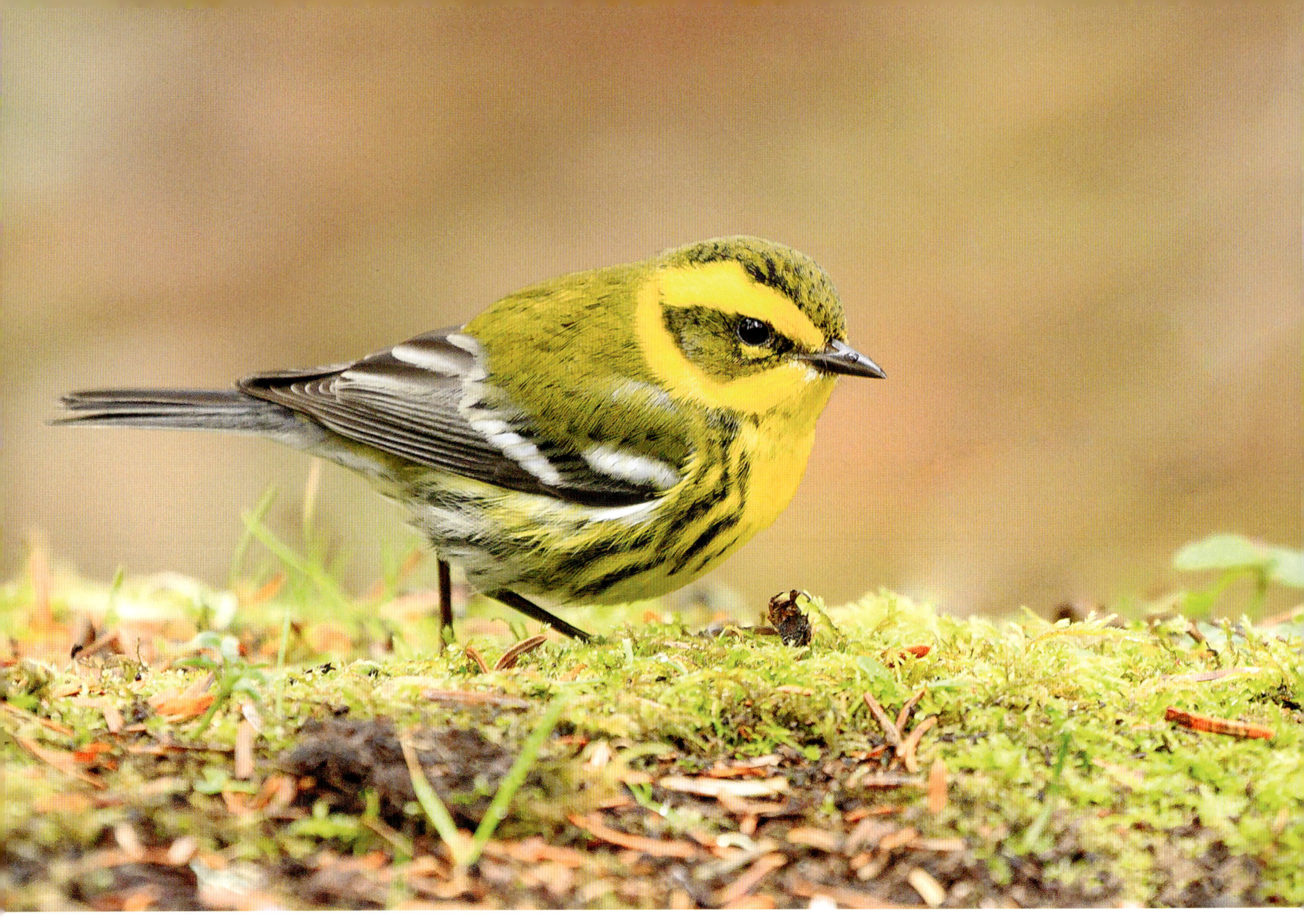

A TOWNSEND'S WARBLER IS JUST ONE OF THE MANY BIRDS I ENCOUNTER IN THE WOODS. THIS PHOTO WAS TAKEN AT CAPE DISAPPOINTMENT STATE PARK IN WASHINGTON.

A CANADA JAY WAITS FOR A HANDOUT IN E.C. MANNING PARK, BC.

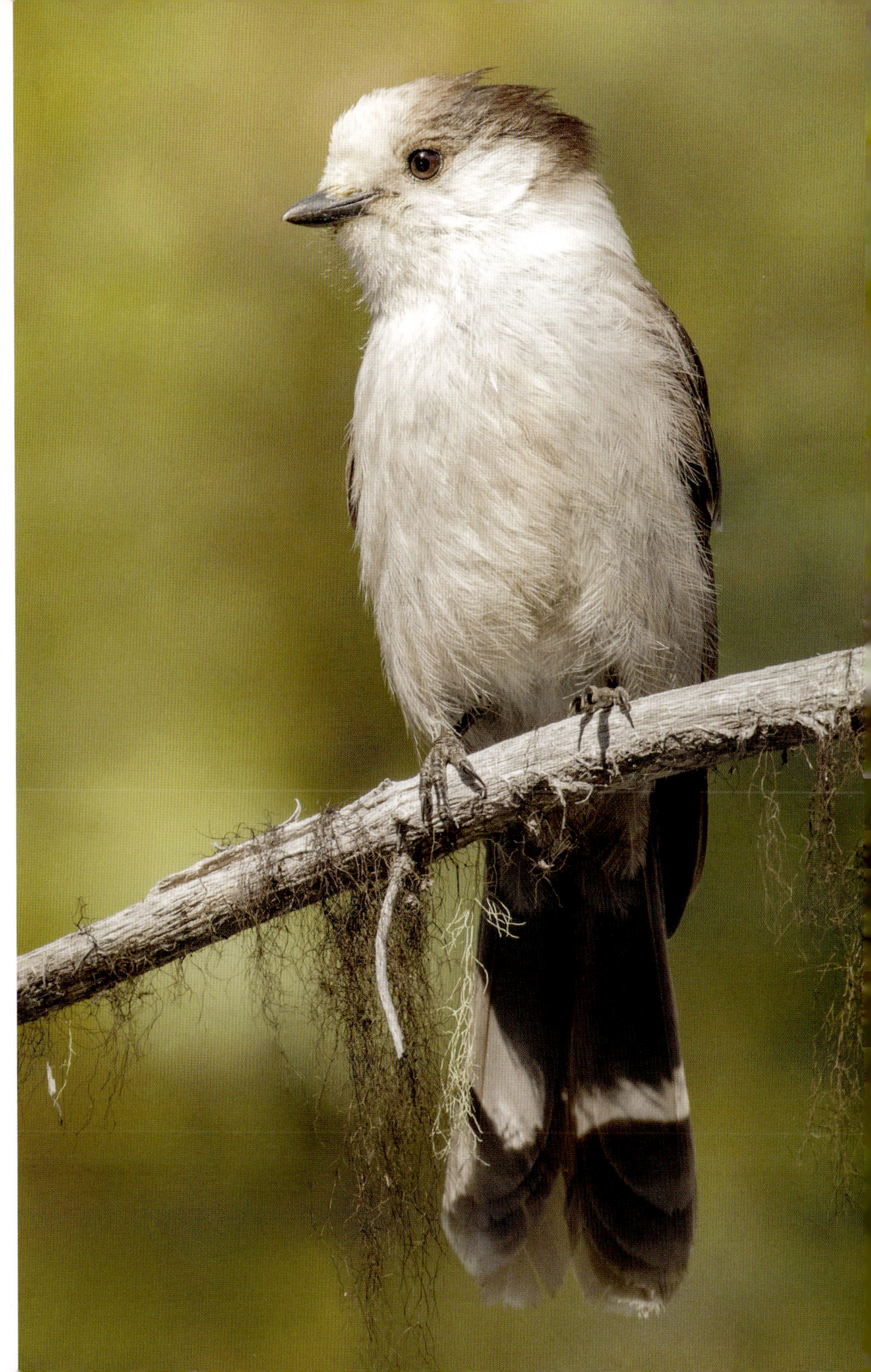

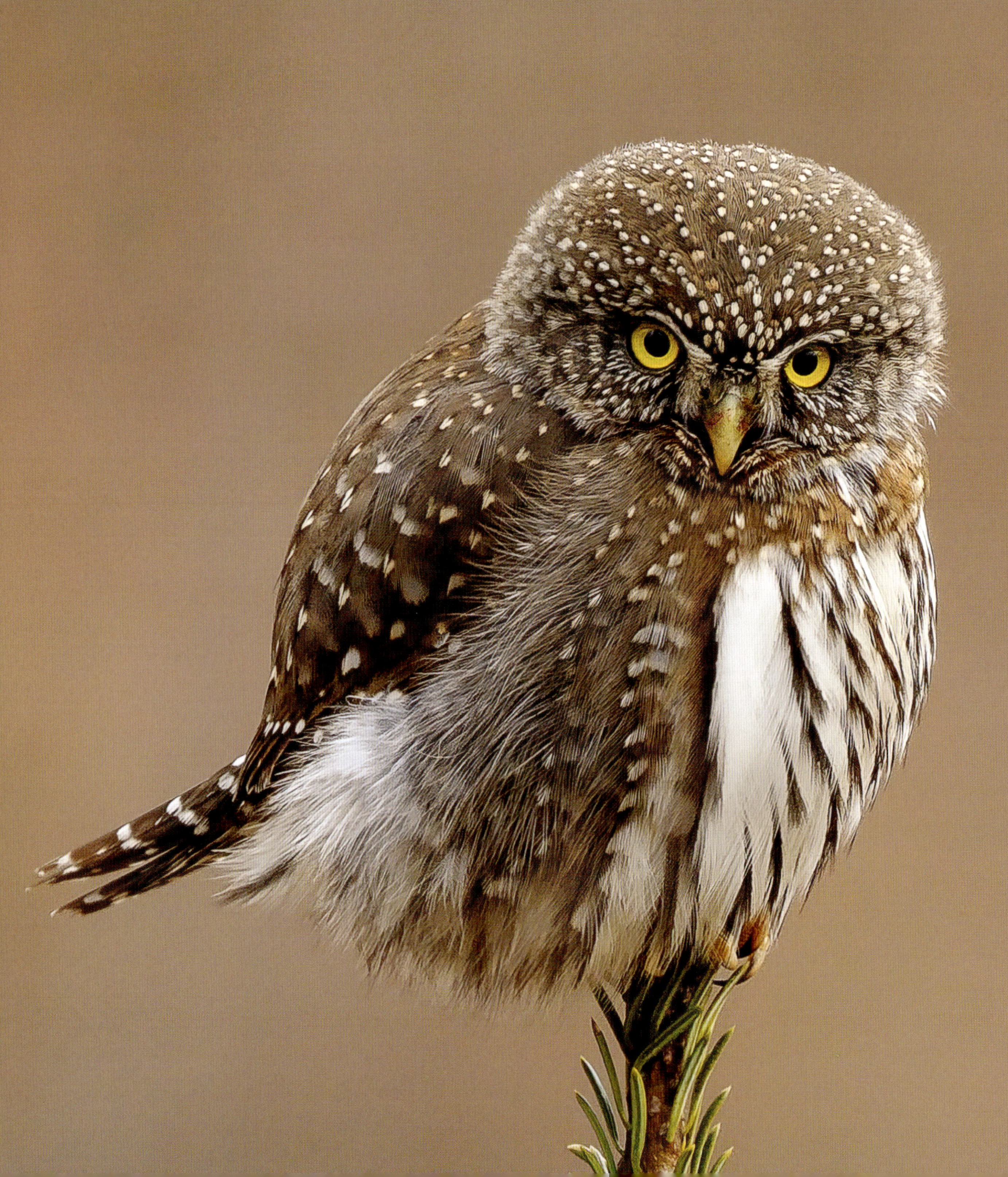

11

Owls

Seeing an owl leaves you entranced. It is truly magical. Watching them take flight on their silent wings, or making eye contact with one of these incredible birds is life-changing. Because owls are so magnificent, they draw many birders and photographers who love to admire them.

Opposite:

A NORTHERN PYGMY-OWL STARES DOWN ITS PREY IN CHILLIWACK, BC.

There are 19 species of owls in North America, and they come in a variety of sizes, from the tiny Elf Owl and Northern Pygmy Owl to the enormous Great Gray and Snowy Owls. I have been lucky enough to see all the breeding owls in North America. It is impossible to pick a favourite, but of the small owls, I love the Boreal Owl, and of the large, the Snowy Owl. Each owl encounter I've had is unique and special. Being granted full, clear views of an accommodating Flammulated Owl with my young birders; having the unique, endangered Ferruginous Pygmy-Owl tooting at me; seeing a family of stoic Great Gray Owls staring back at me; encountering a Northern Hawk Owl hunting in the strangest place have all been one word: MAGIC.

Owls live in such varied habitats, from grassland prairies to arctic tundra. Some owls migrate, such as the Flammulated Owl that leaves BC's interior for Arizona and Mexico, and others stay here all year like the Great Horned Owl. Some owls nest in burrows in the ground like the aptly named Burrowing Owl (who are endangered in Canada), who uses burrows made by other animals like prairie dogs and ground squirrels. Other owls, like Western Screech-Owls, nest in tree cavities excavated by woodpeckers, while Great Horned Owls use large stick nests built by other raptors. Some, like Barn Owls, use nest boxes, whereas Short-eared and Snowy Owls prefer to nest on the ground. All these owls are unique and diverse, making them all the more exciting to look at.

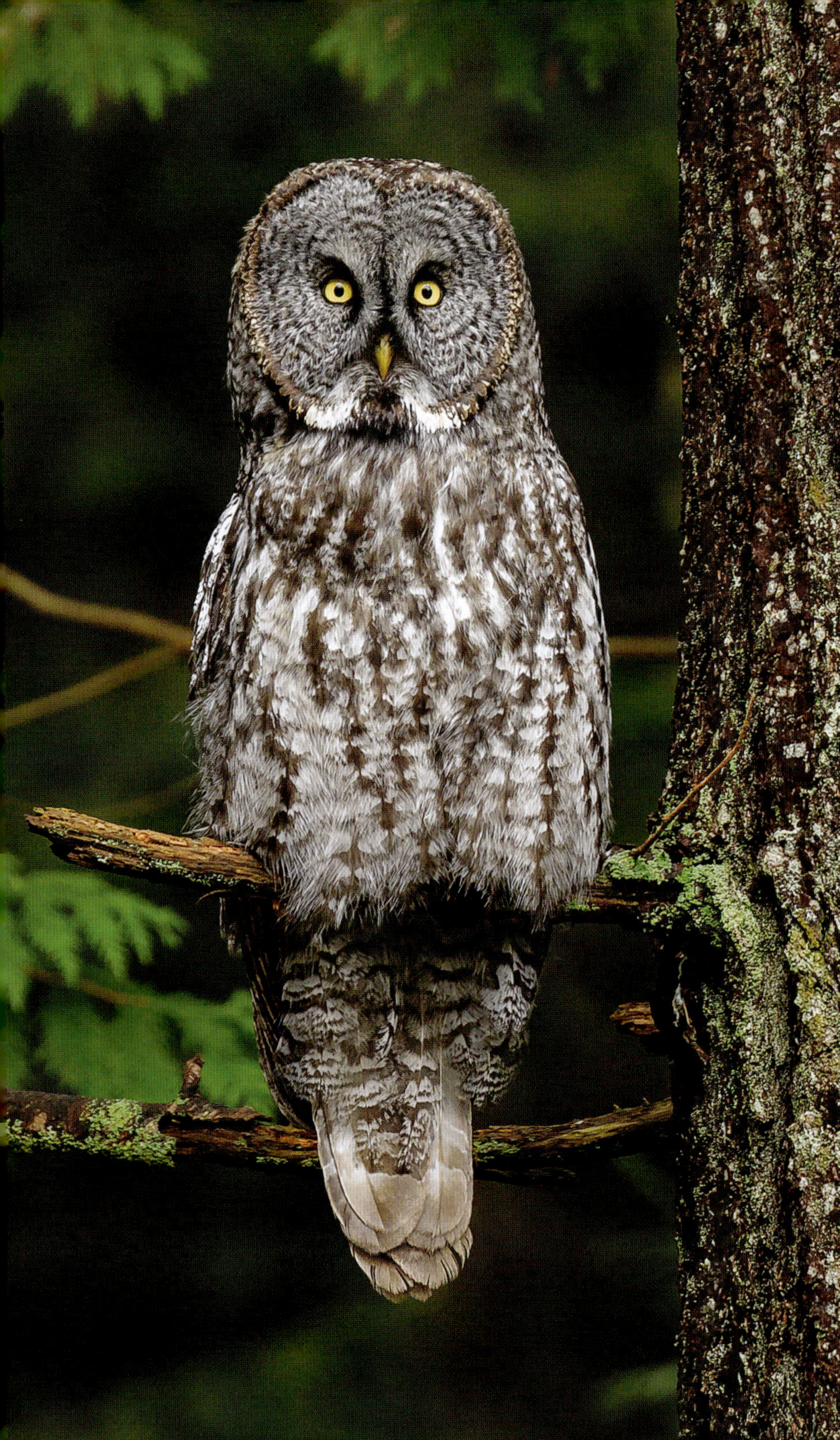

A GREAT GRAY OWL PERCHES IN A SOUTHERN BC FOREST.

One of my favourite encounters has to have been with the endangered Northern Spotted Owl, which I was lucky enough to see a few times in Washington state. One time I even saw two owlets with an adult and that was incredibly special. These owls depend on old-growth forests for the food they eat. When I speak of old-growth forests, I am referring to trees that are over 200 years old! Spotted Owls eat Wood Rats, as well as Northern Flying Squirrels that prefer the high canopy of old-growth forests. These owls also have much larger territories than other owls and require large expanses of unfragmented old-growth forest. These owls almost became extirpated in BC due to logging of old-growth forests. Barred Owls compete with them and have started to move into their territories as well.

A GREAT GRAY OWLET LOOKS AT ME IN BC'S KOOTENAY REGION.

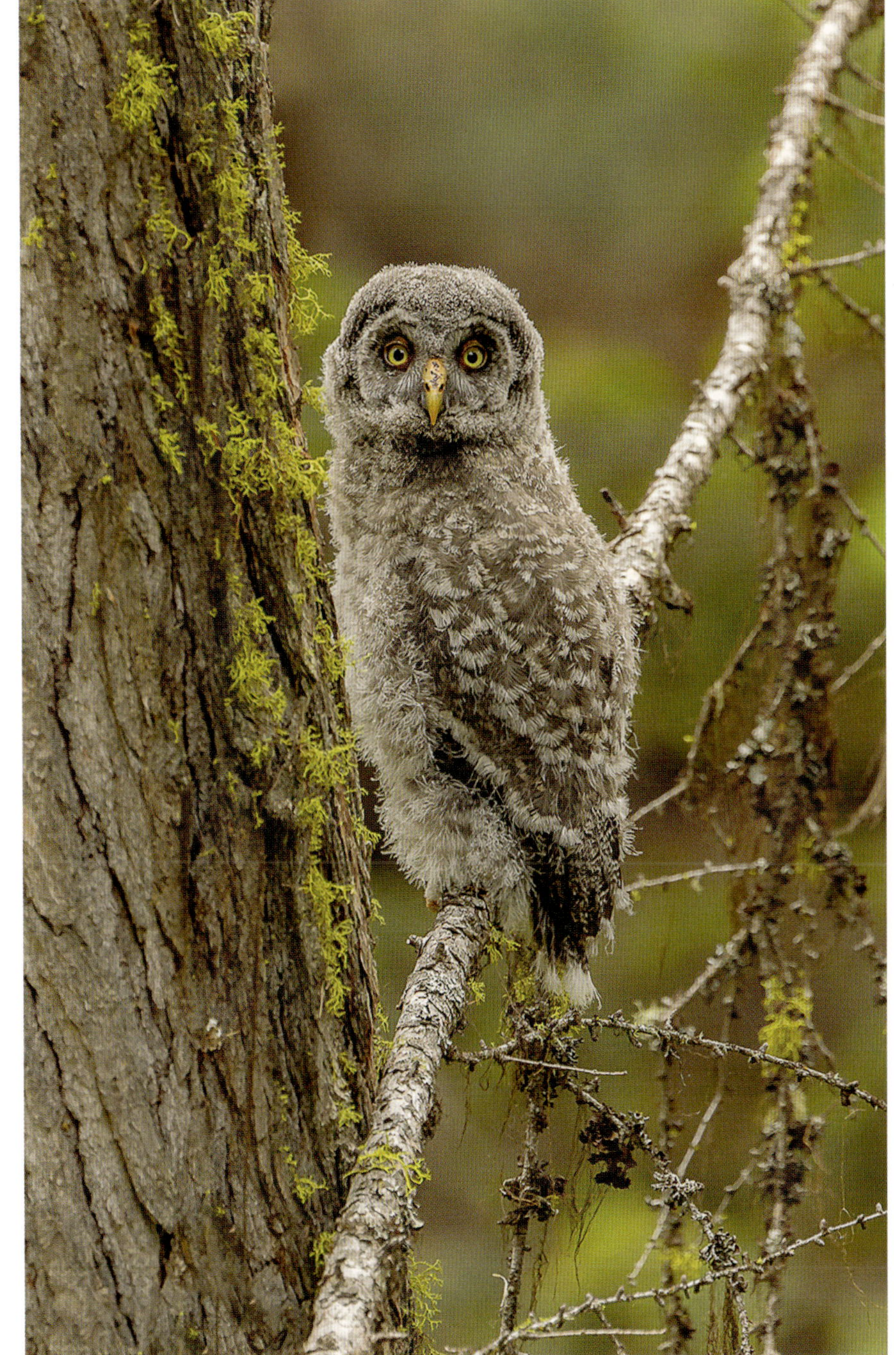

These owls are faring better in Washington state, where the federal government did a better job of protecting old-growth forests, allowing for more continuous, intact forests. By way of doing this, it further protected the Spotted Owl. In 1988, Washington listed the Spotted Owl as endangered. In 1990, the US Fish and Wildlife Service listed it as endangered, giving it special protection. Because BC is at the northern limit of their range, there have always been fewer Spotted Owls here than in Washington state. Despite being listed as endangered in 1986 by the Committee on the Status of Endangered Wildlife in Canada, the Canadian government did not list the Spotted Owl as endangered under the Species at Risk Act (SARA) until 2003. When a species is listed as endangered under SARA, the federal government must

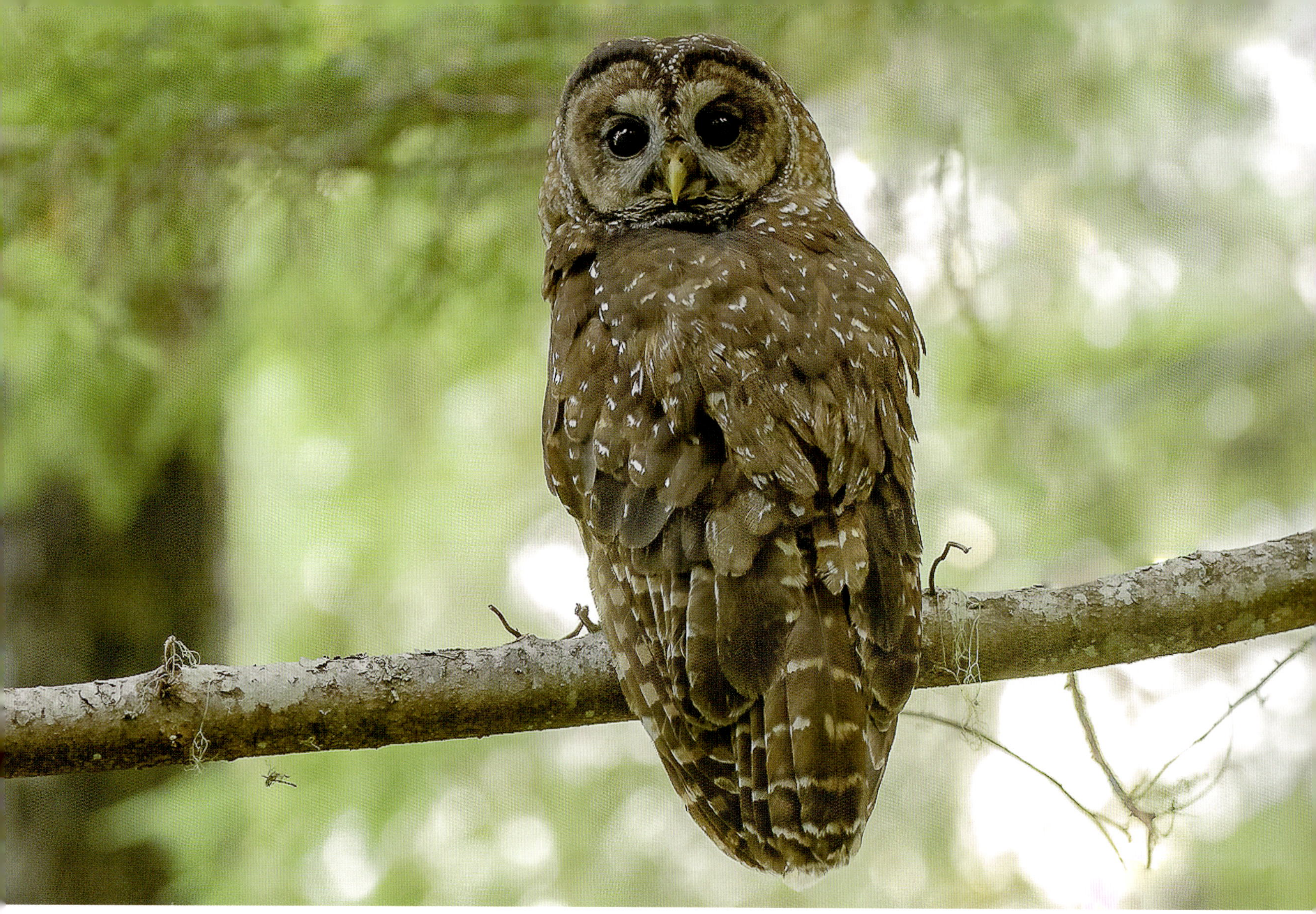

Above and opposite:

AN ENDANGERED NORTHERN SPOTTED OWL IN AN OLD-GROWTH FOREST IN PIERCE COUNTY, WASHINGTON.

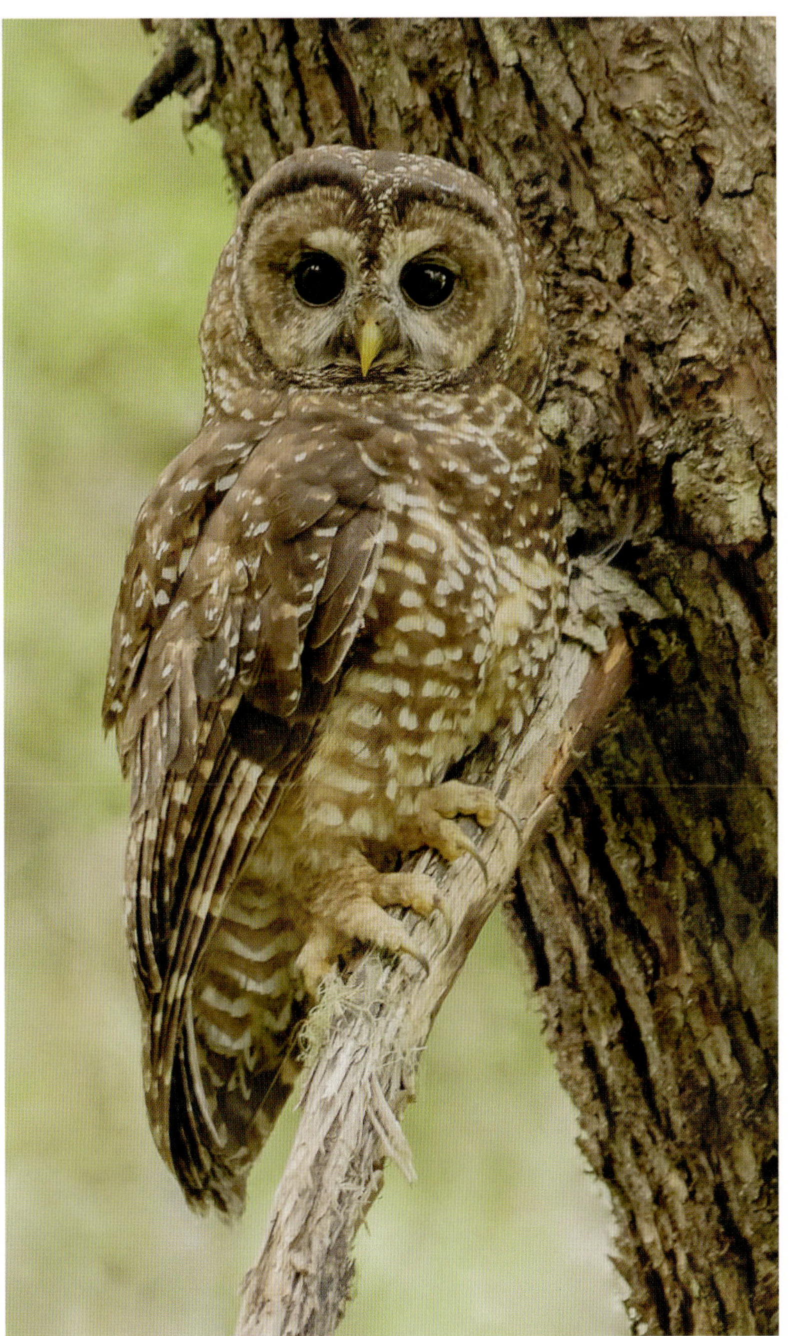

then identify critical habitat for that species, which is then afforded protection. Because of the long lag before Spotted Owls were listed under SARA, and the subsequent lag in identification of critical habitat, many areas formerly occupied by Spotted Owls were not legally protected.

Unfortunately, the BC government continues to allow logging of old-growth forests, breaking up contiguous habitat even in areas the Northern Spotted Owl has historically occupied. When I first saw a Northern Spotted Owl, it felt like I was seeing a ghost of the forest, even more so when I heard one call. The BC population used to be 500 birds, then it was whittled down to only one wild bird until three captive-raised birds were released. One of the captive-release birds had to be returned to captivity after it sadly sustained injury not long after release. It is vital that we

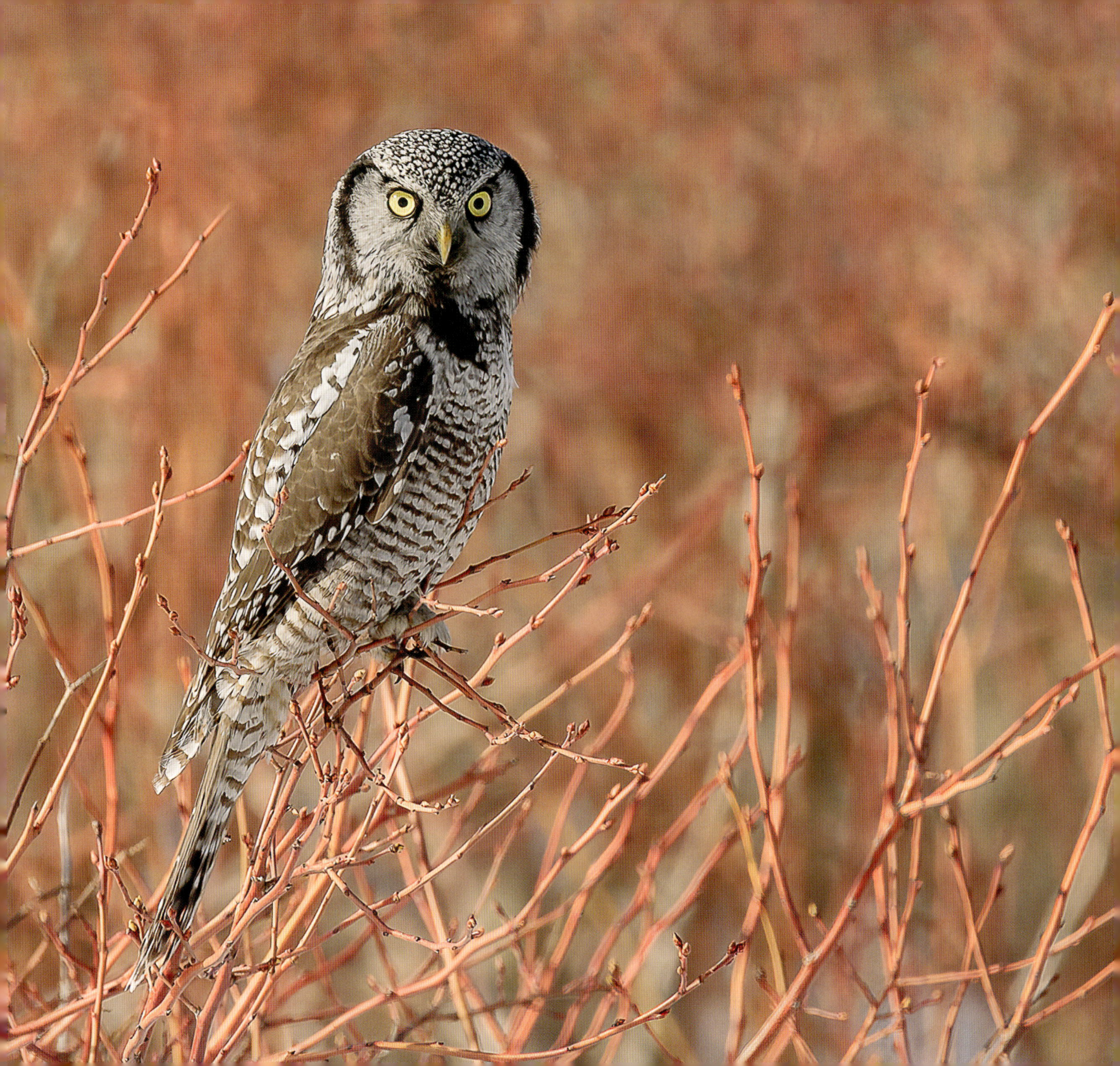

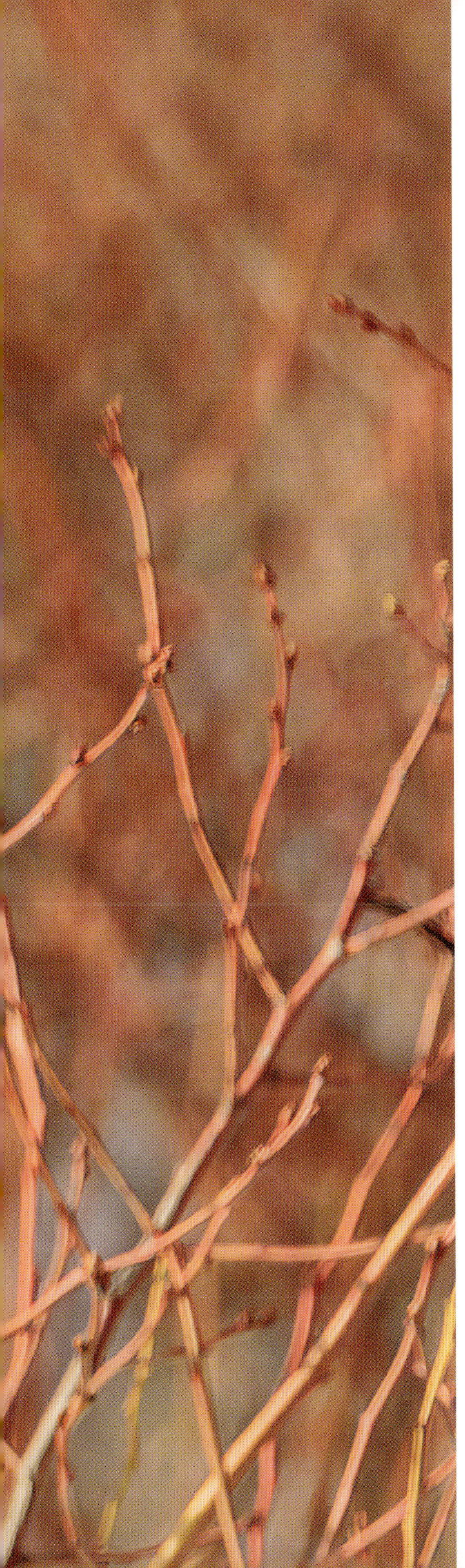

AN ADULT NORTHERN HAWK OWL PERCHES IN MAPLE RIDGE, BC.

hold our governments to account and work to protect old-growth forests so we don't lose the Northern Spotted Owl. If current trends continue, and logging continues, the owl will likely become extirpated despite well-intentioned captive-release programs.

Since most owls are vulnerable to disturbance, it is always important when viewing owls to do so ethically. Sometimes too many people crowd or even chase these birds to get flight shots, or stay by a nest or roost site all day. It is important to give owls plenty of space, especially owls that hunt diurnally and must compete for prey with other species like Northern Harriers, hawks, and eagles. It is also good not to linger long, especially at nest and roost sites, but to enjoy them briefly and then leave, not returning day after day. Audiotapes using the owl's calls should never be used at nest sites nor ever played on a loop. In an era where information spreads online like wildfire, it is vital not to reveal owl and nest locations, so the birds do not become stressed, or their nests fail. Of course, baiting an owl for a photo is extremely unethical and dangerous for the bird. Owls can get hit by cars if they become too habituated to humans and stop behaving in a wild manner. Also, when taking raptor or other bird photos, it is important not to impede normal hunting behaviour. A good approach is to position yourself strategically and stand quietly in one spot to let the animal come to you. This should not cause them stress and is much more rewarding than chasing them down.

If you do all you can to protect an owl from disturbance, you can walk away from the bird with a clear conscience and feel happy with the photos you have taken.

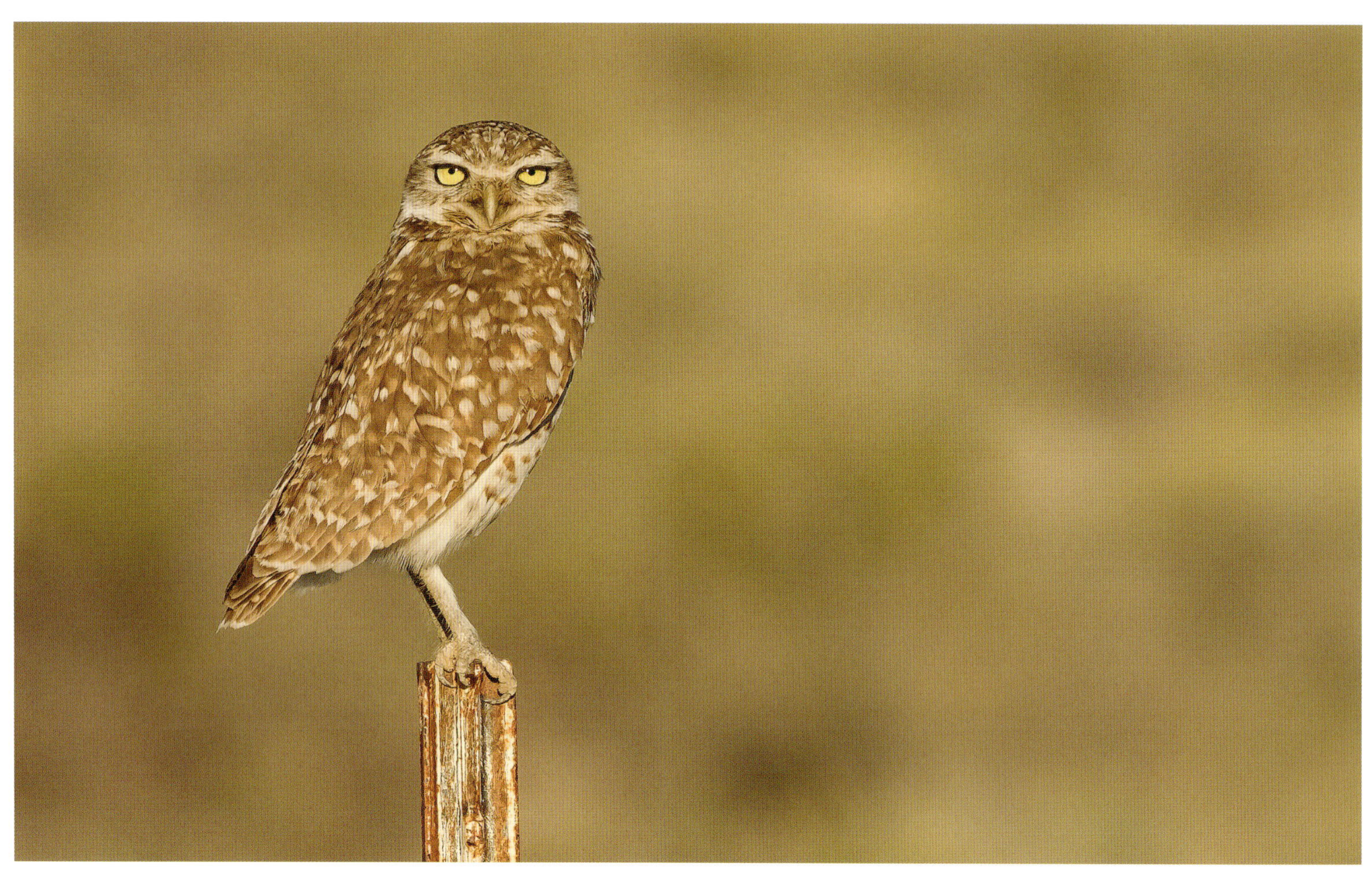

A THREATENED BURROWING OWL SITS ON A POST AT MALHEUR NATIONAL WILDLIFE REFUGE IN OREGON. THESE BIRDS ARE DECLINING DUE TO LOSS OF THEIR GRASSLAND HABITAT, WHERE THEY USE BURROWS TO RAISE THEIR YOUNG AND HUNT.

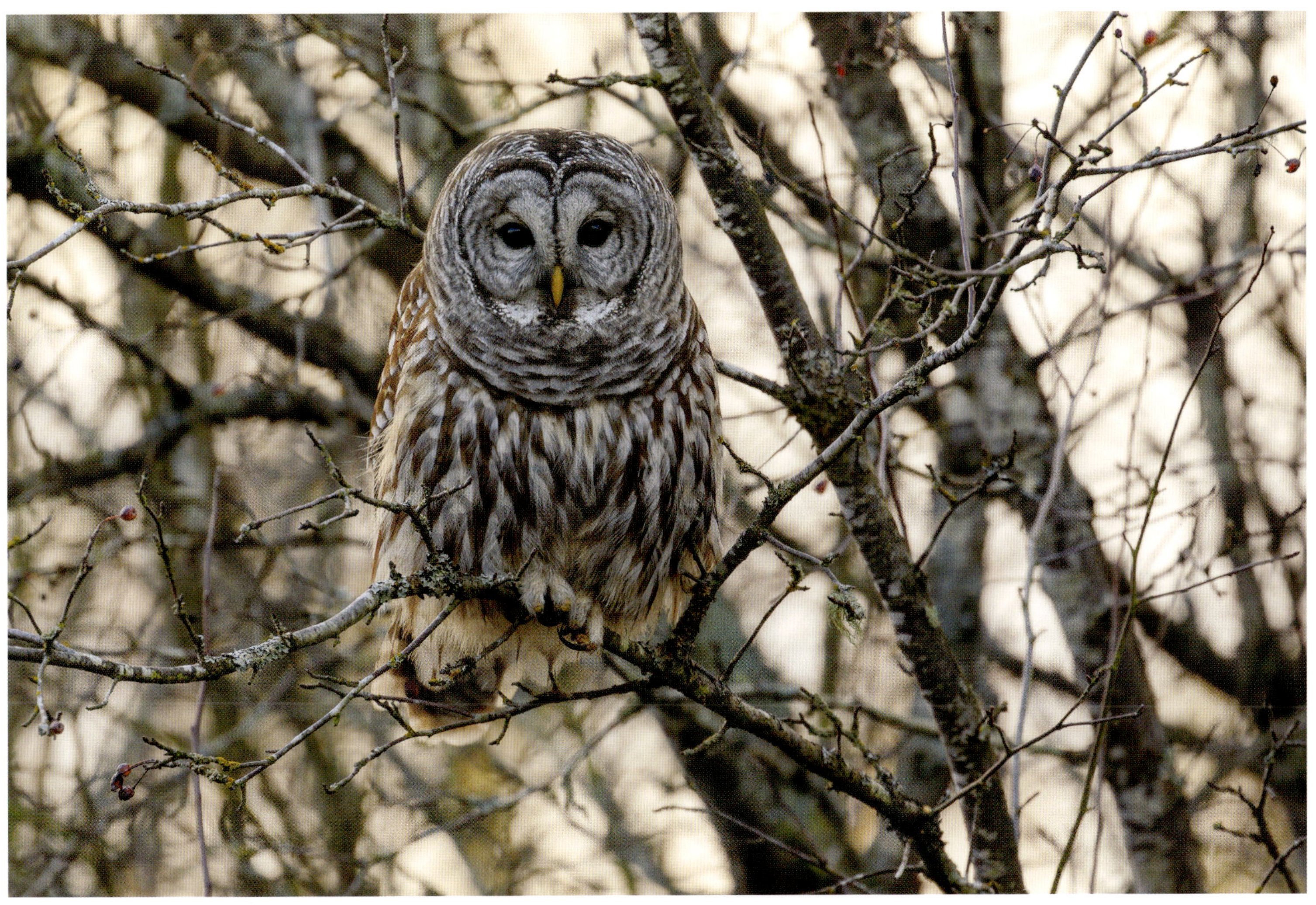

AN ADULT BARRED OWL STARES BACK AT ME IN RICHMOND, BC. BARRED OWLS ARE FREQUENTLY USED AS SCAPEGOATS WHEN IT COMES TO NORTHERN SPOTTED OWL PROTECTION IN CANADA AND THE US. ALTHOUGH THEY ARE MORE AGGRESSIVE AND HAVE TAKEN OVER SOME SPOTTED OWL TERRITORIES AND OUTCOMPETE THEM FOR PREY, LOGGING OF OLD-GROWTH FORESTS REMAINS THE GREATEST THREAT TO THE NORTHERN SPOTTED OWL.

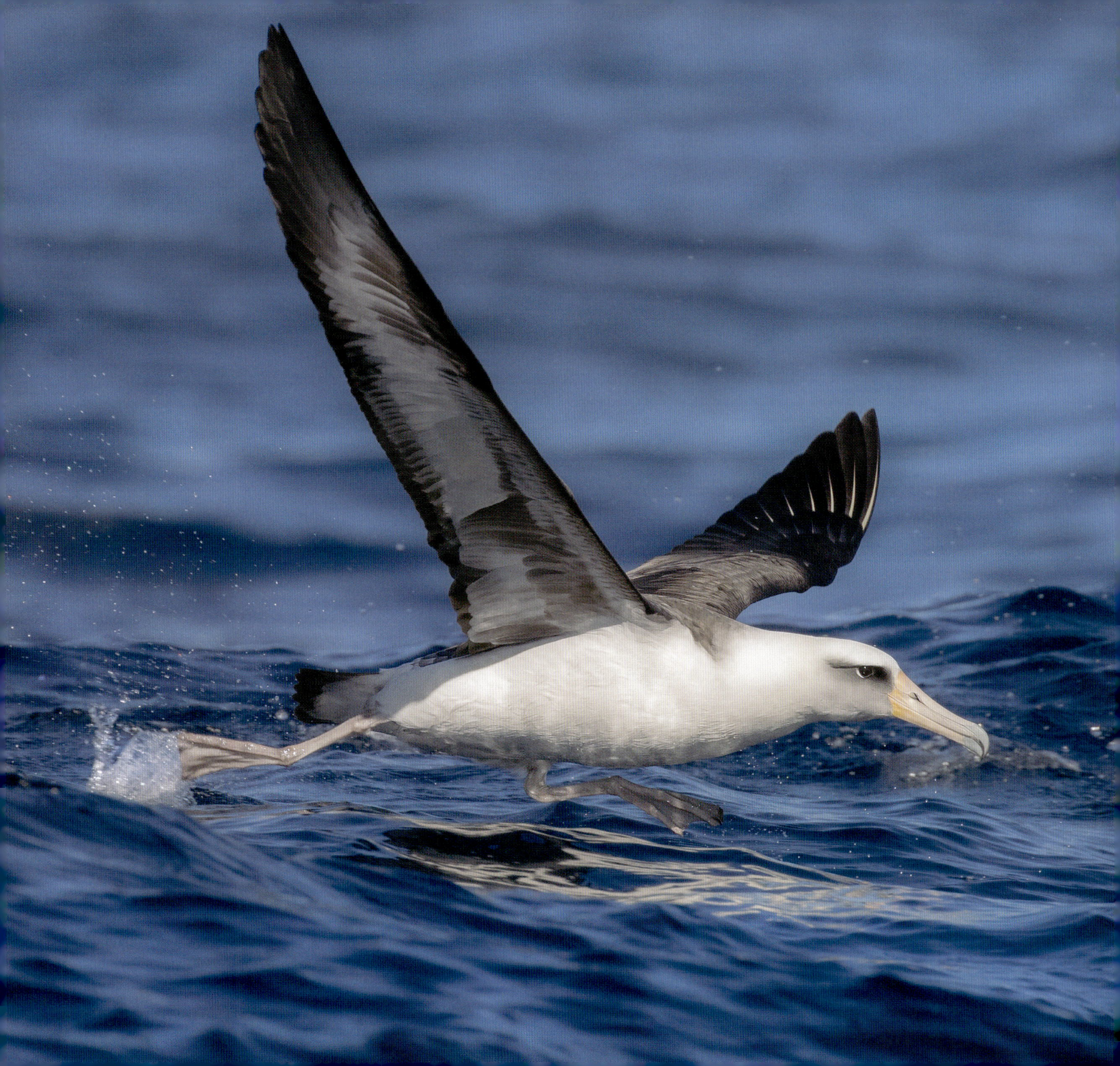

12

The Charms of Albatrosses and Pelagics

I have organized pelagic trips in BC for several years and love to get out on the ocean and look at birds. Pelagic trips are boat trips that take you way offshore to look for seabirds that rarely come close to land except to nest. I have been lucky to see some cool rarities on pelagic trips out of Tofino, including several Short-tailed and Laysan Albatrosses, Guadalupe and Scripps's Murrelets, and Parakeet Auklets. Seeing and hearing an albatross up close is pure magic. When you see their huge 2.29 m (7.5 feet) wingspans, and the way it takes them no effort at all to fly, as they rarely flap but just glide and soar on the wind, you become totally mesmerized by their grace. These birds can fly for months out there on the ocean like this with what may seem like not a care in the world. If we could all be so carefree!

Opposite:

AN ADULT LAYSAN ALBATROSS TAKES OFF NEAR THE BOAT FAR OFFSHORE FROM TOFINO, BC.

The threatened Short-tailed Albatross was brought to near extinction by the feather trade. They used to number at least ten million birds but declined to just 25 birds in 1954. Luckily, they have rebounded to a global population estimated at 4,200 birds following a ban on hunting. Seeing one of these giant albatrosses come close to your boat, with its huge, bubblegum pink bill, is the thing of dreams. One day, I couldn't believe my eyes when we were lucky enough to see three of them all at once! A few of the birds I saw were banded, so we sent the band numbers to researchers and found they were banded on Tori-shima Island in Japan. It takes a Short-tailed Albatross 12 years to reach adulthood. All the birds in BC have been juveniles: large brown birds with incredible wingspans and a large pink bill. Adults are stunningly white with some black wing linings and the signature large pink bill.

On another trip out on the sea, I was lucky enough to see 15 Laysan Albatrosses with one juvenile Short-tailed Albatross. Laysan Albatrosses are incredibly elegant. They nest in places like Hawaii and fly huge distances to find food, including to where I saw them offshore from Tofino. Laysan Albatrosses pair for life but wander the seas separately for years between nesting. When they are reunited with

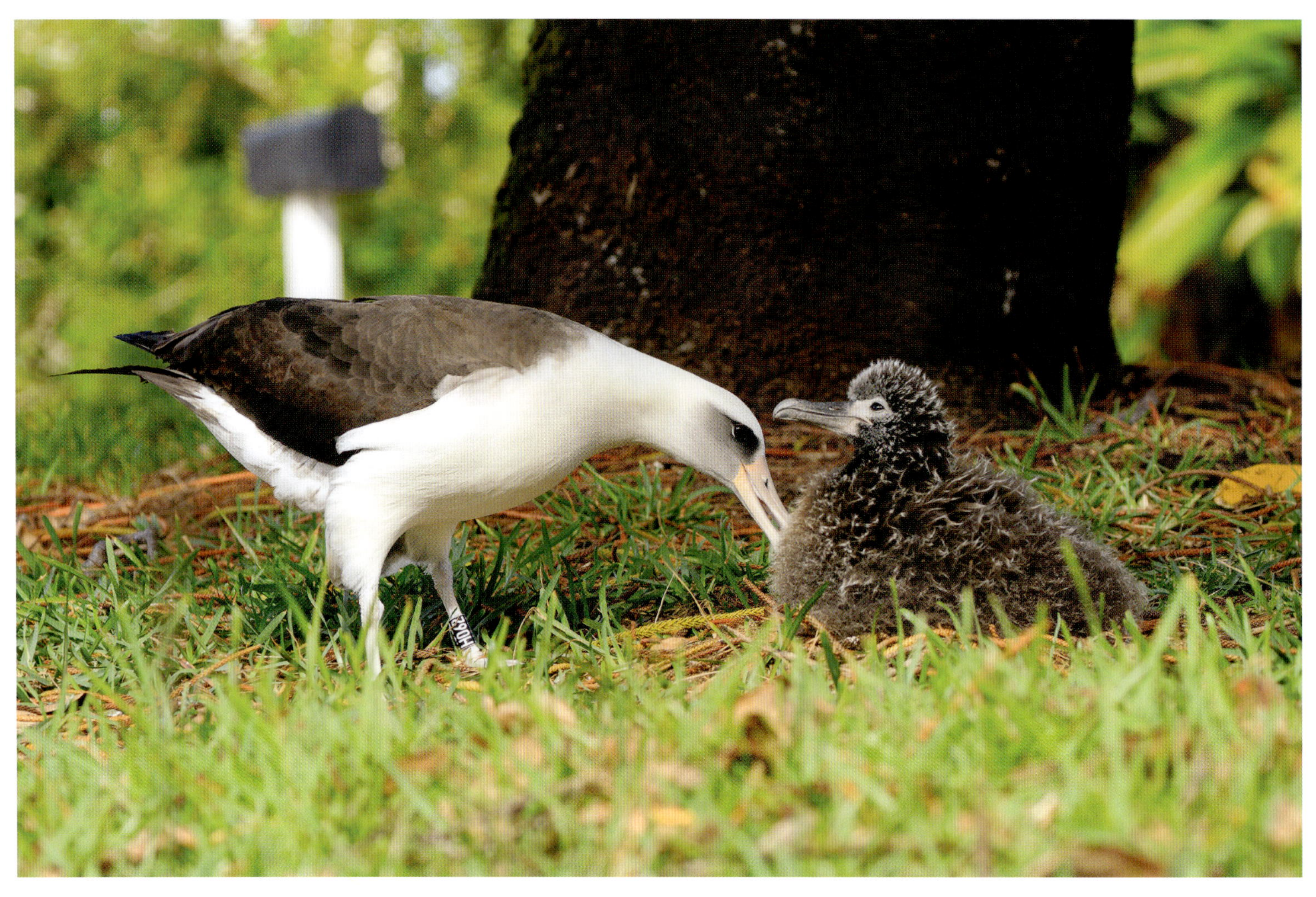

Above and opposite:

A LAYSAN ALBATROSS WITH CHICK, AND THE CHICK BY ITSELF ON ITS NEST IN KAUAI, HAWAII.

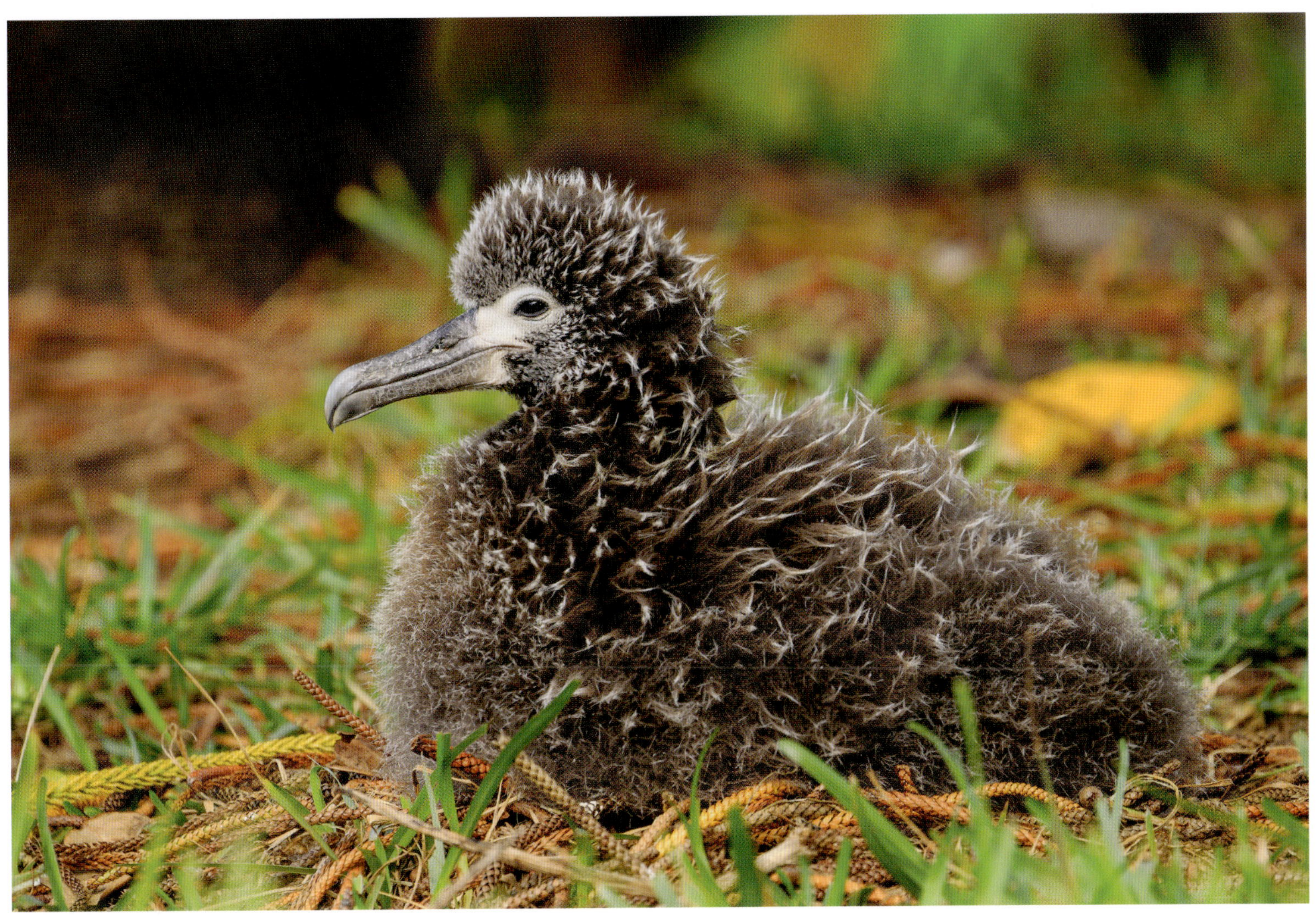

Opposite:

A BLACK-FOOTED ALBATROSS SITS ON THE PACIFIC OCEAN OFF TOFINO, BC.

their mates on their nesting grounds, they engage in elaborate courtship displays where they cock their necks back, slap their bills, and waddle in an amusing type of dance. It almost brings a tear to your eye if you are lucky enough to see it. I have also been lucky enough to see nests with chicks on the island of Kauai in Hawaii.

Longline fisheries, plastic, and invasive species at nesting sites threaten these incredible pelagic birds. Birds can drown from entanglement in drift nets or by ingesting fish on longlines as they get hooked and pulled under water. In addition, pelagic birds frequently ingest plastic because they mistake it for food and also feed it to their young, which can cause blockages and death. Invasive and introduced predators such as mice, rats, cats, and mongoose can prey on eggs and chicks at nests and sometimes even kill or maim adults at the nesting sites.

Being out on the Pacific Ocean is one of my favourite places to be. It is so exciting because you never know what you will see – at any moment, a Short-tailed Albatross can come flying at you! Plus, you don't just have the chance to see amazing pelagic birds but also cool marine mammals. On these trips, I have been blessed with seeing Risso's Dolphins, Northern Right Whale Dolphins, Fin Whales, Orcas, Humpback and Gray Whales, Dall's and Harbour Porpoises, Pacific White-sided Dolphins, Harbour Seals, Northern Fur Seals, Steller and California Sea Lions, and Sea Otters.

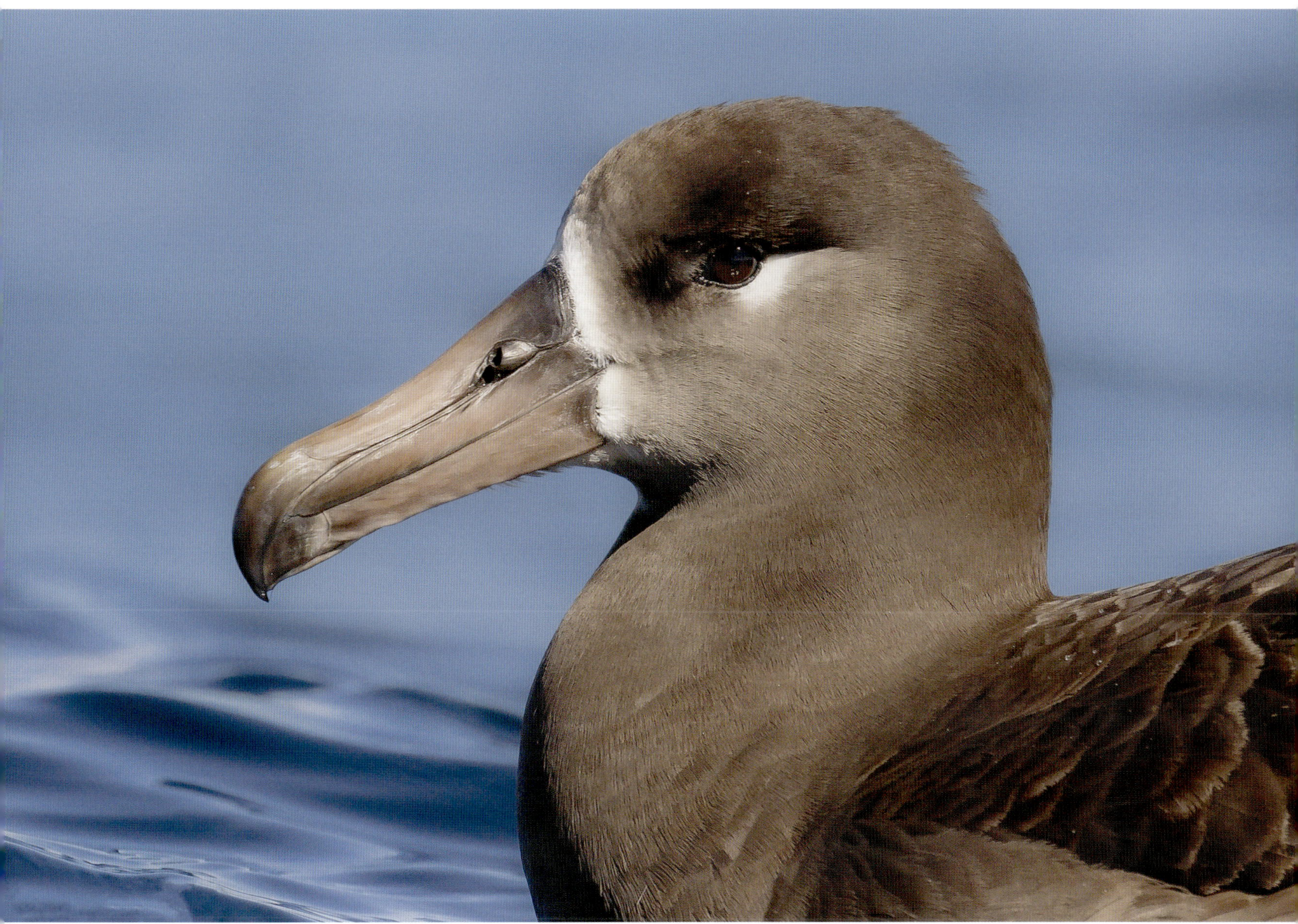

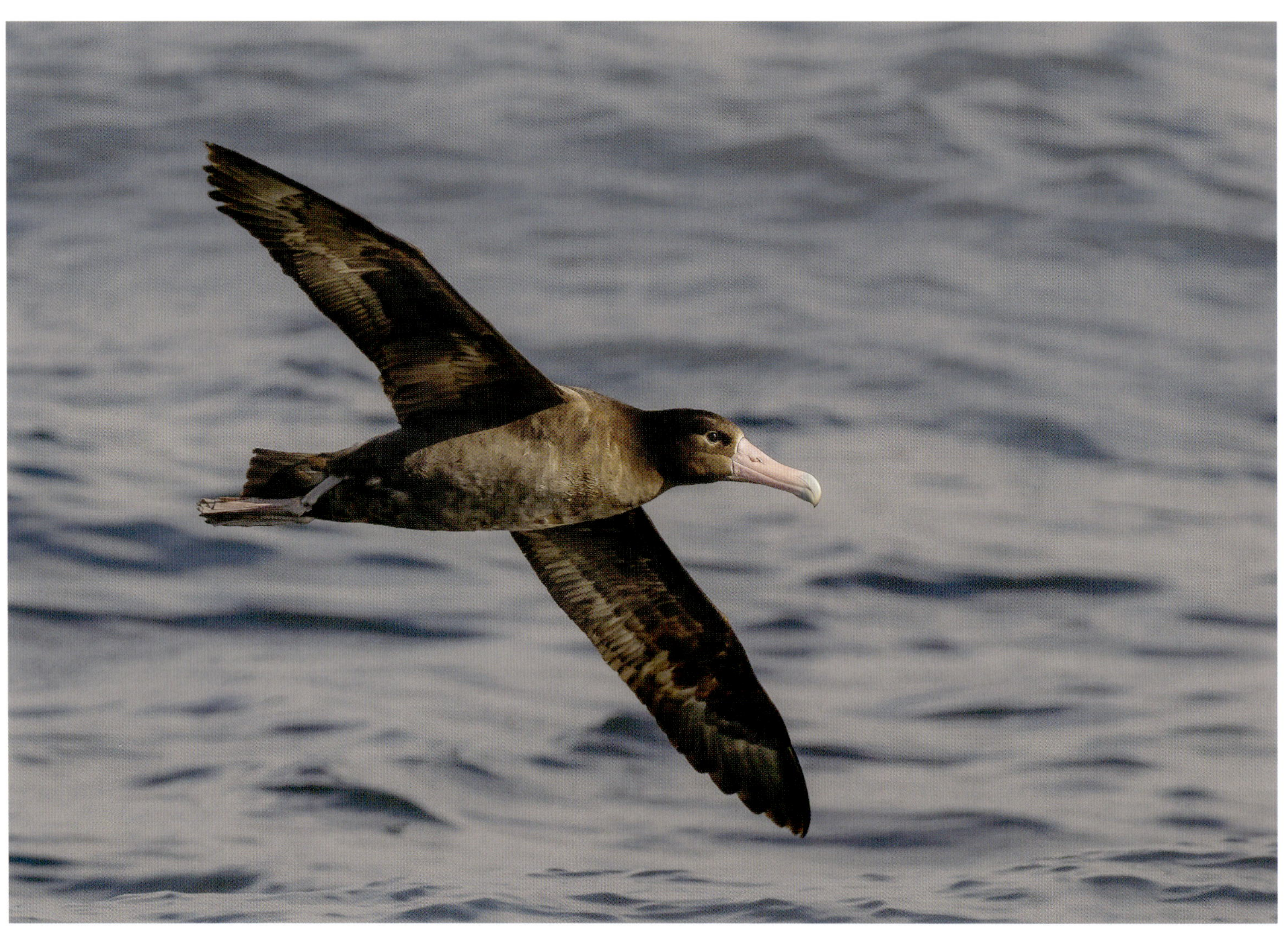

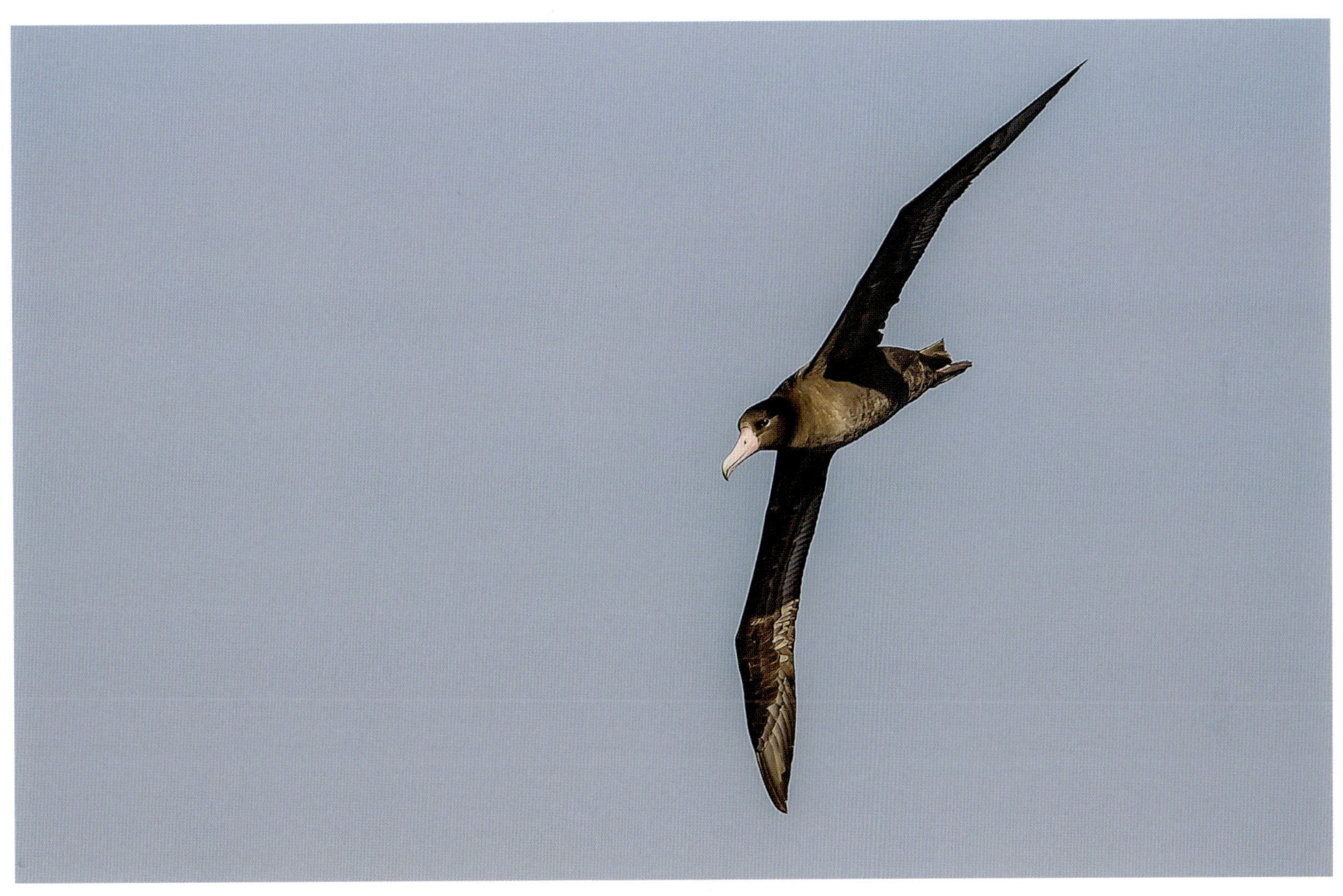

Above and opposite:

A JUVENILE, THREATENED SHORT-TAILED ALBATROSS IS A MEGA RARITY AND A BIRDER'S DREAM TO SEE ON ANY WEST COAST PELAGIC. TAKEN OFFSHORE FROM TOFINO, BC. ONE MY FAVOURITE BC PELAGIC MEMORIES WAS SEEING THREE AT THE SAME TIME!

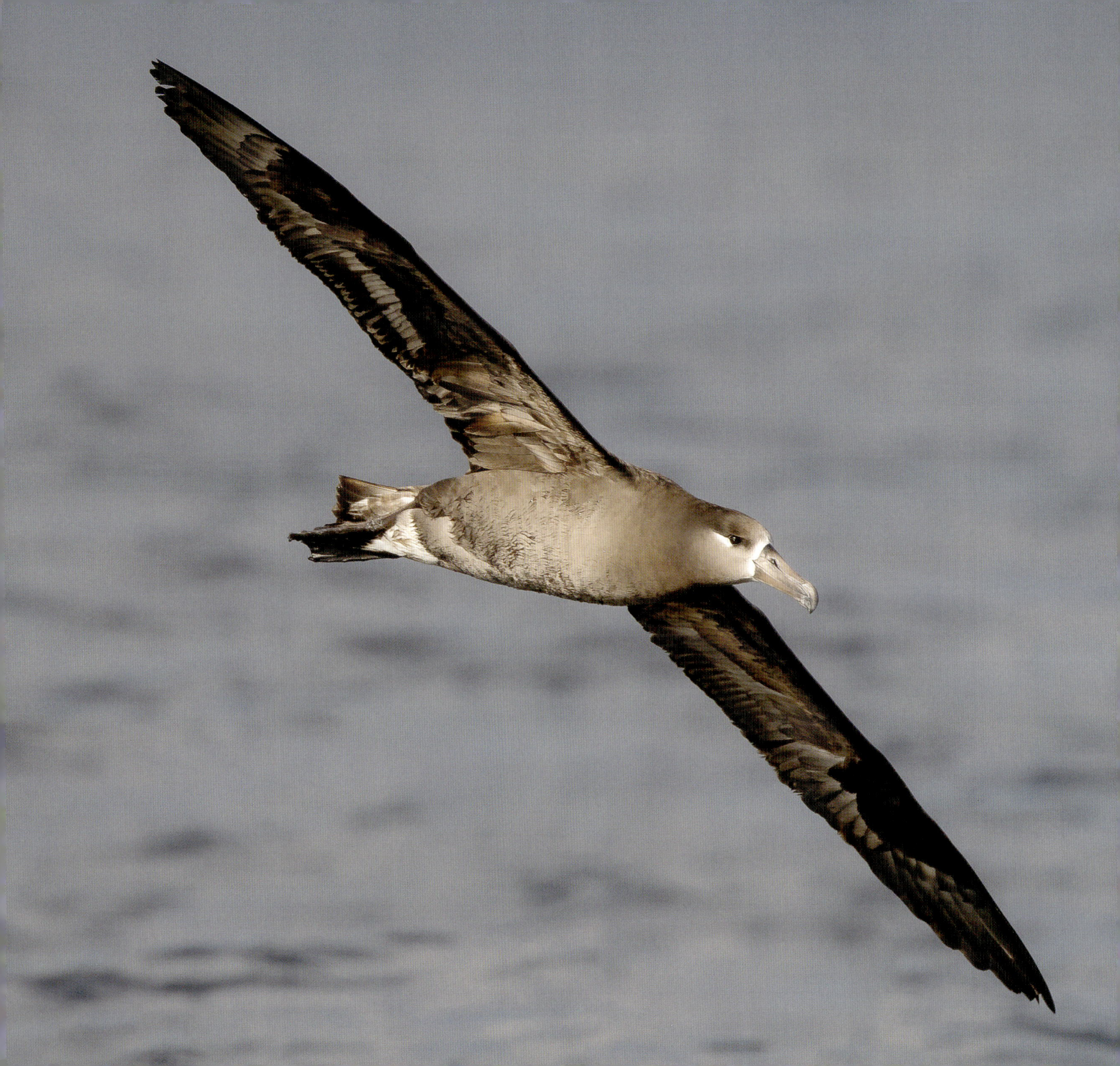

A BLACK-FOOTED ALBATROSS FLIES BY THE BOAT NEAR TOFINO, BC.

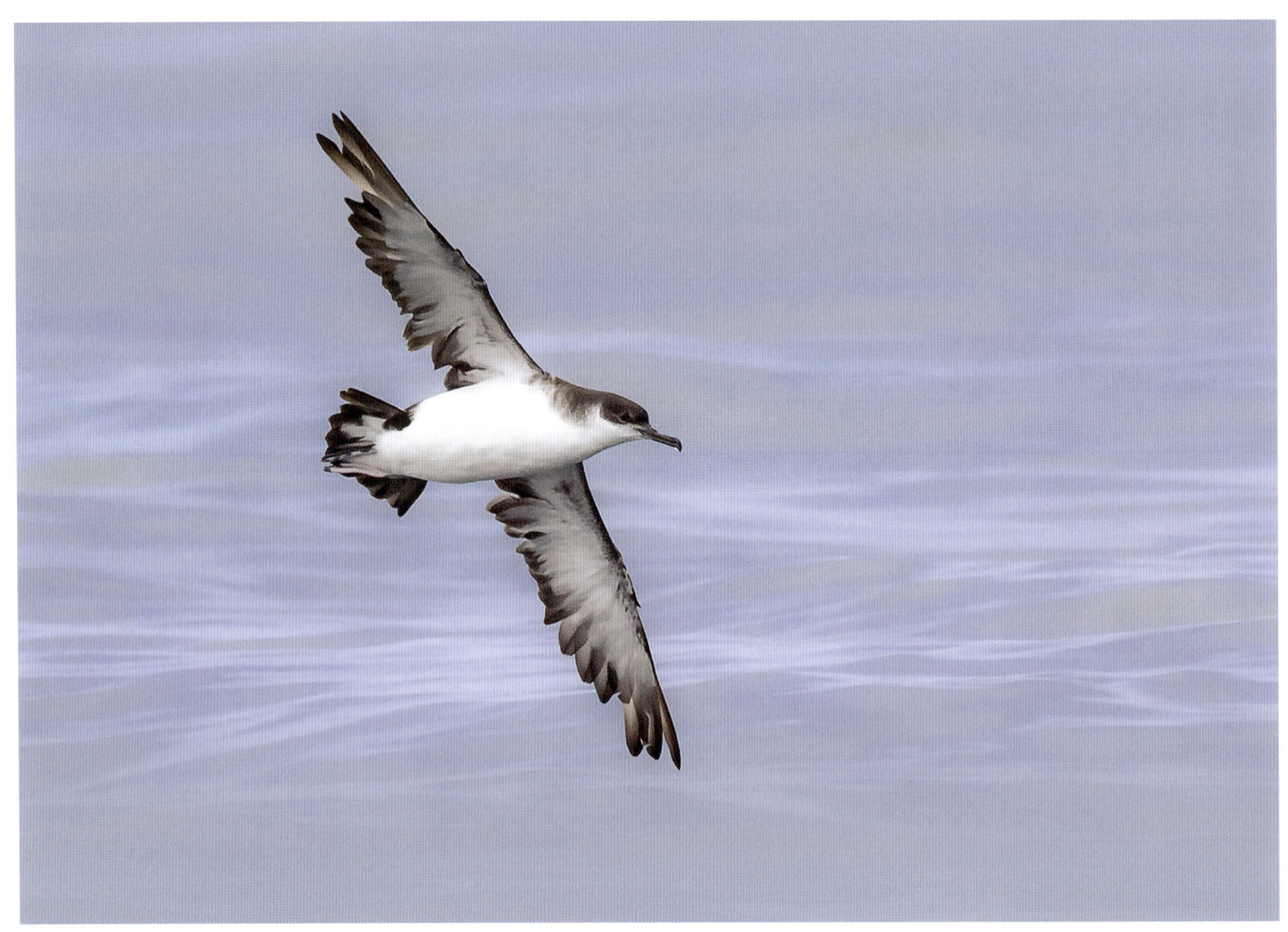

A MOLTING MANX SHEARWATER FLIES BY CLELAND ISLAND NEAR TOFINO ON VANCOUVER ISLAND, BC.

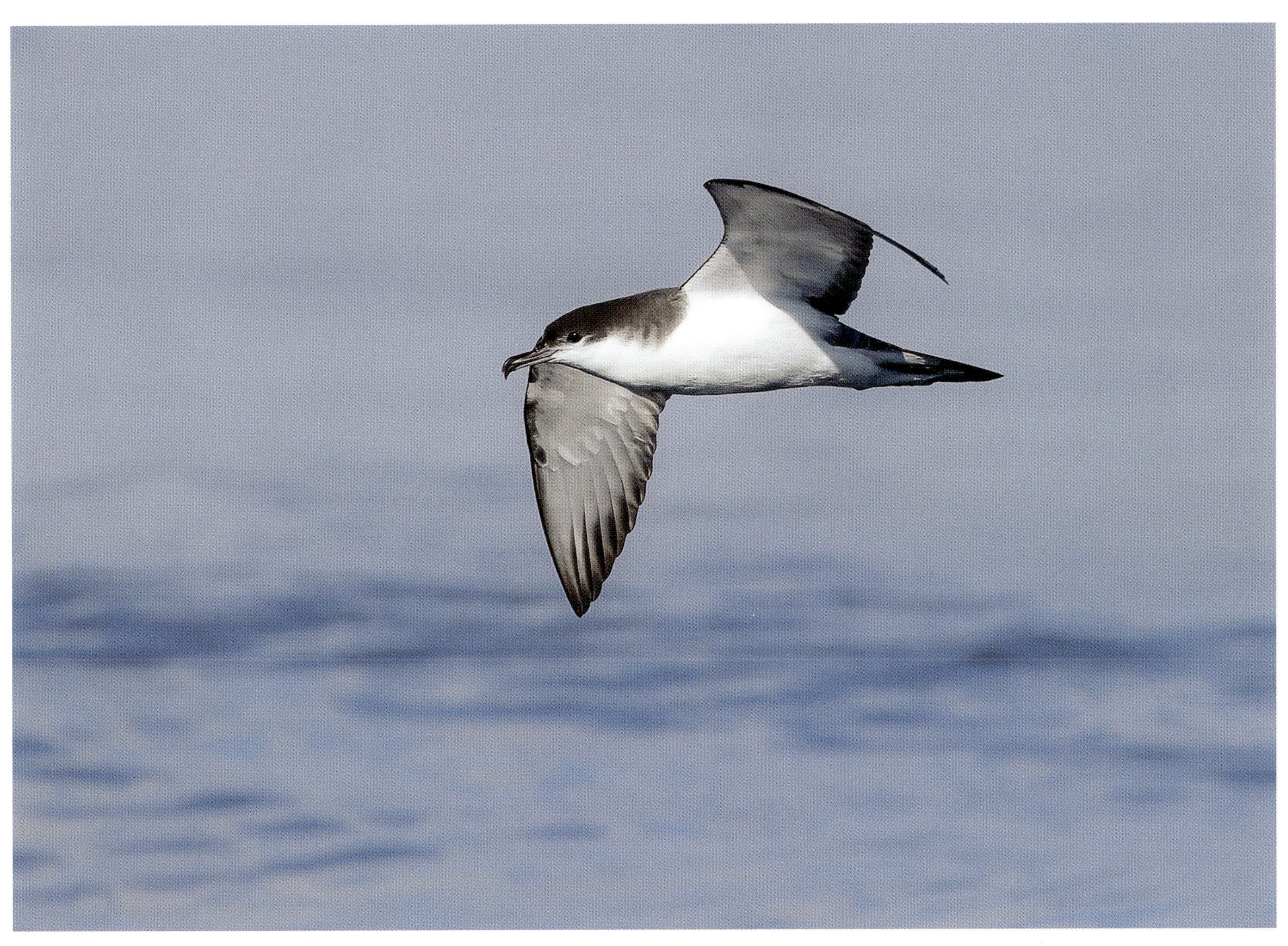

A BULLER'S SHEARWATER FLIES BY ME ON A PELAGIC OUT OF TOFINO, BC.

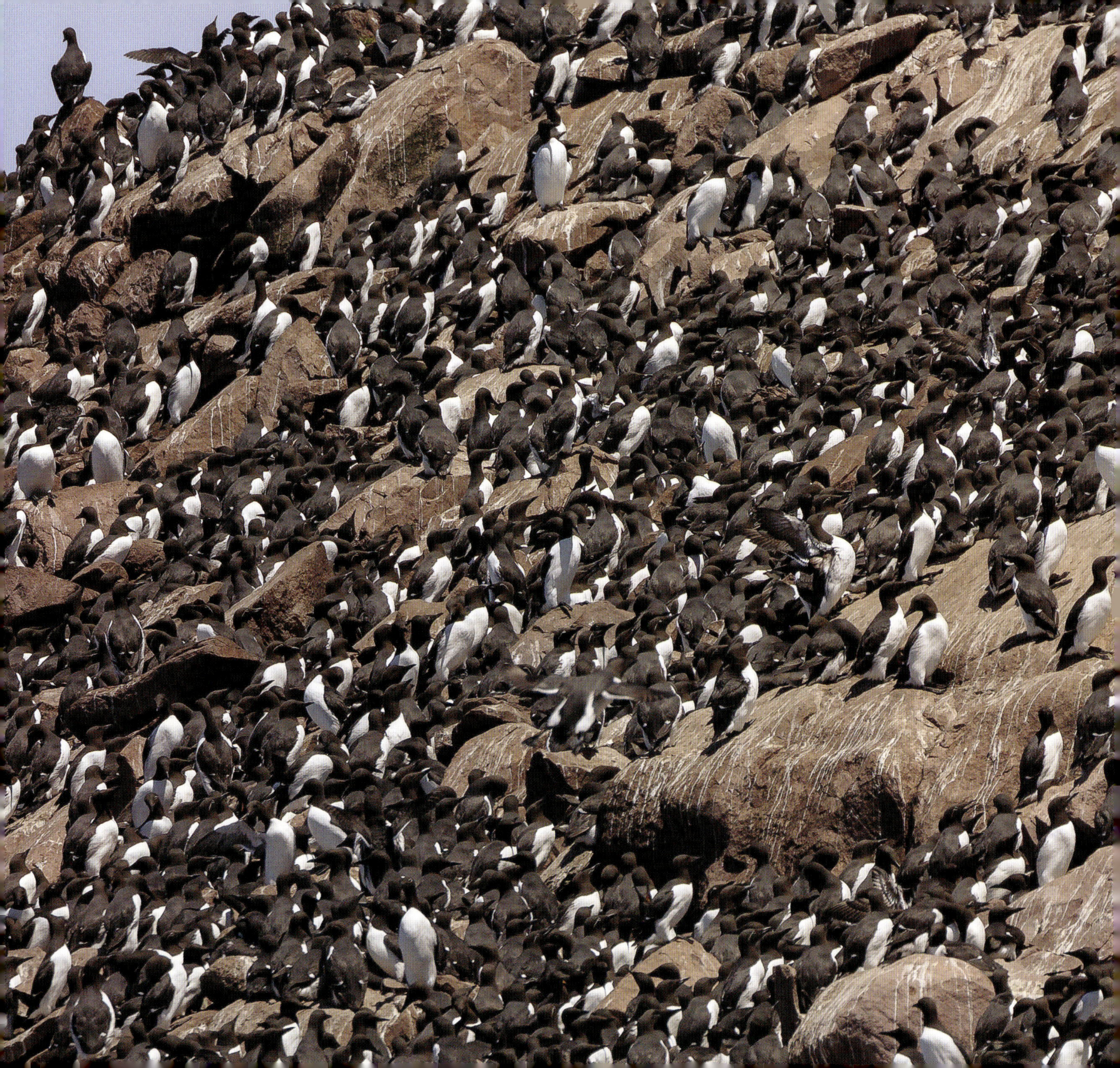

13

Colonies

When I led seven-day bird tours for Avocet Tours in Newfoundland, we visited several seabird colonies from Witless Bay to Elliston, Bonavista, and St. Bride's, where we got to see Atlantic Puffins, Northern Gannets, Great Black-backed Gulls, Common and Thick-billed Murres, Razorbills, Black-legged Kittiwakes, and Black Guillemots nesting. The numbers of birds were mind-blowingly impressive! I had never seen anything like that ever, and the sounds and sights were something every birder should behold. The collective grunting and weird bark-like calls of the alcids and gannets are such an incredible privilege to hear.

Opposite:

A PORTION OF THE 20,000 NESTING COMMON MURRES AT WITLESS BAY IN NEWFOUNDLAND. MURRES NEST ON CLIFF FACES AS PICTURED HERE.

As our boat approached Gull Island at the Witless Bay Ecological Reserve, the sky suddenly appeared as if it were filled with insects. In actuality it was seabirds, mostly puffins and Common Murres, flying to and from their burrows or cliffsides at the colony. I estimated 20,000 Common Murres and 25,000 Atlantic Puffins. There were also a few Thick-billed Murres. Not to mention the 10,000 Black-legged Kittiwakes nesting with 100 Razorbills!

Climate change has dramatically affected marine ocean habitats. It is causing a decline in the amount of fish species seabirds eat, which is negatively affecting their populations. Alcids use their short wings to help them dive underwater to find these fish they need for them and their young to survive. Avian flu has also affected seabird and Northern Gannet colonies around the globe, killing thousands of birds.

SEABIRDS DOT THE SKY LIKE INSECTS
AT WITLESS BAY IN NEWFOUNDLAND.

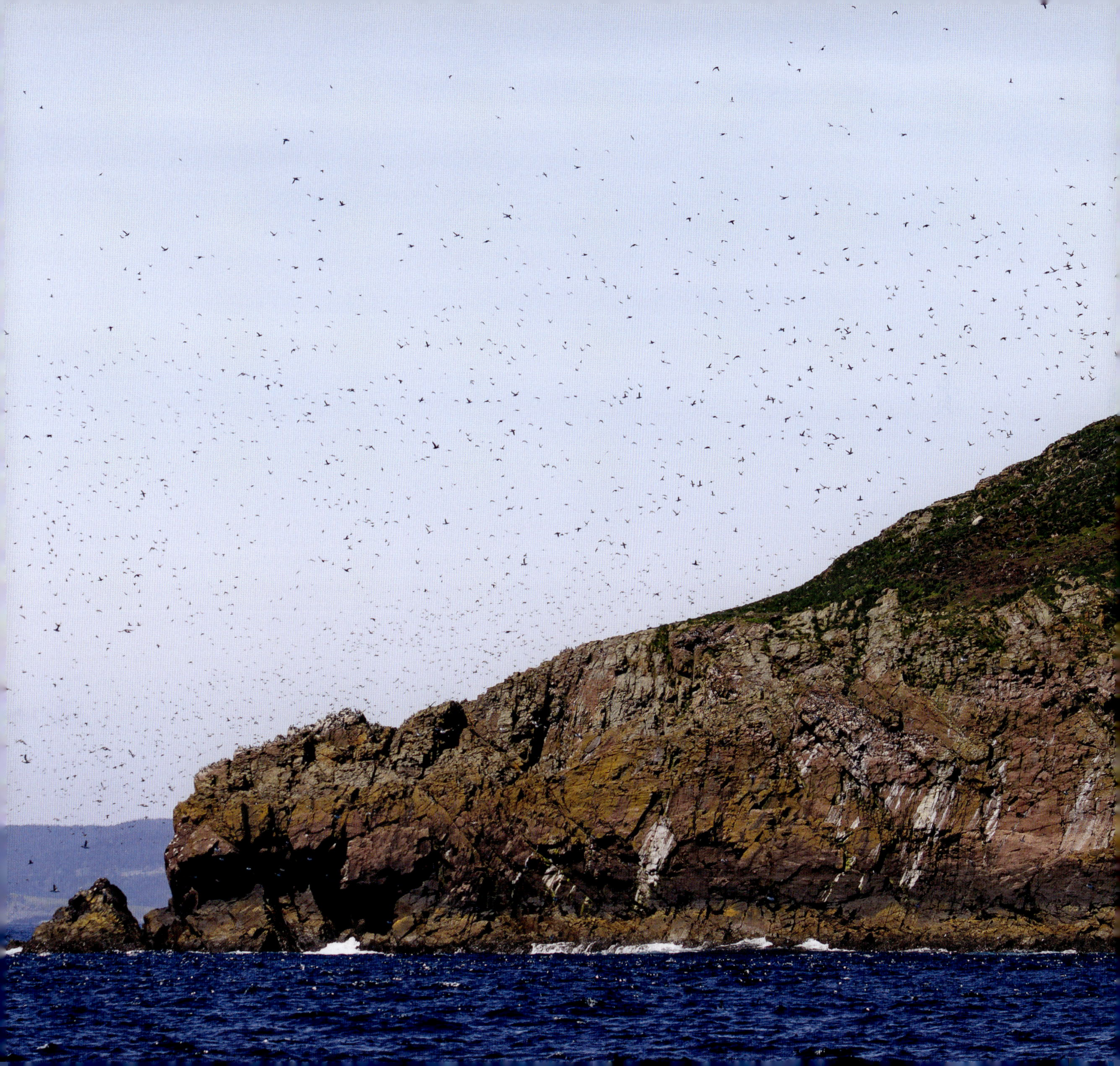

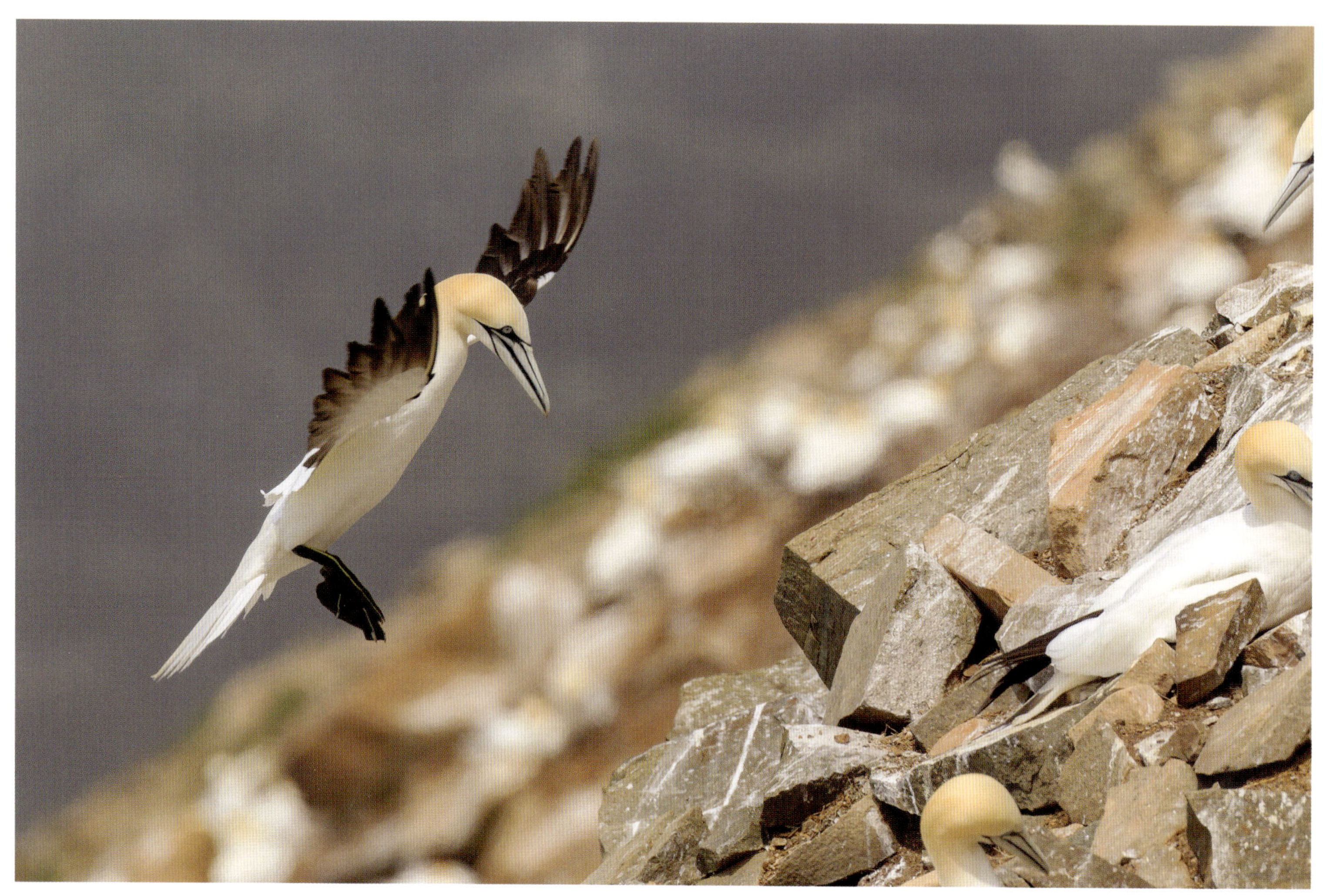

Above and opposite:

NORTHERN GANNETS AT CAPE ST. MARY'S, ONE OF THE LARGEST GANNET COLONIES IN NORTH AMERICA WHERE 24,000 BREED. SADLY, AVIAN FLU RECENTLY IMPACTED THIS COLONY.

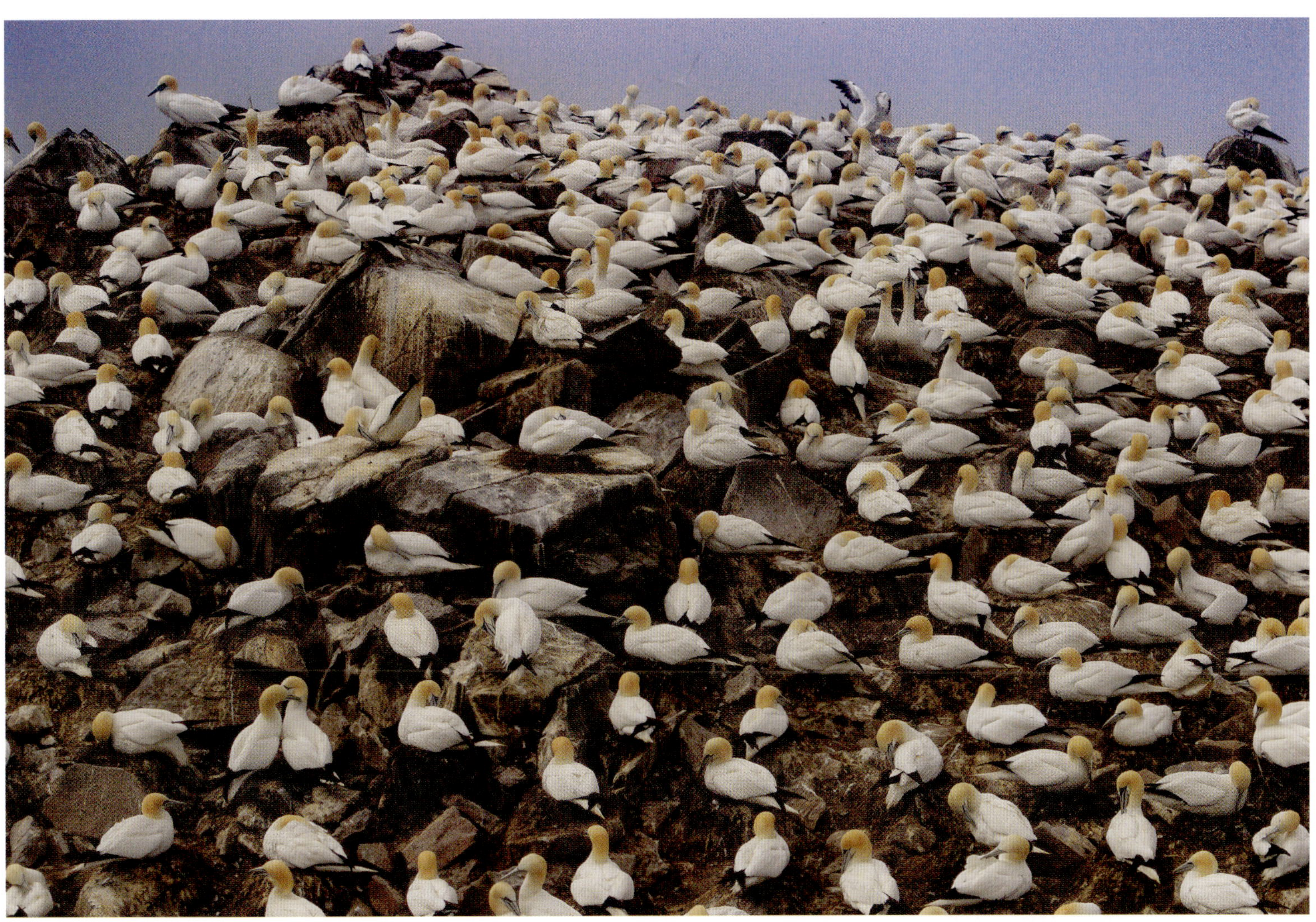

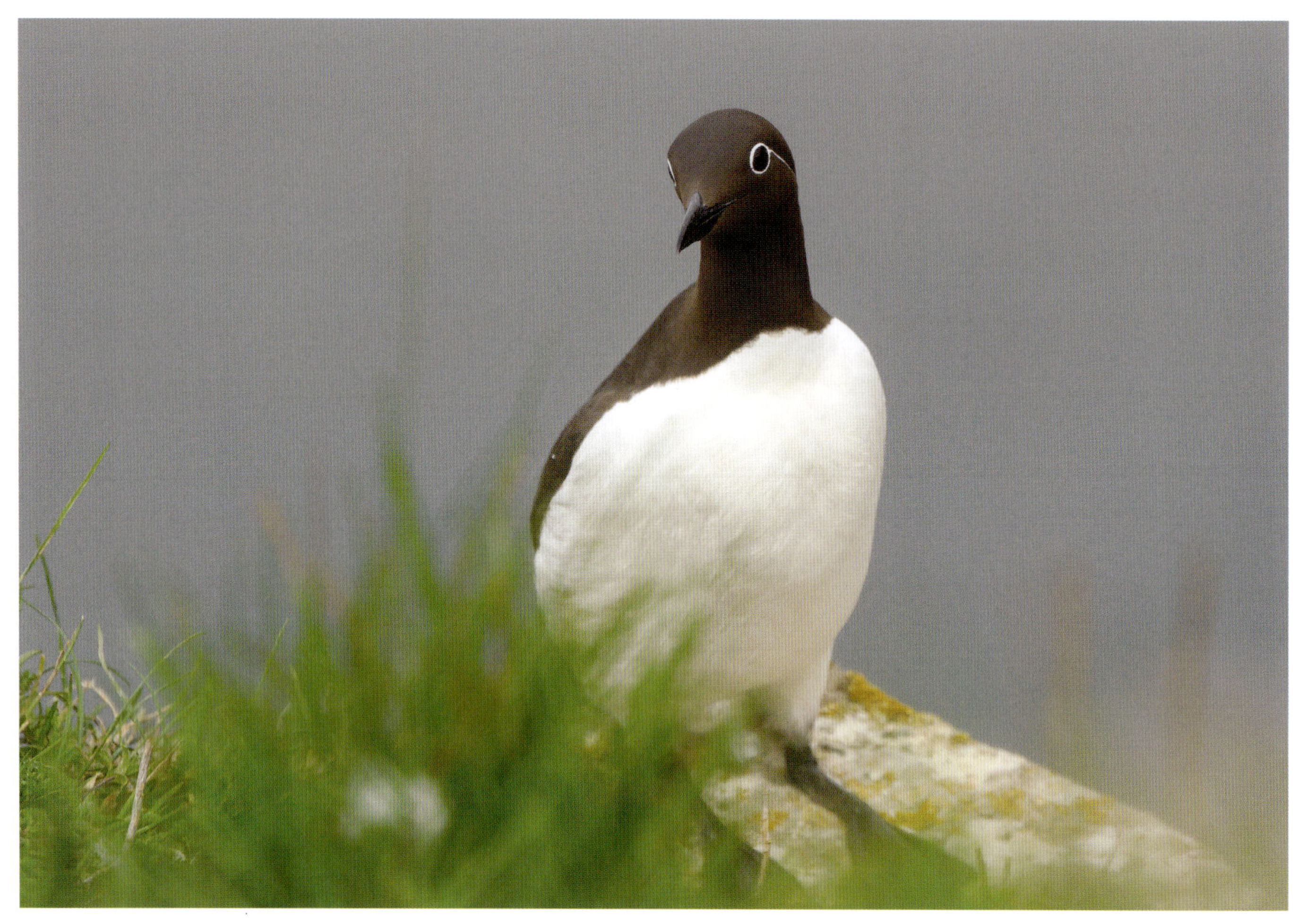

Above and opposite:

A COMMON MURRE SITS ON A CLIFF FACE AT CAPE ST. MARY'S NEAR ST. BRIDE'S, NEWFOUNDLAND. THE ATLANTIC SUBSPECIES IS ALSO CALLED A BRIDLED MURRE. BRIDLED MURRES DIFFER FROM THE COMMON MURRES SEEN ON THE WEST COAST OF NORTH AMERICA AS THEY LACK THE WHITE MARKINGS AROUND THE EYE.

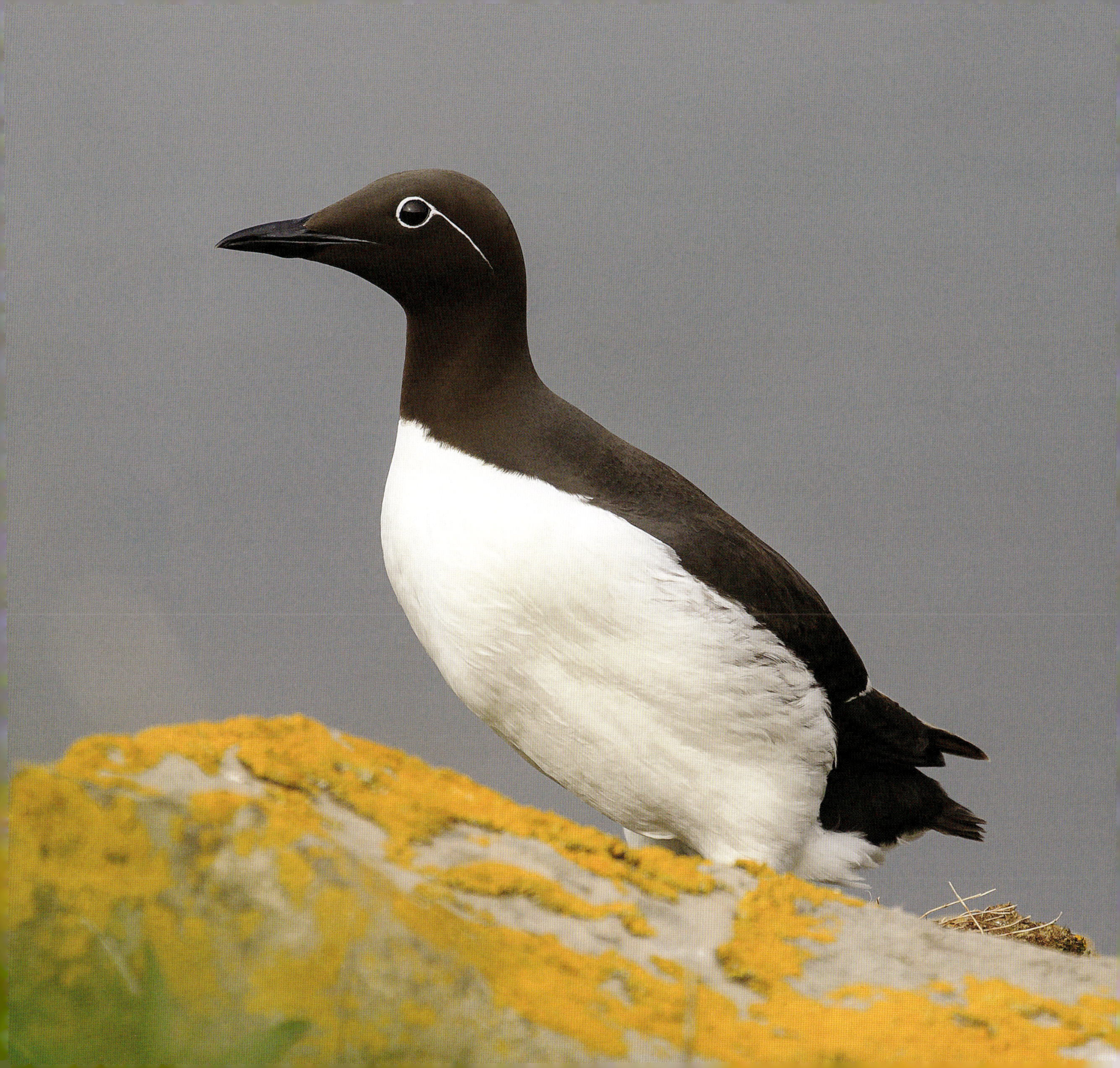

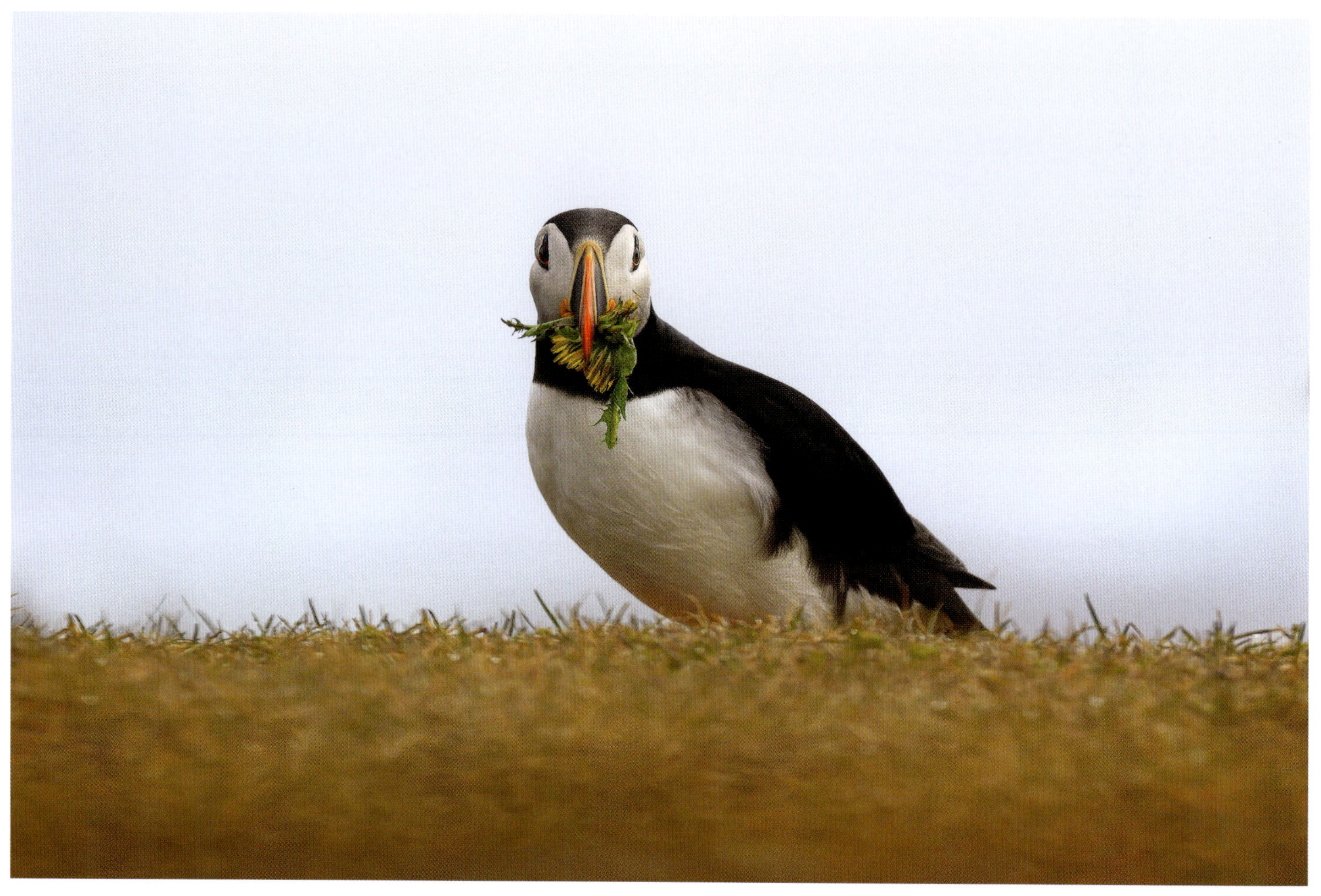

We got to sit and watch puffins dig out their burrows and carry flowers back to their nests to provide cushion and warmth for their eggs and young. They are so cute when they waddle as they walk, with their unique clown-like faces.

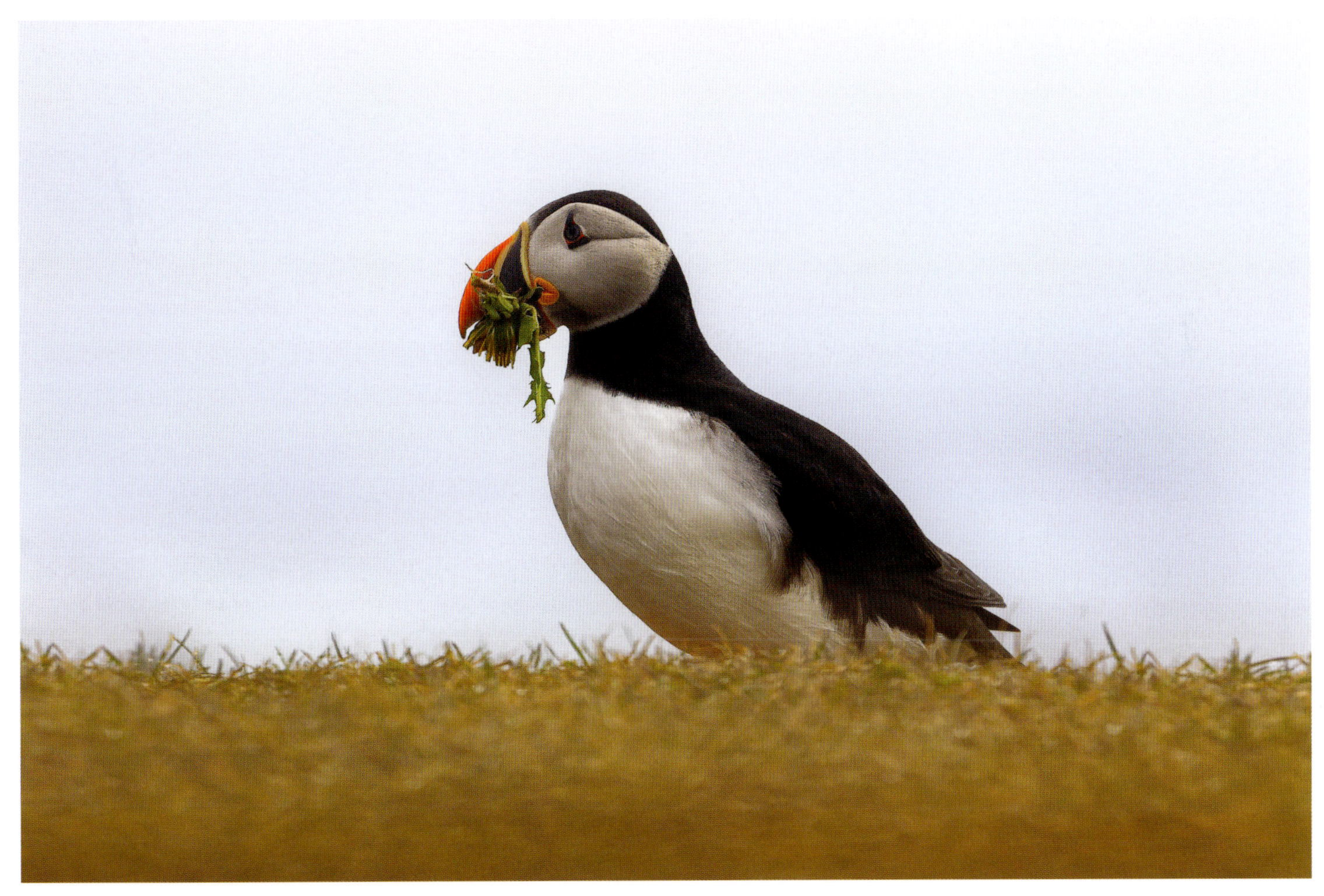

Above and opposite:

AN ATLANTIC PUFFIN AT A COLONY IN ELLISTON, NEWFOUNDLAND, COLLECTS DAFFODILS TO LINE ITS NEST DUG DEEP INTO A BURROW.

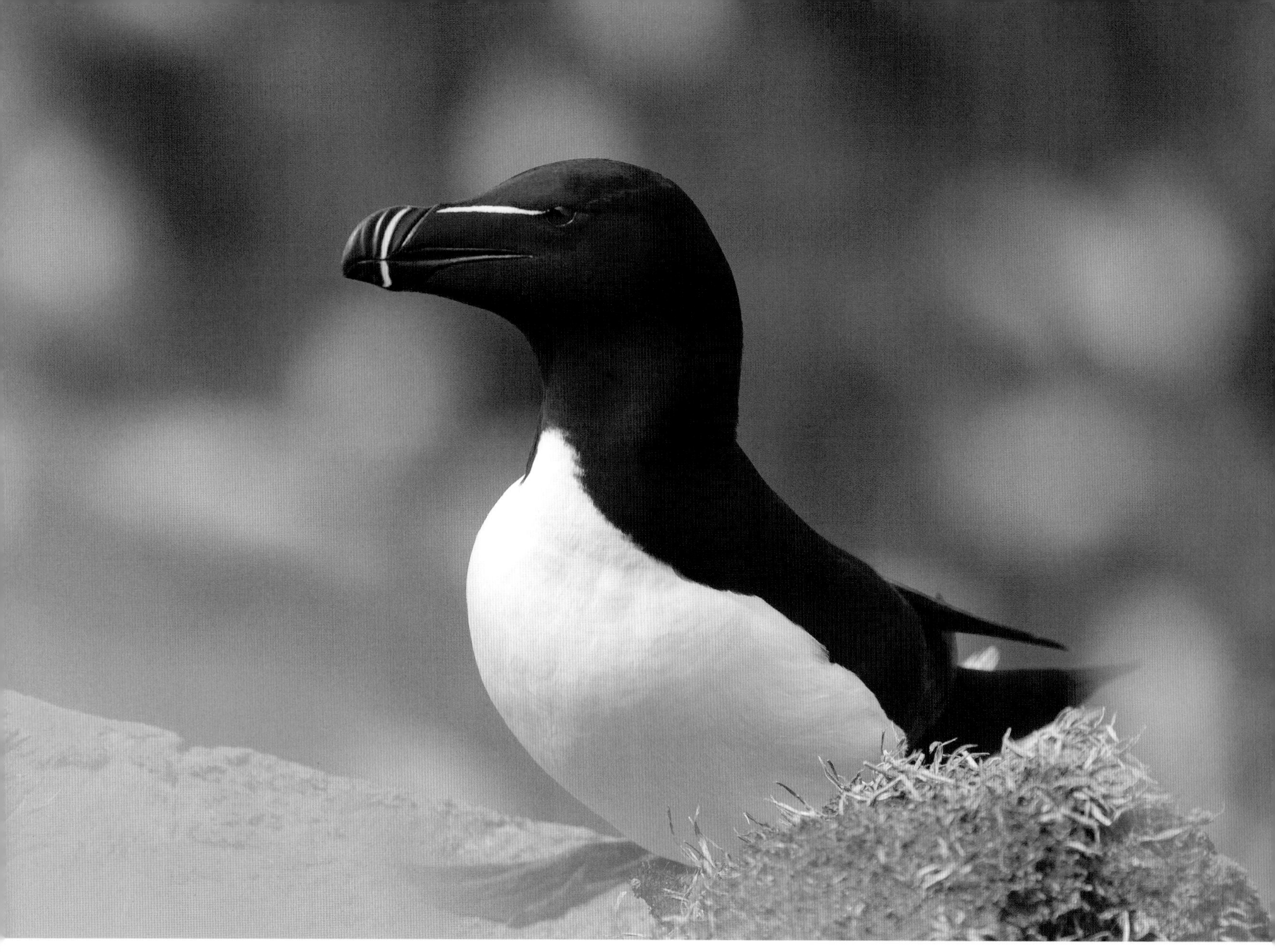

A RAZORBILL, NAMED AFTER ITS UNIQUE BILL SHAPE, DOES A WING STRETCH IN FRONT OF MY CLIENTS AND ME.

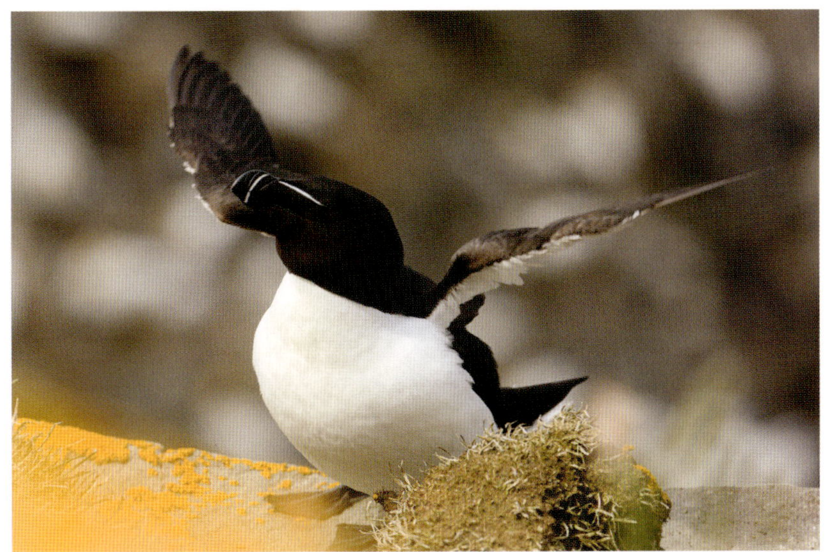

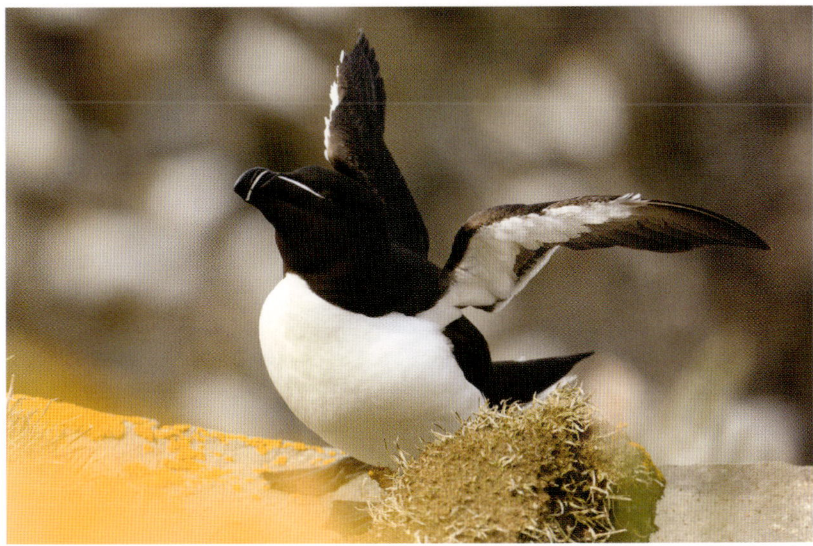

Of all the seabirds, my favourite has to be the very unique looking Razorbill! At Cape St. Mary's Ecological Reserve, one flew and perched on the rock beside us and did a wing stretch, exposing its yellow inner mouth lining. It was truly surreal.

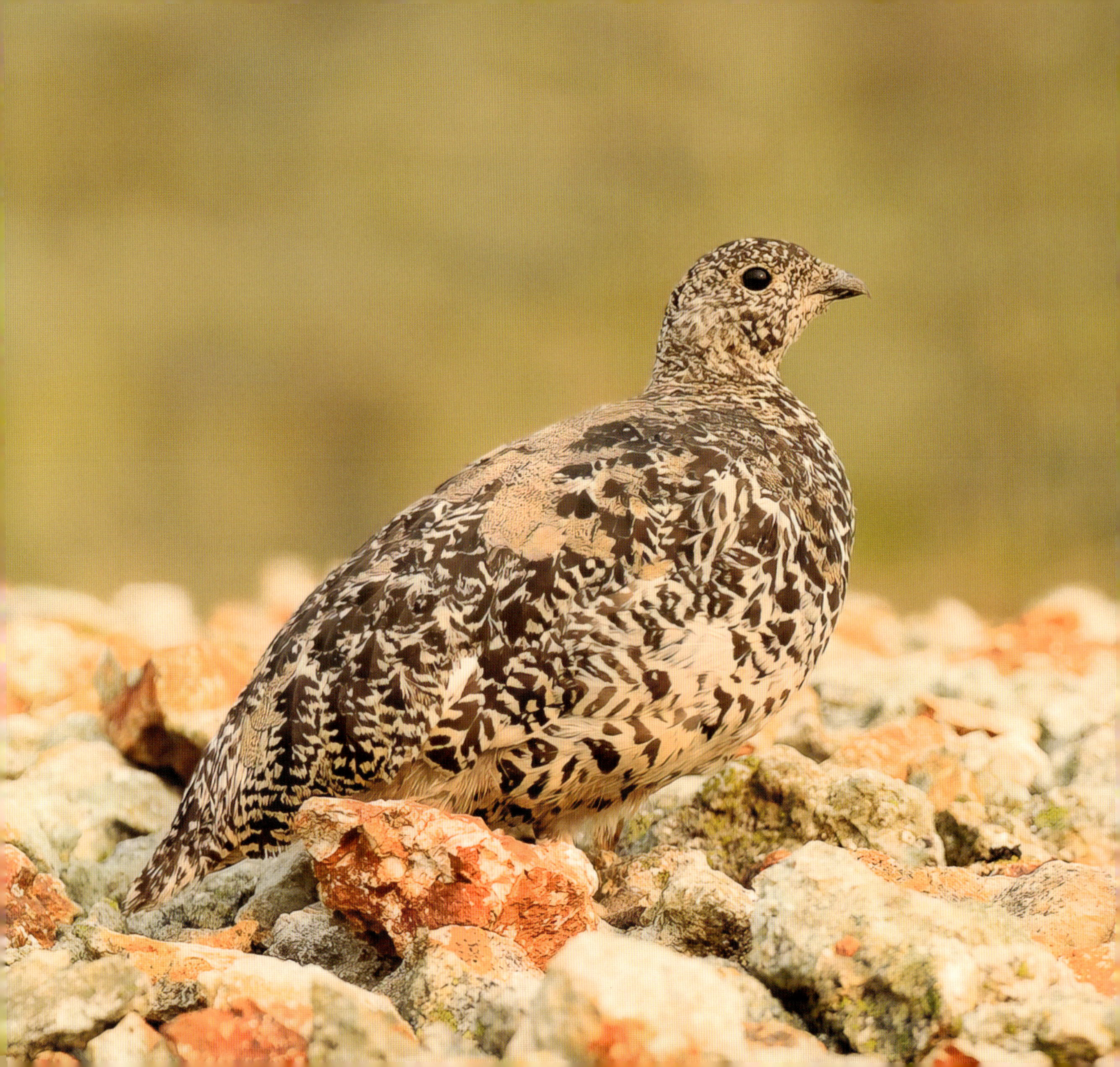

14

Young Birders

In 2014, I founded the BC Young Birders Program. I noticed all these youth birding solo in parks when I went out birding, so I spoke to them individually to see if they would be keen on joining a group that I would form to take them out and see birds near to home and far. The answer was an emphatic YES and "that's so cool!"

Opposite:

AN ADULT WHITE-TAILED PTARMIGAN ON ILLAL MOUNTAIN NORTH OF HOPE, BC, WAS A LIFER FOR MOST OF THE YOUTH IN MY YOUNG BIRDER PROGRAM.

I began taking out youth aged 12-18 years old of all gender expressions and races on group field trips around the province. We have done several overnight and pelagic trips too, which were incredibly fun. Seeing our first Tufted Puffin and Long-tailed Jaeger, Leach's Storm-Petrel and Black-footed Albatross, just to name a few, off of Tofino was so special to share with the kids.

The youth get outside and learn about the benefits of healthy lifestyles and connecting to birds and nature. They also learn about bird biology, identification, and conservation. The youth in our group enjoy the simple joys of watching birds while fostering friendships and future bird conservation leaders. It is a safe and inclusive group for BIPOC and LGBTQ2SIA+ youth. Working with and mentoring these youth has changed my life for the better. They have brought such immense joy and purpose to my life. I truly believe in mentoring youth because they are the future stewards of this land. They will be the ones we leave this planet to long after we are gone, and who have the power to make a difference. The youth I work with are making a difference every day already through their passion for citizen science, such as in their use of eBird and partaking in Christmas bird counts and their volunteer work.

It is so rewarding to work with these youth who have a genuine passion for bird and habitat conservation. Many of the graduates of the program have gone on to become biologists and study ornithology and environmental science in university as well. I have stayed in touch with them and

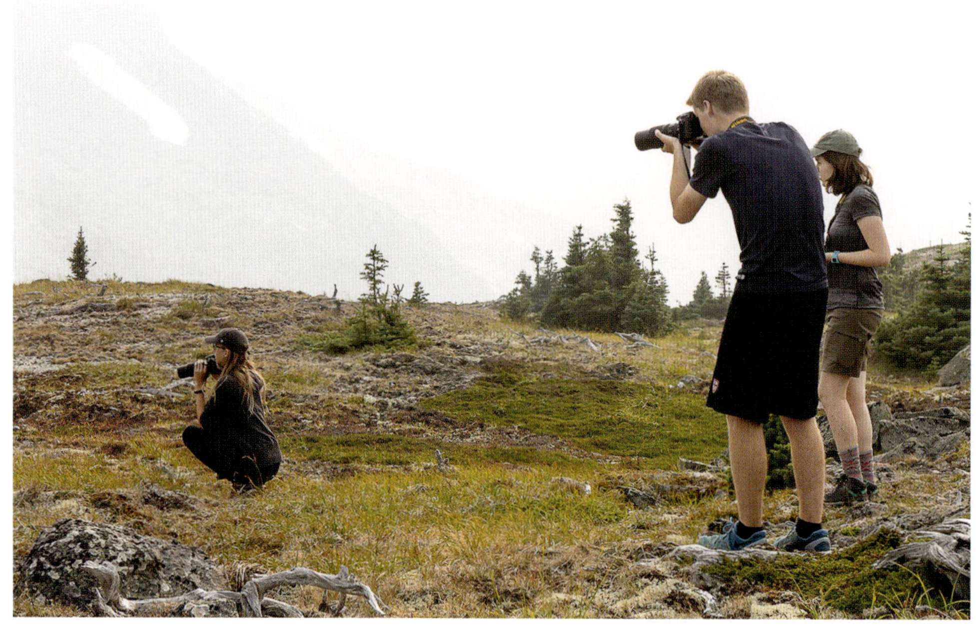

YOUNG BIRDERS LOOKING AT PTARMIGAN ON ILLAL MOUNTAIN NORTH OF HOPE, BC.

still bird with them to this day. Also many of the past graduates have stayed lifelong friends and still bird with one another.

We have seen many great birds together on our adventures, but my favourite of all has to be seeing White-tailed Ptarmigan. We did several field trips on many different mountains to see these so-called fancy chickens. When we finally found them, after a 13-km hike on Illal Mountain near Hope, BC, it was a moment I will never forget. These birds are sometimes called Snow Quails because they turn completely white in the winter. It is pretty cool when the whole group gets a lifer. A *lifer* is the birding term to describe the first time someone sees a specific species of bird. After an intense search, a young birder named Katya spotted them. When we all got eyes on the hen and her four chicks, we hugged one another! The birds were tame because they had seen so few people

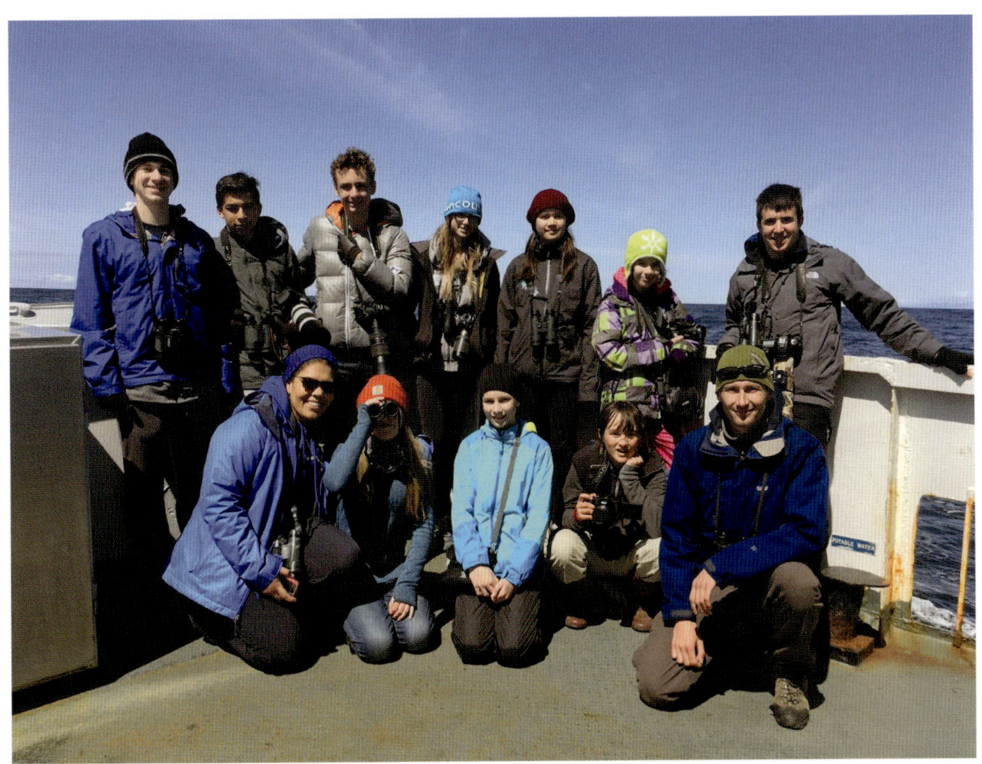

MY YOUNG BIRDERS AND ME ON A PELAGIC OUT OF TOFINO, BC.

in their high-elevation habitat, so as we lay on the ground they clucked and fed right in front of our faces. One of the four chicks even had a dust bath in front of us! It was one of the best field trips we ever had and a memory that will stay with me for a lifetime.

I was honoured to win the 2021 Daphne Solecki Award from BC Nature for my work with youth. I was also honoured by the Canadian Museum of Nature to be an adult finalist for the 2021 Nature Inspiration Awards. A few of the young birders in my program and I were asked to take part in the CBC's 2020 TV documentary *Rare Bird Alert*. It was so much fun to show Ontario birder Paul Riss (the wonderful host and star of the show) and Canadians why birding in BC is so special and why these youth are so incredible.

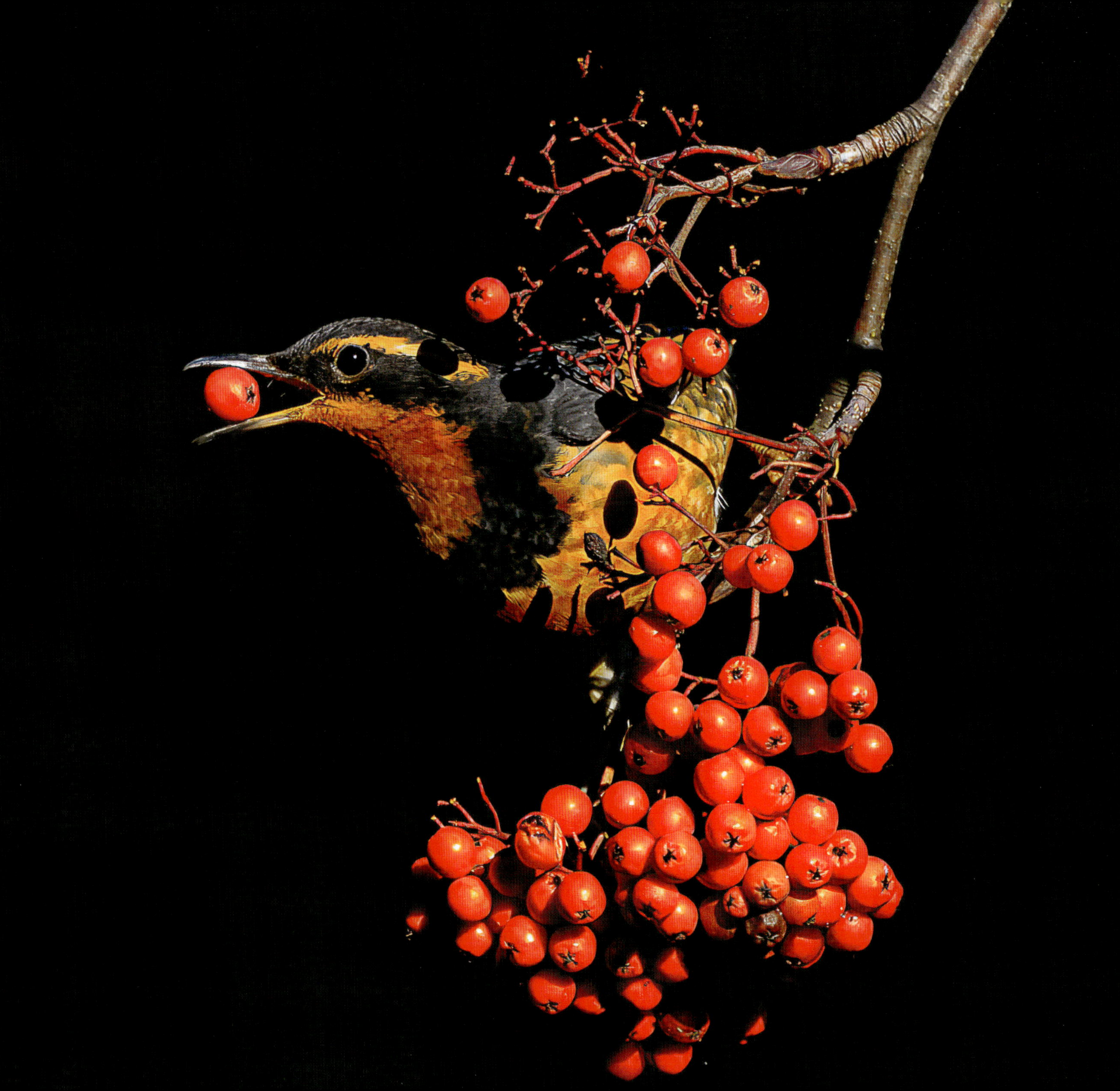

15

Grief, Birds, and Birding with Dad

After losing someone you love, or even if you suffer from depression, you will understand how some days you just feel impossibly low. Talking about grief in our society and even mental health can be taboo. We have a society that tends to think keeping a stiff upper lip is the way to handle loss and to just get on with it. Yes, everyone will experience grief and loss in their lifetime, but that doesn't make it any less painful for the one going through it. No one can truly understand what has been taken from you. For anyone who has lost a loved one, it just isn't that easy.

Opposite:

A STRIKING MALE VARIED THRUSH EATS BERRIES IN VANCOUVER, BC.

Grief is a heavy burden to bear. It is one where you can't just shake it off and keep on going, like with a sports injury. It can come in waves too. One day you are able to feel joy again and function well, and the next day you are shattered, crying on the floor, feeling like the world will eat you up. I lost both my parents just over a year apart and it was crushing, but birds helped me to survive the pain.

When my father died from an acute lung infection, it was so unexpected. He was talking two days before he went into a coma. We could not bring him home, the doctors said, because of the specialized oxygen machine that no hospices had access to. Therefore, he had to die in the palliative care ward of the hospital. When all hope was lost, the doctors discussed removing his ventilation. When the machine was finally turned off, he quickly and peacefully passed away as I held on to his hands, weeping. I kissed his face and hands as he slipped away and left us on a cold, snowy February on my mother's birthday. I was shaking and couldn't comprehend the loss. I was now an adult orphan and would dread Father's Day, and especially Christmas, without both of my parents. My parents made Christmas so special with turkey dinners, love, and togetherness. I knew more than ever I had to now start relying on the gift of birds.

I have found one thing that helps soothe my pain and sadness and that is to get out

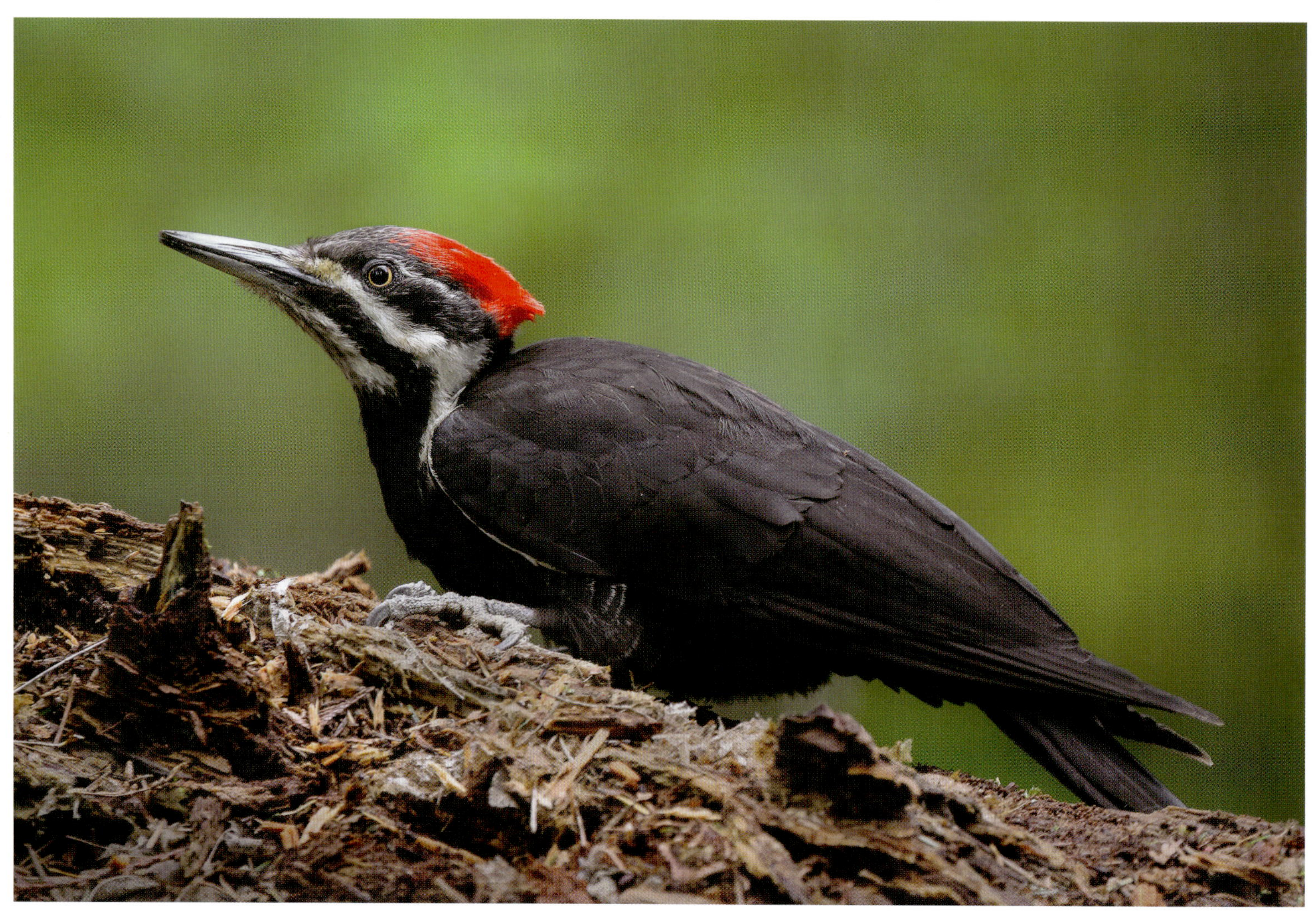

A FEMALE PILEATED WOODPECKER PAUSES FOR A REST AS SHE TAPS THE WOOD FOR GRUBS.

and look at birds. When you are birding, the birds don't care if you cry. They don't judge you at all. It's OK not to be OK with birds. Your tears are welcome at any time. When I look at birds, I get distracted from my inner pain. I see the beauty and hear their songs and I remember so many beautiful aspects of my life. I feel uplifted and remember moments I shared with my mother and father while looking or travelling to look at birds. As I said earlier, I feel a sense of peace when looking at birds and feel grounded to the earth. It is that deep connection we share with animals that helps us to connect with nature.

When I was a little girl, my dad took me out and got me into birding. He is the person who got me into nature and hiking. He taught me how to love and care for animals and the natural environment. He was born in Norway, and most Norwegians are very outdoorsy and adventurous. He taught me how to respect nature and to leave no trace when camping or hiking in the wilderness. I remember feeding Canada Jays and Black-capped Chickadees with him by hand. He bought me my first field guide, the notorious Golden Guide, and we ticked off all the birds we saw together. He also bought me my first camera and binoculars. I still remember my first Rufous Hummingbird and Pileated Woodpecker, both of which I saw with him.

Opposite:

A DRAKE AND HEN WOOD DUCK SWIM BY ME AT PIPER SPIT ON BURNABY LAKE IN BURNABY, BC.

I remember him teaching me how to keep a hummingbird feeder clean and safe for the little hummingbirds. I remember my awe as the orange hummingbird came in to feed. It was so tiny and so fast. He was always dazzled by hummingbirds, and I have fond memories of seeing how excited he was seeing the variety of hummingbirds on our Arizona trips compared to the limited species we get here in BC. We had such great road trips looking at birds, and whenever we spotted an owl together it would make his day. The last owls we saw together were Burrowing Owls in BC's interior. It is a memory I will treasure forever.

I am so grateful to my dad for instilling the love of nature and birds in me, as it has brought so much joy and peace to my life. I believe it is imperative to nurture the love of nature in children from an early age in order that they grow up to value the planet. It also will instill in the child why it is so important to protect the remaining habitat and birds and animals therein.

I will miss looking at Snow Geese every year with my dad. He loved Snow Geese; they were probably his favourite bird and he looked forward to their return to the Vancouver area every year.

One of the last trips I ever did with my dad was in June 2022. I took him on a Father's Day trip to the Okanagan and we saw many great birds together. I was trying to cheer him up after losing his wife of 39 years and was also letting him know how much I loved and appreciated him. We went from Kelowna to Osoyoos, and one memory I will treasure is looking at Common Nighthawks together swirling over the wineries and listening to Common Poorwills at night. Even though he had

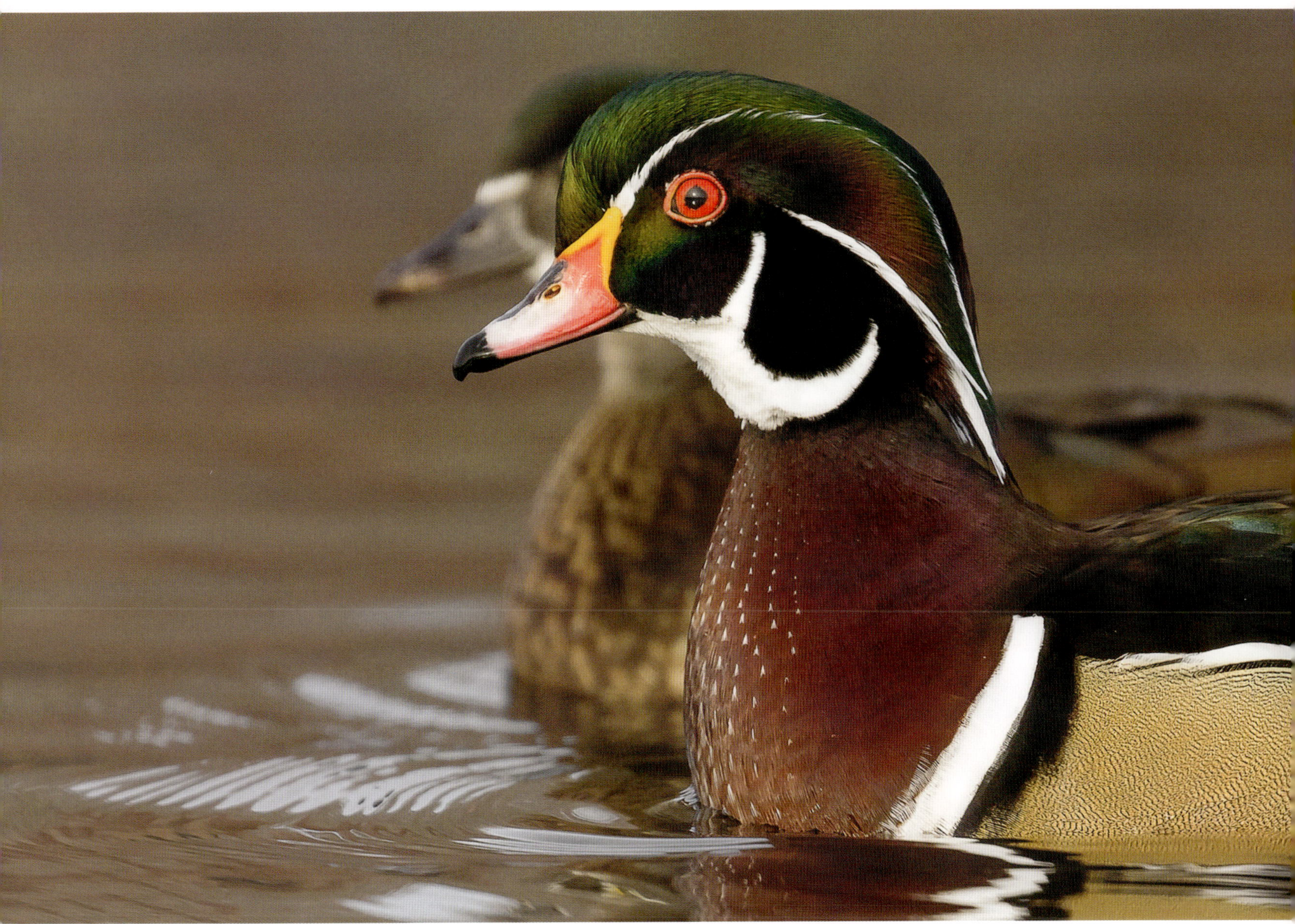

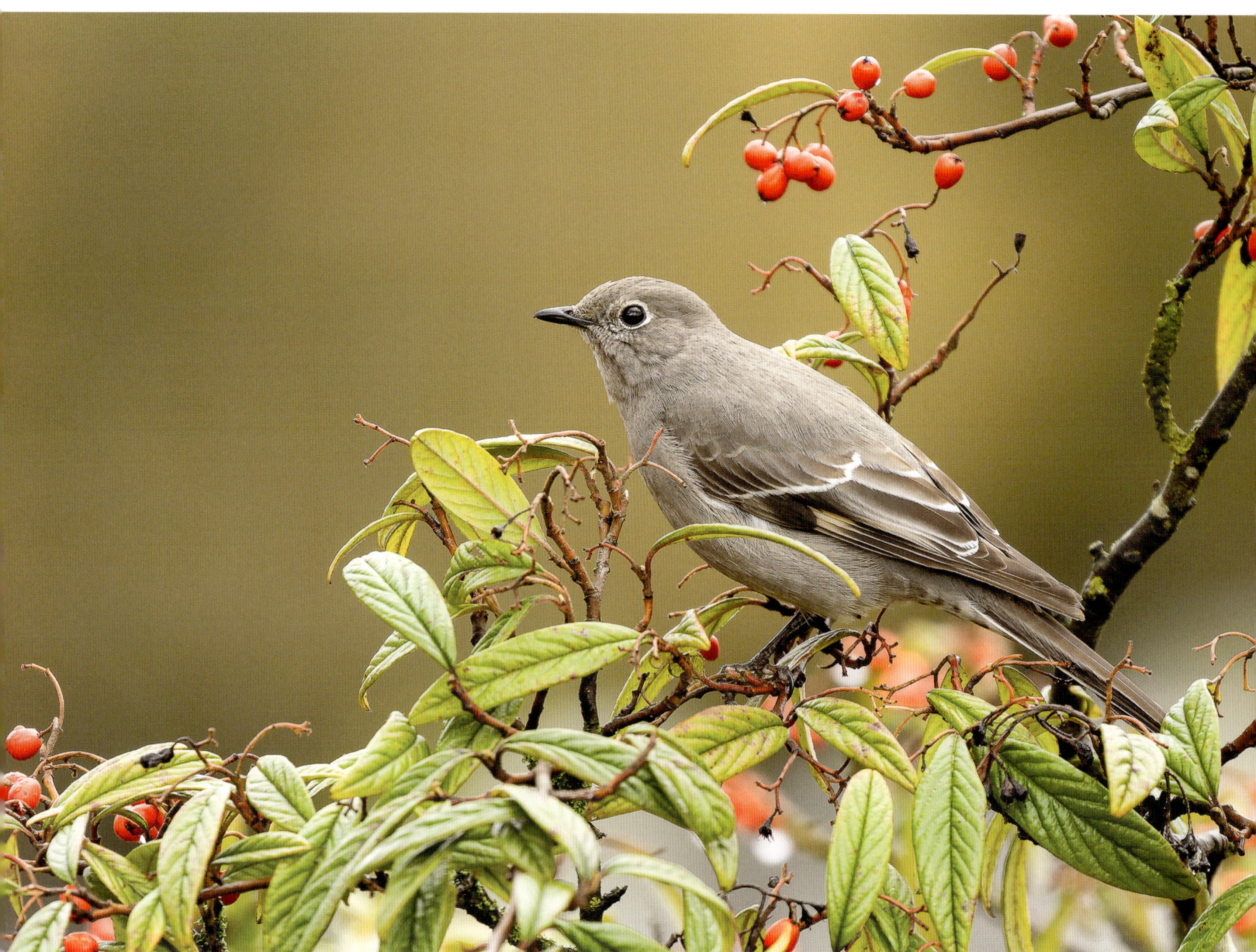

Opposite:

A TOWNSEND'S SOLITAIRE POSES WITH SOME BERRIES IN VANCOUVER, BC.

seen nightjars with me many times before, it never ceased to be special. I will never forget all the incredible moments we shared while looking at birds together and never will forget that moment. I am sure that whenever I look up at the sky and hear that "peent" call of a Nighthawk, he will be there, watching these incredible birds with me once more.

Losing a parent or anyone who loved you so much, and who you loved so much and who made such an impact on your life, is extremely hard. I am grateful I have the birds to help me through life without them. The birds continue to guide me and keep my mental health intact. Most importantly, they soothe me and bring me joy that nothing else can do. Birds help me to continue the relationship with those I lost. I carry them with me in my heart when I go birding, even after their physical bodies are gone. Birding has reinforced that continued relationship with them.

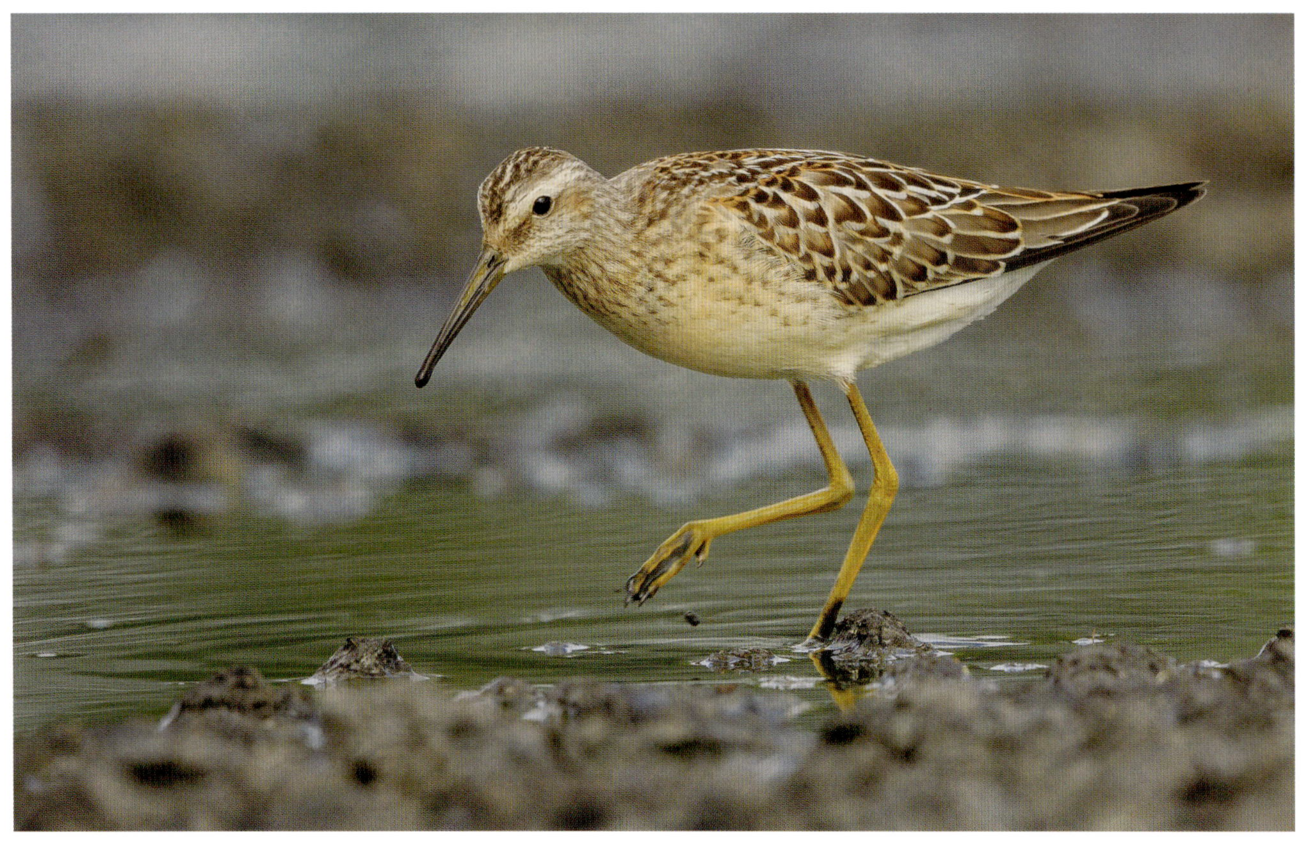

Above:

AN ELEGANT STILT SANDPIPER PROBES THE MUD FOR FOOD IN RICHMOND, BC.

Opposite:

I FIND WATCHING BIRDS LIKE THIS MARBLED GODWIT IN VICTORIA, BC, BRINGS ME PEACE AND RELAXATION.

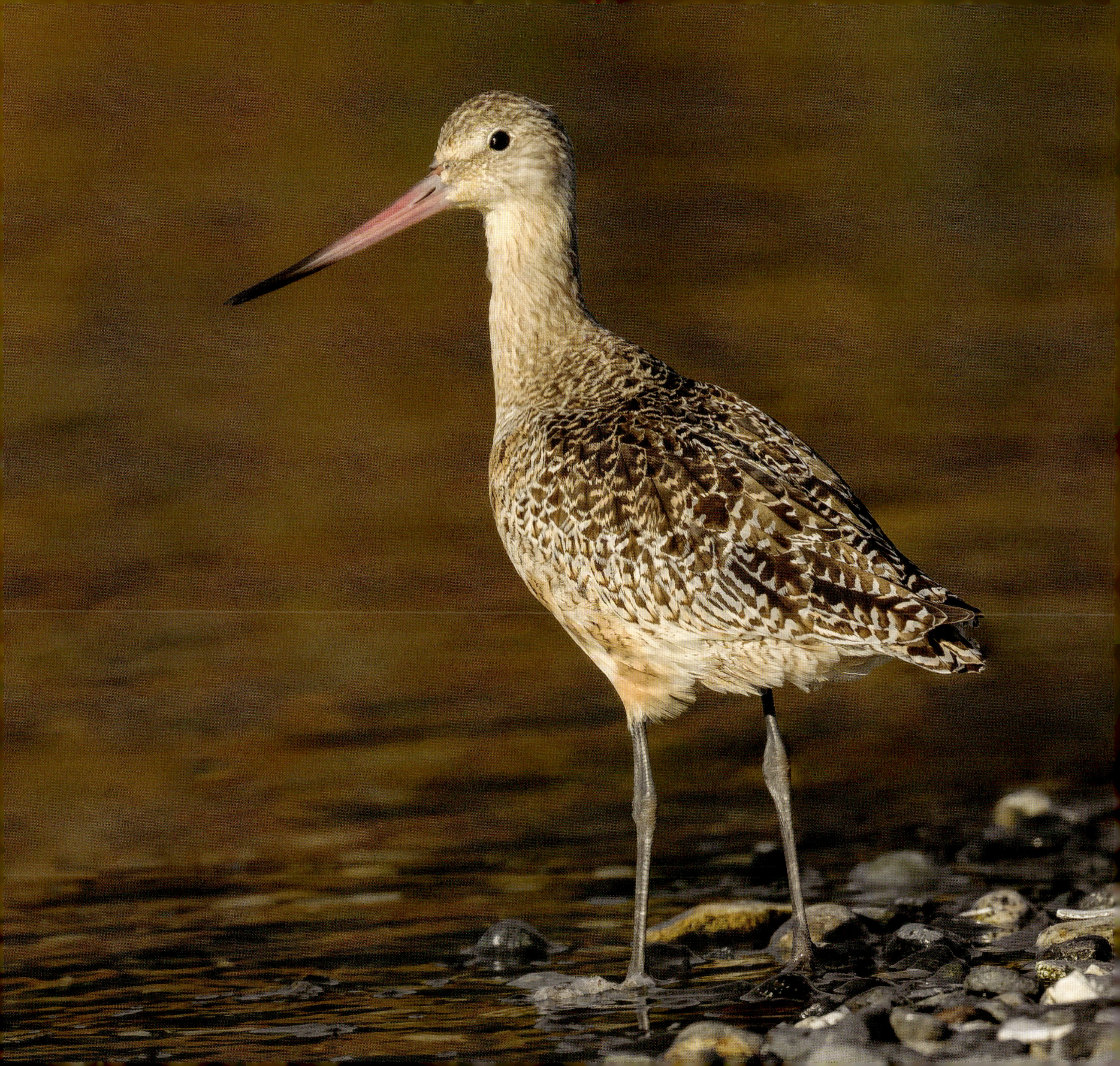

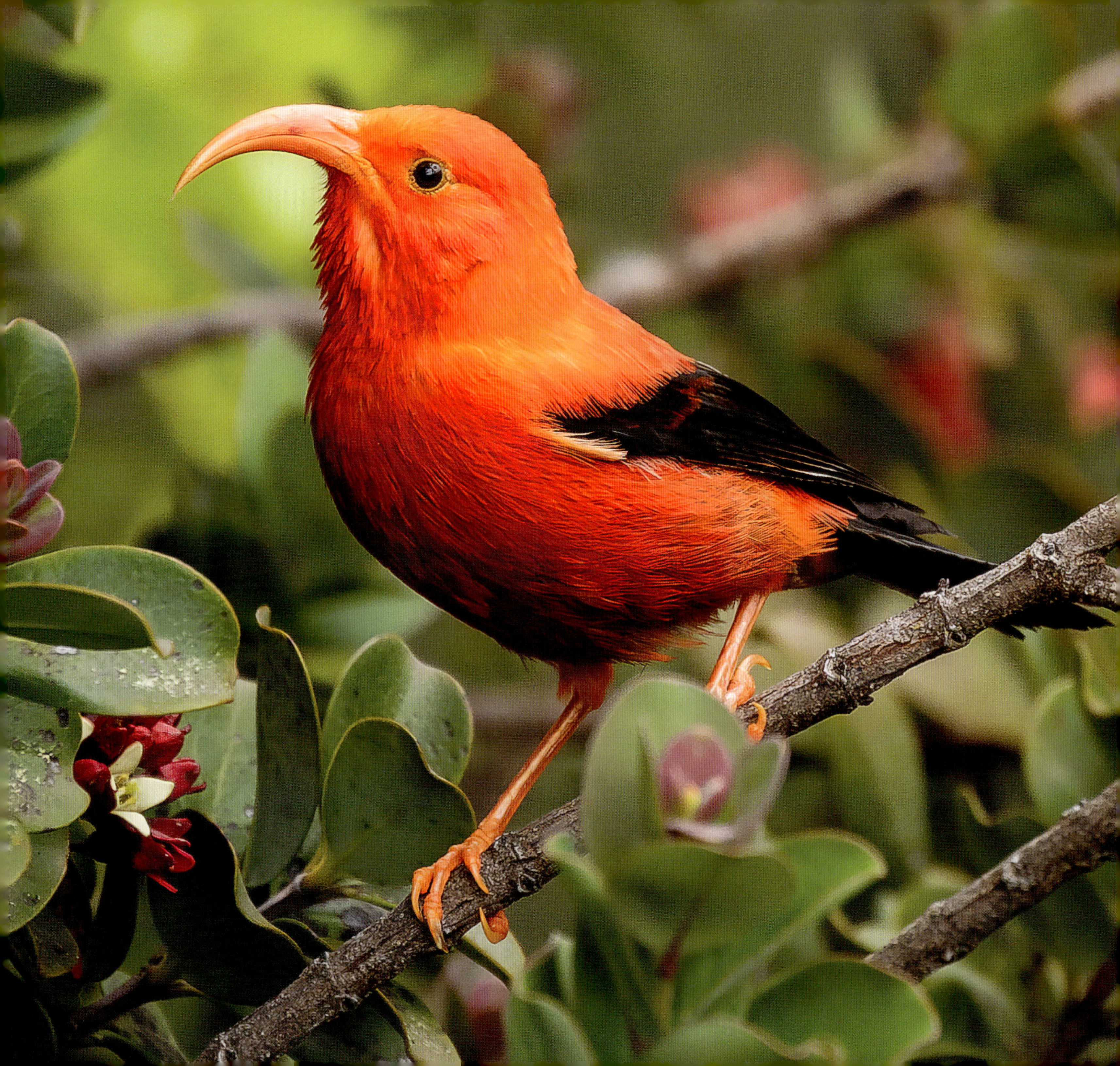

16

The Wonders of Bird Travel

I love to travel around the world looking at birds. Just as birds travel from south to north and vice versa on beautiful, winged migration, I too like to fly to new places to see new birds. I am most keen to see endemic birds in every region I visit, when possible. It is so exciting to see new lifers or life birds when I travel to new countries.

Opposite:

THE ʻIʻIWI IS TRULY ONE OF THE MOST SPECTACULAR BIRDS ON THE PLANET. THESE NATIVE HAWAIIAN HONEYCREEPERS ARE AFFECTED BY AVIAN MALARIA SPREAD BY MOSQUITOES, INTRODUCED BIRDS AND ANIMALS, HABITAT LOSS, RAPID ʻŌHIʻA DEATH, AND CLIMATE CHANGE. THEIR RANGE HAS NOW BEEN CONSIDERABLY RESTRICTED FROM WHAT IT ONCE WAS. PHOTOGRAPHED IN MAUI, HAWAII.

Seeing new bird families, like when I saw antpittas in South America, is mind-blowing. Seeing a Northern Gannet in Newfoundland, for example, is something that stays with you forever. After my mother died, I went to Hawaii and saw some amazing, endangered, endemic Hawaiian honeycreepers and I felt her presence with me the whole time. Every time I saw a new critically endangered bird, I wished for her physical presence but felt she was there in my heart. I remember after an arduous trip to see an ʻAkiapōlāʻau, a rainbow appeared, which I suspect was my mom saying she saw it too.

The ʻIʻiwis and ʻApapanes, with their wing flutters and unique sounds, really entranced me. After I lost my dad, I needed another mental and physical break and went back to Hawaii. Hawaii is a special and spiritual place for me, and seeing some of the world's most endangered birds while walking through the remaining intact native forests was moving. These birds depend on native plants like ʻōhiʻa trees to survive. This is why it's so important to brush and spray your boots with alcohol before hiking in these fragile ecosystems to prevent the spread of Rapid ʻŌhiʻa Death. This is a fungus that kills the trees and detrimentally impacts these Hawaiian honeycreepers. Avian malaria spread by mosquitoes is a huge problem in Hawaii, and so many good people are working with Incompatible Insect Technique (IIT) to try and help save them. IIT is a process in which lab-bred mosquitoes are bred

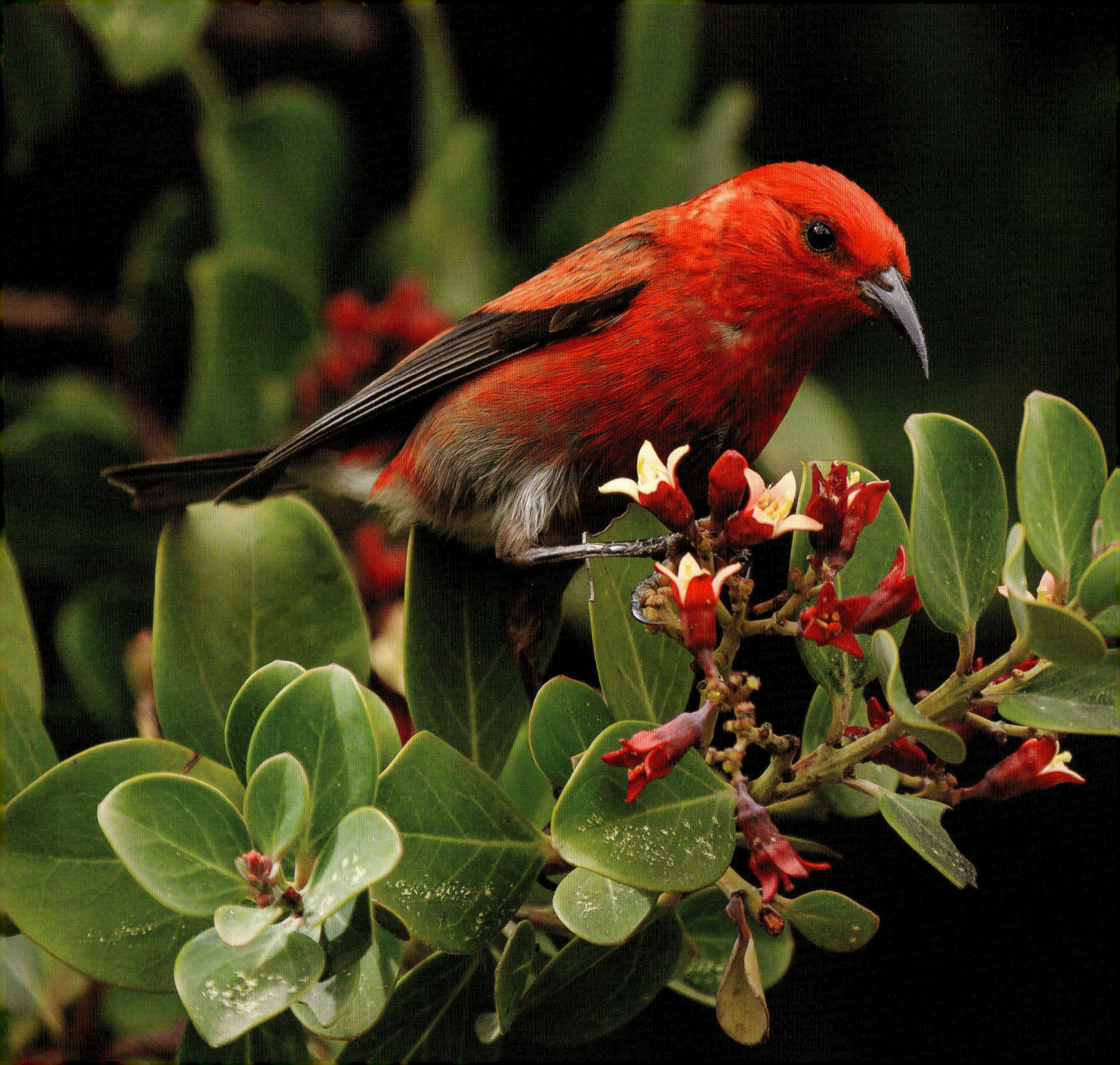

AN ADULT 'APAPANE FEEDING FROM SANDALWOOD, OR AN 'ILIAHI PLANT. PRESERVING NATIVE ENDEMIC PLANTS IS CRUCIAL TO THESE NECTAR-FEEDING HONEYCREEPERS. PHOTOGRAPHED IN MAUI, HAWAII.

with the bacteria *Wolbachia*. Only male mosquitoes get released into the wild, and when they mate with wild females who aren't infected with the bacteria, their eggs are not viable and cannot hatch. These Hawaiian native birds inspire me with their resilience and for hanging on despite it all.

I have been lucky to travel to Thailand, Ecuador, the United States, Canada, the Caribbean, and Europe for birding and can't wait to see where the next adventure takes me. There are so many more birds and places I want to see. I just wish I could physically share them with my parents. I would always call them during my travels, or email them and let them know what I saw. Even when they didn't know what the bird species was, they were always interested and keen to listen. I will miss that. Now I travel with them in my heart wherever I go and they guide me, even though I can no longer see them. It is nice to share the birds with them in another way. I try to reframe it in my mind and create new memories with them as our relationship continues in a new way.

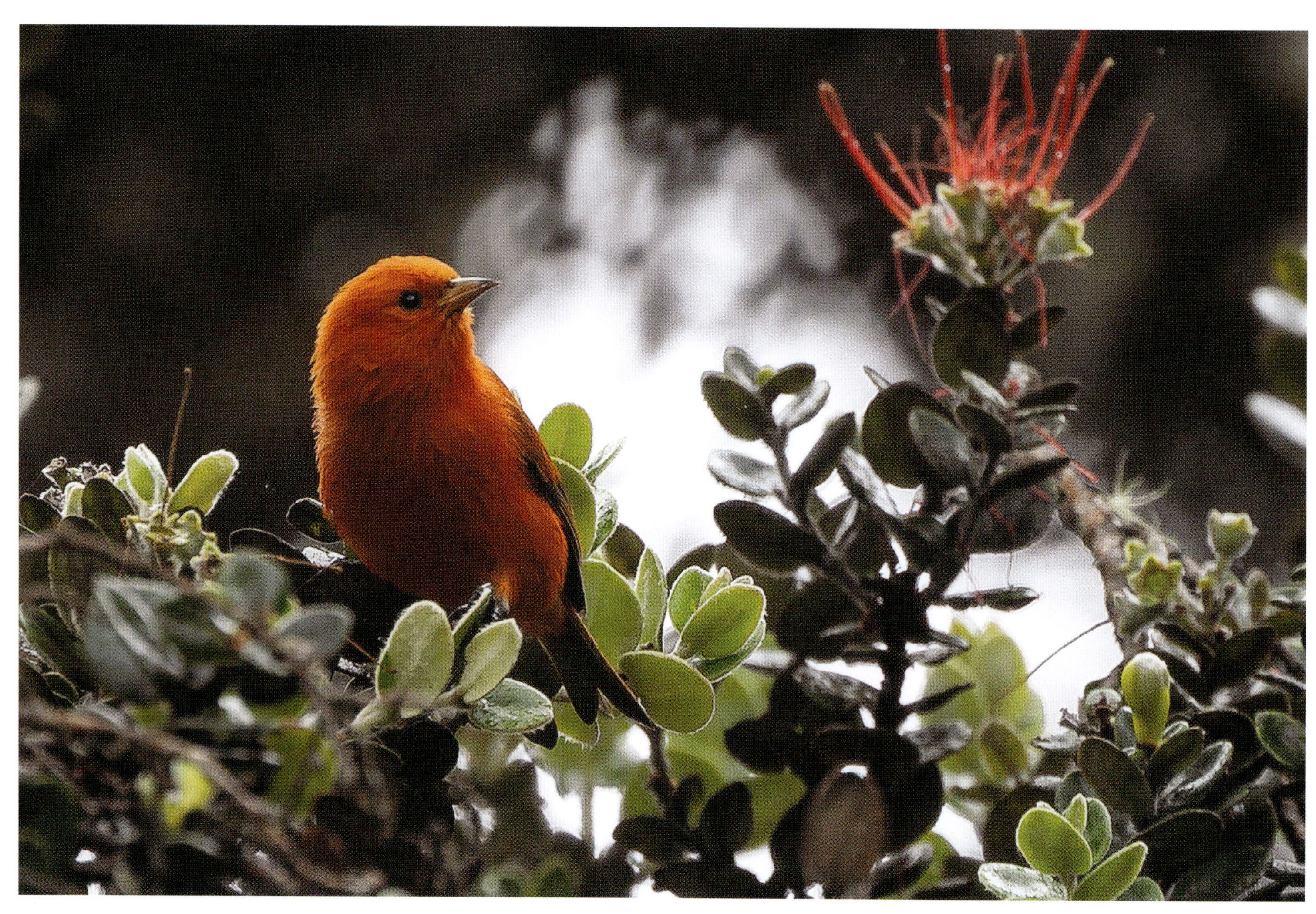

AN ENDANGERED MALE ʻĀKEPA ON THE BIG ISLAND OF HAWAII.

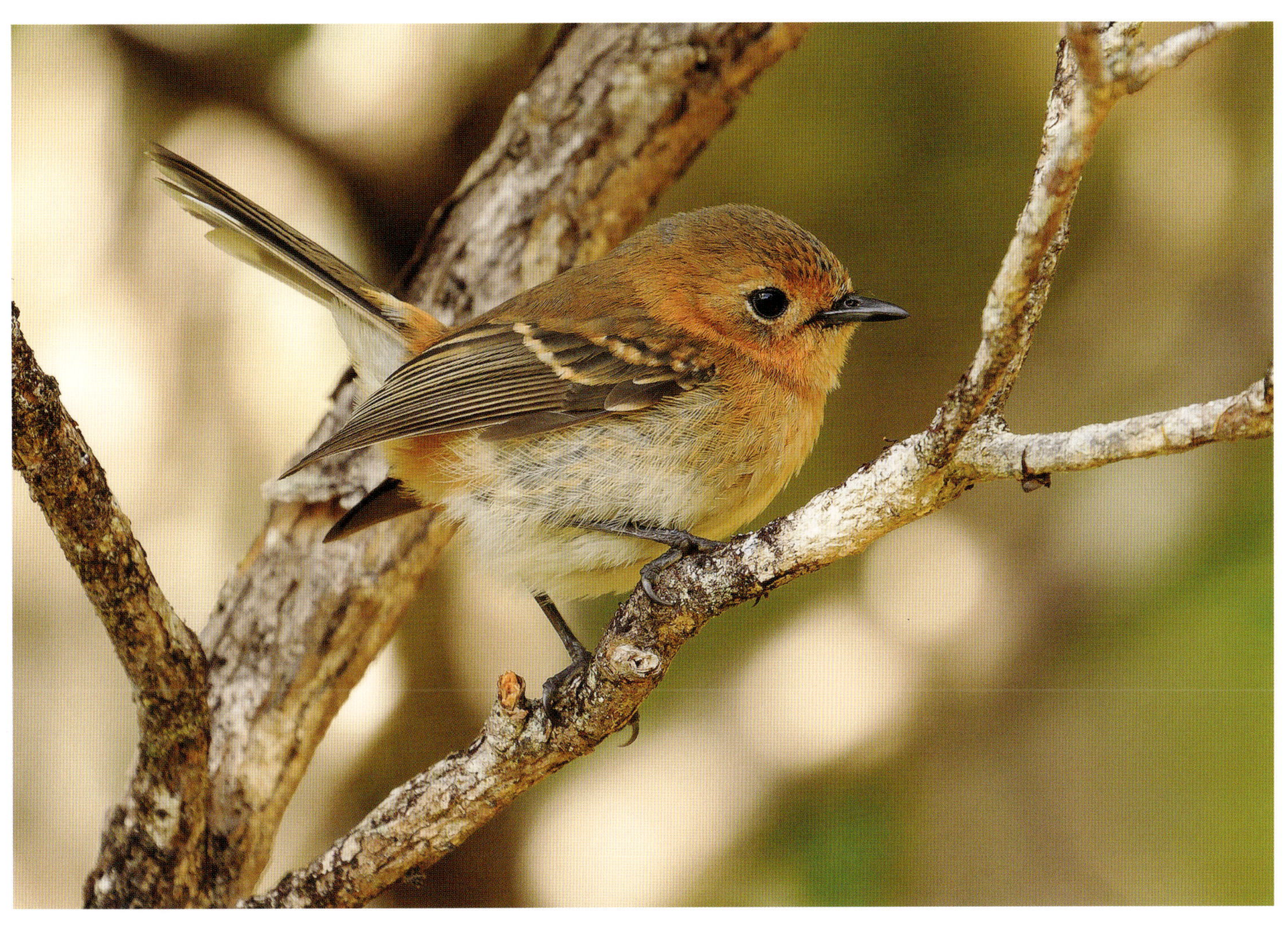

A THREATENED KAUA‘I ‘ELEPAIO ENDEMIC TO THE ISLAND OF KAUAI DELIGHTED ME IN THE ALAKA‘I WILDERNESS PRESERVE.

A WHITE TERN CHICK SITS ON A BANYAN TREE SLEEPING AND WAITING FOR ITS PARENT TO RETURN AND FEED IT. WHITE TERNS DO NOT MAKE NESTS BUT LAY THEIR EGGS PRECARIOUSLY ON BARE TREE BRANCHES. PHOTOGRAPHED IN WAIKIKI, OAHU, HAWAII.

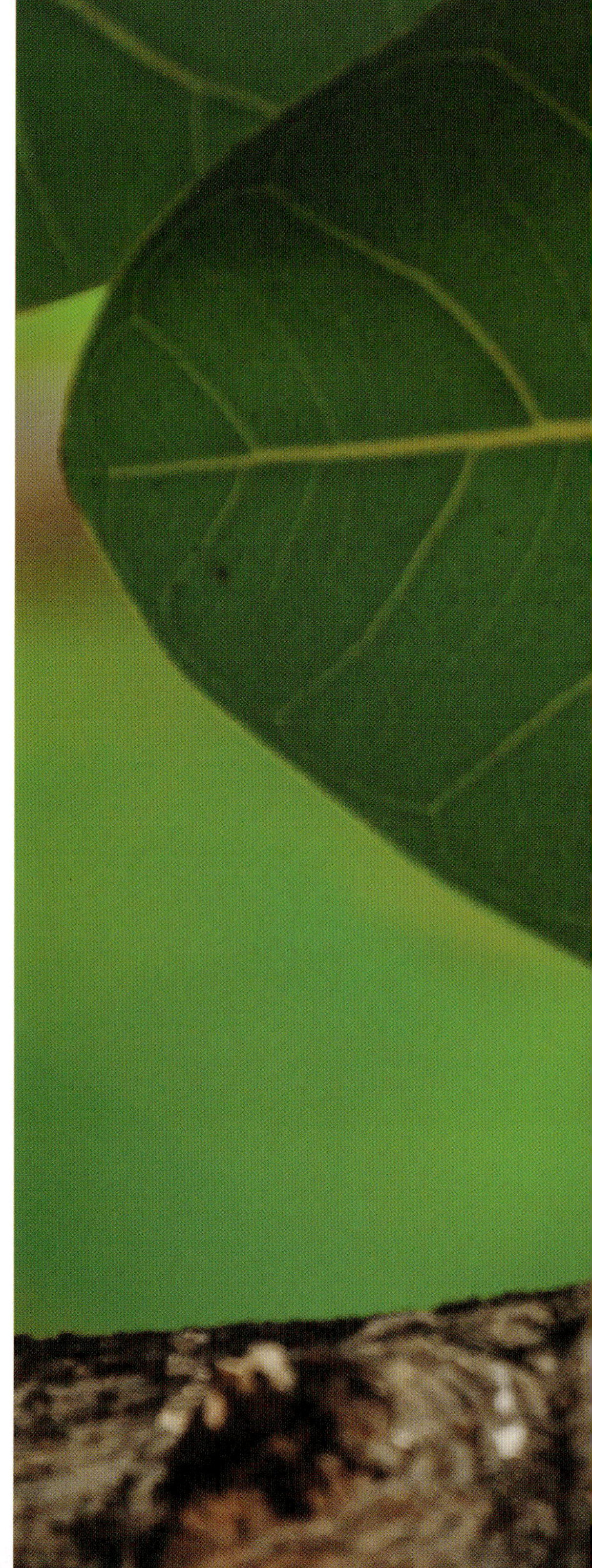

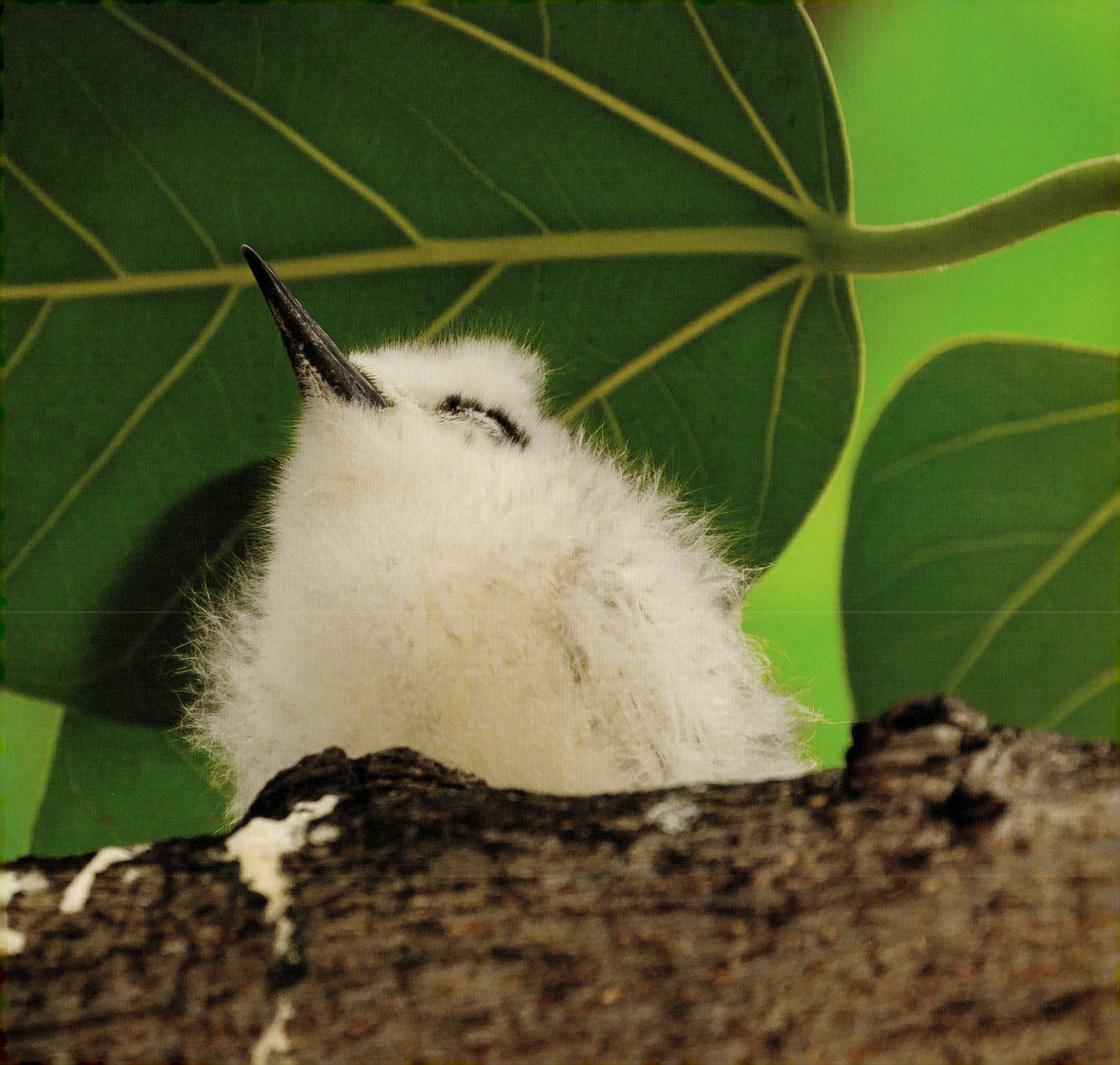

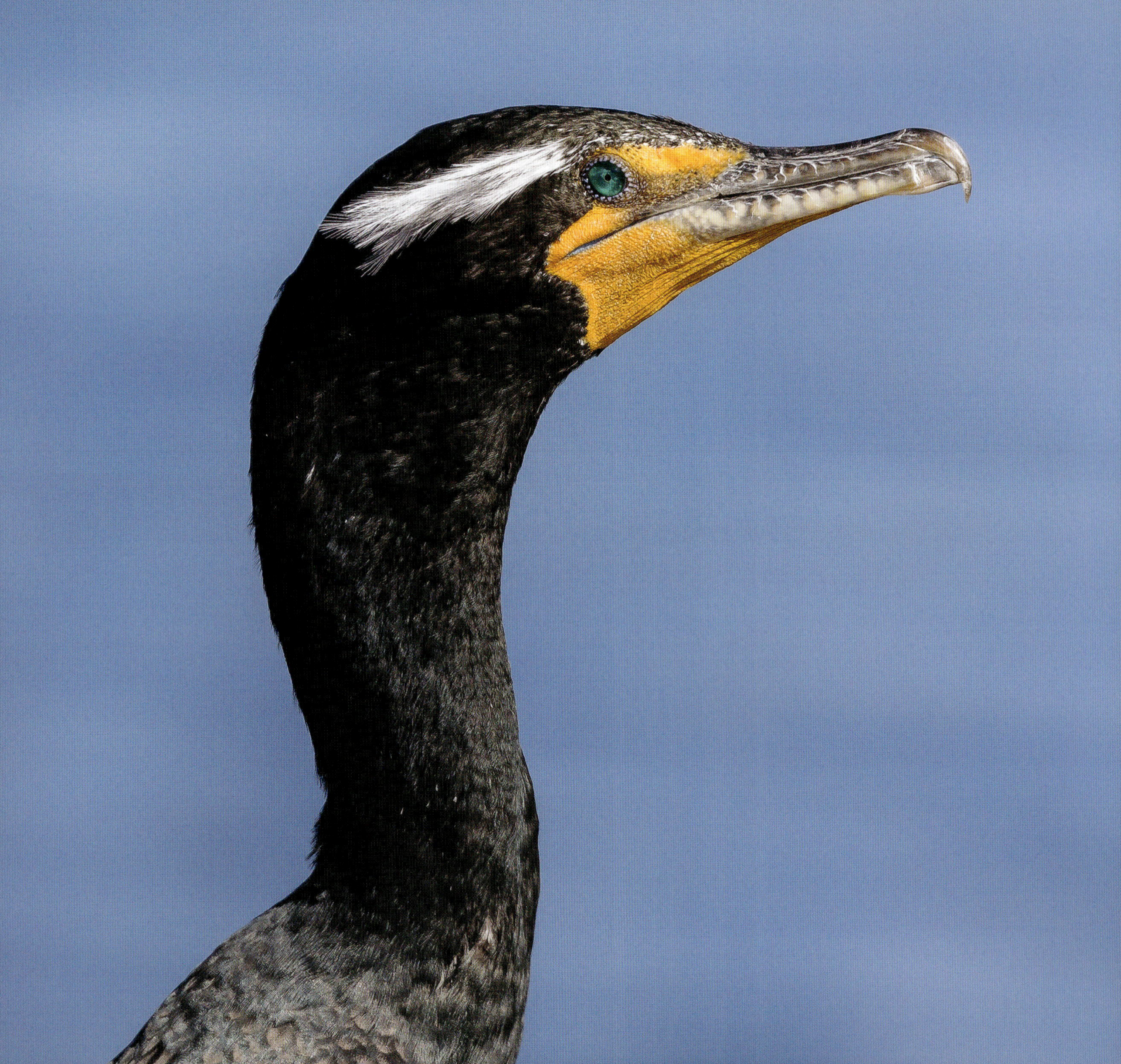

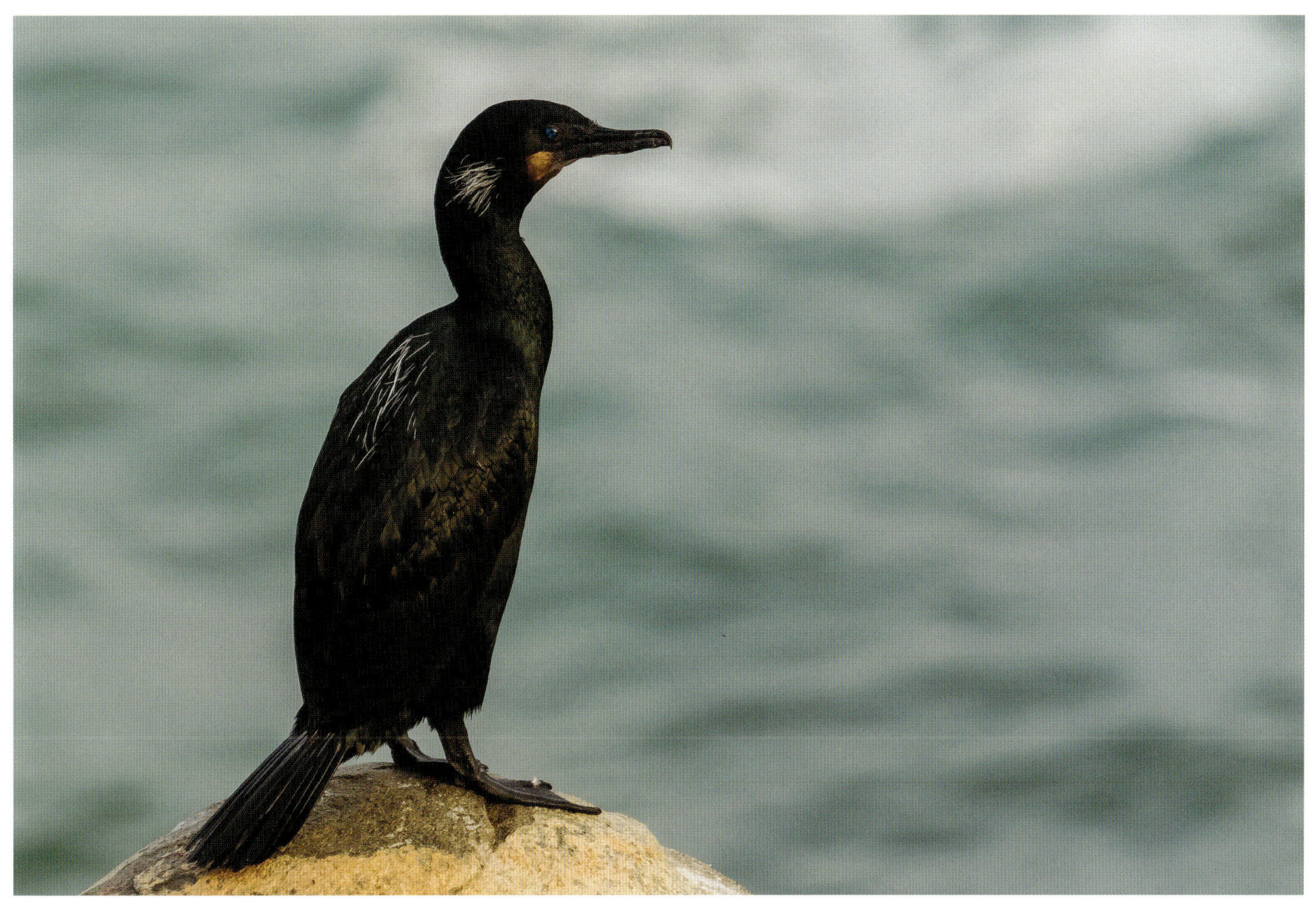

Opposite:

A DOUBLE-CRESTED CORMORANT IN BREEDING PLUMAGE HAS STUNNING EMERALD EYES AND WHITE CROWN TUFTS. TAKEN IN SAN DIEGO, CALIFORNIA.

Above:

A BREEDING-PLUMAGED BRANDT'S CORMORANT STANDS ON A ROCK AT LA JOLLA IN SAN DIEGO, CALIFORNIA.

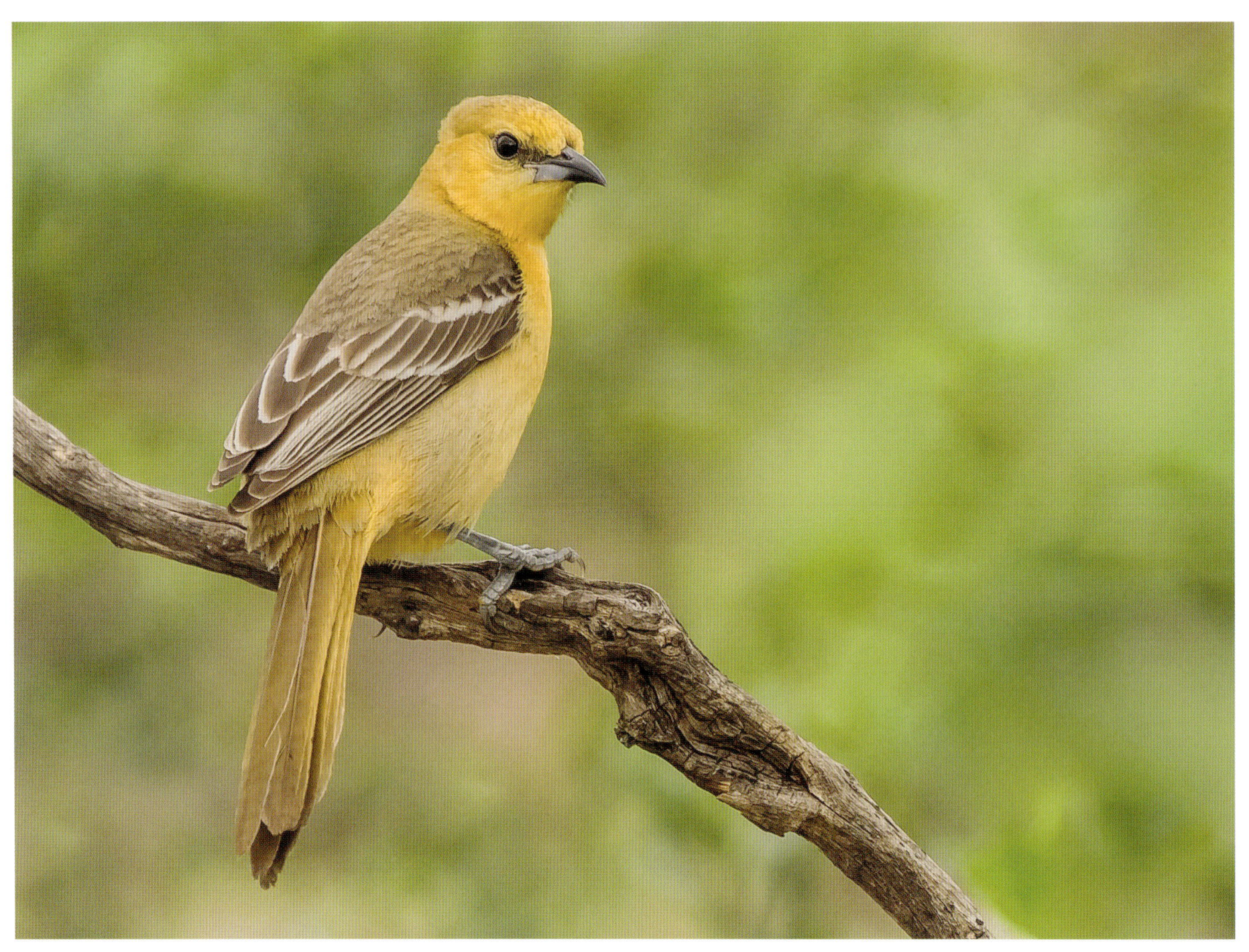

A FEMALE HOODED ORIOLE IN TEXAS HILL COUNTRY, NEAR UVALDE.

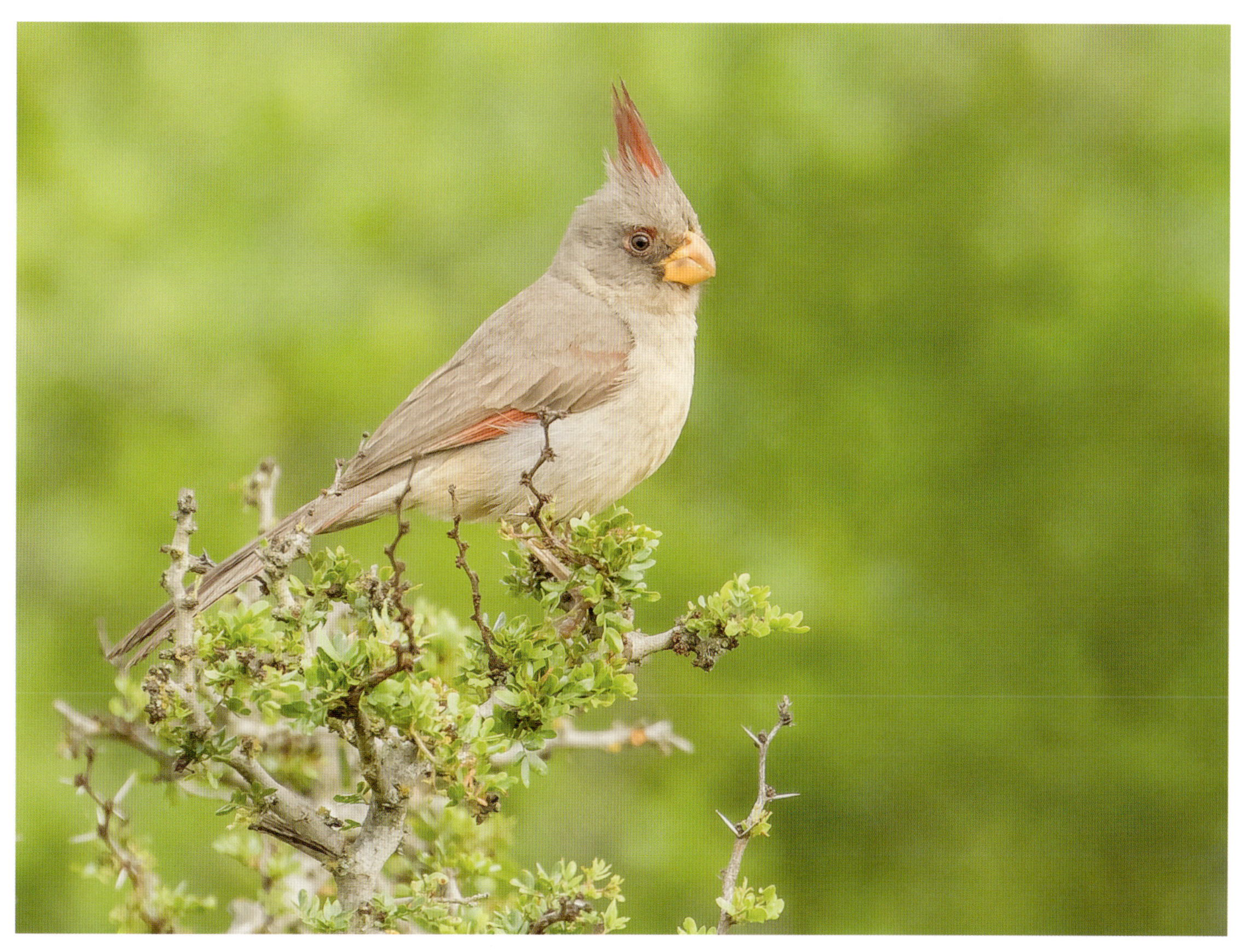

A FEMALE PYRRHULOXIA, OR DESERT CARDINAL, IN TEXAS HILL COUNTRY.

A LONG-TAILED JAEGER RESTS ON ITS BREEDING GROUNDS IN THE ARCTIC TUNDRA IN NOME, ALASKA.

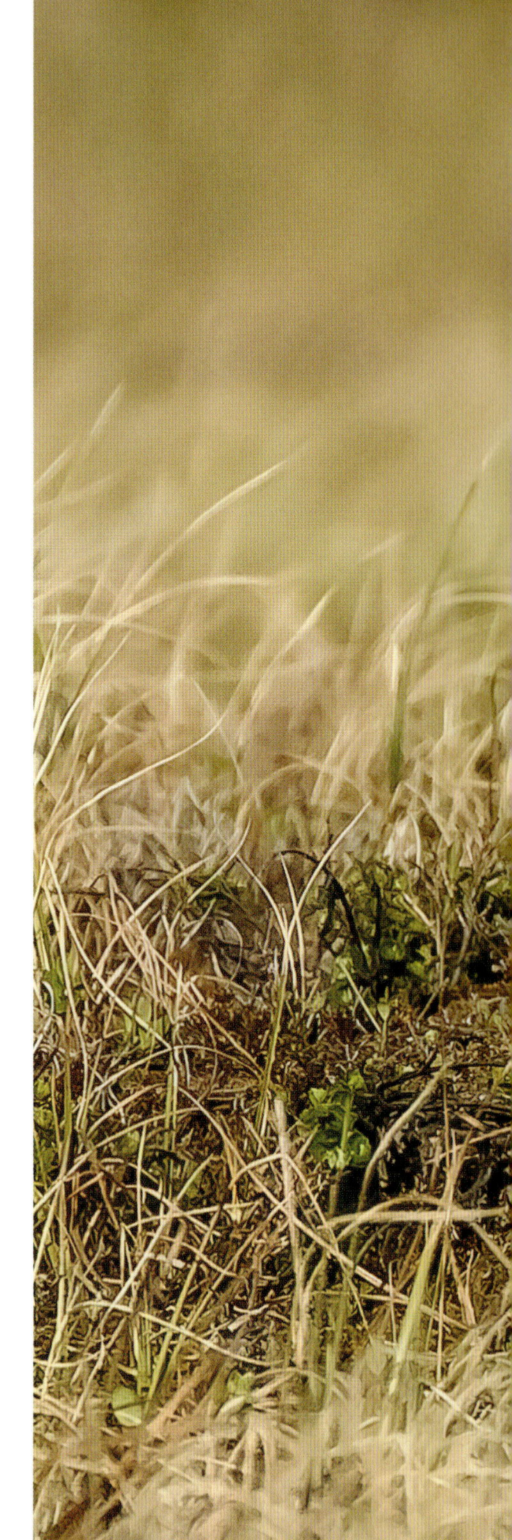

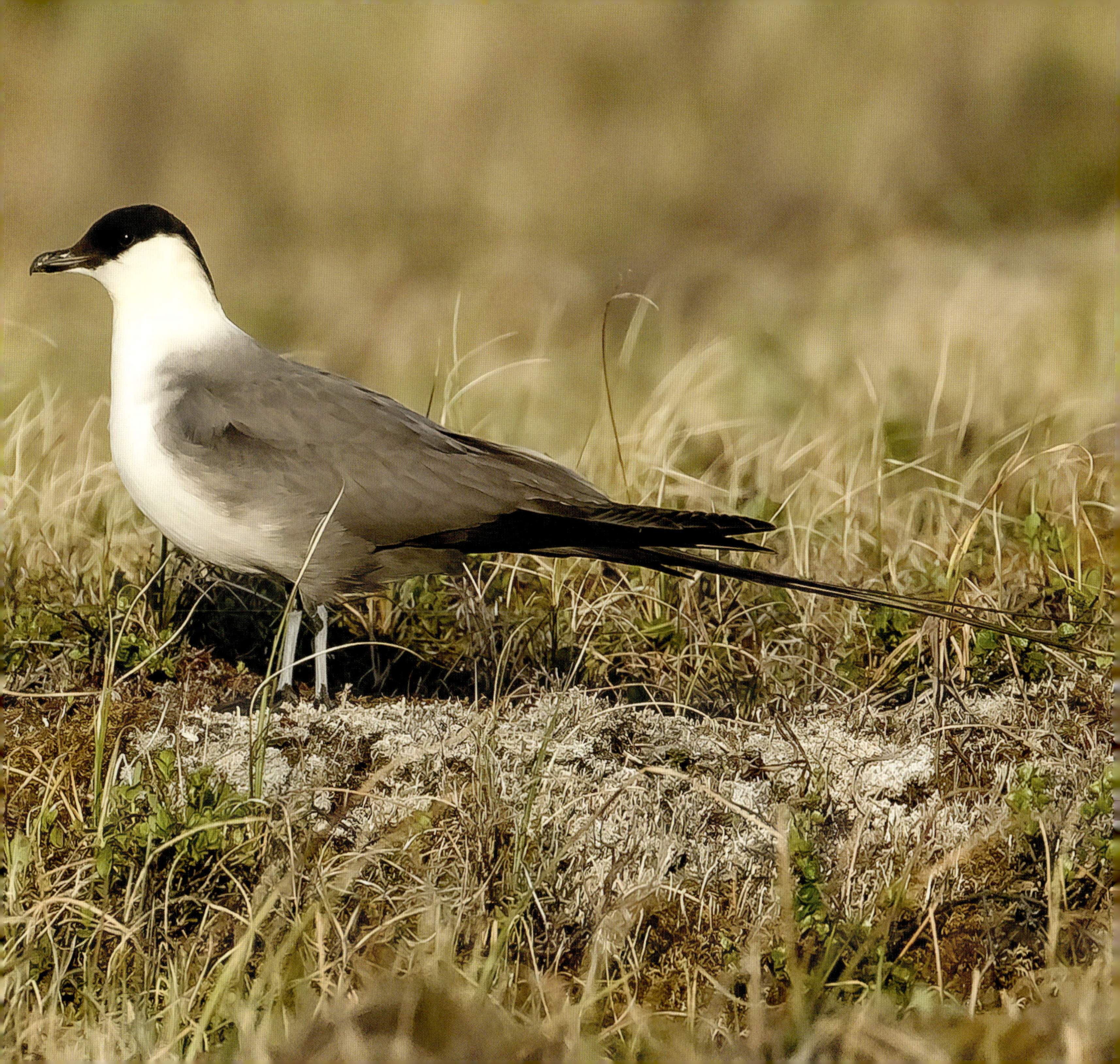

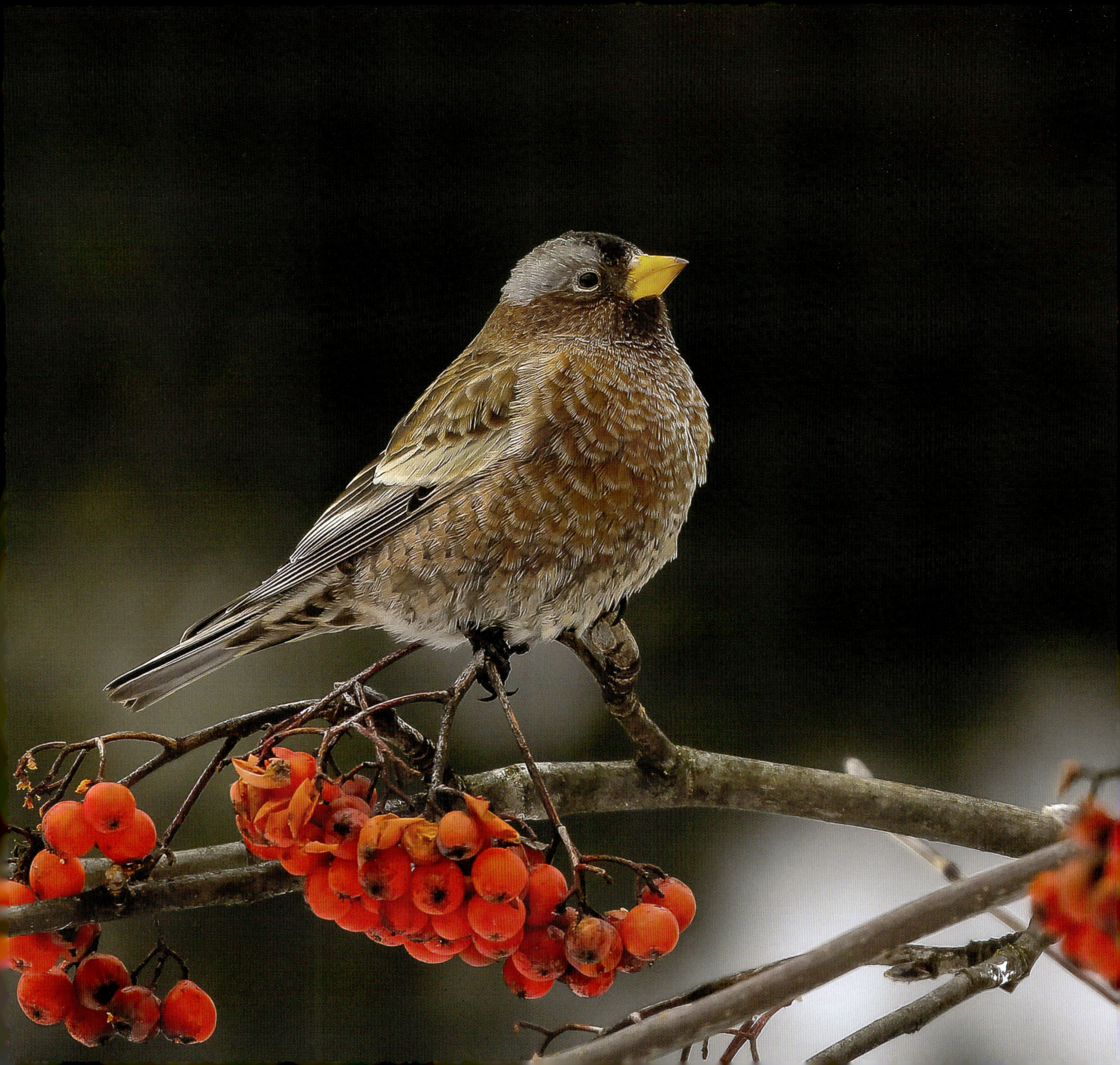

17

How Birds Can Save Us

After my mom died, my heart was broken. When my dad died, I thought I had died too. My whole body hurt. My spirit broke. I couldn't move for many days. I felt numb. I felt pain in my heart like never before. I was bereft without both my parents. The fact that they were gone, and the immediate reality my dad wasn't coming back, hit me like a freight train.

Opposite:

A GRAY-CROWNED ROSY-FINCH WAS ONE OF THE FIRST BIRDS I SAW AFTER MY MOM DIED, AND IT HELPED ME GET THROUGH MY FIRST CHRISTMAS WITHOUT HER. TAKEN IN REVELSTOKE, BC.

My dad got sick quickly. I was talking to him up to two days before he died. The immense weight of losing the most important person left in my life crushed my spirit. I was told I had to be strong for my younger sister, and I knew we had to do so much to settle his estate and would have to pack up and sell his house. I didn't want to go through all the motions again with cold banks and lawyers like we did with my mom. And, unlike with my mother who knew she was sadly terminal, this time nothing was prepared. This was much more stressful. Everything about my current world immediately stopped. The world kept swirling and moving faster than ever. I remember after I left the hospital room when he died. I saw some nurses laughing about something down the hallway, unaware of the pain that had just befallen me in another room. A huge amount of work and stress dropped in my lap when all I wanted to do was grieve, stop moving, and cry about my dad. Unless you have lost someone you loved, you can empathize but can't really understand the magnitude of pain that occurs in one's being. You are changed for life.

Birds saved me. Whenever I felt sad (which was honestly all the time), and when I really couldn't breathe or couldn't stop crying, I would force myself to get outside and watch and listen to birds. I watched them in every season after my parents' passing and they helped me to cope. They brought some peace and uplifting moments into my crushed heart and helped a little

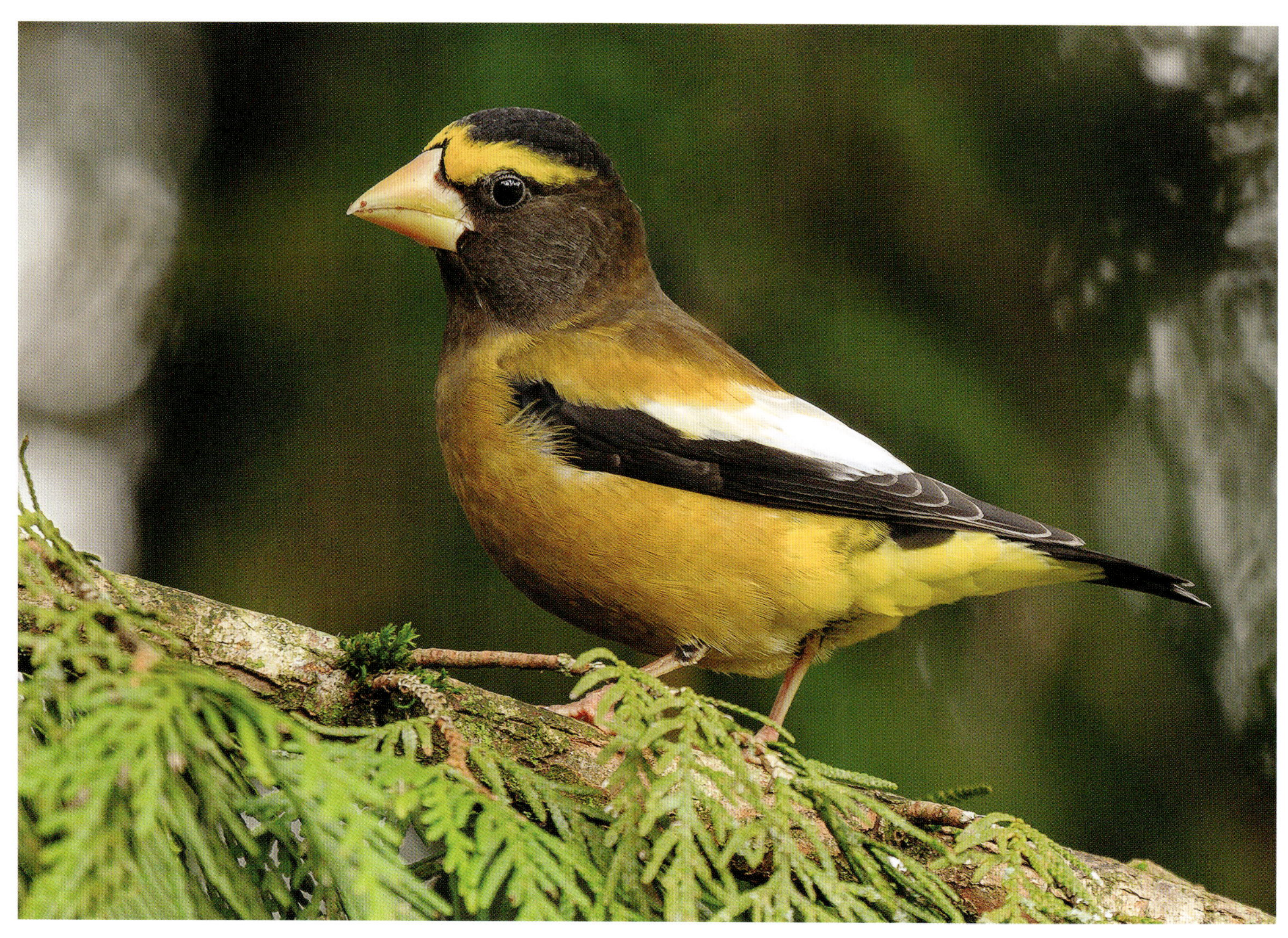

A MALE EVENING GROSBEAK DAZZLED ME IN MAPLE RIDGE, BC.
IN CANADA, EVENING GROSBEAKS HAVE HAD DECLINES OF OVER 80 PER CENT SINCE THE 1970S.

bit with my sadness. They helped me to smile again and to share some lovely moments with friends, young birders, and other important people in my life. As I said earlier in the book, whenever I see a Mountain Bluebird now, I think of my mother who loved them so much, and whenever I see a flock of Snow Geese, I think of my father who adored them. I sure miss watching the geese with him. Birds will always help to ground me and relive memories I shared with my parents, whom I adored and who loved me with a love that was so unfailing it crushes me to never embrace them again. The birds have given me hope and have helped me to survive. So I thank the birds for giving me strength to keep on getting out the door. Despite the trauma and pain, the birds are a light for me in the darkness. They force me to keep fighting for change and to not only survive but thrive.

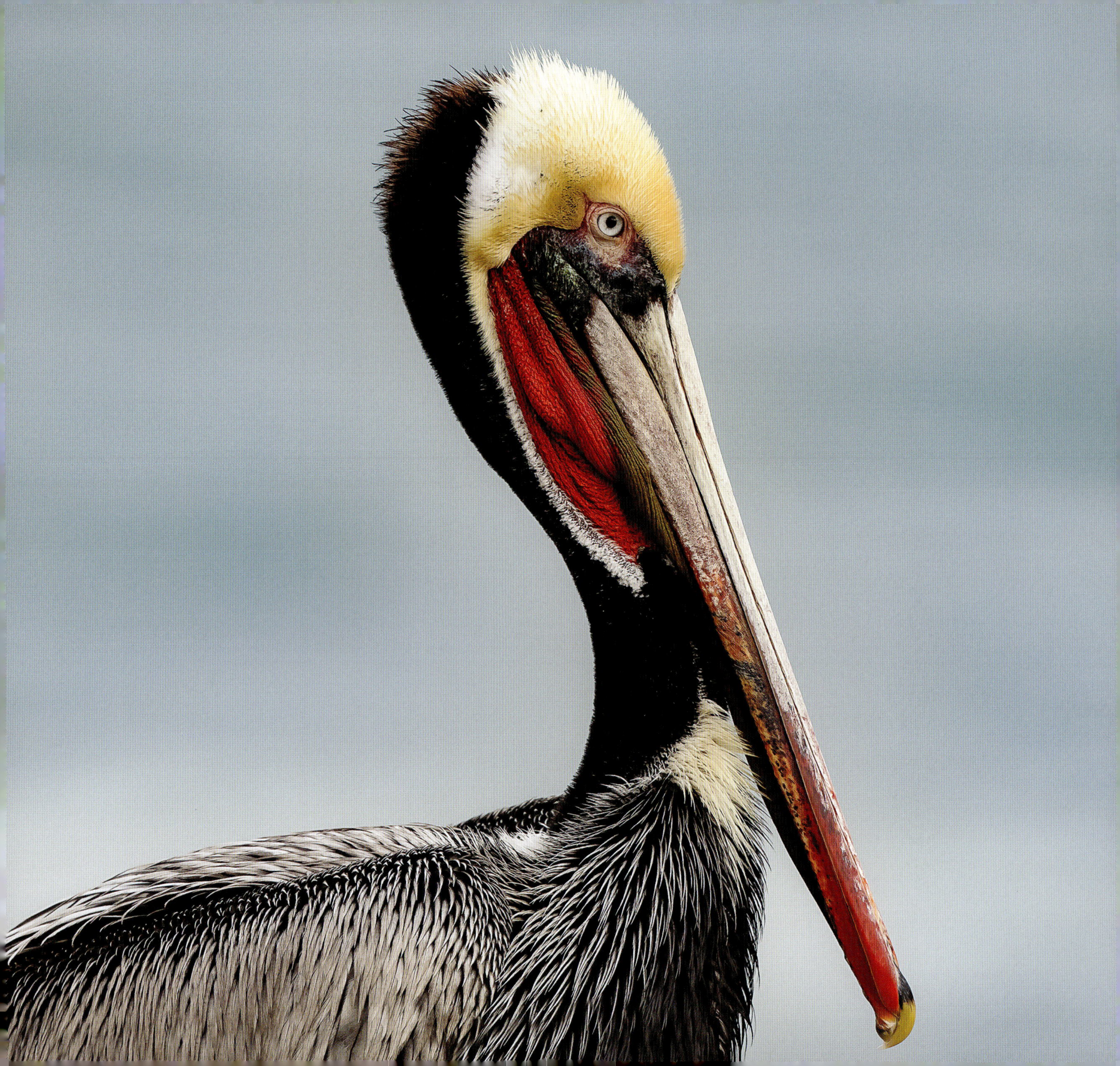

A BROWN PELICAN AT LA JOLLA COVE IN SAN DIEGO, CALIFORNIA, SHOWS OFF HIS STUNNING BREEDING PLUMAGE AND RED-COLOURED GULAR POUCH.

A BELL'S VIREO IN BRACKETTVILLE, TEXAS.

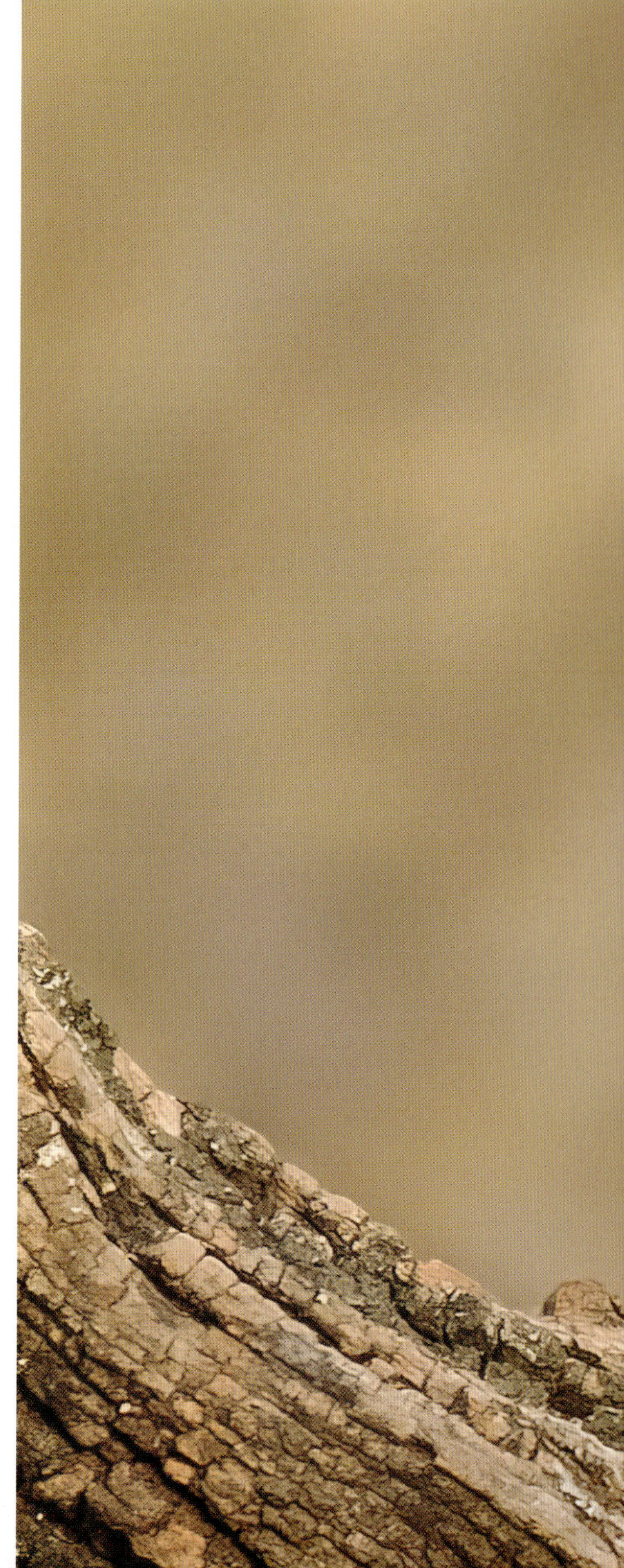

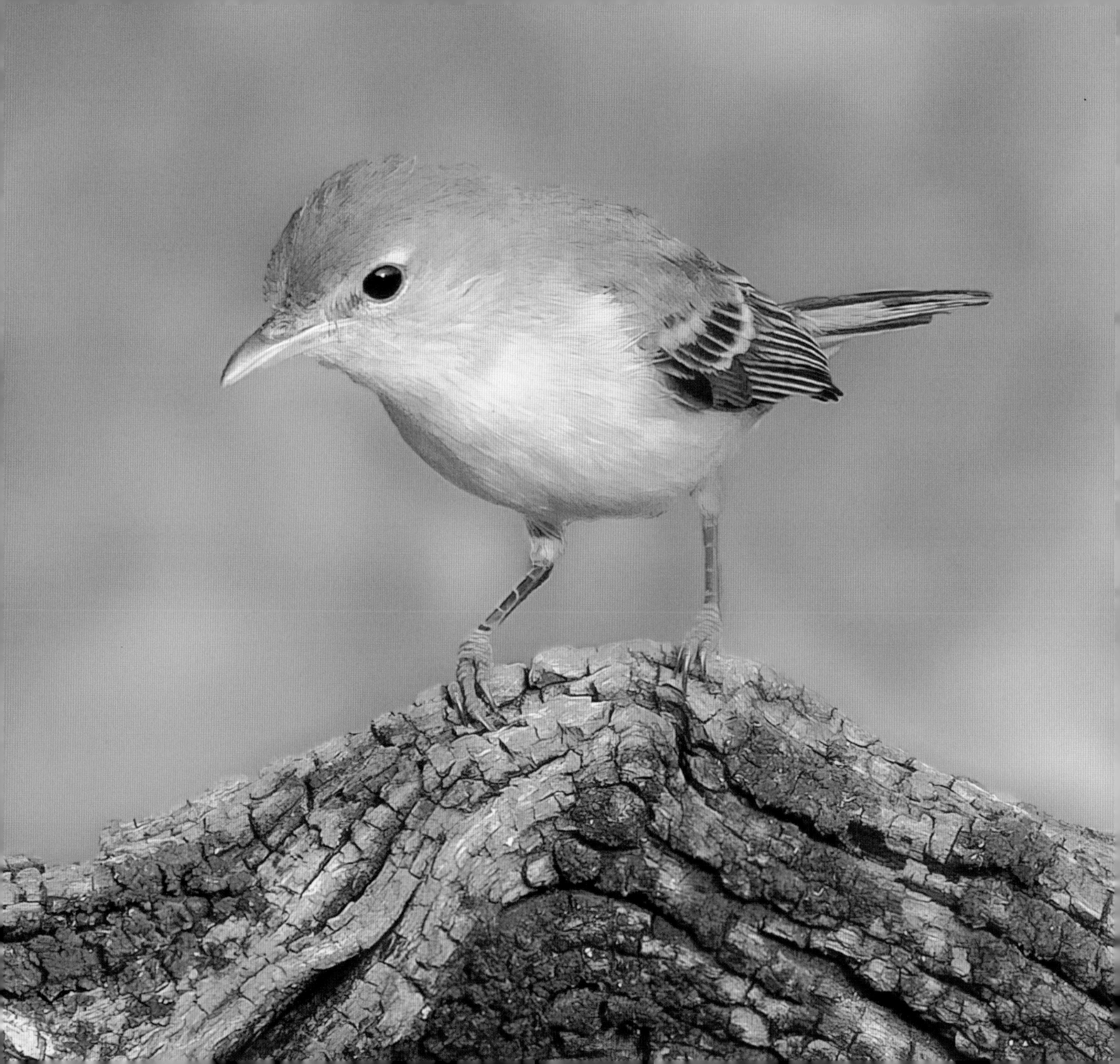

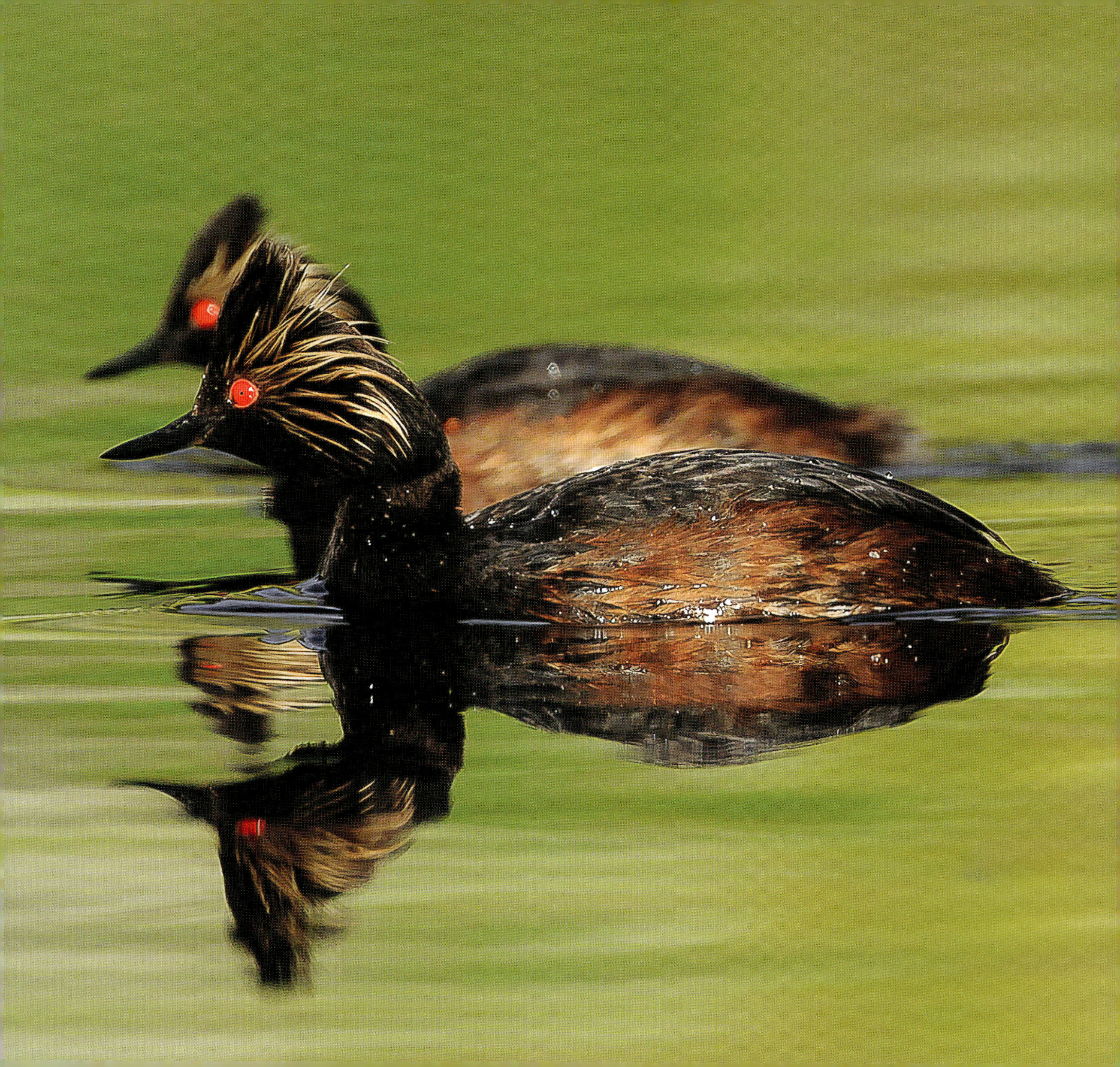

18

Friendship and the Social Aspect of Birding

When you are grieving, much of the time you want to self-isolate because you are so sad and don't want to bring others down. Also, some people just don't understand your deep grief and want to fix you or get you over it. Some say unhelpful comments when they are trying to make you feel better, despite their very good intentions. However, sometimes you really want to get out and be with your friends.

Opposite:

A PAIR OF EARED GREBES GLIDES TOGETHER IN KAMLOOPS, BC.

It's OK to have joy while also carrying immense sadness. The two things can exist together. There are days when I just want to talk about birds and be so-called normal again. On these days, I just want to look at birds in the company of good friends. I am lucky to have met many good friends in BC. During my travels, I have enjoyed meeting birders from across the province. As an eBird reviewer for several areas in BC, I am so grateful to the birders who take the time to submit their sightings to eBird and participate in citizen science to help protect and track birds.

Many people are working hard to protect the natural areas in their regions and have specific concerns about the birds there. There are close communities of birders who are doing great work here and in all provinces and states in North America, as well as around the world. This is one hobby that allows young people to connect with the elderly and vice versa. You can do birding at any age and make long-lasting friendships with people of all ages. I find that to be a unique and beautiful thing about birding. You will be hard-pressed to find more empathetic and caring people than birders.

One of the best things I have got out of birding is the friendships and great people I've met during my life. Not only here in BC but also the lifelong friends I've met in the rest of Canada, the United States, and around the world. I look forward to meeting more birders in my journeys throughout my life through this incredible pastime.

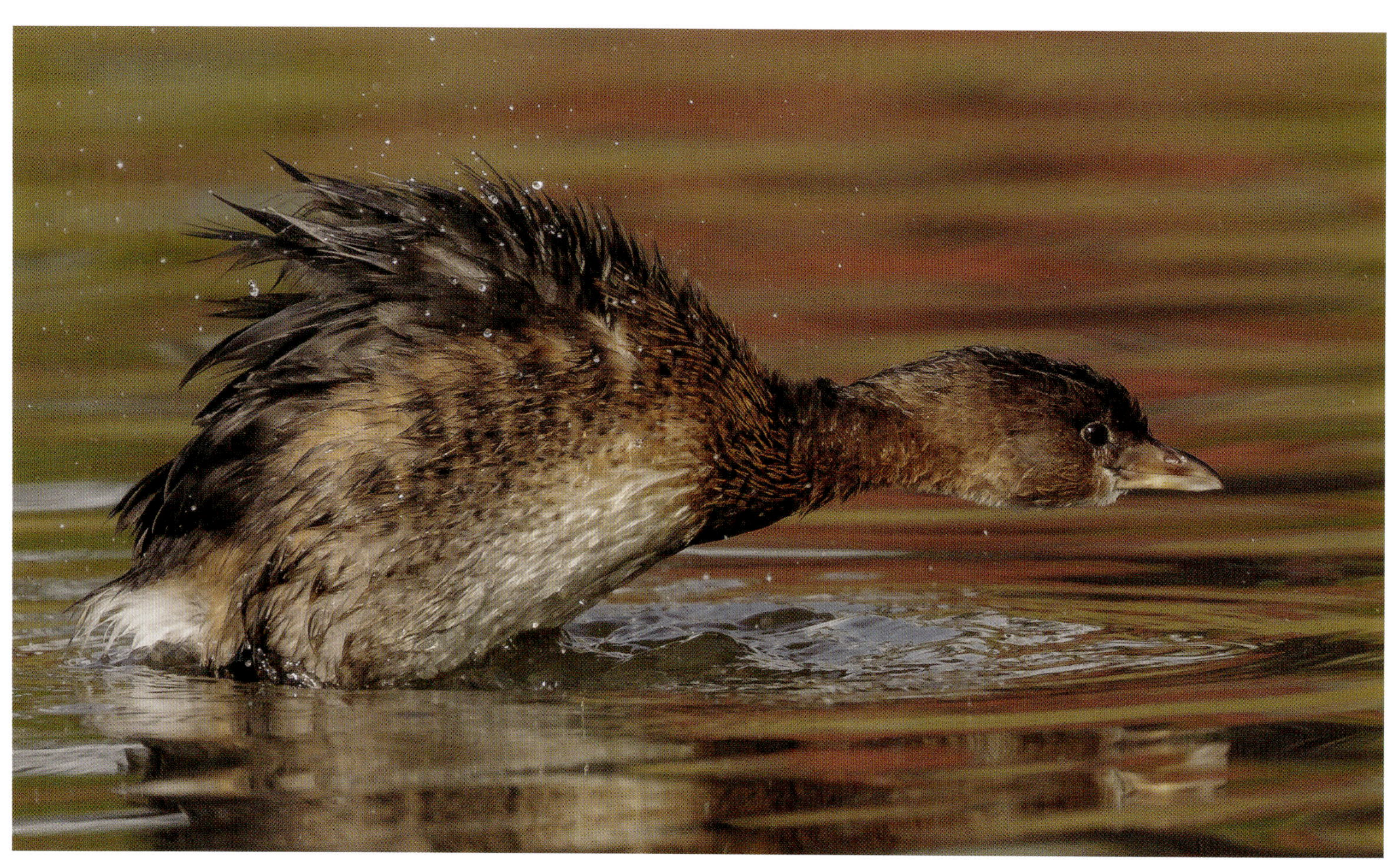

A PIED-BILLED GREBE GETS READY TO DIVE FOR A FISH IN LANGLEY, BC.

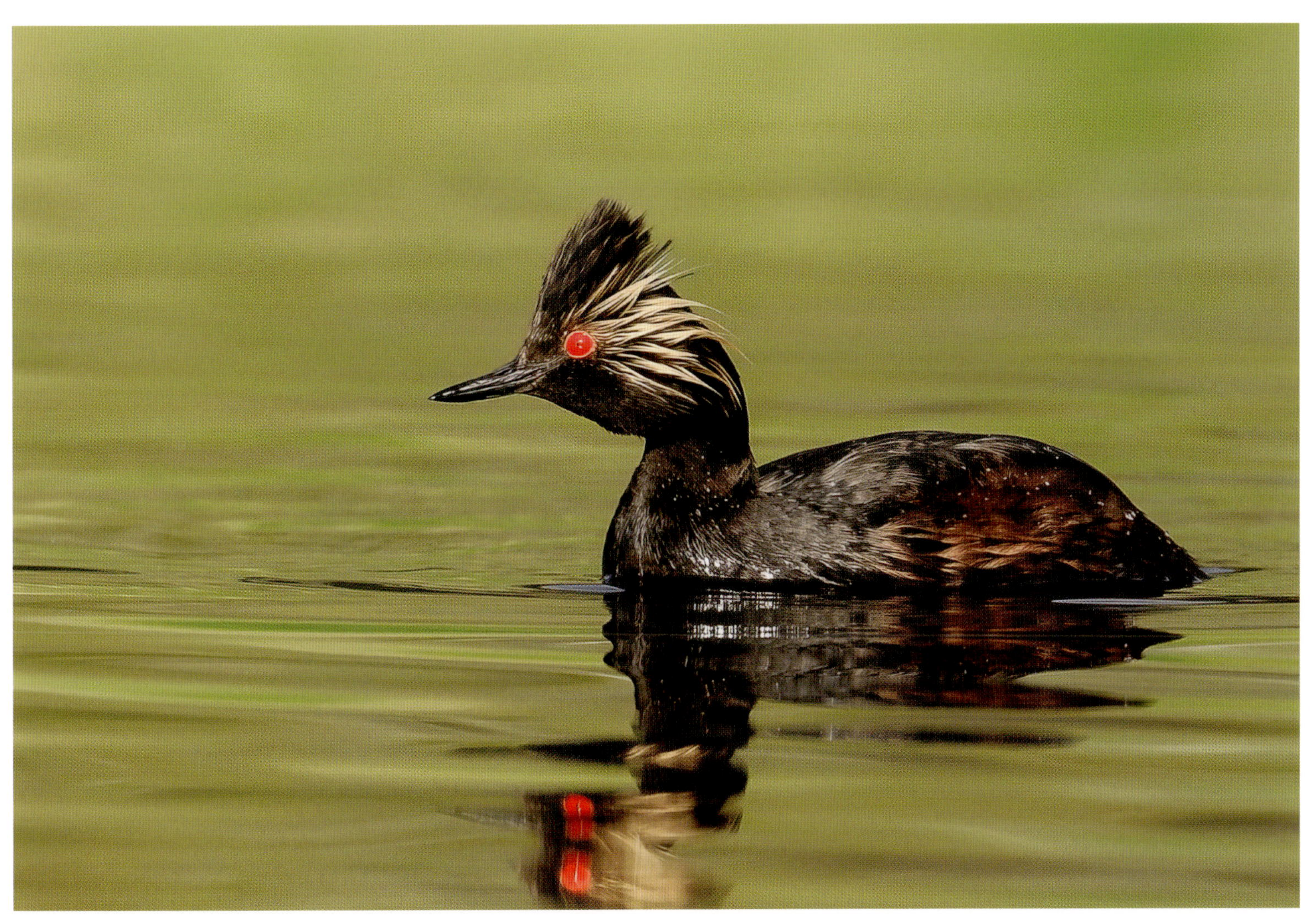

AN EARED GREBE GETS READY TO DO A COURTSHIP DISPLAY IN KAMLOOPS, BC.

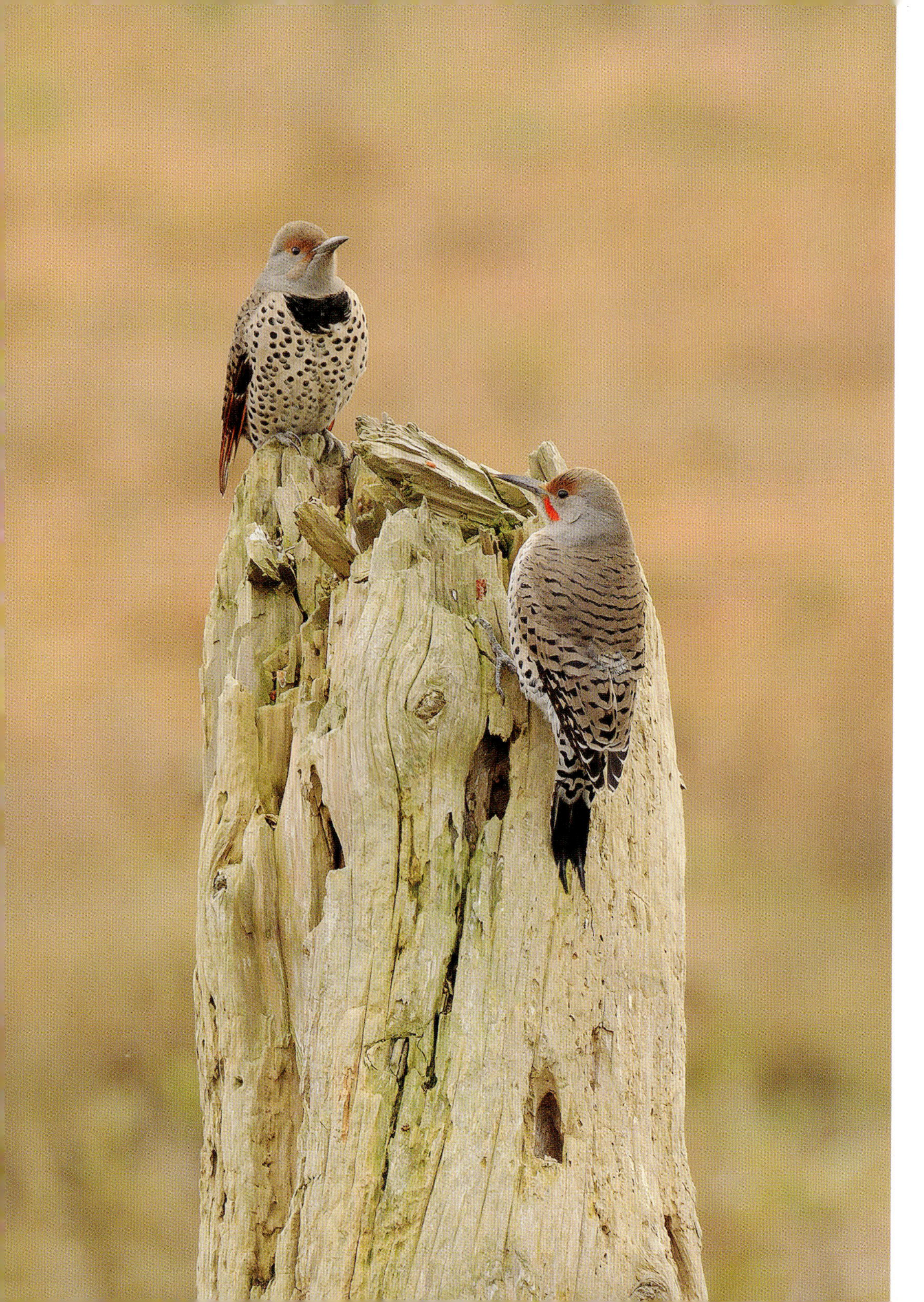

Left:

A PAIR OF NORTHERN FLICKERS CHECKS OUT A LOG IN DELTA, BC.

Right:

A MOUNTAIN CHICKADEE POSES FOR ME IN SISTERS, OREGON.

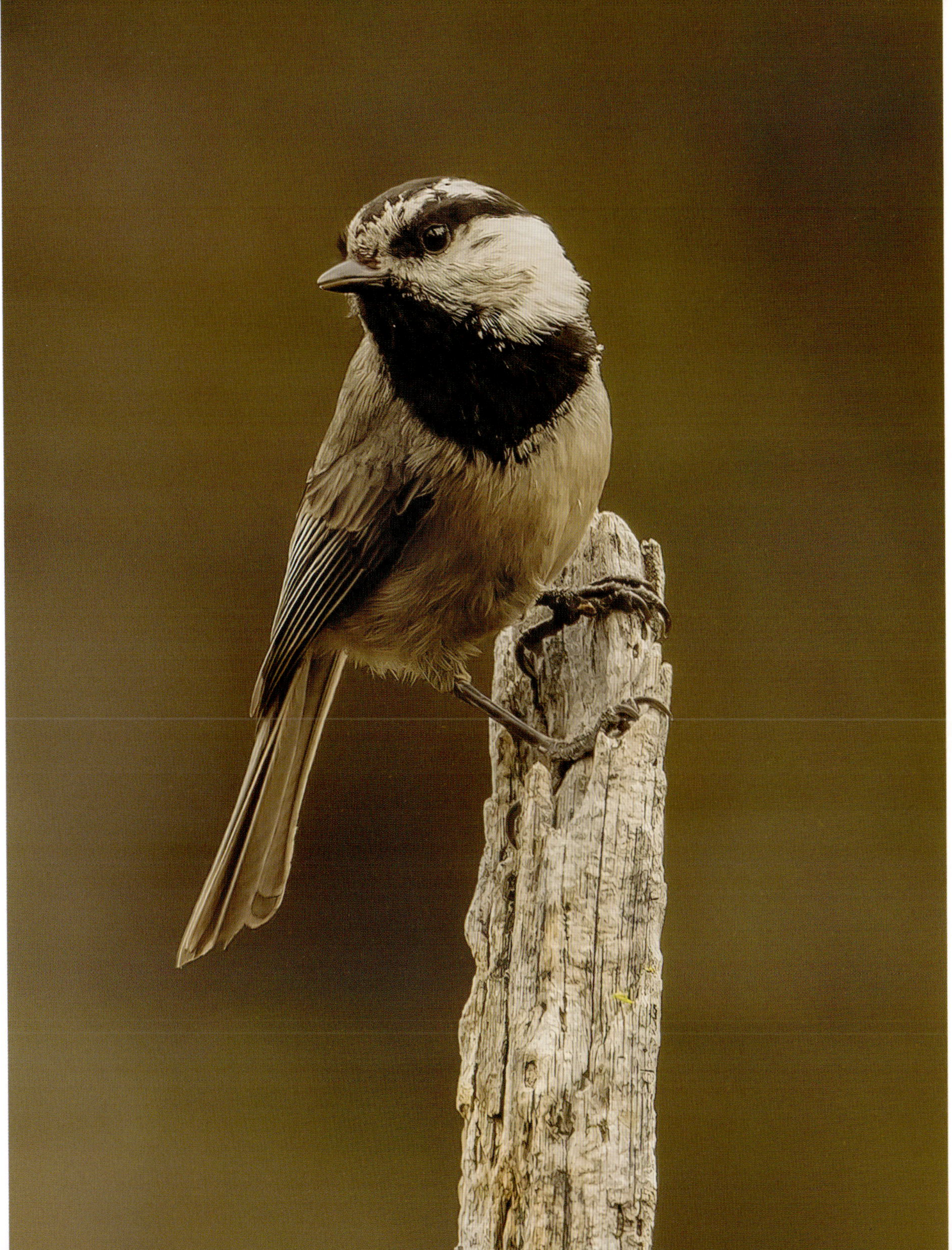

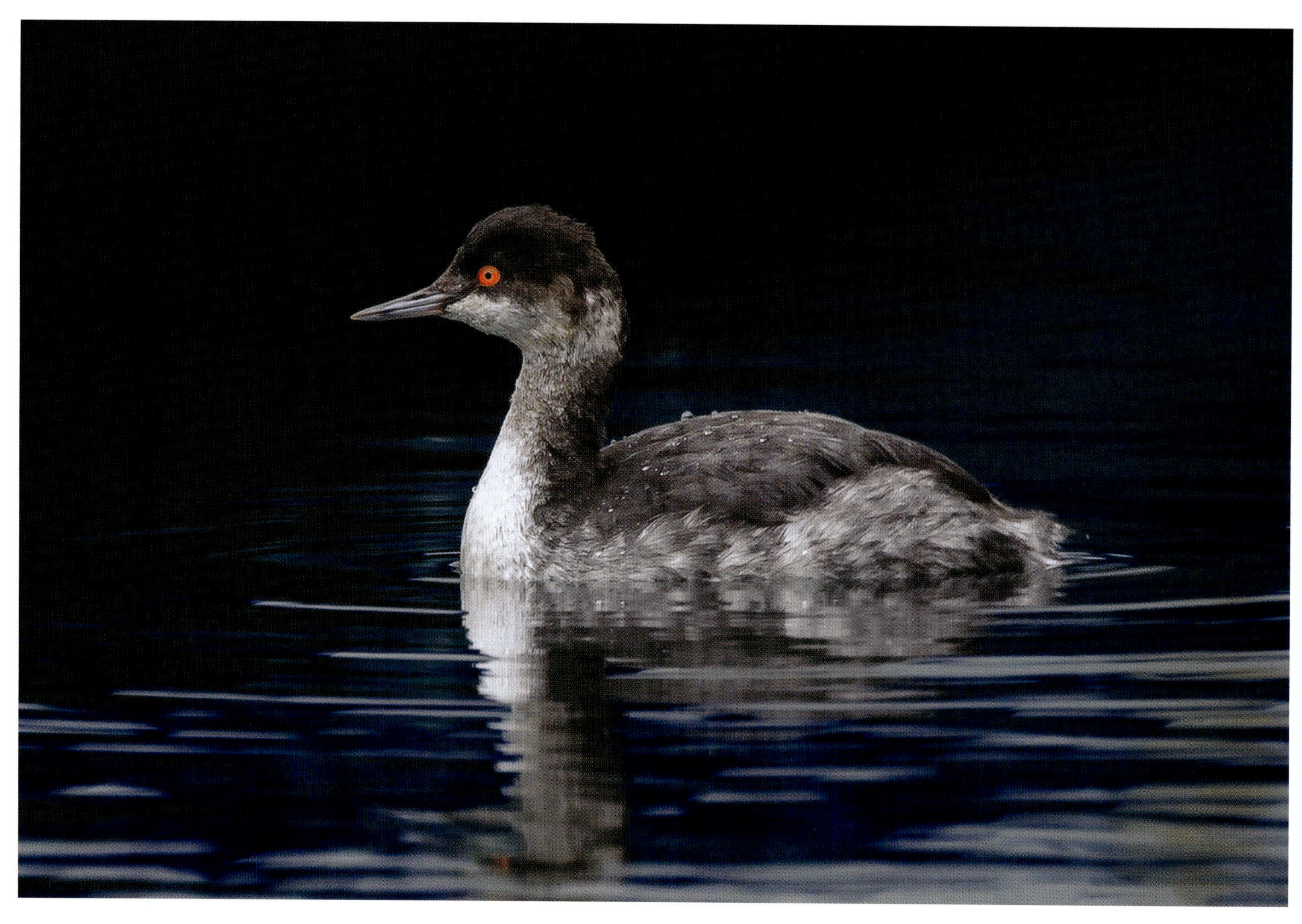

Above and opposite:

AN EARED GREBE IN NONBREEDING PLUMAGE SWIMS IN THE HARBOUR AT GRANVILLE ISLAND IN VANCOUVER, BC.

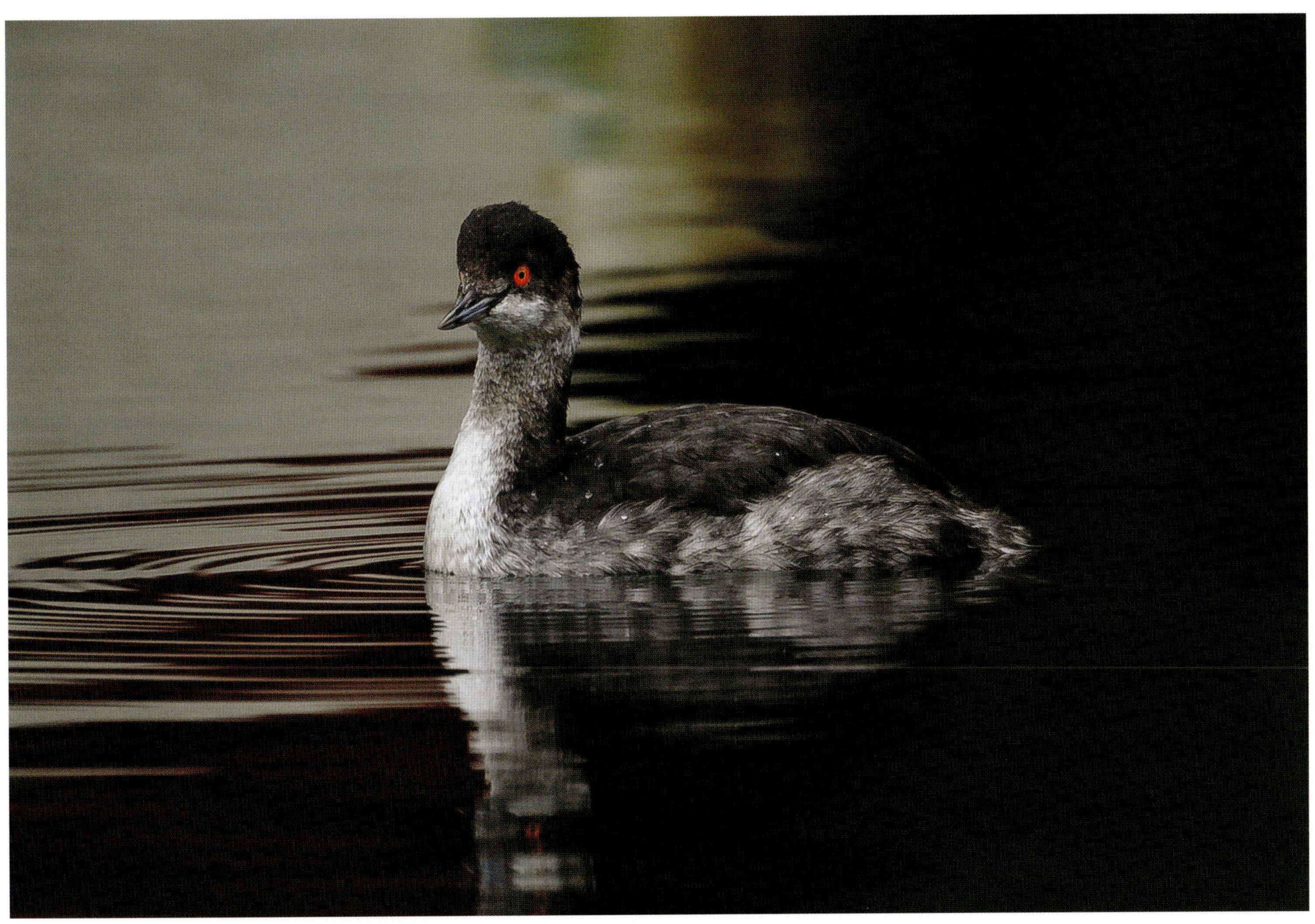

A PHAINOPEPLA IN PALM SPRINGS, CALIFORNIA.

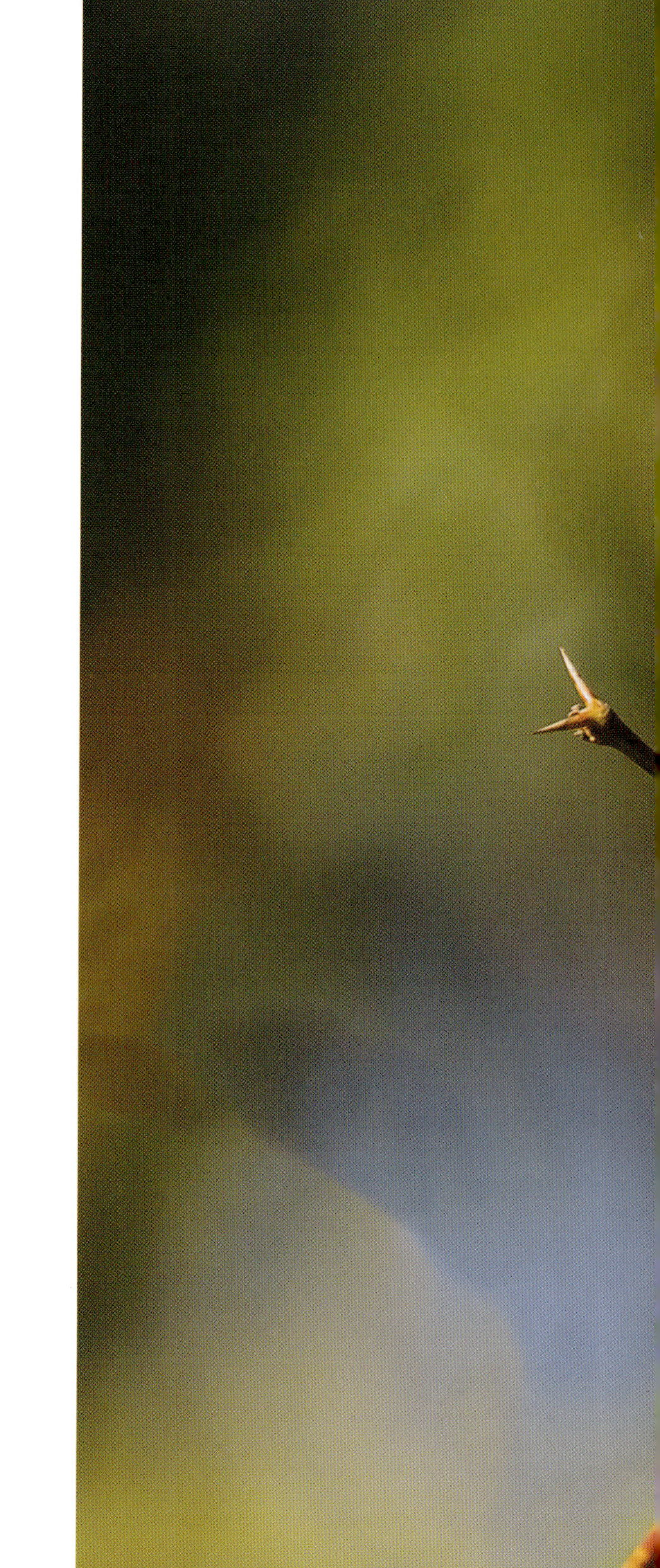

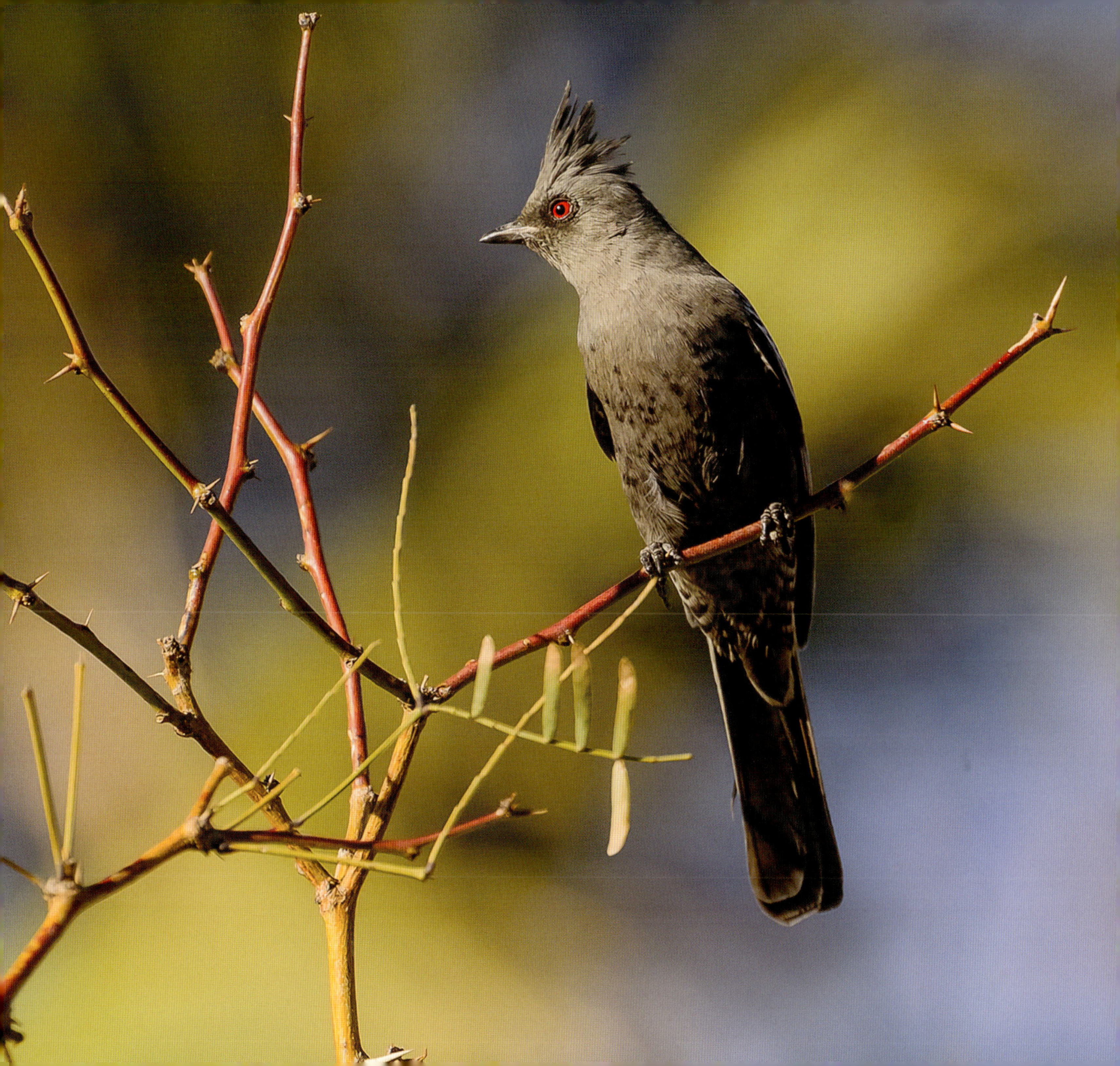

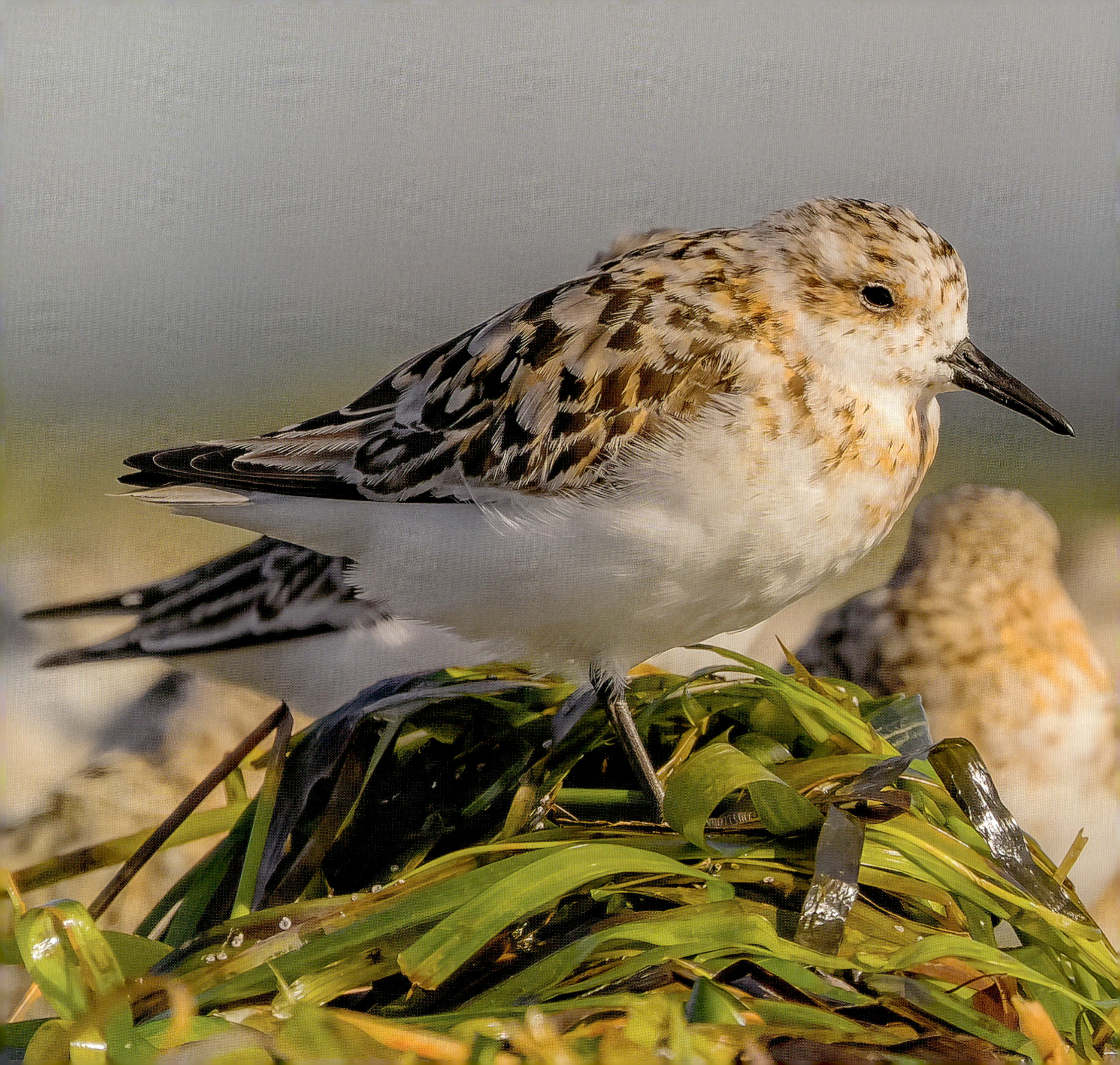

19

Birding with a Dog

A lot of birders do not like dogs in birding areas. There are some places dogs should never go. For example, taking your dog to mudflats where shorebirds need to refuel, feed, and rest on migration is not good, or where large flocks of migratory waterfowl like Brant Geese rest. Too often I see unleashed dogs running through these flocks and constantly flushing them.

Opposite:

A SANDERLING IN POINT ROBERTS, WASHINGTON.

Dogs should always be kept on leash and under control where they are permitted in birding areas. If you have a well-trained dog and take them where their presence is legally allowed, it can be really good. Dogs offer protection, especially as a BIPOC woman hiking alone in the mountains or in lonely areas. They can alert you to danger. Dogs should always be on lead when hiking in bear or cougar country. Dogs get you out to exercise, and if you can bird at the same time as you walk the dog, it's a win-win for both parties.

Dogs can also help prevent loneliness. Since I lost both of my parents, my dog Pipit (named after the American Pipit) has really helped me to keep going. I have had dogs most of my life and have trained them not to chase birds. I used to have a Border Collie–Blue Heeler cross named Sammy who would go out and help me find Common Nighthawk nests. She would gently lie down and point to where the nest was with her nose and never once flushed a bird. She would also find roosting nighthawks. I know that was rare, and I miss that dog every day. A Border Collie is generally thought to have a high prey drive, but not this dog. Even so-called high-prey-drive dogs can be trained to respect and not chase or kill birds, which Sammy proved. Honestly, I think there are no bad dogs, only bad dog owners – it's all about how you train your dog.

There are many situations where even a well-trained dog's presence can scare off a bird. Never bring dogs to an area where threatened shorebirds like Snowy Plovers nest. Their mere presence can cause chicks

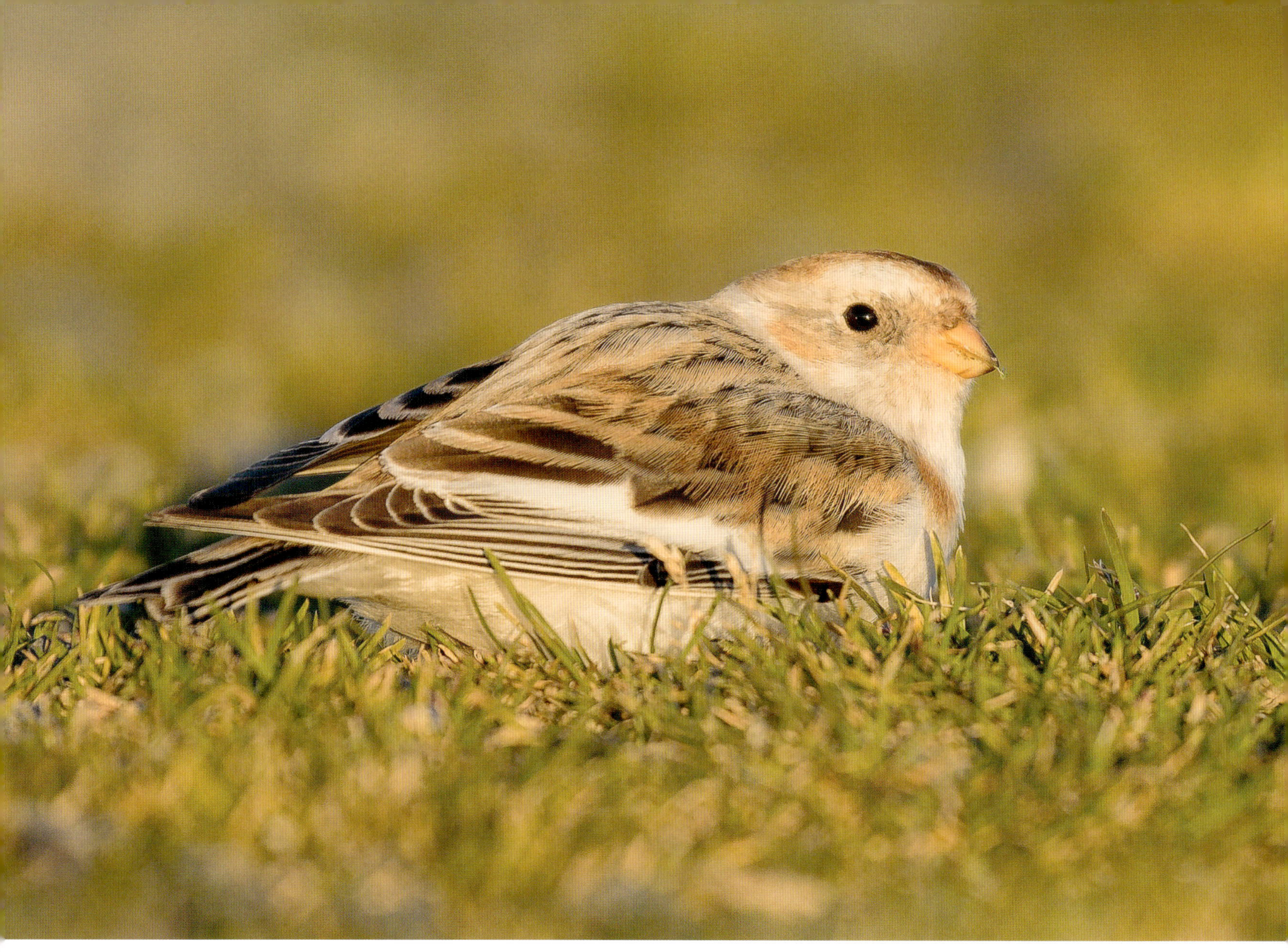

I'VE SEEN MANY SNOW BUNTINGS WITH MY PUP PIPIT. TAKEN IN DELTA, BC.

to be separated from parents, resulting in them being picked off and killed by other predators. Don't take dogs to areas where endangered or sensitive species are breeding. I have watched dogs catch and kill young geese and grouse and this is never to be tolerated.

A well-known birder named Laura Erickson wrote an article titled "Training a Good Birding Dog" about how she birds with her dog and the ways birders can train their dogs to respect birds. You don't want a dog barking at and scaring birds or people, or having them jump on people. It may be funny to dog lovers, but not everyone loves your dog and some people are scared of dogs from past experiences. When you go birding with a dog, you must make sure you are responsible by only bringing your dog to birding areas where it is legally permitted to do so. You must have good control of your dog. It's also important that you clean up after your dog to keep the environment as unspoiled as possible.

If you like to chase rare birds and would like some company, why not bring your dog? Of course, you will need to make more pit stops when you have a dog and are driving long distances, but you may find the benefits outweigh the small inconveniences. Dogs and cats can really help with loneliness and grief. They certainly have for me. I own both, and they have brought warmth and purpose. Now, when you embark on long-term, overseas birding trips that is a downside. You will need to kennel your dog or find someone to home-sit, which can be costly.

When I am birding seriously with my dog, I use a hand-free leash tied to my waist so I can use my hands for holding my binoculars. I have found birding with a dog to be especially good on days I want to do casual, relaxed birding. I wouldn't take him on a big day or all-day birding; it just wouldn't be fair to the dog, and, to be frank, I'd see a lot less. Often, though, especially when one is grieving, you just want to be alone with your thoughts. So often I go to the beach, especially to one of my favourite spots in Point Roberts, Washington, where I would often go with my parents, and just sit with my dog and watch the water birds on the ocean. I watch the tranquility of the tide ebbing and flowing and the Sanderlings running on the beach and it brings me peace and tranquility.

I've started to keep a fun life list for my dog, detailing the birds he has seen with me, as well as the important moments we've shared together. One day, we went to a dog-friendly beach in the winter and watched an owl roosting on the logs at sunset. It was a moment with him I won't soon forget. He laid his head on my lap and I watched the owl till dark. It was a cold, wintry day and no one was about. I shed some tears because I wished my dad was with me, but now that I think about it, I think he was there beside Pipit and me, watching with us, and perhaps he brought the owl to me.

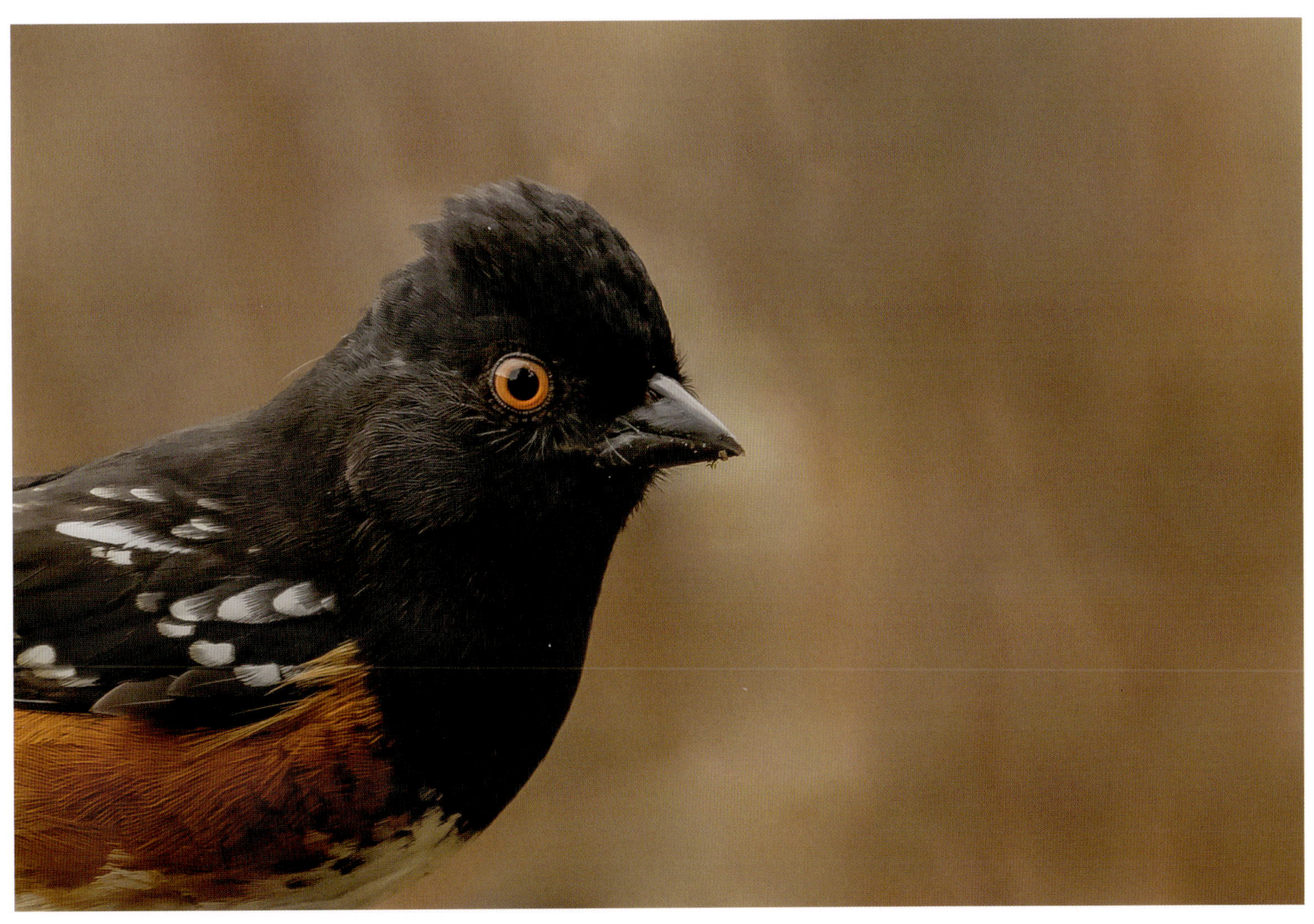

SEEING A SPOTTED TOWHEE IS PRETTY COMMONPLACE IN VANCOUVER AND IS SEEN ON ALMOST EVERY OUTING WITH MY DOG. TAKEN IN VANCOUVER, BC.

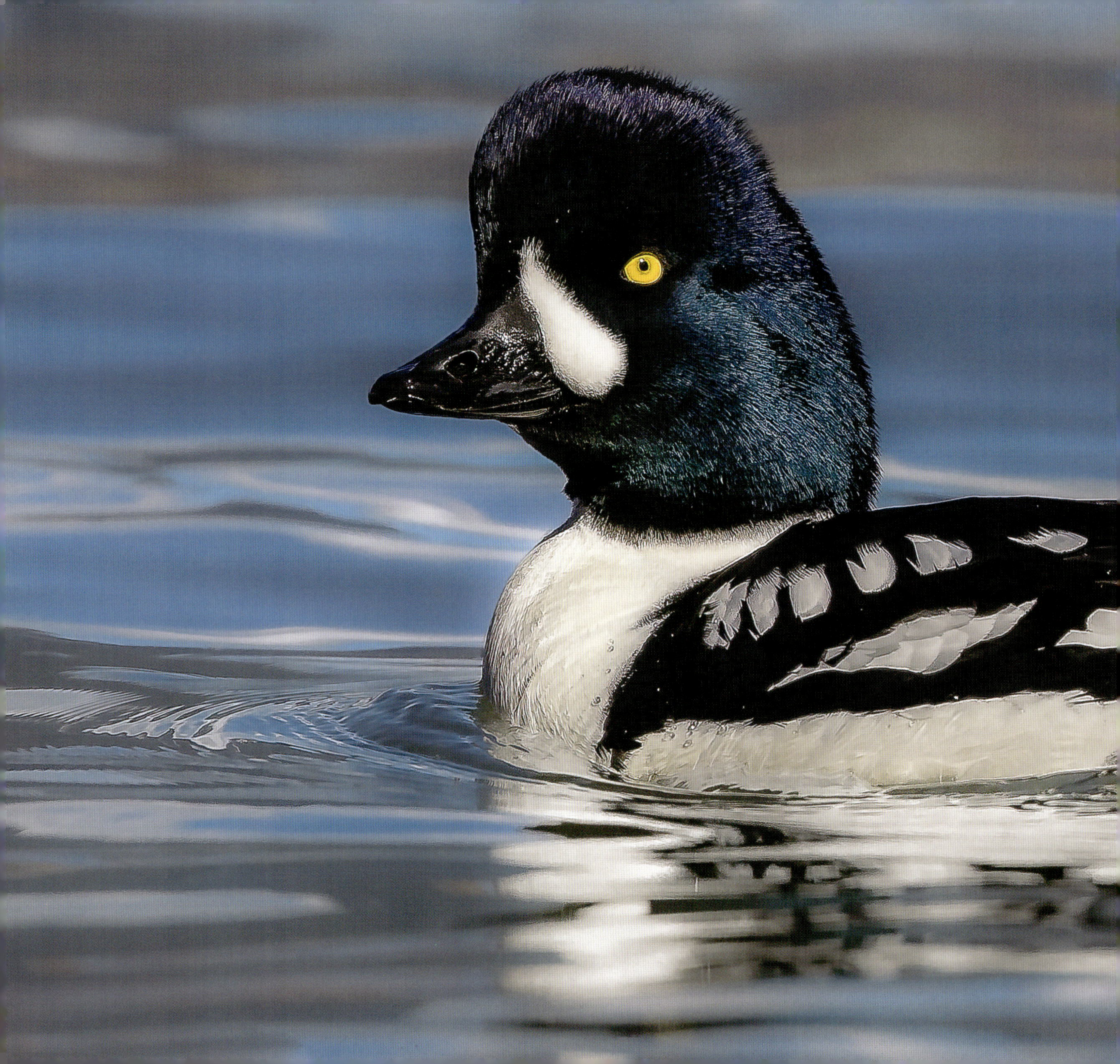

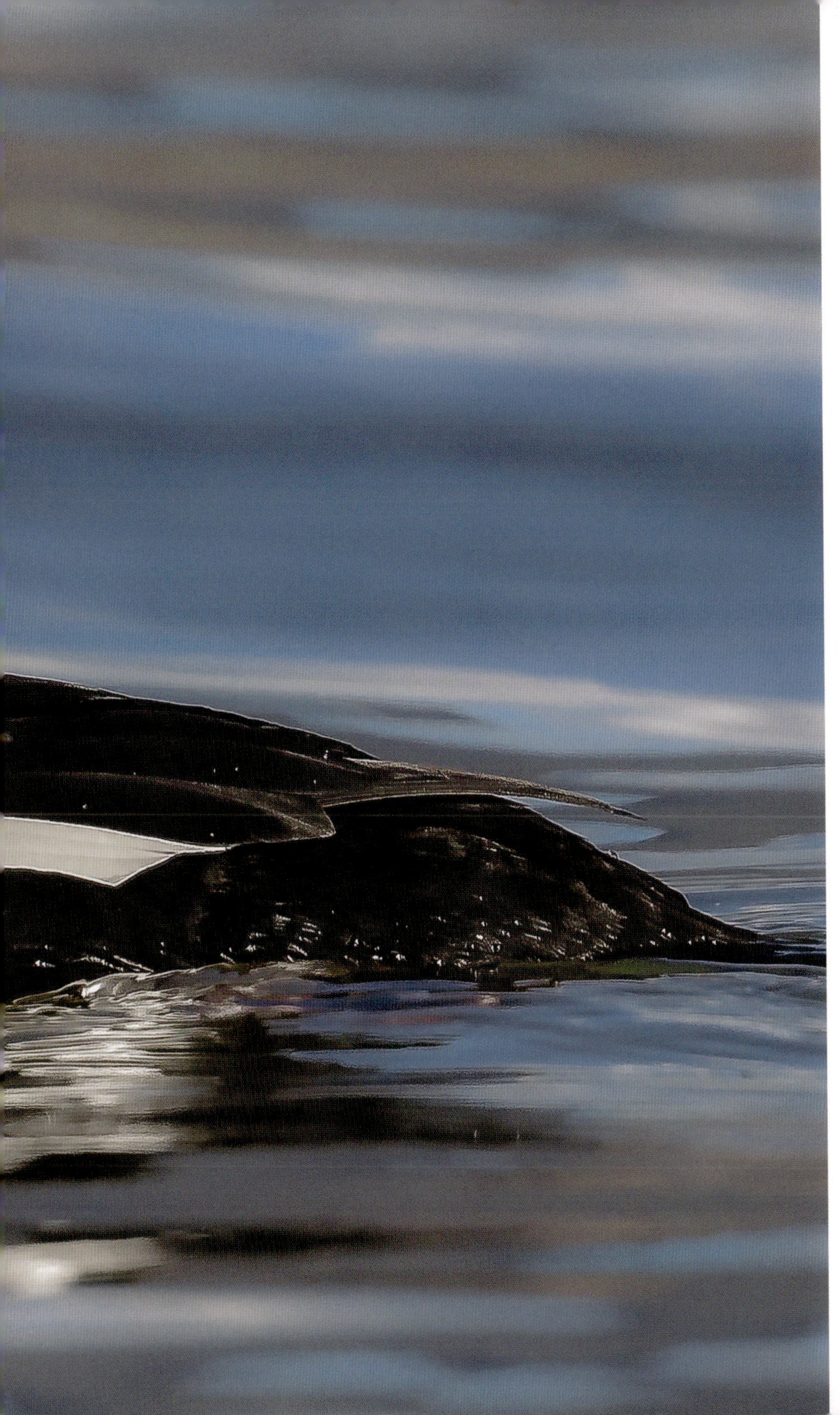

I LOVE TO SIT BY THE OCEAN AND WATCH BARROW'S GOLDENEYES, LIKE THIS DRAKE IN THE WINTER, WITH MY DOG. TAKEN AT STANLEY PARK IN VANCOUVER, BC.

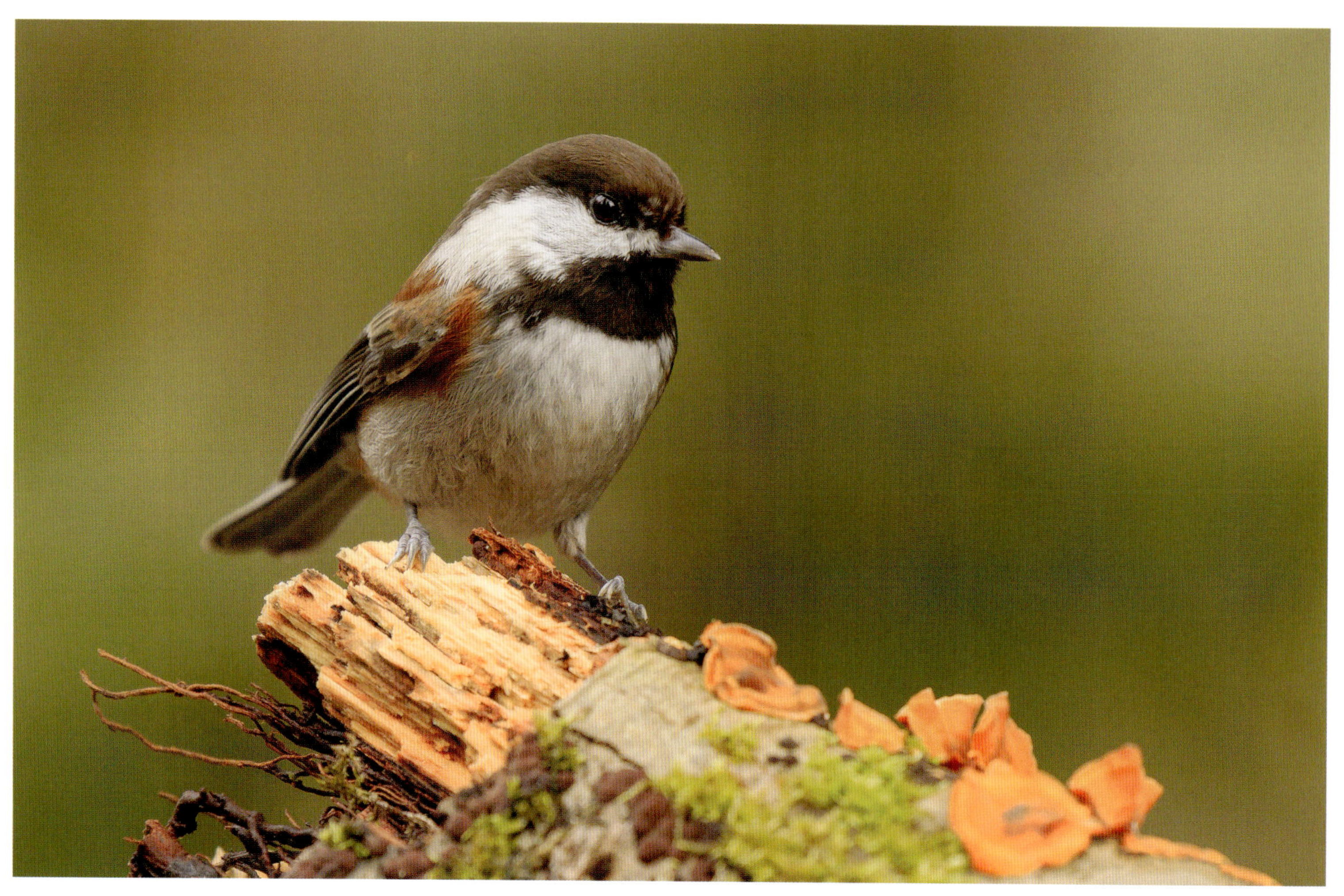

Above and opposite:

A CUTE CHESTNUT-BACKED CHICKADEE IS OFTEN SEEN ON WALKS WITH MY PUP IN VANCOUVER, BC.

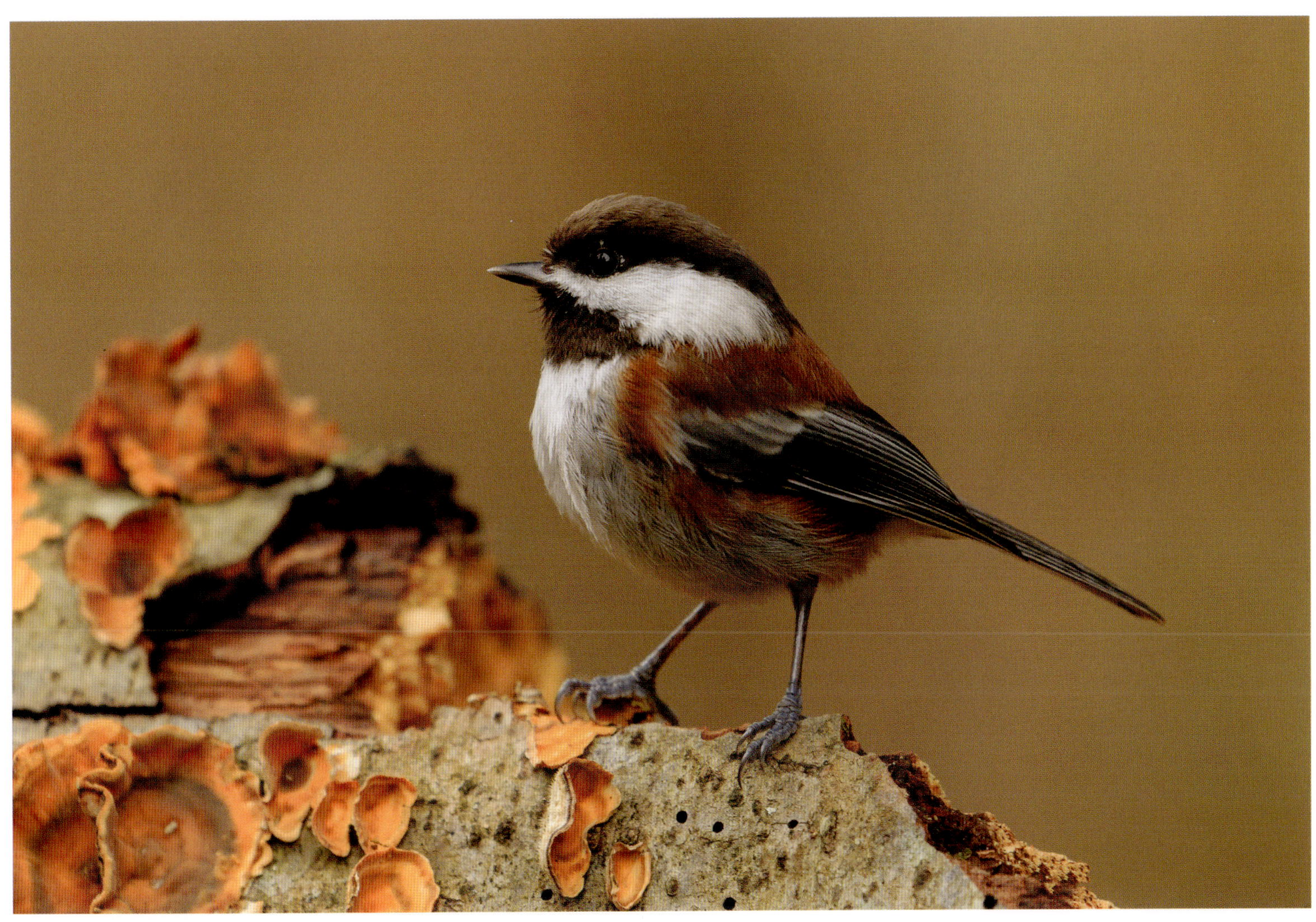

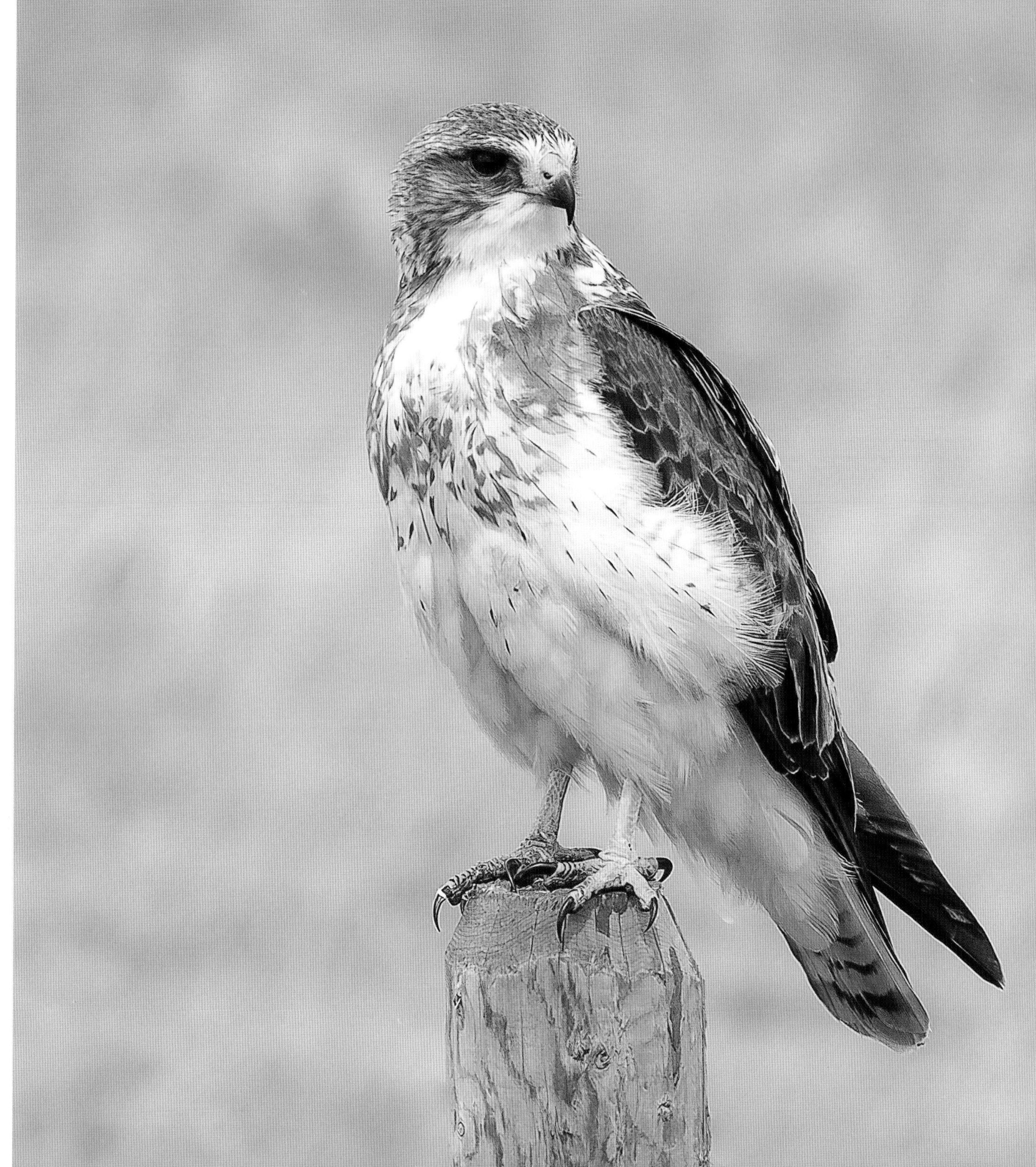

CAR BIRDING AND SEEING RAPTORS LIKE THIS SWAINSON'S HAWK ON A POST IN MEDICINE HAT, ALBERTA, IS A GREAT WAY TO BIRD WITH A DOG FOR COMPANY.

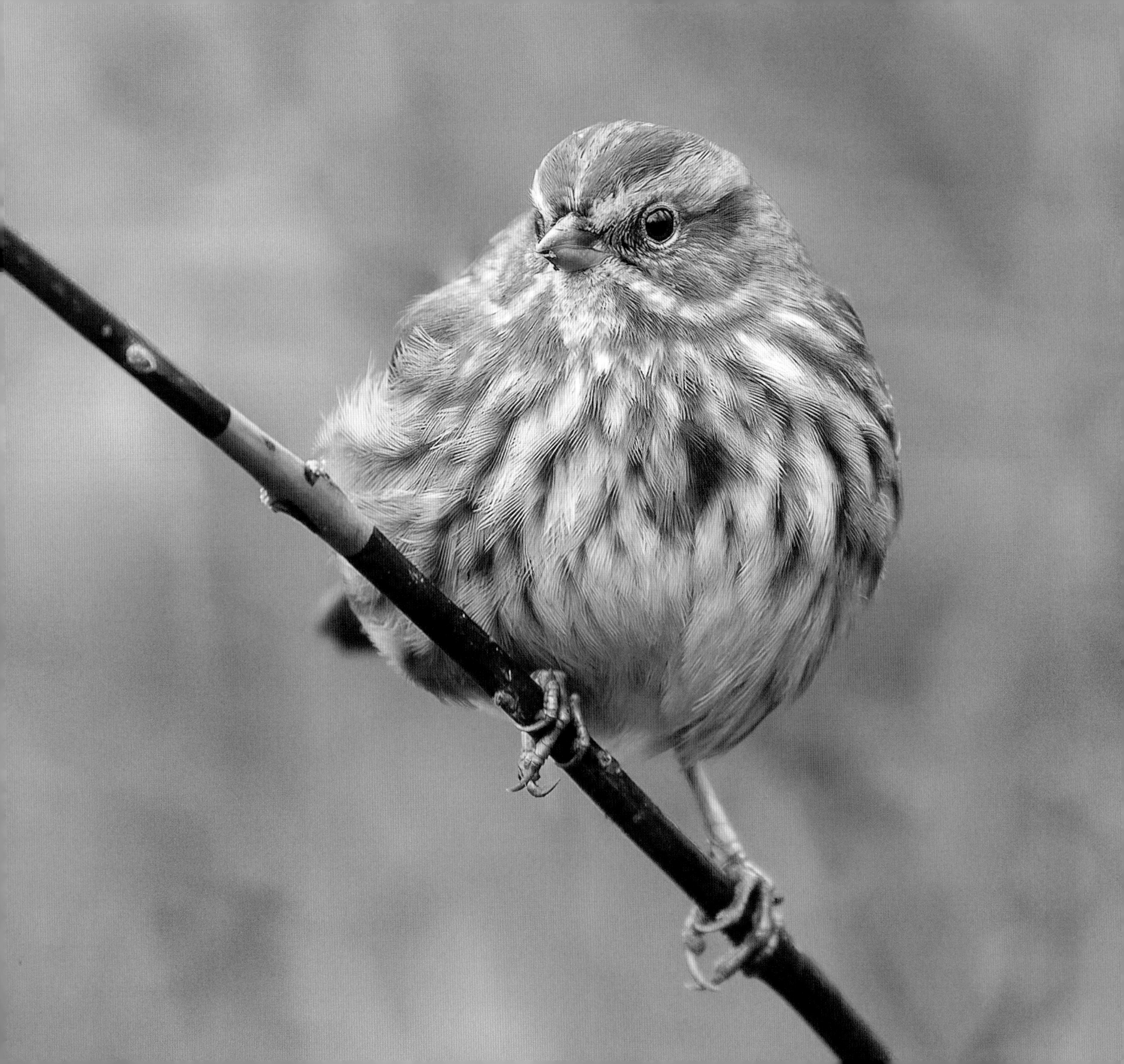

20

Hope

Birds give us hope. When we look up and see them in flight, it inspires freedom. They lift us up when we are feeling down. Just like us, birds go through trauma and loss. They must go through long, arduous migrations. They must withstand storms, fight for survival on their breeding grounds, and surmount an ever-changing warming climate. They must survive great difficulty, as we humans must. As I said earlier, we are all connected.

Opposite:

A SONG SPARROW MAY BE KNOWN AS A "LITTLE BROWN JOB," BUT IT EXPRESSES SO MUCH BEAUTY WITH ITS VOICE. TAKEN IN DELTA, BC.

Birds force us to examine our lives. To try and live our best lives and get as much out of them as possible, for as long as we can. When you are a BIPOC birder like myself, you need to fight for equality and inclusion. All of us need to fight for protection for the birds. The more people who feel included in birding, the more people there will be to protect and care for the birds.

After I lost my parents, I would go outside and not be able to see any beauty. The skies were darker, the world felt colder, but when a bird appeared, it helped me to see there was still some light.

Birds help us to understand ourselves better, to focus on what is truly important to us. They help us to put things into perspective. When we watch birds with genuine awe, we see the beauty that is all around us. If we all loved birds, it would surely be a better place. With more young birders joining my young birder program, and seeing more and more people join the hobby during the pandemic, I have great hope in my heart for more people getting passionate about birds, and in turn passionate about protecting their critical habitats.

Birds help us to discover new places and people and bring new wonders into our lives. The exciting spark of electricity of not knowing what new bird is around the next corner during travel or our everyday lives is what keeps me going.

When we watch birds, we discover new things about them, but we also discover

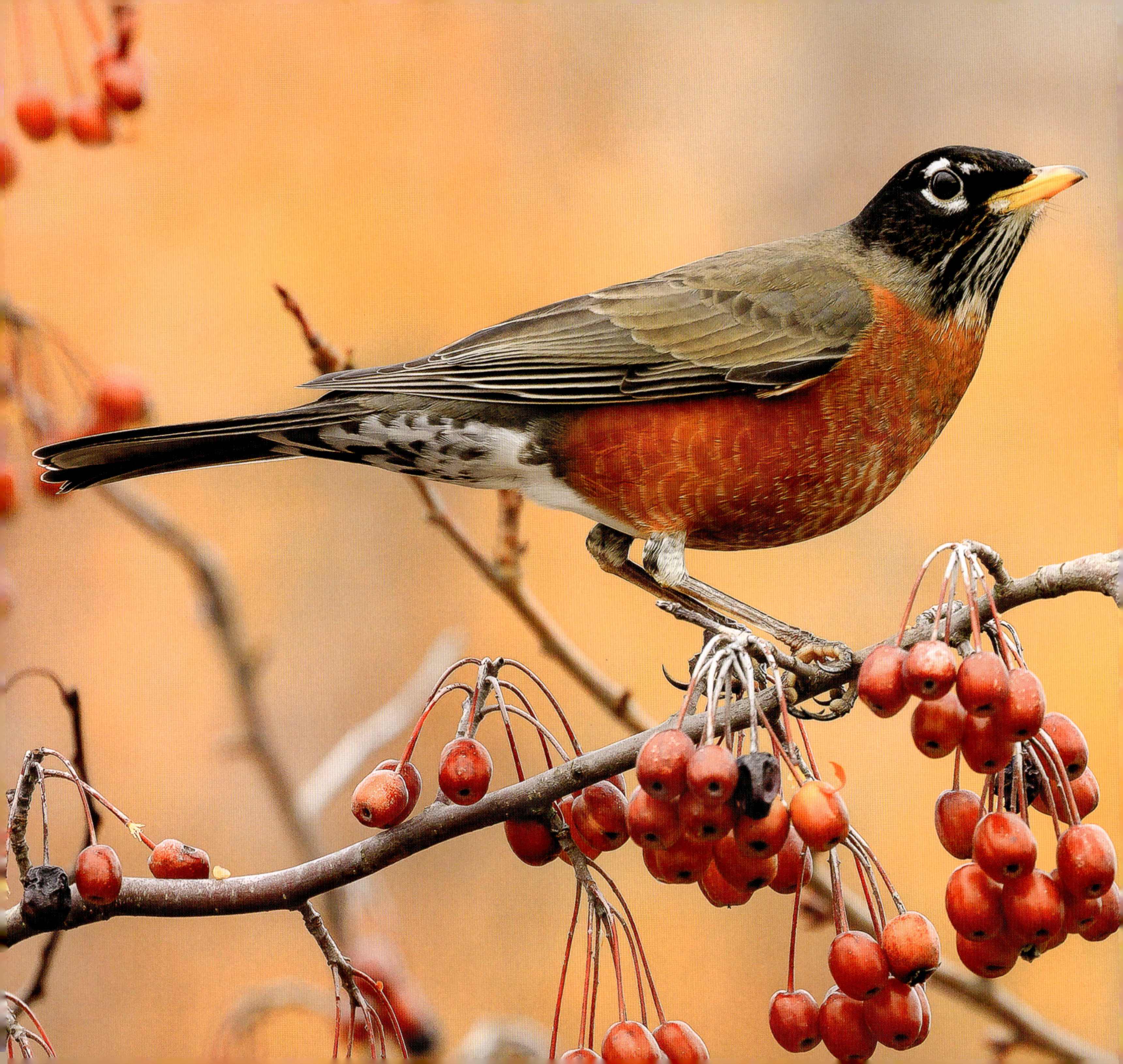

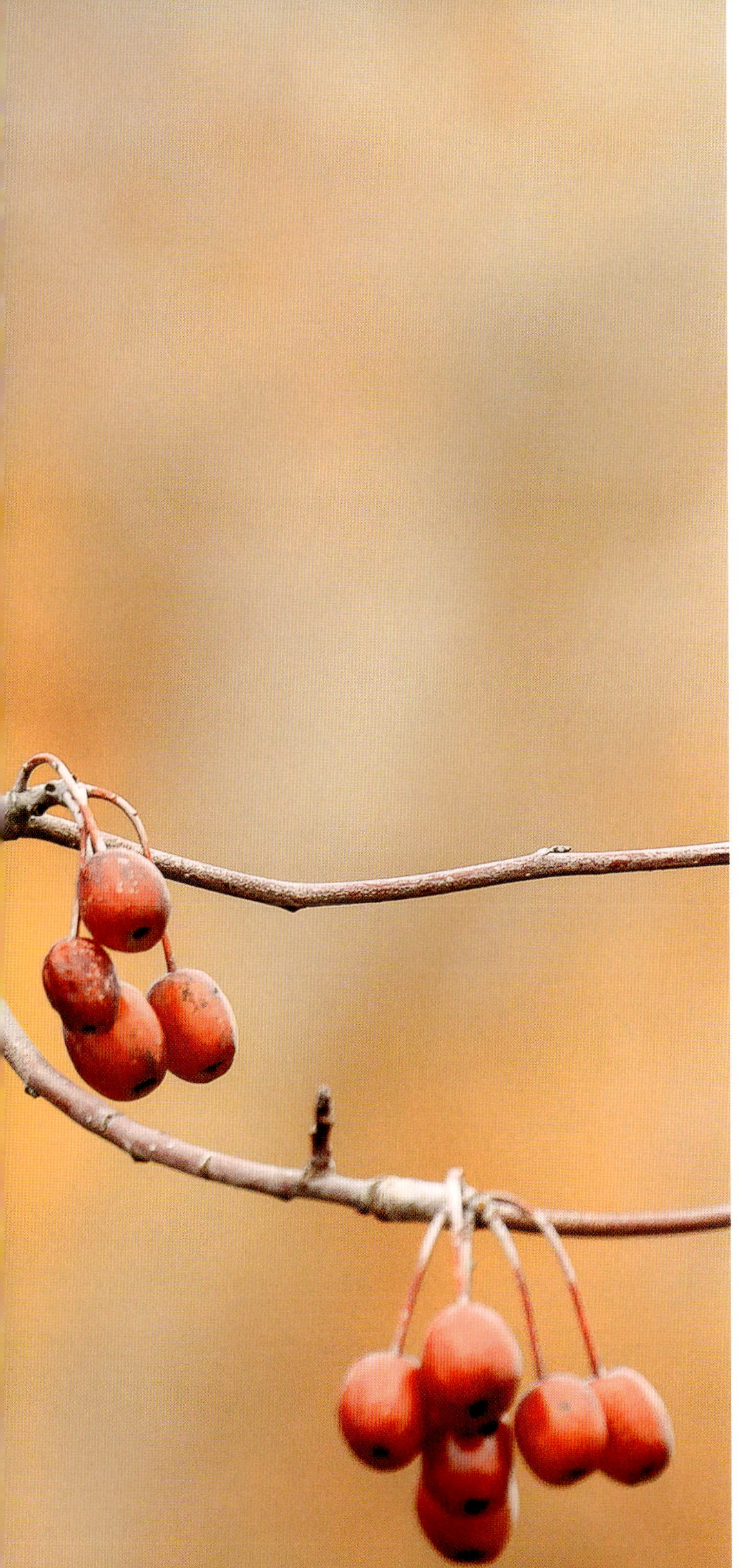

A MALE AMERICAN ROBIN EATS BERRIES IN FRONT OF MY FRIEND AND ME IN RICHMOND, BC.

new things about ourselves. They help us to grow as people, to seek out new things and experiences and to strive for light.

I have been through heartbreaking pain and loss in my life, as many of you reading this book have as well. Loss in any form is not easy, but I still count all the many blessings the birds have given me.

I remember after my dad died, I stayed with his body until dawn. When I left the hospital, the first bird I heard singing was a little Song Sparrow. Tears began streaming down my face. When I came out of that dark room that morning, my eyes hurt from the bright sunlight and blue sky. My tears almost hurt as they came out and touched my face. The little bird continued to sing and showed me that, despite the betrayals in life I have suffered, and the pain of

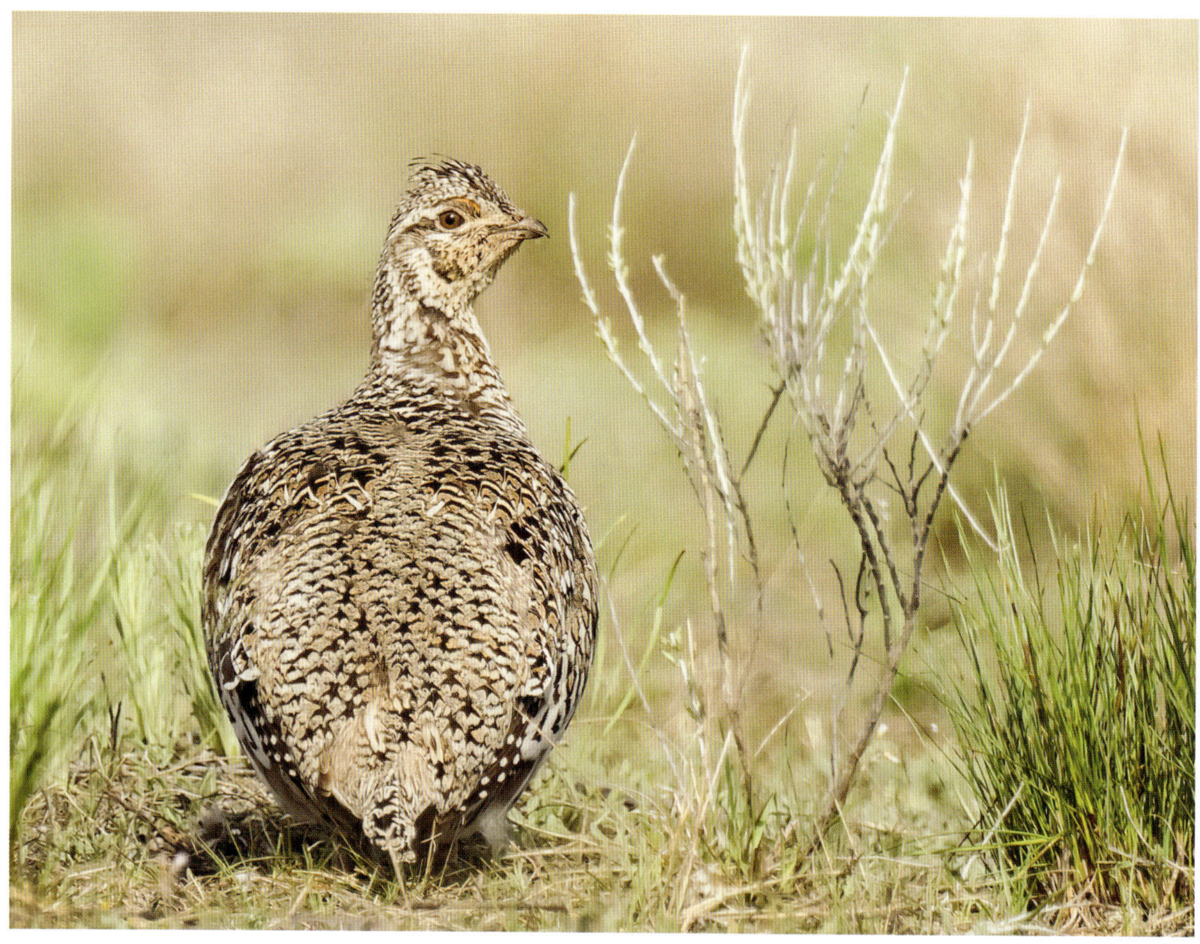

losing my beloved dad and mom, life will be brighter again. The birds will always be there to comfort me. I felt just a little less alone. The sparrow may have been just a drab little brown bird, but it had a beautiful song that lifted me up.

In the early days right after I lost my dad, when the compound, complex grief of losing both my parents hit me, I thought not even the birds could help me make it. I felt like my body couldn't hold me anymore. Yet, like a rallying ally, they

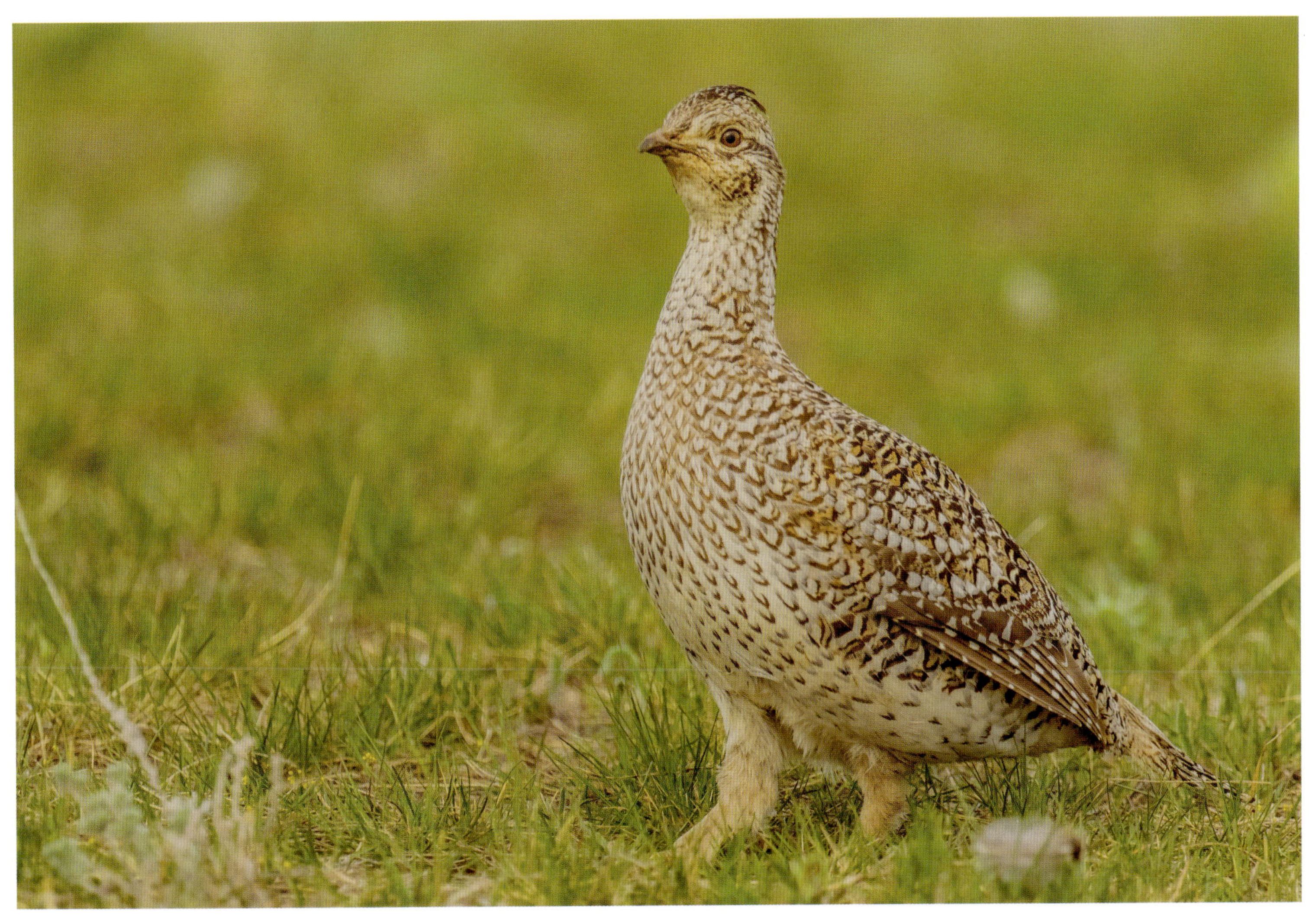

Above and opposite:

A FEMALE COLUMBIAN SHARP-TAILED GROUSE ON THE LEK IN THE THOMPSON-NICOLA REGION OF BC.

Opposite:

A MALE COMMON YELLOWTHROAT HOLDS ITS BEAK FULL OF INSECTS THAT IT WILL TAKE BACK TO ITS NEST TO FEED ITS YOUNG IN RICHMOND, BC.

showed up for me, and the first one to do so was that small Song Sparrow. Life isn't fair and can be very cruel. It can be incredibly lonely, even for those who are constantly surrounded by many people. When you have deep pain like I do, I invite you to try and channel it into growth because it will help to bring you inner peace and maybe just a little joy. So get out there and create new experiences and memories, despite all the challenges. This is what is so imperfectly beautiful about being human.

I remember after my mom died I went back to Grant Narrows Regional Park in Pitt Meadows, BC – a place I went with her often to watch large numbers of Black and Vaux's Swifts in the summer. They would fly over and dazzle us, stopping us in our tracks. Every time I see a swift there now, I think of her. When I am in the mountains, and a Canada Jay lands on my hand, I immediately think of my dad, who showed me my first Canada Jay that we fed on our hands. These memories live on in the new bird species I see. Although it's painful not to share them with my parents in person, I can relive those special moments every time I see birds that provide keys to my most treasured memories. The longer my parents are gone from me, the more I realize I need them here, but luckily I can keep a tie to them through the birds. In that way, my mom and dad constantly return to me.

I will be forever grateful to birds. The birds have never given up on me, and I never will on them. I don't know with any certainty of the tides that will come my way, but I do know one thing: birds will be a focal point of my life. I will continue to advocate and fight for them in return for all the continued gifts they give me. They will feature with great magnitude in my life until I too pass away and join my dear parents. I thank the heavens for the birds now and always, as they guide me blindly but peacefully into my future. I lift my own wings in solidarity with these winged creatures who have truly helped save my life and helped me weather the worst of possible storms.

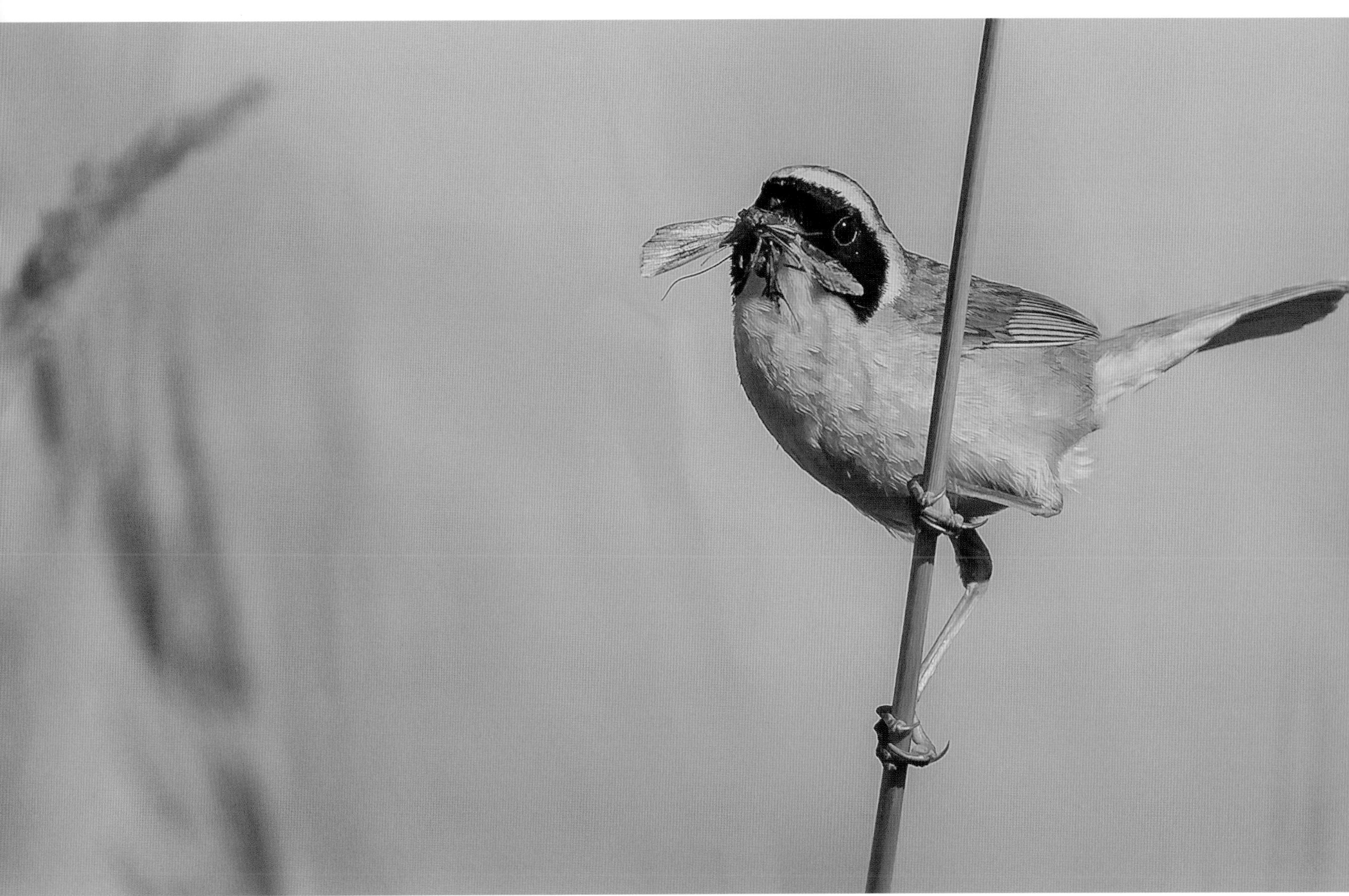

A COMMON LOON SHAKES OUT ITS WINGS IN BLAINE, WASHINGTON.

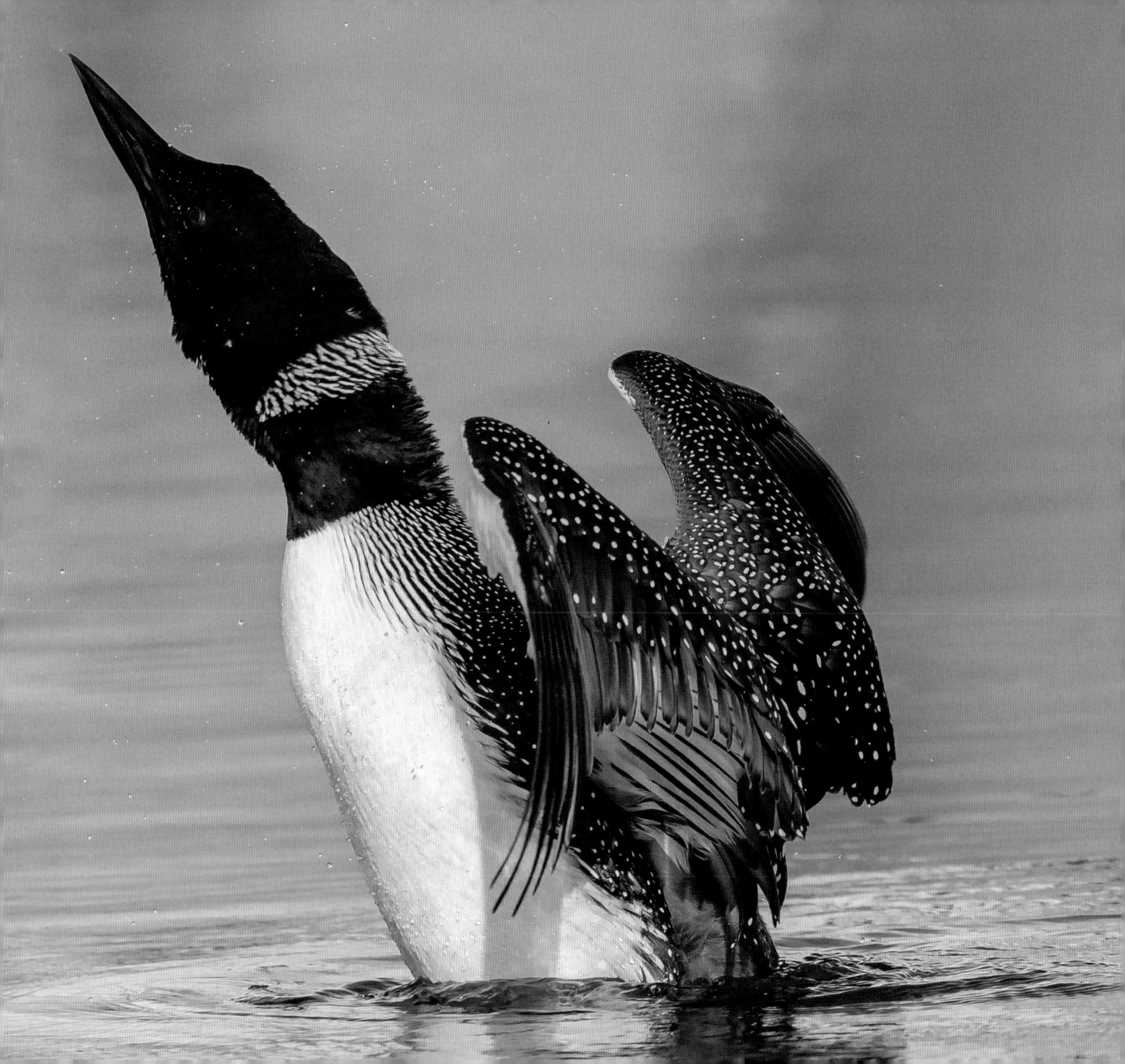

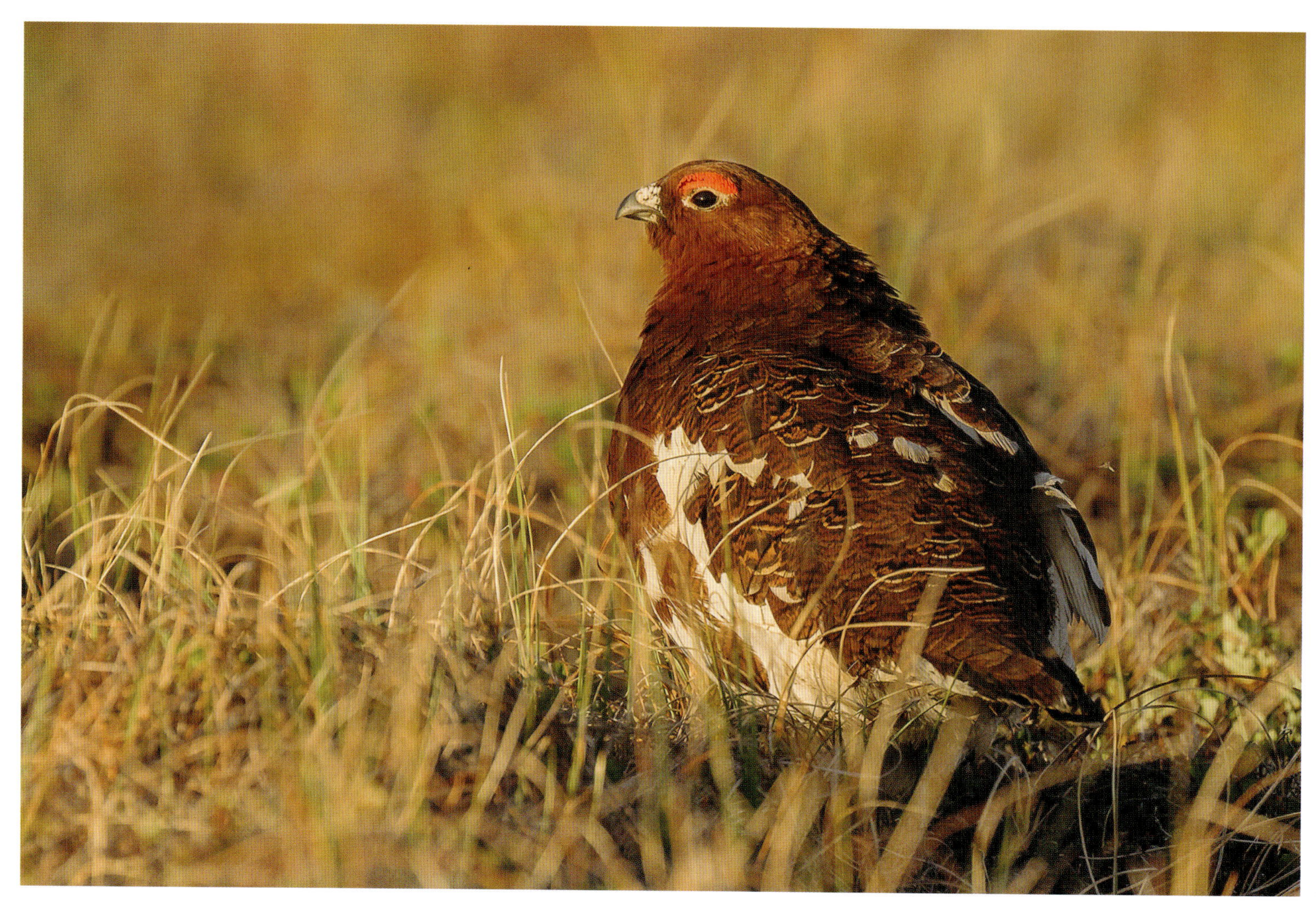

A MALE WILLOW PTARMIGAN IN NOME, ALASKA.

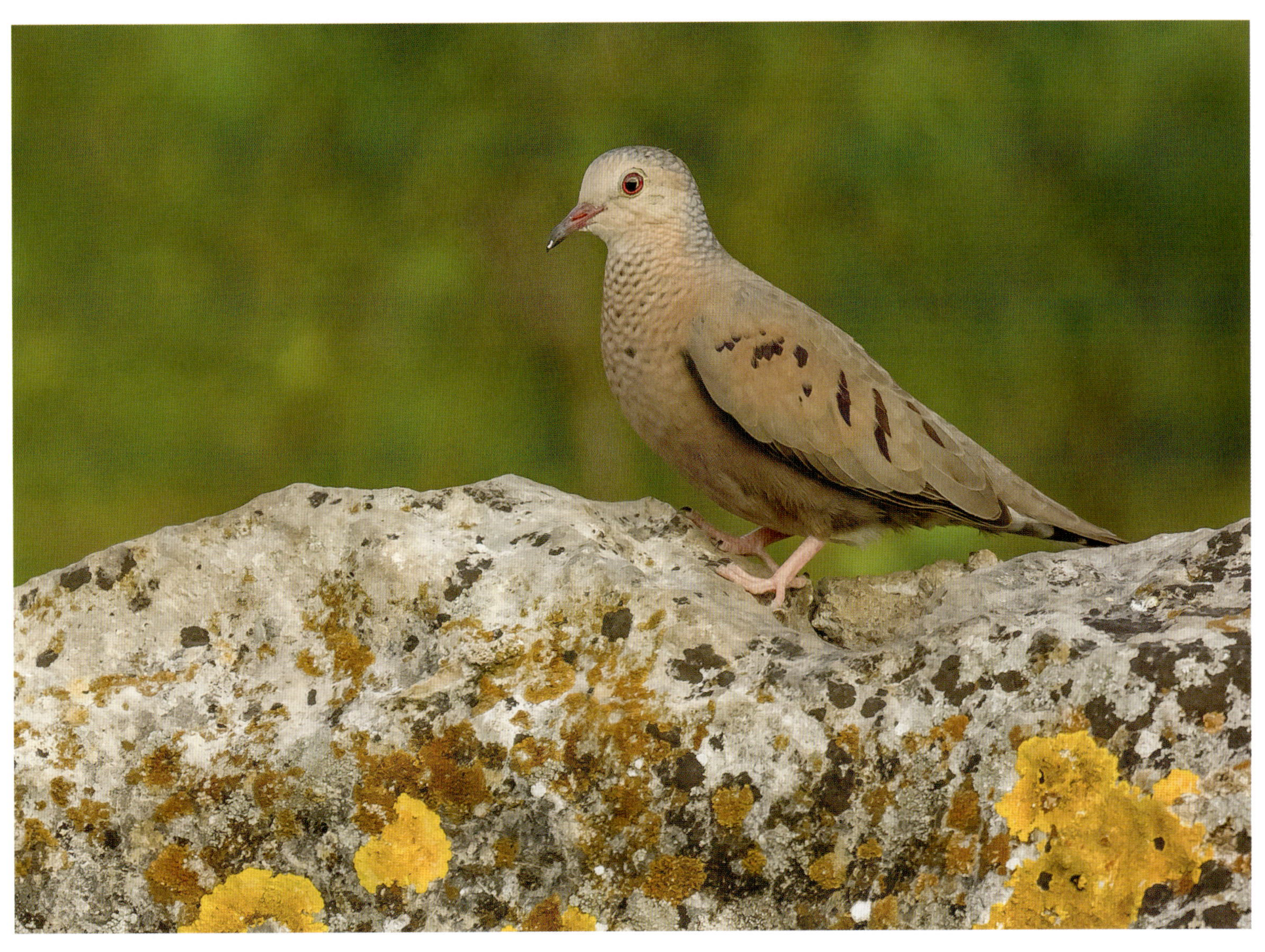

A MALE COMMON GROUND-DOVE NEAR UVALDE, TEXAS.

A VEERY (A TYPE OF THRUSH) PERCHES IN FRONT OF ME IN PEACHLAND, BC. THE VEERY GETS ITS NAME FROM THE ETHEREAL CALL IT MAKES, WHICH IS A DESCENDING "VEER."

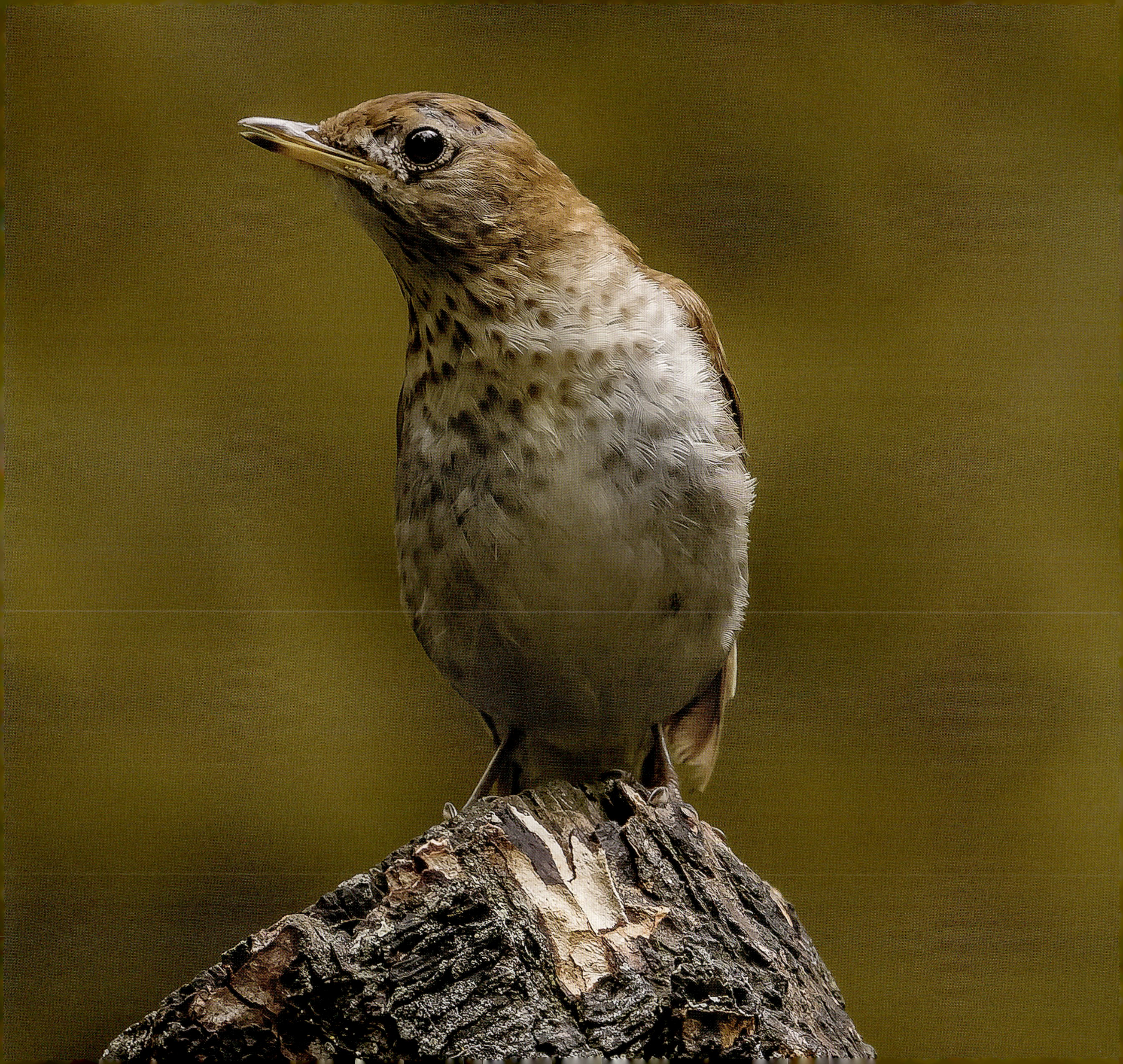

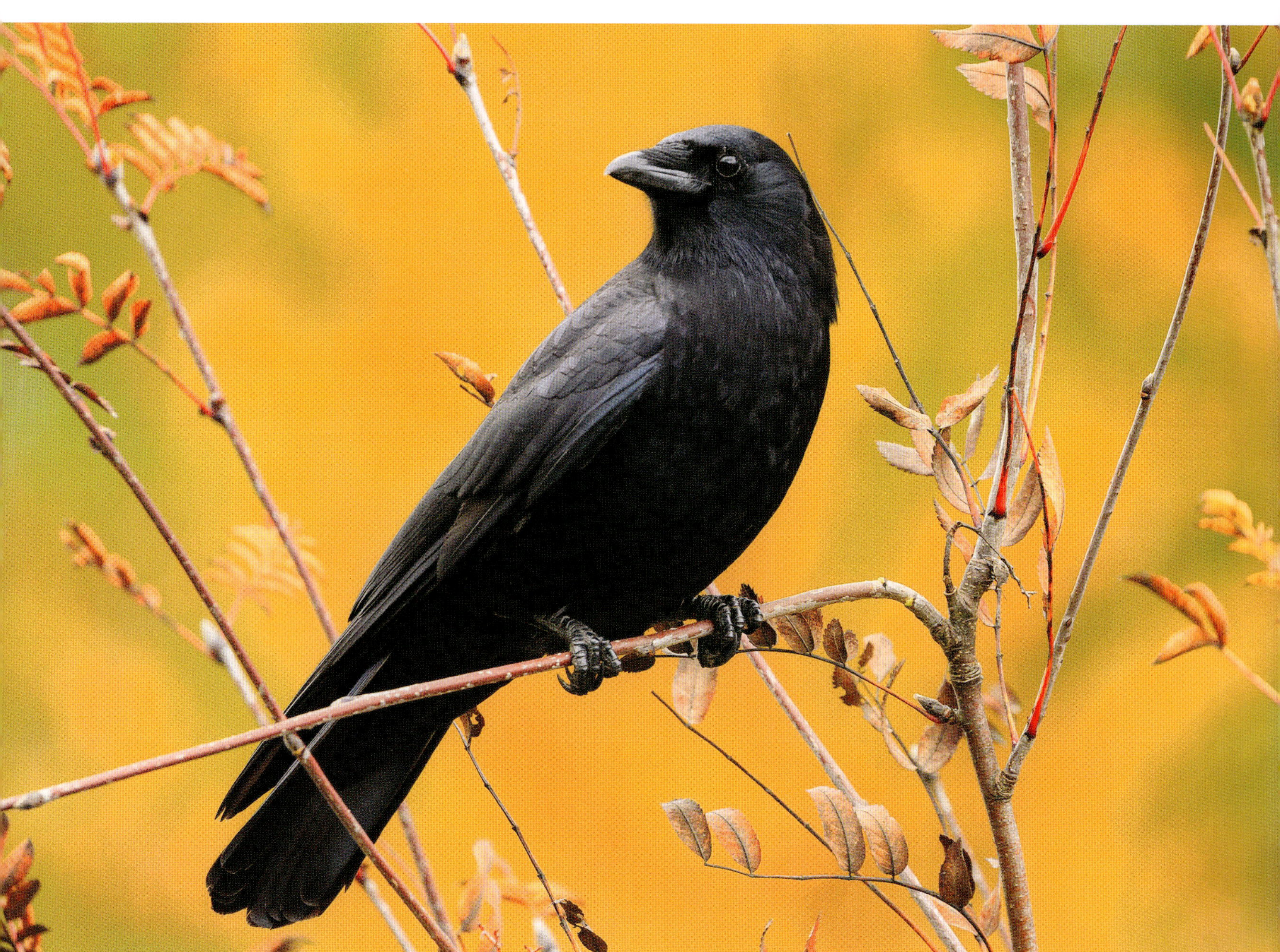

AFTERWORD

Opposite:

AN AMERICAN CROW PERCHES IN FRONT OF ME IN RICHMOND, BC. THESE BIRDS ARE SOMETIMES VILIFIED AS PESTS BUT ARE INCREDIBLY INTELLIGENT. THEY CAN TRAVEL AS FAR AS 65 KM EVERY NIGHT TO SLEEP IN LARGE ROOSTS THAT NUMBER BETWEEN 100 TO OVER 10,000 BIRDS.

Birds have intrigued and inspired poets, authors, artists, and musicians for thousands of years. I think that is why musical and artistic people are so attracted to birding. I do believe birds are one of the most wonderful gifts human beings have access to. They can and do evoke so much heartfelt emotion. Birds create bonds and connect us to the land and other people tied to that land. Birds inspire us to study and learn more about them and their environments, and in turn our own environments.

The way birds sing, move, fly, migrate, and interact with one another is magic. Their amazing colourful plumage delights us, and their diversity and differentiation of species leaves us enthralled.

That is why it is imperative that we self-reflect to see the damage we have caused to these sensational creatures. We must do more than saving a few parks in cities of cement. Even the largest national parks and wildlife refuges are being affected by human-induced climate change. We must remember that our actions, which may seem far away from northern areas and arctic climates or warm tropical islands, will impact these environments and the people who live there. These are often people who contribute the least amount of greenhouse gasses to the planet. It is the marginalized and Indigenous Peoples who will suffer the most from Western industrialism. We must do our part to combat environmental racism in our everyday lives.

We have completely changed pristine landscapes across the world and in turn have dramatically sliced bird populations by more than half in some species, and even caused extinctions in some locales. We have done so by spreading disease and destroying habitat through deforestation, mining, agriculture, pesticides, and more. We have introduced invasive bird and animal species that have killed off native

AN ADULT TUFTED PUFFIN FLIES OVER MY YOUNG BIRDERS AND ME DURING A PELAGIC TRIP IN TOFINO, BC.

birds, either indirectly or directly. Cattle, pigs, and sheep have degraded grasslands to the point that some birds can't survive or nest there anymore. We have killed off bird species for feathers and meat. Some are still here, but others have gone extinct like the Dodo. We have pushed birds that used to be further south to go up further north and forced them up into higher elevations. There soon will be a point where these species can't survive anymore – they will run out of space and habitat to exist.

In trying to make the world more hospitable to humans, we have made it worse for the natural world. Fires due to intense heat have destroyed countless areas of wild bird habitat and the birds therein.

The fact that birds persist at all in these environments is awe-inspiring and shows that their resilience is worth fighting for. They are still holding on in the most inhospitable of places. The birds are fighting, so we must too.

The destiny of birds is held right in the palm of our hands. Across the world, we must strive to protect the land, sea, and air they need to survive. Birds are resilient and can make comebacks but still need our help to do so. We can do well to keep our cats inside (cats kill massive numbers of birds) and to decrease our use of pesticides, rodenticides, and fossil fuels. We need to recycle and dramatically reduce our use and reliance on plastics. Since we have cut down so many natural nesting sites, we should erect nest boxes and monitor the birds through citizen science. A great place to start is your local park. If you can, donate to bird conservation organizations. When you see people behaving unethically or illegally, endangering birds or their habitats, report it to conservation or Fish and Wildlife officers. Try and support petitions and politicians that support bird and habitat conservation initiatives.

You can make small differences to bird mortality by turning your lights out at night, putting graphics on your windows, choosing "bird-friendly" coffee, and picking up fishing line you see outside. If you are a

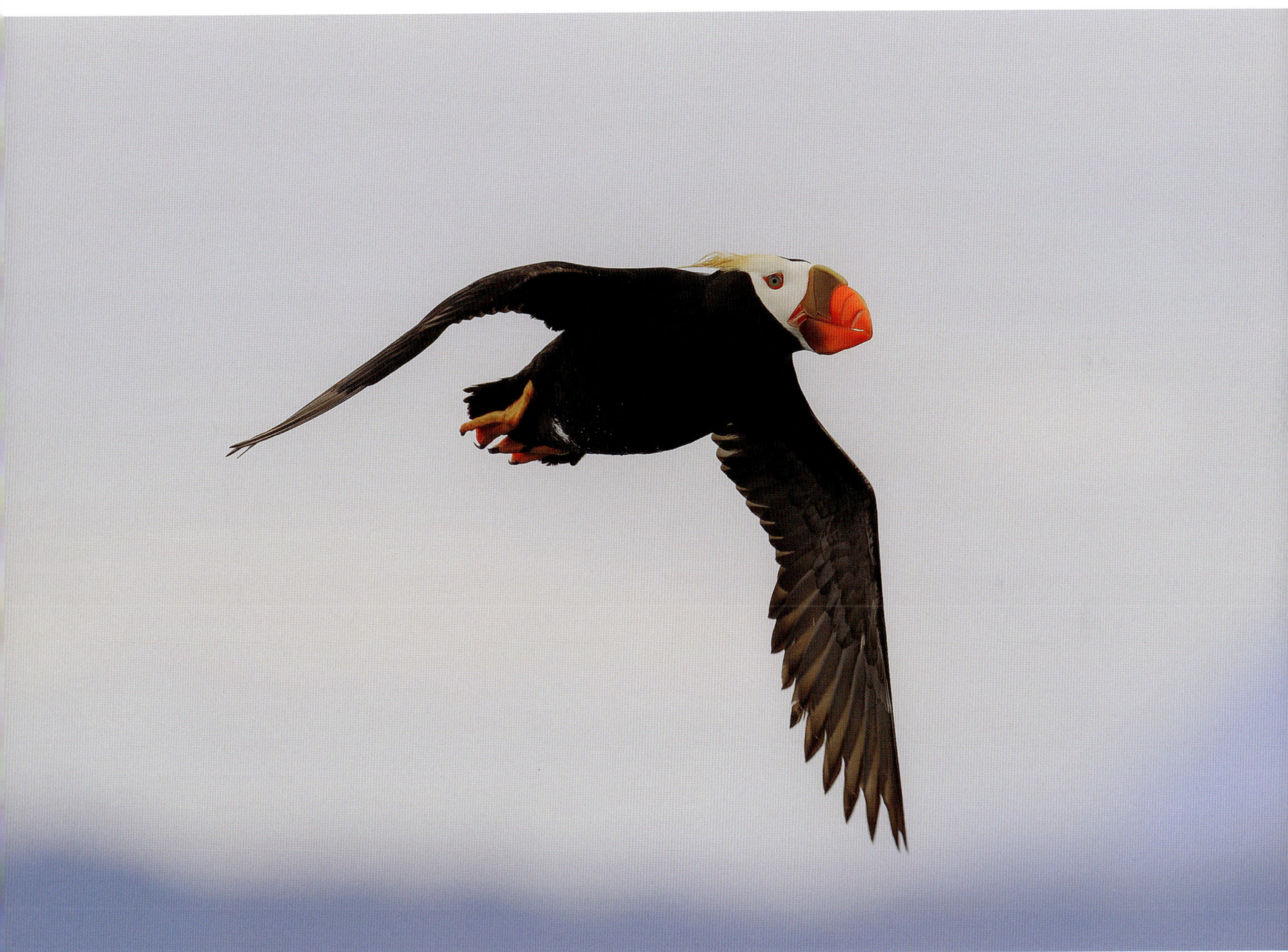

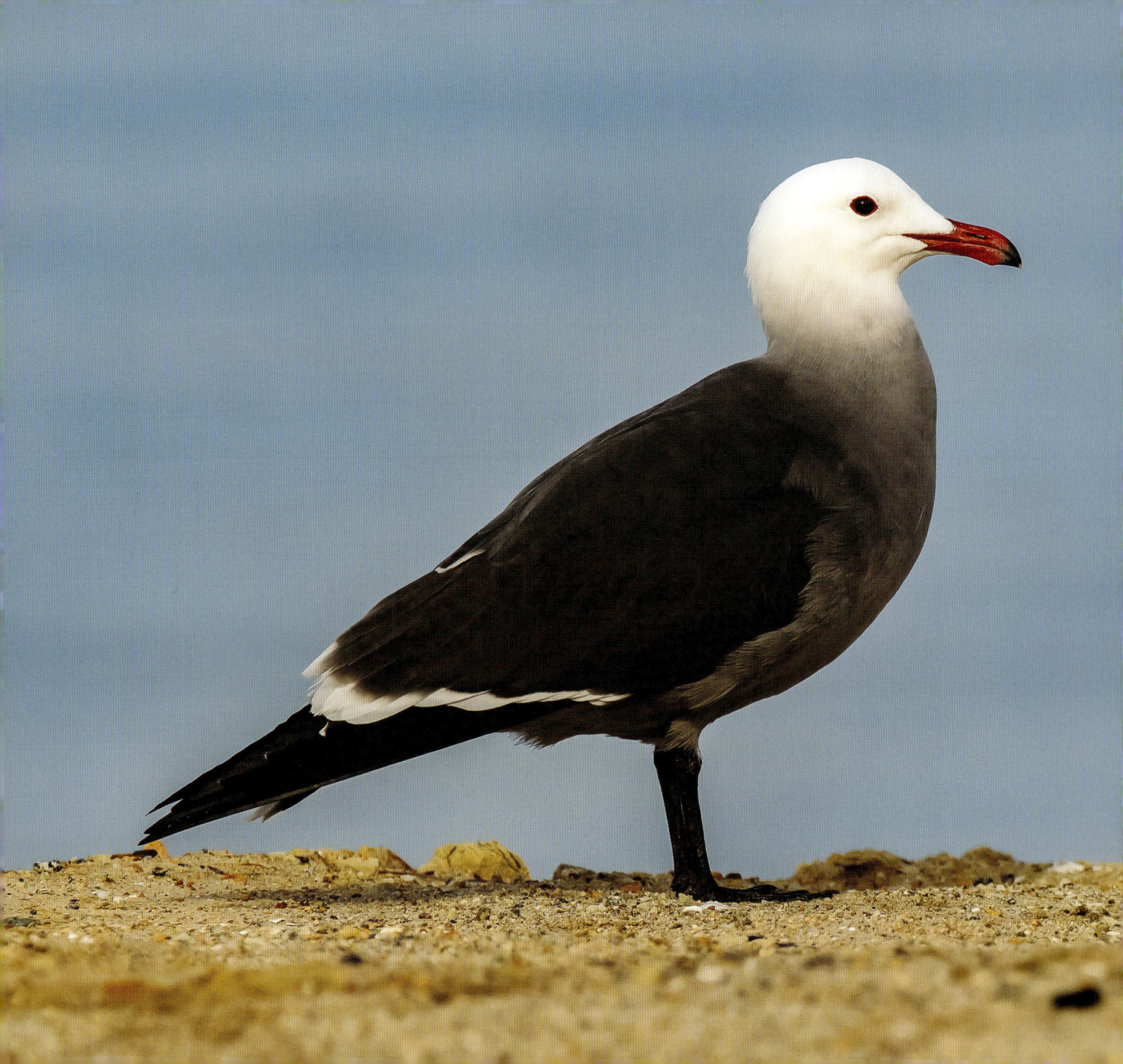

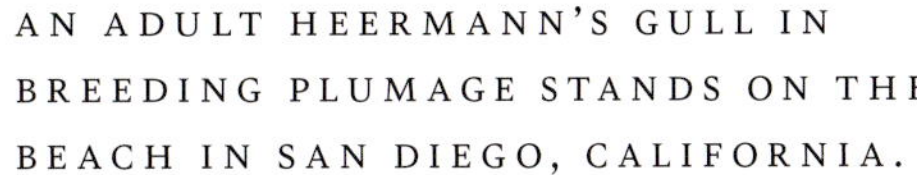

AN ADULT HEERMANN'S GULL IN BREEDING PLUMAGE STANDS ON THE BEACH IN SAN DIEGO, CALIFORNIA.

hunter, you should switch to copper bullets from lead bullets, which poison many vultures and raptors like eagles.

Share your knowledge with friends who aren't birders. You will find that once people know just how many bird species are declining and why, they will want to take an active role in changing their own behaviour in order to protect birds and the environment. Mentor a young person, or better yet a group of young people, because getting the youth out into nature is another key factor in having a more successfully protected, greener planet. Youth have a vested interest in wanting to protect the planet they will inherit.

Most of all, please, NEVER GIVE UP. Never give up fighting for the birds and, frankly, for yourself. The birds deserve better and so do you. As the Bald Eagles and Whooping Cranes have come back from near extinction, I know the future can be bright, if we come together as one to do the work that is required to make us all thrive. The many habitats and birds protected because humans have cared give me much needed hope. We have the technology and science in this day and age to forewarn us of what negative impacts are to come if we don't make the changes now. It is up to us all to show the world just how much we value our avian friends. Let the challenge begin.

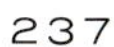

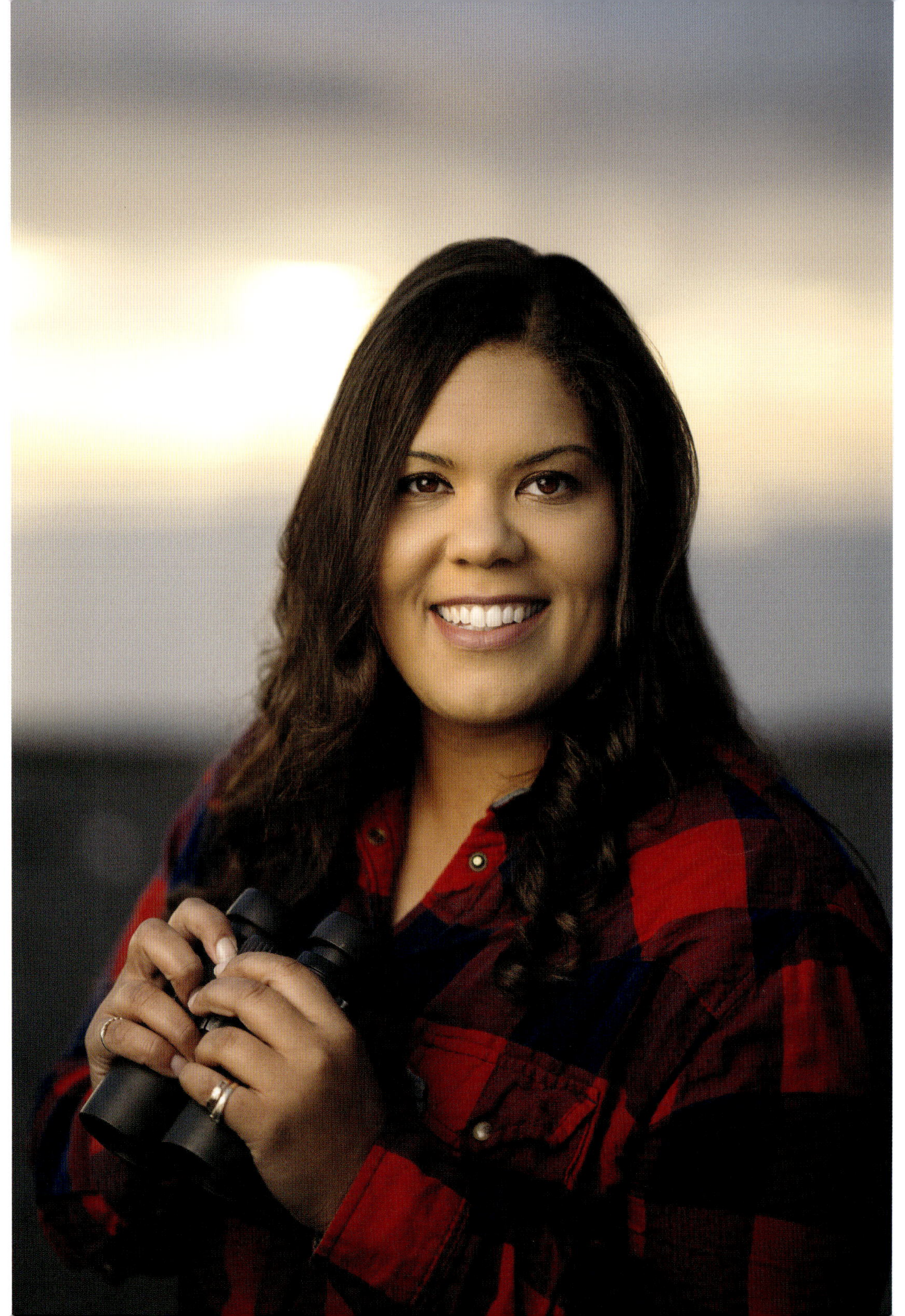

ABOUT THE AUTHOR

Melissa Hafting is an ecologist, bird guide, author, and photographer. She founded the BC Young Birders Program in 2014, which aims to bring together youth of all races, sexual orientations, and genders to look at birds on fun excursions in the natural world. The program also helps teach youth about citizen science and the importance of bird conservation. She is also passionate about making birding more inclusive for all, especially for BIPOC birders like herself. She is an avid traveller and loves to explore the world looking for birds. Melissa is an eBird reviewer for the province of BC and sits on the board of directors of the Frontiers in Ornithology Association and Wild Bird Trust of BC. She was also a judge for the 2022 and 2023 Audubon Photography Awards, the recipient of BC Nature's 2021 Daphne Solecki Award for contributing to nature education for children in British Columbia, a finalist for the 2021 Nature Inspiration Awards for the Canadian Museum of Nature, and a lead in the 2020 CBC TV documentary, *Rare Bird Alert*. Her photography can be viewed on her Instagram account @bcbirdergirl (+10,000 followers). Melissa lives in Richmond, British Columbia.

Opposite:

MELISSA HAFTING.
PHOTO: IAN HARLAND.

Overleaf:

A ROCK SANDPIPER FORAGES NEAR DAVIS BAY BEACH IN SECHELT, BC.

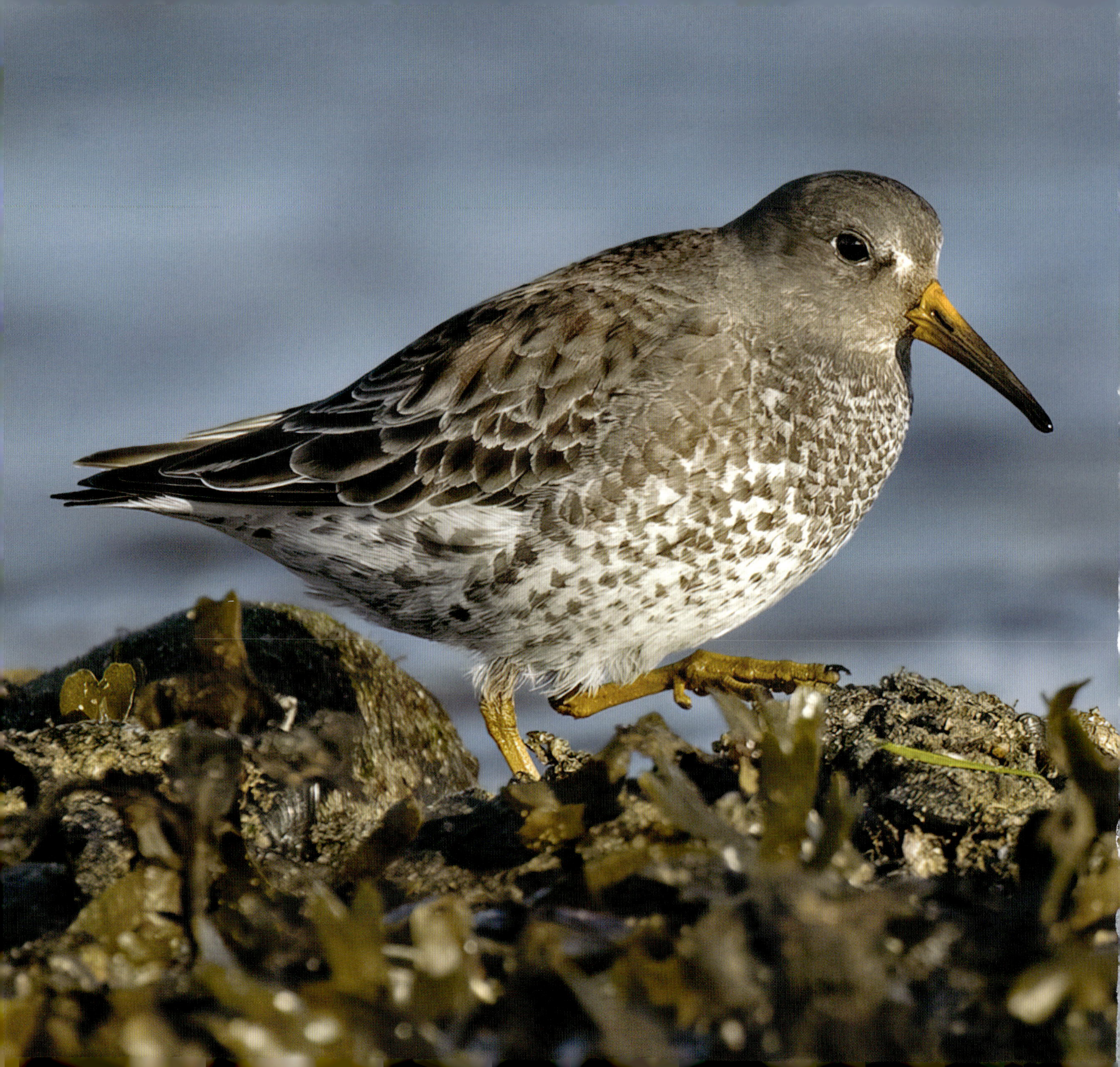

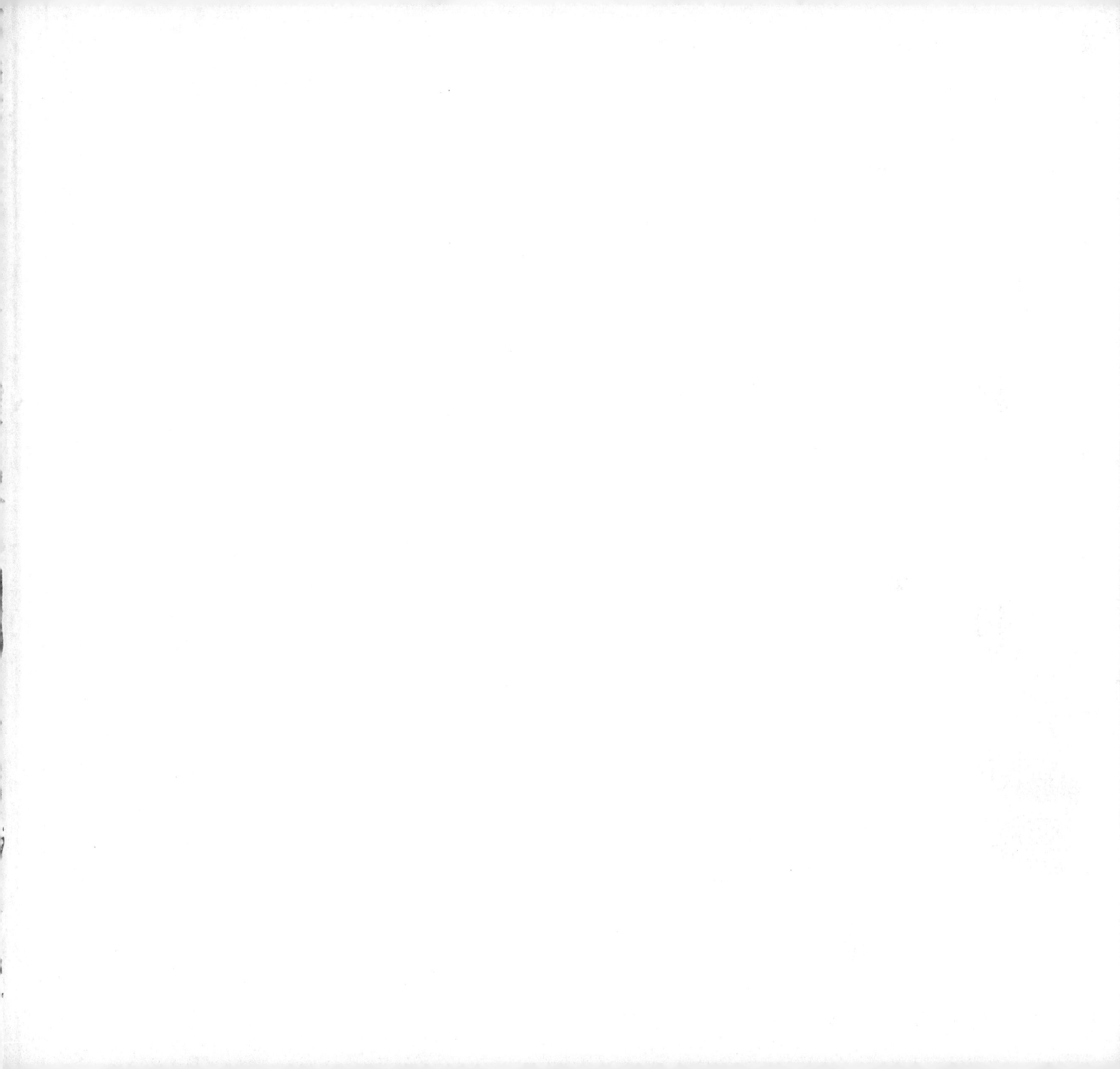